GENERAL THEORY OF LAW

Modern Legal Philosophy Series: IV

GENERAL THEORY OF LAW

By

N. M. KORKUNOV

LATE PROFESSOR OF PUBLIC LAW
UNIVERSITY OF ST. PETERSBURG

ENGLISH TRANSLATION

By

W. G. HASTINGS

DEAN OF THE LAW FACULTY, UNIVERSITY OF NEBRASKA

SECOND EDITION

GYAN

Published by

Gyan Publishing House
5, Ansari Road
Daryaganj, New Delhi-110002
Phone: 011-47034999, 9811692060
E-mail: books@gyanbooks.com

Distribution Network
gyanbooks.com
India, USA, Canada, UK, Australia, France

ISBN : 978-81-212-6360-3 (PB)
First Published, 1922

2nd Impression 2022

Printed at: Gyan Press, Delhi.

GENERAL THEORY OF LAW
Author: N. M. KORKUNOV

THE MODERN LEGAL PHILOSOPHY SERIES

General Theory of Law

THE MODERN LEGAL PHILOSOPHY SERIES

Edited by a Committee of the
ASSOCIATION OF AMERICAN LAW SCHOOLS

INTRODUCTION TO THE SCIENCE OF LAW. By KARL GAREIS of the University of Munich. Translated by ALBERT KOCOUREK of Northwestern University.

THE WORLD'S LEGAL PHILOSOPHIES. By FRITZ BEROLZHEIMER of Berlin. Translated by RACHEL S. JASTROW.

COMPARATIVE LEGAL PHILOSOPHY, applied to Legal Institutions. By LUIGI MIRAGLIA of the University of Naples. Translated by JOHN LISLE of the Philadelphia Bar.

GENERAL THEORY OF LAW. By N. M. KORKUNOV of the University of St. Petersburg. Translated by W. G. HASTINGS of the University of Nebraska.

LAW AS A MEANS TO AN END. By RUDOLF VON IHERING of the University of Berlin. Translated by ISAAC HUSIK of the University of Pennsylvania.

MODERN FRENCH LEGAL PHILOSOPHY. By A. FOUILLÉE, J. CHARMONT, L. DUGUIT and R. DEMOGUE of the Universities of Paris, Montpellier, Bordeaux and Lille. Translated by MRS. F. W. SCOTT and JOSEPH P. CHAMBERLAIN.

SCIENCE OF LEGAL METHOD, SELECT ESSAYS. By Various Writers.

THE FORMAL BASES OF LAW. By G. DEL VECCHIO of the University of Bologna. Translated by JOHN LISLE of the Philadelphia Bar.

THE PHILOSOPHY OF LAW. By JOSEF KOHLER of the University of Berlin. Translated by ADALBERT ALBRECHT.

Modern Legal Philosophy Series: IV

GENERAL THEORY OF LAW

BY

N. M. KORKUNOV

LATE PROFESSOR OF PUBLIC LAW
UNIVERSITY OF ST. PETERSBURG

ENGLISH TRANSLATION
BY

W. G. HASTINGS

DEAN OF THE LAW FACULTY, UNIVERSITY OF NEBRASKA

SECOND EDITION

1922

EDITORIAL COMMITTEE OF THE ASSOCIATION OF AMERICAN LAW SCHOOLS

LIST OF TRANSLATORS

ADALBERT ALBRECHT, South Easton, Mass.

ERNEST BRUNCKEN, Washington, D. C.

JOSEPH P. CHAMBERLAIN, Columbia University.

WM. G. HASTINGS, Professor of Law, University of Nebraska.

ISAAC HUSIK, Professor of Philosophy, University of Pennsylvania.

RACHEL SZOLD JASTROW, Madison, Wis.

ALBERT KOCOUREK, Chicago, Ill. (of the Editorial Committee).

JOHN LISLE, Philadelphia, Pa. (of the Philadelphia Bar).

MARTHA MC. READ, Washington, D. C.

ETHEL FORBES SCOTT, Urbana, Ill.

JOHN SIMPSON, New York, N. Y. (of the New York Bar).

GENERAL INTRODUCTION TO THE SERIES

BY THE EDITORIAL COMMITTEE

"Until either philosophers become kings," said Socrates, "or kings philosophers, States will never succeed in remedying their shortcomings." And if he was loath to give forth this view, because, as he admitted, it might "sink him beneath the waters of laughter and ridicule," so to-day among us it would doubtless resound in folly if we sought to apply it again in our own field of State life, and to assert that philosophers must become lawyers or lawyers philosophers, if our law is ever to be advanced into its perfect working.

And yet there is hope, as there is need, among us to-day, of some such transformation. Of course, history shows that there always have been cycles of legal progress, and that they have often been heralded and guided by philosophies. But particularly there is hope that our own people may be the generation now about to exemplify this.

There are several reasons for thinking our people apt thereto. But, without delaying over the grounds for such speculations, let us recall that as shrewd and good-natured an observer as De Tocqueville saw this in us. He admits that "in most of the operations of the mind, each American appeals to the individual exercise of his own understanding alone; therefore in no country in the civilized world is less attention paid to philosophy than in the United States." But, he adds, "the Americans are much more addicted to the use of general ideas than the English, and entertain a much greater relish for them." And since philosophy is, after all, only the science of general ideas—analyzing, restating, and reconstructing concrete experience—we may well trust that (if ever we do go at it with a will) we shall discover in ourselves a taste and high capacity for it, and shall direct our powers as fruitfully upon law as we have done upon other fields.

Hitherto, to be sure, our own outlook on juristic learning has been insular. The value of the study of comparative law has only in recent years come to be recognized by us. Our juristic methods are still primitive, in that we seek to know only by our own experience, and pay no heed to the experience of others. Our historic bond with English law alone, and our consequent lack of recognition of the universal character of law as a generic institution, have prevented any wide contact with foreign literatures. While heedless of external help in the practical matter of legislation, we have been oblivious to the abstract nature of law. Philosophy of law has been to us almost a meaningless and alien phrase. "All philosophers are reducible in the end to two classes only: utilitarians and futilitarians," is the cynical epigram of a great wit of modern fiction.[1] And no doubt the philistines of our profession would echo this sarcasm.

And yet no country and no age have ever been free (whether conscious of the fact or not) from some drift of philosophic thought. "In each epoch of time," says M. Leroy, in a brilliant book of recent years, "there is current a certain type of philosophic doctrine—a philosophy deep-seated in each one of us, and observable clearly and consciously in the utterances of the day—alike in novels, newspapers, and speeches, and equally

[1] M. Dumaresq, in Mr. Paterson's "The Old Dance Master."

in town and country, workshop and counting-house." Without some fundamental basis of action, or theory of ends, all legislation and judicial interpretation are reduced to an anarchy of uncertainty. It is like mathematics without fundamental definitions and axioms. Amidst such conditions, no legal demonstration can be fixed, even for a moment. Social institutions, instead of being governed by the guidance of an intelligent free will, are thrown back to the blind determinism of the forces manifested in the natural sciences. Even the phenomenon of experimental legislation, which is peculiar to Anglo-American countries, cannot successfully ignore the necessity of having social ends.

The time is ripe for action in this field. To quote the statement of reasons given in the memorial presented at the annual meeting of the Association of American Law Schools in August, 1910:—

The need of the series now proposed is so obvious as hardly to need advocacy. We are on the threshold of a long period of constructive readjustment and restatement of our law in almost every department. We come to the task, as a profession, almost wholly untrained in the technic of legal analysis and legal science in general. Neither we, nor any community, could expect anything but crude results without thorough preparation. Many teachers, and scores of students and practitioners, must first have become thoroughly familiar with the world's methods of juristic thought. As a first preparation for the coming years of that kind of activity, it is the part of wisdom first to familiarize ourselves with what has been done by the great modern thinkers abroad—to catch up with the general state of learning on the subject. After a season of this, we shall breed a family of well-equipped and original thinkers of our own. Our own law must, of course, be worked out ultimately by our own thinkers; but they must first be equipped with the state of learning in the world to date.

How far from "unpractical" this field of thought and research really is has been illustrated very recently in the Federal Supreme Court, where the opposing opinions in a great case (*Kuhn* v. *Fair-*

mont Coal Co.) turned upon the respective conceptions of "law" in the abstract, and where Professor Gray's recent work on "The Nature and Sources of the Law" was quoted, and supplied direct material for judicial decision.

Acting upon this memorial, the following resolution was passed at that meeting:—

> That a committee of five be appointed by the president, to arrange for the translation and publication of a series of continental master-works on jurisprudence and philosophy of law.

The committee spent a year in collecting the material. Advice was sought from a score of masters in the leading universities of France, Germany, Italy, Spain, and elsewhere. The present series is the result of these labors.

In the selection of this series, the committee's purpose has been, not so much to cover the whole field of modern philosophy of law, as to exhibit faithfully and fairly all the modern viewpoints of any present importance. The older foundation-works of two generations ago are, with some exceptions, already accessible in English translation. But they have been long supplanted by the products of newer schools of thought which are offered in this series in their latest and most representative form. It is believed that the complete series will represent in compact form a collection of materials whose equal cannot be found at this time in any single foreign literature.

The committee has not sought to offer the final solution of any philosophical or juristic problems; nor to follow any preference for any particular theory or school of thought. Its chief purpose has been to present to English readers the most representative views of the most modern writers in jurisprudence and philosophy of law. The series shows a wide geographical representation; but the selection has not been centered on the notion of giving equal recognition to all countries. Primarily, the desire has been to represent the various schools of thought; and, consistently with this, then to represent the different chief countries. This aim, however, has involved little difficulty; for Continental thought has lines of cleavage which make it easy to represent the leading schools and the leading nations at the same time.

To offer here an historical introduction, surveying the various schools of thought and the progress from past to present, was regarded by the committee as unnecessary. The volumes of Dr. Berolzheimer and Professor Miraglia amply serve this purpose; and the introductory chapter of the latter volume provides a short summary of the history of general philosophy, rapidly placing the reader in touch with the various schools and their standpoints. The series has been so arranged (in the numbered list fronting the title page) as to indicate that order of perusal which will be most suitable for those who desire to master the field progressively and fruitfully.

The committee takes great pleasure in acknowledging the important part rendered in the consummation of this project, by the publisher, the authors, and the translators. Without them this series manifestly would have been impossible.

To the publisher we are grateful for the hearty sponsorship of a kind of literature which is so important to the advancement of American legal science. And here the Committee desires also to express its indebtedness to Elbert H. Gary, Esq., of New York City, for his ample provision of materials for legal science in the Gary Library of Continental Law (in Northwestern University). In the researches of preparation for this Series, those materials were found indispensable.

The authors (or their representatives) have cordially granted the right of English translation, and have shown a friendly interest in promoting our aims. The committee would be assuming too much to thank these learned writers on its own behalf, since the debt is one that we all owe.

The severe labor of this undertaking fell upon the translators. It required not only a none too common linguistic skill, but also a wide range of varied learning in fields little travelled. Whatever success may attend and whatever good may follow will in a peculiar way be attributable to the scholarly labors of the several translators.

The committee finds special satisfaction in having been able to assemble in a common purpose such an array of talent and learning; and it will feel that its own small contribution of this unified effort has been amply recompensed if this series will measurably help to improve and to refine our institutions for the administration of justice.

TABLE OF CONTENTS

BOOK II

TRANSLATOR'S PREFACE

In the year 1905 there came into my hands a catalogue of a Paris publisher in which was advertised an International Library of Public Law. The English and American works were excellent selections. My attention was attracted to the fact that these French publishers of "international" books, in whose own country Boistel's work had lately appeared, and where Fouillée and Renouvier were still writing, had taken for their work on General Theory of the Law that of a Russian writer of whom I had never heard. The whole field of English, German, and Italian theorists seemed to be passed by, in thus going outside of France, by these French publishers who were, evidently, seeking the best works in their several departments. The curiosity thus excited resulted in an order for the French version.

It was found to have a preface by Prof. Larnaude of the University of Paris, sketching briefly the development of legal theory in Western Europe and England in late years, and justifying the selection of Prof. Korkunov's work, as representing most fully the tendencies of that development, notwithstanding the "*œuvres maîtresses*" in France, Germany, England and Belgium, which the Paris professor cited. The book, on examination, seemed to justify its selection, and Prof. Larnaude's declaration that it is not a "simple reflection of German science," but that "it has originality of its own, and above all a surprising clearness of form and expression."

Another statement of Prof. Larnaude's preface was entirely justified by the French copy. "They (the readers) will make some discoveries not lacking in interest. Notably they will see that Korkunov, though teaching in a country of absolutism and of the censorship, does not fear to attack the most delicate problems of public law. If it were not published under a Russian name, no one would suspect that it was written in Russia. It has boldnesses which perhaps will astonish a little the Russians themselves. Who would believe that ideas like the following are taught in Russia? 'The regular development of social life will be seriously fettered if conditions which are indispensable to it are sacrificed to the present hour, to that interest, for example, which offers to assure external order; as in stifling the manifestation of all ideas in order to restrain the propagation of dangerous ones, order might be re-established more readily, but society would long feel the disastrous consequences of suppressing freedom of speech and of the press.'"

"There will be no less astonishment at this passage: 'Though the government is the representative of all the people, yet the people can also act sometimes directly on their own behalf. It is probable that rules which grow up of themselves are better applicable to the people's interests than are those which the government might propose.' Individual liberty, too, is characterized as 'playing a great rôle in Modern Law,' and modern law itself as 'giving the preference to solutions the most compatible with individual liberty.'"

"Those searching carefully will find in Prof. Korkunov's book the theory of popular sovereignty and everywhere the refutation of the dogma of the historical school that law is a development purely national, and that a bird can as easily become a mammal, or *vice versa*, as a state can change its institutions, the organization conformed to its national genius."

"'This opinion of the historical school,' says Korkunov, 'is false, since we have seen that a change brought about in the social ideal may bring on a change in social development itself. By studying the origination of another people and its political development the members of a given society can bring about the formation of a political ideal like that of such other people.'"

"When I have stated that this passage refers expressly to the attempts made at the end of the XVIII century to bring into Russia English political institutions, I shall have shown how strong a spirit of liberalism undoubtedly animates the instruction given by the faculties of law in Russia. It must be so, since we find the clearest expression of it in the work of one of the most famous of professors in the Russian Universities, consequently in the official instruction itself, but it is in curious contrast with the administrative practices which are at least said to prevail in Russia."

The interest excited by such statements from Russian official legal instruction was succeeded by scepticism as to the authenticity of some of them. It seemed desirable to test, by comparison with the original Russian, some of these "surprising" passages. It happened that I have lived for a good many years in a Czech, or Bohemian, community and had a somewhat extensive acquaintance with that language. I had been informed that its relationship with Russian was close. After getting the Cyrillic Alphabet, it was found that the pronouns and prepositions in the two languages are almost identical, the verb structure and inflection nearly so, and the other inflections are much alike, and the vocabularies in large part the same.

There is in Lincoln, Nebraska, a Russian population of several thousand. An instructor was found who was a graduate of the University of Nebraska, and the French version was carefully compared with the Russian, and the liberal sentiments were found to be all in the original and stated with even more pith, condensation and force than in the French. It seemed desirable that a translation should be made, and the one here offered was prepared.

Free use has been made of M. Tchernoff's French version, and I have had the assistance of my instructor, Mr. Felix Newton, a born Russian, without whom this rendering would never have been attempted, but the responsibility for the English form of the work is my own. It is hoped that no injustice is done to the distinguished Russian teacher or to his work, the first Russian edition of which was published in 1887.

The author was at that time a professor in the University of St. Petersburg, having in 1878 succeeded Prof. Redkin to the chair of Legal Encyclopedia. He had been previously a teacher of the same subject in the Imperial Alexandrian Lyceum at St. Petersburg. In 1889, on the death of Prof. Gradovsky, he succeeded to the chair of Public Law in the University of St. Petersburg. This he held till his death in 1902 at the age of forty-nine. His distinction in his own country rests largely on his Russian Public Law, of which the sixth edition by his surviving colleagues appeared in 1908.

A Russian Biographical Dictionary says that his work "is distinguished by penetrating analysis, and abundant originality of view."

Of his General Theory of Law, which is here translated, an eighth edition was published in 1908, which I have not seen. The one used in making this translation was the sixth, published in 1904, the first after his death, and stated to be "without change."

Besides its interest as the authoritative statement of the head of legal instruction in the Russian Empire at the close of the XIXth century, the book seems fully to deserve Prof. Larnaude's claim for its originality and clearness, above given. The author's studies and teaching while holding the chair of "Encyclopedia of Law," made him familiar with the writings, ancient and modern, of the theorizers of all nations. He seems to have been most strongly drawn to English writers and thinkers on law and government, especially J. S. Mill.

His point of view is certainly much less individualistic than theirs. He seeks to harmonize their conceptions with his own inclination to see all problems from the point of view of society instead of that of the individual. He is permeated with the evolutionary philsophy and tries to bring social and legal development within it. To what extent he has succeeded will, of course, be a matter of controversy.

He has at all events given a singularly lucid, though condensed, perhaps lucid because condensed, statement of the various views which have prevailed as to the elements of law and its functions in human society, and has added many acute observations of his own. His work would seem to go far towards justifying the recent declaration of a learned writer, Brückner, in his History of Russian Literature, that if the Russians have no great philosophers they have great legists as well as great theologians.

Prof. Larnaude in his preface to the French version, which has been already quoted at length, says that no competent instruction is even yet to be found in the French schools upon this "Cours," designed to show "the object and end of juridical science, the different parts of which it is composed, the connection of all these parts, the order in which they ought to be successively treated, and, above all, the method which ought to be employed to fill this gap." He adds: "For the moment they (the publishers of the French version) are giving us a book which, while not especially Russian, is from many points of view excellent."

"Korkunov's General Theory of law contains in truth parts of rare vigor and originality. As to natural law, the origin of law, legal norms, the distinction between public and private law, the theory of the three powers, moral persons, the nature of society and of the state, and a good many other questions, there will not simply be found, formulated with great precision and uncommon force of reasoning, the chief theories which are at the bottom of universal legal thought. There will be found, too, Russian theories, often very ingenious. Russian thought is not, even in the legal domain, though profoundly influenced by German science, a mere reflection of it. From these different points of view Prof. Korkunov's book will be read I think with very great interest by all those who for the first time penetrate into Russian juridical thought."

It is hoped that in its English form the book will inspire some such interest in others as its Russian and French forms have in the translator. The Russian, in its condensation, seems to lend itself to re-expression in English even better than in French. If the English version does not do justice to the author's thought, the fault must be laid at the translator's door. The need for such teaching in English is not less than Prof. Larnaude says it is in French.

W. G. HASTINGS.

LINCOLN, NEBRASKA, July 23, 1909.

TRANSLATOR'S PREFACE TO THE SECOND EDITION

The exhaustion of the edition of this work, printed in 1909, and the necessity of setting it up in type again, as there were no plates of the former printing, have furnished an opportunity to correct a few obvious typographical errors in the first edition.

In truth, Prof. Korkunov's book seems to have justified its translation into English. The call for a reprinting is very gratifying. The St. Petersburg law teacher, who has been dead for nineteen years, was evidently a phenomenal man in his power of intellectual detachment and analysis, combined with moral earnestness. The breakdown, for the time, of the legal system under which he worked does not of course in any way impair the philosophic value of his conclusions. That the official head of Russian legal instruction at the close of the nineteenth century was capable of forming, and was permitted to teach, such opinions as are here represented is a vindication of at least some parts of that Czaristic régime. That the downfall of the imperial system was in some degree precipitated by Czaristic reaction against the legalist movement which developed the Duma of 1905, seems now clear.

Prof. Korkunov would surely, had he lived to see them, have been as disappointed as any of us at the terrible consequences of the collapse at once of the official government and the official church throughout the vast empire. That the breakdown is only temporary, and that there will follow a reorganization which will embody sound practical principles of justice and political administration, the presence of such work as Korkunov's in the great body of Russian literature is certainly a strong guarantee.

W. G. H.

STATE UNIVERSITY, LINCOLN, NEBRASKA,
June 1, 1921.

General Theory of Law

THEORY OF LAW

INTRODUCTION

NEED FOR GENERAL KNOWLEDGE

SCHELLING. Vorlesungen über die akad. Studium, 1802.
COMTE, AUG. Cours de philosophie positive. Tome 1. (Première leçon.)

Section 1. Human knowledge as shown in the separate sciences presents itself only as divided into fragments. Observation by itself gives us nothing general. We gain from it, directly, only knowledge of isolated, partial facts. Meanwhile, for practical life, a purpose not to be left out of view by any living science, fragmentary knowledge does not answer. The life, even of a single individual, presents at every step very broad and general questions, and answers to them he expects precisely from science. One for whom even a little corner of existence has opened, disclosing henceforth to him the world of scientific comprehension, does not easily reconcile himself again to surroundings of total darkness. Moral satisfaction in the complete finishing of his separate work he will experience only in the connecting of that isolated work with the universal, fundamental questions of life. A fully comprehended and satisfactorily finished work is possible only under the condition of being performed as a vitally connected part of the work of all humanity; and for such an understanding of his own isolated labors, that of each special one does not suffice the man. Every one involuntarily shows the tendency towards enlarging his knowledge, giving it the character of generality, so that all questions which life raises may receive scientific treatment and solution as far as possible.

But how shall we attain this purpose? Under what form turn fragmentary into systematic science? The simple means for that purpose at first view would seem to be the augmenting of the quantity of knowledge. To arrange so that I should know all the science attainable by any one and serve myself with the general knowledge held by all mankind, would seemingly solve the problem. If the bulk of this knowledge seems too great, and passes the strength of any individual man, it is possible to lighten it at the expense of quality. Though an imperfect, superficial knowledge, yet it would be unrestricted and all-embracing. Reaching this aim, we attain an all-embracing universal science.

To settle the question in this manner is to resort to the encyclopedic method. But whatever the importance of an encyclopedic science, it is not that which is to furnish our solution. The encyclopedic method can give no science as a whole. The different elements of human knowledge will all be found grouped as one may arrange the elements of science acquired by a single individual. But the comprehension of this mass of matters through the construction of an articulated system is not the immediate result of the encyclopedic method. It can bring us to know in one domain the small details, and by the side of this our ignorance may be complete as to other questions of much greater importance. We have found by the aid of spectral analysis the chemical contents of the most distant stars. But how is it with obscure points as to the organization of our own bodies? Comparative philology shows us the degree of civilization of the oldest Aryans, while the question of the origin of Russia remains as insoluble for us as when the comparative method was not even a name.

Human science is a book with leaves gone. Here on one page we have read all which has been written, but the pages which precede and those which follow do not exist and that which we have read only irritates us as an undecipherable enigma. Moreover, human science in its final results shows itself fragmentary. Even if I should attain to the assimilation of all which men know, my science would not exhibit a unified system. Even in antiquity when the mass of material facts of science was not yet so great, and minds were not uncommon which embraced the entire stock of human knowledge, its fragmentary character made itself felt. Even then generalization of knowledge and its co-ordination into a general system was struggled for. As a means to this came the thought of changing the very method of study. Among the Greeks, accordingly, appeared philosophy as a special form of science. Not in the extending of empirical knowledge did the Greek thinkers find the means for giving to our science generalization and completeness. They sought it in the analysis of primary conceptions found in all men, in decomposing them into their ultimate elements, and in bringing them into more general conceptions, so as to form a systematic, independent whole, detached from the accidental frame of empiric notions. Thereby the very source of knowledge was changed. Observation gave only fragmentary science and therefore they filled in with deduction. I can observe only accessible phenomena. Meditation, however, knows no exterior bounds. Everything may be the subject of meditation. Freed from necessity of observation, it can go forward to the establishing of an entire, complete system, to what is called a philosophic system.

Since Plato's time the thinkers among mankind have worked out not a few such systems. But their very number and the impossibility of finding a sufficient objective reason for preferring any one of all these different ones, could not fail to produce doubts of the utility of metaphysical paths towards a genuine science of real things and not merely a collection of opinions. And so in positivism appeared the absolute denial of any help from metaphysics. But even the positivists were compelled to recognize the imperative necessity of generalizing this special knowledge gained by empirical method. Even the founder of positivism, Auguste Comte, explained in great detail the insufficiency of simple special knowledge.

In the very beginning stage of our science, declared he, it is not possible to recognize any determinate division of intellectual labor. All the sciences are cultivated at the same time by the same men. This stage of human knowledge, inevitable at first, changes little by little according as separate branches of science develop. By virtue of a law of evident necessity, each branch of the scientific system separates itself insensibly from the stem just far enough to enlarge itself so as to be the subject of a separate science, that is, to occupy by itself the activity of certain minds. It is to this division of scientific research into distinct categories, divided out to distinct groups of savants, that we owe the remarkable development which is taking place before our eyes in each branch of knowledge. From this new state of science there results for the modern savant an evident impossibility of beginning again those encyclopedic studies which were so easy and common in antiquity. In a word the division of labor, becoming more and more marked, is one of the distinguishing characteristics of modern scientific development. But in fully recognizing the advantages of such a division one cannot avoid, on the other hand, being struck with the disadvantages resulting from this excessive subdivision of the studies with which the learned are occupied. These disadvantages are in a degree inevitable, but we may be permitted to seek an alleviation of that in them which is most troublesome, while leaving in its entirety the division itself. The golden mean, evidently, consists not in a return towards antiquity with its absence of all division. This would result in hindering the future progress of knowledge. It consists, on the contrary, in developing this division. Let a group of savants deemed fit for such work, instead of devoting themselves to some one of existing separate sciences, consecrate themselves to the exclusive examination of their present state, their tendencies with regard to each other, the explanation of their connections and mutual relations, the reduction, so far as possible, of their leading principles to a less number of more general ones; let other savants guide themselves by these general principles so that by harmony with those who established them, they may verify by a common effort their results, and thus the division of labor in the domain of scientific activity can be developed to its extreme limits without science losing itself in the accumulation of details, "without the trees preventing our seeing the forest."

If this scientific method is used, a synthetic science will be reached which in its method will not differ from the special sciences. Science so constituted will not reject the teachings of daily experience, nor be metaphysical, nor claim to have attained to the absolute. It will propose but one task, to reach the highest point of a generalization founded upon acquaintance with phenomena, consequently upon that relative knowledge which is the subject of the special sciences.

All which has just been said of science in general can be applied particularly and specially to the study of law. Among all the branches of science it is precisely in law that the compelling necessity for a generalized system is felt. This arises from the fact that we cannot observe law in its entirety. The vault of heaven with its stars, or an animal's body, we conceive before all as a whole, and it is only scientific analysis that teaches us to regard them as complex aggregations of a multitude of special elements. This is not the case with law. We directly perceive only separate laws, distinct transactions, and it is only by scientific synthesis that we combine these separate elements into a single conception of juridical order, into a single idea of law considered as the norm of social life. Therefore in the study of law the fragmentary condition of the elements of our knowledge is so much the more serious because we do not recognize its unity by observation, by direct perception. To be sure, legal relations, the peculiar relations which men have with each other, are not without connection between themselves. But these relations, and the bond which unites them, are not evident nor palpable and, moreover, lawyers do not study them directly. They study, to tell the truth, custom, laws, judgments, transactions between individuals. But all this matter is at first view extremely varied, and the greater the development of social life, the greater is this variety. The development of social life gives birth to a larger and ever larger number of extremely diverse interests, which struggle together and whose delimitation and determination form the task of law. In a social life, so complex and entangled, the same interests may give rise to a multiplicity of relations, and each form which they take demands for its control a special legal rule. For example, the rules as to individual inheritances in modern legislation are not controlled by a single general law, but by a multitude of different ones, distributed among various branches of legislation. Therefore, a comprehensive view of the legal organization of the rules of descent of property can be secured only by the aid of scientific synthesis embracing the numerous different rules which make up such legislation.

At the same time no science touches more closely upon the immediate questions of life than does that of law. You can find, perhaps, in our social organization a man who has never concerned himself with natural science or history. Well, search the age, there is no one wholly unconcerned with legal questions. It is something quite unthinkable. Be ever so misanthropic, avoid mankind however carefully, yet legal questions shall not pass around you. In any event there is one domain of law, that of personal liberty, which shall imperatively demand your attention. In shunning men you must say to them, "Here commence the bounds of that domain where I am free; you have no right to encroach upon it." For all these reasons, it is in legal science that the tendency to generalize ought to manifest itself more imperiously than anywhere else; and, in fact, there has been for a long time an idea of creating by the side of the special juridical sciences one which should give a complete knowledge of the law. It has chosen the first of the means which we have indicated for reaching generalization in science, the encyclopedic method. Its task consists in multiplying and expanding the different elements of the science, in reuniting into a single branch various concrete facts, and in arranging these branches. The philosophy of law in its turn seeks to establish a science of law by the deductive method. This science, because of the end which it seeks, strives towards a unified system. Finally, the general theory of law which finds birth in our day has for its purpose the creating of a unified theory out of the concrete, empiric elements, furnished by the special branches of the subject.

The encyclopedia and the philosophy of law ordinarily form part of the instruction in faculties for legal training. In Germany both are taught; in England and France philosophy alone. In Russia at present we concern ourselves only with encyclopedia, though formerly, before the university crisis of 1835, it was the philosophy of law which was obligatory, but now, as we have said, it is encyclopedia which has replaced it. These three forms of science having the same object, we must give some effort for the attentive examination of each of them and shall estimate them in turn in the following sections of this introduction.

ENCYCLOPEDIA OF LAW

FRIEDLANDER. Juristische Encyclopädie oder System der Rechtswissenschaft. Heidelburg, 1847.

ORTLOFF. Die Encyclopädie der Rechtswissenschaft in ihrer gegenwärtigen Bedeutung. Jena, 1857.

ORNATSKY. Comparative examination of Modern, with Ancient Greek and Roman ideas of "Encyclopedia." – Collection of January 12, 1855. Art. 7. Moscow.

REDKINE. Review of Legal Encyclopedic Literature. Redkine and Janevich-Janovsky's Juridical Memories. Vol. 5. St. Petersburg, 1860.

KARASEVICH. Encyclopedia of Law. Lectures, given at Laroslavl, 1872. In Demidoff's Journal of the Juridical Lycee.

ZWAIREV. Encyclopedia's place in the organization of Juridical Science. Juridical Messenger, 1880, No. 1.

Section 2. Encyclopedia in its usual meaning does not denote a special science. It ordinarily means not a science but a circle of sciences. We speak, for example, of the Encyclopedia of Bacon, of Wolf, or of Comte, meaning by that the modes of classification of the sciences which those writers have adopted. If we apply the term to a book we mean by it a work containing in some order, often merely alphabetic, a review of a more or less extended group of sciences, sometimes of all the sciences at once. This understanding of the term is based on its etymology. It comes from a Greek expression meaning a circle of sciences answering to a program of the secondary education of that time. The Romans kept the same meaning. In reality the words "Encyclopedia," "Cyclopedia," the form it usually has in English, or simply "Pedia," were not in use before the sixteenth century. The first book bearing this title was Ringelberg's Lucubrations vel potius Absolutissima Kyklopaideia, 1541. The author has combined some studies upon grammar, rhetoric, dialectics, and in a distinct part, "Chaos," he placed what would not go under the other three rubrics.

When we apply this meaning of the word to the encyclopedia of law in particular we mean by it only a general and succinct résumé of materials of all the juridical sciences. The first book bearing the name of Encyclopedia of Law was Hunnius', 1638. But he was only the first to make use of the name. A book whose subject was the same was published before his, under another title. It is claimed, indeed, that the first encyclopedic work on law was the Speculum Judiciale of Durantis, 1275. This is not to be accepted. The assertion of it rests upon the fact that the nature of his subject includes Roman as well as canon law. This, however, is not sufficient ground for calling Durantis' Speculum Judiciale encyclopedic. First: It does not embrace all law. Feudal law is not treated. Roman law is, moreover, so closely bound up with canon law that the common study of both parts was necessary aside from any encyclopedic purpose. Second: Durantis' Speculum was intended to serve as a manual not for the study of law as a whole, but for lawyers in judicial employments. The author sets forth his general views in a little preface in which he distinguishes among other six laws after the number of wings of the cherubim: "*Per sex alas sex leges intellige: prima est lex naturalis, secunda mosaica, tertia prophetica, quarta evangelica, quinta apostolica, sexta canonica.*"

It is more correct to place the origin of encyclopedic literature in the XVI century when we can show the coming of many works of a systematic, methodical character, covering all branches of the law. Among them that of Lagus, a German jurist, Lagus' Methodica Juris utriusque Traditio, 1543, deserves special attention. It had up to the end of the century six editions and afterwards two more which later were revised by Freigius. This proves the book had an unquestionable success. It ought to be considered as the first systematic encyclopedia of law. It includes not only law, public and private, but also positive law and the philosophy of law. It is divided into two parts, first, *pars philosophica;* second, *pars historica.* The first part embraces the origin of law, legislation, manners, the commentary and application of law, the theory of analogies, and that of fictions, and, besides, natural law. In the second part is positive law. He describes, too, the different sorts of legal relations, *forma juris*, and for each of them sets four questions: Who is the owner of the rights? How does he get a right? How lose it and how keep it?

The expression "Encyclopedia of Law" as we have said does not appear till the XVII century and the first work bearing the name was Hunnius' Encyclopedia Juris Universi, Cologne, 1638. It was re-edited in 1642, 1658 and 1675. The book is divided into five parts and contains a review of law under an artificial system. First, Jus personæ. Second, De Judiciis et processu Judicario. Third, De contractibus. Fourth, De Materia ultimarum Voluntatum.

All the historians of encyclopedic literature of the law consider Hunnius as not only the first to employ it, but as the only one of that century. This latter is incorrect. Two years after his book, in 1640, there was published at Frankfort a work entitled, Encyclopedia Juris, publici privatique, civilis, criminalis, feudalis, Autore Joanne Philippo a Vorburg. At the head of the book is found a discourse of Hallutius upon the importance of encyclopedia in general. Then comes a preface by Vorburg himself upon Juridical Encyclopedia. The book has two very unequal divisions. First, Collection of legal rules,—Nux regularis Juridica sive Accurata et articulosa enucleatio atque expositio omnium Juris civilis regularum, by Wolfgang Sigismond of Barburg, Dean of Ashfenburg; and second, A Legal Dictionary. Besides this work of Vorburg, one, which is not mentioned by any encyclopedist, appeared in 1675, that of Unverfarth, Pædiæ Jurisprudentiæ. The author defines his "Pedia" thus: "*Pædiæ vocabulum proprie significat institutionem puerilem, qua, si bona sit animi ad virtutes et bonas artes capessendas subiguntur.*" He assigns to "Pedia" seven ends, among them: First, Determination of sources and criteria of scientific truth; third, of the scientific method also; fourth, a table of books and documents for the use of the learned. The book is divided according to this scheme. It has twenty-three chapters devoted exclusively to setting forth the general questions just mentioned without going into the detailed development of any branch of juridical science. For this reason Unverfarth's book ought to be credited with much more value than that of Hunnius.

In the XVIII century two diametrically opposing tendencies show themselves in juridico-encyclopedic literature. This was the time when the rupture was most complete between the philosophic and the positive sciences. Some were written under the dogmatic or positive tendency, as it was then called. Such, for example, was Stephane (Pütter's) Entwurfeiner Juristischen Encyclopädia, Göttingen, 1757, which really brought the term encyclopedia into current use, and which also separated methodology from encyclopedia, which cannot be reckoned, to tell the truth, as a merit. Others belong to the philosophic tendency. Such are the works of Nettelbladt, Wolf's celebrated pupil, who wrote several encyclopedic manuals, well known at that time. The encyclopedias written under this influence remained, as before, brief compends of the contents of the special sciences and nothing more. The philosophic system gave to summary expositions of this kind a suitable form, some ready made plans, some rubrics and categories, but did not bring forth the intrinsic unity, the general idea which should dominate the whole.

It is only with the commencement of the XIX century that the characters of legal encyclopedias change. Some new and enlarged requirements were made of them. The encyclopedists were not satisfied with brief expositions of the materials of special juridical sciences. They aspired to make of encyclopedia an independent science having its own task. This new tendency, which sees in encyclopedia not only a special manner of setting forth a science, but a distinct and independent science, was formed under the immediate influence of Schelling's and Hegel's doctrines, who first had spoken of encyclopedia as a science.

The need of raising encyclopedia to the level of an independent science is recognized when the insufficiency of the notion of it till then prevailing is observed. Encyclopedia was certainly designed in the thought of its inventors to remedy those inconveniences which lie at the commencement of legal study in its special branches, civil and political law for example; the study of special parts supposing always a knowledge of a series of general juridical notions, such as law in the subjective and objective sense, the state, capacity of persons, etc. Even the history of law supposes this knowledge, since all history is essentially the translation of historic phenomena into the language of modern notions and the history of law into the language of modern juridical ideas. So, indeed, one feels the need of an introduction to the study of law which shall not leave the professor under the necessity of beginning to study certain parts of a science whose outline remains unknown. But it is doubtful whether the means proposed would answer the purpose; whether a brief sketch of all the parts of the science can serve as a satisfactory introduction to the study of law. If it is difficult to begin by a detailed study of some of the parts, it is equally so, to begin by a superficial study of more. The difficulty consists not in the abundance of details but in the too fragmentary character of the study itself. A rational study of law does not consist simply in recognizing the meaning of the principal terms, the division of the science into distinct branches and investigating the material with which each of them deals. To get brief notions of details is not to get the idea of a whole. To join parts into a whole is not simple and easy even to those who are acquainted with the parts. The controversies of which the general system of law is the subject, are, as we shall see, the proof of this. A rapid review of all parts of law makes an even more defective preparation for legal study than does an elaborate and detailed study of a separate branch. A special study sufficiently thorough permits of studying some part in its relations to the whole. In showing him to the bottom all the materials of one branch of the law, the student is at a stroke introduced *in medias res*. The richness of the content interests, attracts him, and a rigorously scientific study accustoms him to scientific observation and analysis. A rapid study, condensed like a manual, is incapable of interesting him because of the poverty of its content; superficial, it does not go to the bottom of the subject and instead of fruit gives him the bark.

With these considerations, which are suggested to us by the conditions of instruction, a good many others unite. It is not merely the beginners who feel the need and difficulty of conceiving science as a whole. A specialist who studies only some particular scientific question experiences the same necessity. The development of science brings with it greater and greater specialization. In legislation, as in other things, specialization unceasingly increases. One finds quite frequently among the ancient lawyers, authors devoted to studies bearing upon all branches of legal science. So in the first half of this century there were savants equally perfect in two or three branches of legal study. For example, K. S. Zachariä, who treated of public and private law; Heffter, who employed himself upon both criminal and international law; Bluntschli, who taught international, public and private law, etc. Now by pressure of things in the domain of law the learned are compelled to restrict their field of research. But this concentration of scientific effort upon a more limited domain, this concentration required by the development and specialization of science, ought not to have as a result, it goes without saying, the restricting of the jurist's horizon. As we have said, special and particular research upon a determinate matter can produce, if well conducted, extensive results which throw a new light on man's conception of the universe. The best example is Darwin's. Being, and always remaining, a mere zoölogist, he nevertheless reached, in his study upon The Origin of Species, the establishment of a vast and profound system which gave birth to a new conception of the Universe called by good right "Darwinism."

But that a special study may have this fruitfulness, the desired direction must be given it. It is necessary in working upon individual questions not to lose sight of general principles, and to consider the development of parts a means and not an end. In a word, every specialist, however peculiar his subject, ought to have as his aim science considered as a whole. To attain this aim the savant must be inspired with a fixed conception embracing all the progress realized by science at a given moment; but, by what means is he to reach such a conception? He cannot create it himself. This would require a preliminary labor which would prevent his devoting himself to his special studies, since a rapid review of different materials of science is absolutely helpless to bring out the idea of unified knowledge. A rapid review of this kind never determines the connection between the particular question of the savant's studies and other scientific questions.

So we think we have established that encyclopedia, as ordinarily understood, cannot satisfy the requirements of scientific instruction. It gives no general notion of a science conceived as a whole.

It is these defects of encyclopedia, regarded as a rapid superficial review of materials, as a manual of other sciences, which have given birth to the idea that it must be allowed standing as a separate science, designed to show the general connection between the different questions which the special sciences study separately. Schelling developed this idea in his Discourse upon Academic Studies conformably to his conception of the Universe, according to which the whole is organically bound together. He considered science as a living organism. Its distinct parts are not, for him, dead mechanical portions, but living parts of a living whole. Just as an organ of any organism can be understood only on condition of being studied in its relation with the entire organism, so one can suitably study and comprehend each branch of a science only in its connections with the whole of it. It is this purpose that "Encyclopädie" ought to serve, having as object the study of all human science. It appears then not as one of the special sciences but as the science of sciences which commands the rest, as a "potential" science containing in itself all the essentials which the special sciences develop in detail.

Hegel's doctrine offers a synthesis even more harmonious and more audacious. For him the whole universe is only an uninterrupted dialectic development of absolute thought. He has extended this synthetic view to science, which, being itself one of the phases of dialectic development, presents, also, in its branches phases of this movement. This is why he demands that special sciences be studied in their connection with the whole, since they are for him only phases of methodic development of a unified science,—"The One."

These ideas set forth by Schelling and Hegel induced a considerable movement in encyclopedic literature. The best of more recent legal encyclopedias have all been made more or less under the influence of these ideas. Among those thus made are Karl Pütter's Der Inbegriff der Rechtswissenschaft, oder Juristische Encyclopädie und Methodologie, 1846, which first introduced into the encyclopedia the study of the general history of the law, and Friedlander's Juristische Encyclopädie oder system der Rechtswissenschaft, 1847, which gives in a little book the best attempt yet made to present "Encyclopädie" as a special science. The encyclopedias which show the direct influence of Schelling's system like that of Rudhart, Encyclopädie und Methodologie der Rechtswissenschaft, 1823, do not shine by any special qualities. But the organic conception of the Universe, the main point of Schelling's doctrine, has given birth to the three best later German Encyclopedias, Ahrens', Warnkönig's, and Walter's. In that of Ahrens, Juristische Encyclopädie, 1857, the organic conception of the Universe appears with the modifications which Krause, one of Schelling's successors, had brought in. Warnkönig, Juristische Encyclopädie, 1853, shows himself a partisan of the same organic system as the younger Fichte. In Walter's Juristische Encyclopädie, 1856, the organic tendency is joined with Stahl's theological one. All the encyclopedias of the XIX century which we have cited follow, then, the philosophic tendency; but it has not been the only one. Even in the XVIII century there was observed besides it a contrary tendency which has now everywhere a historic character. To it belong Falk's Juristische Encyclopädie, 1821–5, Ausgab. v. Jhering, 1851, and Bluhme's Encyclopädie der in Deutschland geltenden Rechte. First, Ausg. 1847–54. Second, Ausg. 1855–69. For the XIX century the period from 1840 to 1860 marks the time of greatest development of encyclopedic literature. The following period marks its decline. If we leave out Goldschmidt's book, Encyclopädie der Rechtswissenschaft, 1862, which does not set forth an "Encyclopädie" but gives only a résumé of matters embraced in university instruction, with notation of authors to be consulted, no attempt was made in Germany after those mentioned till the period from 1870 to 1880 to set forth the "Encyclopädie" of law as a whole. Holtzendorff's Encyclopädie der Rechtswissenschaft, 1889, is only a collection of articles by different authors. They are in two separate volumes. In the first the author has set forth a short exposé of the special juridical sciences preceded by a brief study of the general history of law by Merkel. The second volume is a juridical dictionary. So we do not recognize it as an "Encyclopädie" as Schelling and Hegel conceived one. It is only in 1885 that a new systematic study of "Encyclopädie" is attempted. Merkel in his Juristische Encyclopädie, 1885, does not follow, to say the truth, the tendencies of the encyclopedists of 1850 to 1860. He does not make of his "Encyclopädie" an independent science. It consists of a review of the special juridical sciences and has not, consequently, the character of an independent one. This does not reduce its value. The first part, especially where he gives a brief sketch of the General Theory of Law, is a very precious and interesting contribution to legal literature. It is the same with Gareis' Encyclopädie und

Methodologic der Rechtswissenschaft, 1887. It is still more like a simple review of special juridical matters, for its general part is less developed. Gareis, himself, defines "Encyclopädie" as a systematic review of the law.

The little book of Ratkovsky, Encyclopädie der Rechtswissenschaft und Staatswissenschaften als Einleitung in deren Studium, Vienna, 1890, is divided into three parts. In the first part are explained the leading legal conceptions. In the second is found a review of sciences rigorously juridical, and in the third a review of the political sciences, all in a hundred pages. Thus the authors of the most recent works on "Juristische Encyclopädie" have not sought to make of it an independent science. How explain this fact? Why, after such a series of efforts to raise it to the level of a science, is there a return to the old conception long since condemned? Why is "Encyclopädie" considered again as a mere brief résumé of special matters without any intrinsic unity, made generally upon an arbitrary plan, alphabetic at need? There is only one explanation. Lawyers no longer believe that it is possible to realize Schelling's and Hegel's ideas. They no more admit that "Encyclopädie" can be made a science of sciences distinct and independent and embracing the content of all the special sciences. The German philosophers thought to inspire themselves with the idea that each special question ought to be studied in its connections with the whole; otherwise the study would have no living value, would be sterile. Meanwhile, this is the general condition necessary to all science which seeks to keep a character genuinely scientific. It is a condition which every science ought to fulfill and not merely the pretended encyclopedic one. Only, this last, it is said, to constitute a science must bear upon special and independent matter. What is that matter? We are told that "Encyclopädie" embraces the materials of all the sciences. To this we may object with Konopake,—either "Encyclopädie" is not a science or it is incapable of embracing the materials of all the sciences, for the sum cannot be equal to each of the parts taken separately. Aside from this entirely formal argument, we must observe that the existence of "Encyclopädie" as a science of the sciences would render these other sciences absurd and objectless. It would swallow up in itself all the matters of which they treat. On the other hand it is the division of our scientific studies that makes necessary most of the special sciences and impossible the existence of a distinct and independent one embracing all human knowledge. So, it is necessary to recognize in the decadence of encyclopedic literature no passing phenomenon; it is rather a proof of the sterility of the encyclopedic idea itself.

In setting forth the history of encyclopedic literature we have spoken only of Germany, for German literature alone presents on this subject a regular development prepared by a current of preceding ideas. If some encyclopedias of law have been published in other countries they have been only imitations of the Germans, and are to be considered as accidental facts without importance. In Russia "Encyclopädie" was taught for the first time at the end of the eighteenth century by German savants at the University of Moscow. The first professor of it was the celebrated Bause, who was inspired with the principles of Wolf's philosophy; after him came Purgold. But encyclopedic instruction at this period was optional. It was only after the legislation of 1835 that it was introduced into the University's programme as obligatory. From this time date the Russian encyclopedias of law. Down to 1835 there had been published only Degai's, entitled, Advice and Rules for Applying Russian Law, or materials for the Encyclopedia, Methodology, and History of Russian Law, 1831. This book is only a compilation and has now only one interest, that of showing us our own jurisprudence before the promulgation of the code. The next following book was Nivoline's Encyclopedia of Jurisprudence, 1839, second edition, 1857, decidedly better in scientific quality. At its head is a short philosophic introduction where the author explains the notion of law. He tries to base this part upon Hegel's and Stahl's philosophic doctrines, defending with Stahl the existence of a personal God who governs at his will the fate of the philosophy of legislation and then that of positive legislation. In the history of the philosophy the author gives a detailed analysis of philosophic doctrines founded upon a direct study of the sources. The history of positive legislation is treated with less personal care.

Rojestvensky's Encyclopedia of Law, 1863, is concerned in quite a different order of ideas. The author excludes absolutely from his book philosophic doctrines of the law and all history of positive law. The book, simply dogmatic, contains a sketch of materials of juridical sciences and is found preceded by a general philosophic introduction inspired by the doctrines of the younger Fichte.

Rojestvensky's book is, moreover, the only Russian encyclopedia giving an outline of matters of juridical science. The work of Kapoustine, published in 1868, Juridical Dogmatics, and that of Rennenkamp, Outline of Juridical Encyclopedia, 1880, second edition, are only general studies in the law. They present no application of fixed philosophic ideas. They are eclectic in character. Yet they are the best two manuals of encyclopedia of law in Russian literature. Unfortunately, they are no longer in current use. In the last twenty years many new works in legal literature and upon legislation have appeared, but the Juridical Dogmatics of Prof.

Kapoustine is still in its first edition. Prof. Rennenkampf's book, republished in 1880, appeared again in 1889 in briefer form, under the title Juridical Encyclopedia. But even the last is not brought up abreast with current legislation. Thus in the 1889 edition the author declares that our legislation contains no enactments concerning Catholic and Protestant churches, although such regulations were incorporated into the code of 1857. The author, and this is more strange, employs the edition of the code of 1857 even for questions treated in the editions of 1876 and 1886. The old theories, for example Hegel's distinction between the false in criminal and in civil matter, are accepted as absolute verities.

In the period from 1870 to 1880 appeared two new works upon encyclopedia, Karasevich's Encyclopedia of Law, 1872, and Delarov's Outline of Encyclopedia of Law, 1878, but they remain unfinished. Karasevich had one fascicule published, containing little more than the preface. Delarov's work according to the author's plan was to have three volumes. In the first, law is considered as one of the factors of social life. To speak properly, the author has concerned himself little with positive law. The first is the only volume published. The other two which have not appeared were to contain an exposition of the general theory of law, Vol. 1; and the application of this theory by means of the civil law, Vol. 2. In the literature of other countries are scarcely found, so far as I know, works upon legal "Encyclopädie." Holland must be excepted, for there is found Anne den Tex. Encyclopædie Jurisprudentiæ, 1835, and also the Belgian Roussel's Encyclopédie du droit, 1813. Second edition at Namur, 1874. One might also cite two French works, Eshbach's Cours d'introduction générale à l'étude du droit ou Manuel d'encyclopédie Juridique, third edition, 1856, and Courcelle-Seneuil's Preparation à l'étude du droit, 1897.

PHILOSOPHY OF LAW

MASARYK. Versuch einer Konkrete Logik, 1887. Wundt Logik, Section 619.

HARMS. Begriff Formen und Grundlegung der Rechtsphilosophie, 1889.

BERGBOHM. Jurisprudentz und Rechtsphilosophie 1, 1892.

Section 3. With the ancients philosophy was universal science. For them it was a science which generalized the others in bringing out the traits common to them. So Aristotle's philosophy embraces mathematics, physics, ethics and poetics. What the author called "primary philosophy," πρώτη φιλοσοφία and his ancient commentators "metaphysics," because it followed physics, had as object the study of the fundamental principles of the Universe. The word "metaphysics" indicated to them only the order of succession of Aristotle's studies, but, subsequently, it took another signification. It designates *a priori* studies. In England philosophy still usually means science in general, as with Aristotle. On the continent, however, and above all in Germany, philosophy means a particular transcendental view both of the object of study and of the source of the science. As to the first, it regards philosophy as the science of supranatural phenomena; for example, those of the soul, of the supreme cause of general phenomena, of the absolute, in contradistinction to relative knowledge of sensible phenomena. As to the second, philosophy can have the same object and the same content as the empirical sciences on condition that the method applied to the study of these phenomena be not empirical. According to this method, which has especially prevailed since the time of Chr. Wolf, each thing can be the subject of a double study, one empirical—finding its matter in sensible experience, the other philosophical—seeking knowledge of the supra-sensible; so, for example, by the side of empirical science of nature is philosophy of nature, and by the side of empirical psychology is philosophic, rational psychology, etc.

As law is not a phenomenon of external material nature, but one of the consequences of man's rational activity, it has been for a long time classed among the subjects of philosophical research. The setting forth of the idea of law, the determination of its origin, and other such questions, are studied in that philosophy styled "practical" or "ethical." Antiquity ignored legal philosophy as a distinct branch, in the same way in which it failed to recognize elsewhere the divisions of science. As for the middle ages, philosophy of law as a distinct branch of learning distinguished from ethics appeared only in the XVII century. Starting with the XVII century, it passed in its development through two entirely distinct phases. At first the philosophy of law differed from the science of positive law not only by its method, but by its very object, which was not positive law, variable and changeable as we find it, but the invariable, eternal, natural law on which positive law, it was thought, should rest. It was only at the end of the XVIII century, when the new historical school had shown the insufficiency of the conception of natural law, that philosophy applied itself to the explanation of positive law. Briefly, the philosophic study of law was known to the XVII and XVIII centuries under the name of natural law—*Jus naturale*, and to the XIX century under the name of philosophy of law.

The beginnings of natural law are found in the celebrated treatise of the learned Hollander, Hugo Grotius, De Jure Belli ac Pacis Libri Tres, 1625. The fundamental idea of his doctrine is, that there should be recognized beside or beneath the variable positive law established by the will of God or of men (*Jus Voluntarium*), an invariable natural law derived from the nature of man regarded as a reasonable being, and especially from his inward need for living in society. (*Appetitus Societas.*) "That is just,' proclaimed Grotius, "which is conformed to the nature of society among reasonable beings. Such law is absolutely natural and independent of time and place. No one can change it. It would exist and remain the same even if there were no God."

Grotius' doctrine was presently a good deal extended Already, in the XVII century some new theories of natural law appeared. Such was, first, the theory of Thomas Hobbes in his Elementa Philosophica de Cive, 1842, which repeated Grotius' principle of sociability and recognized as humanity's leading trait, fear, upon which he established his fundamental natural law, "Pax est Quærenda." Samuel Puffendorf applied to natural law the doctrine of the Cartesians. With him as with Grotius the principle of sociability is the primary natural base. His doctrine was very popular in the law schools of the time because it was the first to set forth natural law according to a well ordered system and also because he had connected his theory with the more philosophic doctrine of Descartes. His book, De Officiis hominis et Civis, 1673, translated into several languages, became a current manual of natural law.

The theories of the XVII century did not yet distinguish morality from law, at least from natural law. So in these theories the opposition between natural and positive law is not yet very clear. It was confused with the scarcely recognized distinction between law and morality. But at the beginning of the XVIII century Chr. Thomasius first distinguished definitively law from morality. He went so far as to oppose the one to the other, giving to the theory of natural law a more precise and rigorous character.

Starting from this time, natural law is only law as opposed to moral rules. About the middle of the XVIII century Chr. Wolf and his disciples gave to the theory of natural law a systematic form, but in the spirit of the doctrine of Leibnitz. The theorists of the XVII and XVIII centuries all alike employed in developing the natural law a deductive method. It is, however, necessary to observe that the elements on which they build were not created *a priori*, were not innate ideas. Kant (1714–1804), in his Metaphysische Anfangsgrunde der Rechtslehre, had sought to give to the theory of natural law the absolute, *a priori* character, which it lacked. He deduced all its principles from an absolute *a priori* category of our reason, which can be formulated in the following terms: Act in such a manner that your liberty shall accord with that of all and of each.

The doctrines of natural law penetrated into Russia at the commencement of the XVIII century. That of Puffendorf was particularly esteemed. In 1726 there was printed a translation of his book made by order of Peter the Great. Ch. F. Gross, professor of moral philosophy at the academy of sciences (1725–1731), and the first professor of the law faculty at Moscow, Diltei, used this book in their classes. From 1790 to 1800 Prof. Skiadan used it also. We might cite, too, an original attempt to set forth the theory of natural law by V. Zolotnitsky in his Abridgment of Natural Law, Extracted from Various Authors for the Use of Russian Society, 1764. The author gives as the foundation of his science the rule "know thyself," which leads us to a comprehension of our dependence upon God, and our neighbor and the necessity of guarding our own preservation.

However, the taste for the doctrines of natural law was not at that time general. On the contrary, from 1760 to 1770 one observes in Russian savants a tendency to study legal history. We might name among those who showed this, Polenov, and especially Diesnitzky, the first Russian law professor to criticise the theory of natural law severely in his Opinion Concerning the Most Direct and Shortest Means for Studying Jurisprudence. "The work of Puffendorf is really useless," says he, "for writing upon imaginary states of mankind without showing how property, possession or inheritance take birth and are regulated, does not answer to our ideas or purposes."

It was the foreign savants who contributed to spreading in Russia the doctrine of Wolf. Kant's doctrine represents the culminating point in the natural law theory in its first phase. He presses to its extreme limits the opposition between natural and positive law. But at the same time that his doctrine was spreading, an Historical School of Legislation was forming in Germany, having as its principal representatives Gustave Hugo (1798–1844), Fri. K. Savigny (1779–1860) and Geo. Fr. Puchta (1798–1846). This school declared energetically against the existence of natural law as a special norm having its place beside the positive law. It claimed to show that all law is a historical product of the people's life, that it is not created by the will of a legislator and is not a code of eternal, absolute, invariable principles. According to this school, law is a historic element in the life of a people, capable of a regular evolution.

The blow to the theory of natural law given by the historical school was a heavy one. In philosophic literature, too, a reaction appeared against the extreme abstraction of the rationalist doctrines. With Schelling (1775–1854) the philosophers abandoned the study of empty abstractions, to turn towards concrete and living realities. In opposition to the abstract systems of the rationalists who did not concern themselves with concrete reality, contemning the positive law which they considered as only a mutilation of the eternal principles of natural law, Schelling elaborated his system of positive philosophy which was to explain the meaning and inner reason of all that exists. The late representatives of German philosophy followed Schelling. Among them we will cite the three who have had most influence upon modern philosophy of law: Hegel, Grundlinien der Philosophie des Rechts, 1821; Krause, System der Rechtsphilosophie, 1874, and Herbart, Analytisch Beleuchtung des Naturrechts und der Moral, 1836. None of them maintain the existence of a natural law by the side of positive law. They follow a different purpose, that of comprehending the positive law in its historic forms and explaining their basis. If they employ still sometimes the words "Natural Law," they no longer mean the famous code of natural and eternal laws, but the philosophic basis for positive law. The disciples of Hegel (Michelet, Gans, L. Stein, Lasson, Lassalle, Max Stirner), taking for starting point the identification of laws of being with laws of thought, have struggled to present the development of different systems of positive laws as a dialectic development of a general idea, that of liberty. Krause's disciples, who form what is called the organic school where can be ranked Röder, Ahrens, and a good many Italian writers like Pepere, Lioy, and others, think to find in the harmonious development of the individual the definitive ideal towards which the development of positive law tends. Lastly, the disciples of Herbart (Thilo, Geyer, Ziller) seek to draw all the great variety of historic forms of law from two ideas, that of right, resulting from conflict, and that of justice (remuneration), which are, according to them, the absolute base of all which we deem just and equitable.

Among all these schools the most influential one in Russia has been Hegel's. Chitcherin followed it, making original applications of it: History of Political Doctrines, 1878. Property and Government, 1882–1883. Principles of Logic and of Metaphysics, 1894.

Although the philosophy of law in its latest form has turned towards the explanation of positive law, it is, nevertheless, not to be confused with the science of positive law. It keeps its own method. It employs neither observation nor induction. It continues to suppose that an explanation of eternal principles of positive law can be given, not by the empirical method, but by way of metaphysics with the aid of principles conceived immediately by our reason without aid from experience. It thinks this peculiarity of method allows philosophy to reach not only an absolute knowledge of law, to explain not merely legal relations, but also, the profound reasons of the law.

The conception of legal philosophy regarded as a special science supposes, first, the possibility of a knowledge not founded upon any experimental system; second, the necessity, or at least desirability, of separating the *a priori* elements of the science from the empirical ones. I do not wish to pass upon the first proposition. It belongs to the theory of knowledge, a theory having no special connection with law and offering still a vast field of controversy. We will say only that in these last days, the theory of knowledge *a priori* is more and more combatted. Whatever opinion one adopts as to the theory of knowledge, I do not think it possible to maintain the necessity of a legal philosophy, conceived as a metaphysical science of law.

If metaphysical knowledge of absolute truth is possible, why separate it from empirical study of the variable and the relative? In this case, the relative deserves study as a special manifestation of the absolute. The metaphysical knowledge of the absolute and the empirical knowledge would both gain much from such a combination. The notion of the absolute explained by the knowledge of the special and relative form of its manifestation would become more concrete, more living. Knowledge of the relative, illuminated by understanding its absolute and fundamental principles, would become more profound and more rational. This is why, if there are several methods of knowledge, there is no reason for separating them. They ought all to be combined into the scientific study of the object.

Moreover, it is necessary to declare that in our day we are more and more led to refuse to admit the existence of philosophy as a special metaphysical science bearing upon the elements which constitute the domain of the empirical sciences. If philosophy has still pretensions to being a special and independent science, it is not as an *a priori* knowledge of being, but as a theory of knowledge, or as a general theory having, nevertheless, the same sources as the different special sciences.[1]

[1] Wallaschek Studien zur Rechtsphilosophie 1889. S. 107. Die Zurückführung des in der Rechtsordnung formulierten Inhalts auf allgemeine Denkformen ist die Aufgabe der Rechtsphilosophie, sie ist die Wissenschaft vom Juristischen Denken.

THE GENERAL THEORY OF LAW

MERKEL. Ueber das Verhältniss der Rechtsphilosophie zur positiven Rechtswissenschaft (Grünhut's Zeitschrift, Sec. 1, 1874).

SCHUETZE. Die stellung der Rechtsphilosophie jur positiven Rechtswissenschaft. Id. Sec. 6, 1879.

BERGBOHM. Jurisprudentz und Rechtsphilosophie, 1892. Vol. 1, pp. 90–100.

MUELLER. Die Elemente des Rechts und der Rechtsbildung, 1877.

POST. Bausteine fur eine Allgemeinen Rechtswissenschaft, 1880.

MERKEL. Elemente der Allgemeinen Rechtslehre, 1889. (Holtzendorff's Encyclopädie der Rechtswissenschaft.)

Section 4. As seen in the last section we maintain that neither the encyclopedic method which seeks a remedy for the excessively fragmentary condition of our science in a review, superficial it is true, of the whole of it in all its branches, nor the philosophic system which attempt to find the deepest source of the science in some *a priori* principles, have reached their object. In our day no one any longer believes they can. Both the encyclopedic and the philosophic literature of the law are going through a phase of decadence. Philosophy, which was conceived as a science having its own peculiar source and distinct method, is regarded in our time as a more general science, but one supporting itself by experimental proofs like all the rest. Its actual task extends only to the generalization of materials furnished by the various special sciences.

Consequently, the philosophy of law, the metaphysical science of absolute legal principles, is replaced little by little with general theory of law, which has as its base positive and historic proofs. This tendency is very marked in England where it is known under the name of the analytical school. John Austin is considered its founder with his Province of Jurisprudence Determined, 1832, and Lectures on Jurisprudence or Philosophy of Positive Law, 3d Edition, 1869. He has at the present time a good many followers.[1]

In Germany, too, the necessity of replacing metaphysical construction by a general theory of positive law is recognized. As early as 1820–1830 Falk had demonstrated the need of the change. In contemporary German literature this view is especially sustained by Merkel, who thinks it absolutely necessary to eliminate from all serious study of the law, that of the metaphysical philosophy of it, or at least no longer to recognize it as drawing its proofs from any special source. It is to be considered only as general theory with the rank such theory holds in all other sciences. Meanwhile, this opinion has not been approved by all the world. It meets numerous adversaries who present various objections. Schütze, for example, defends the old separation between positive law and the philosophy of law. According to him Merkel's general theory is "Encyclopädie." "The philosophy of law is a branch of practical philosophy, that is, of that philosophy which applies deductively the formal laws of thought to the establishing of the absolute and its ideal content. It is precisely that part which is to concern itself with law in drawing it out from a higher conception and studying it in its logical development." This sufficiently obscure distinction Schütze explains by some examples which show in what consists for him the difference between a philosophic, and a positive study of legal institutions. For this purpose he passes in review the most important institutions, contract, property, the state, and penalties. "For the lawyer or the historian," said he, "the obliga-

[1] Markby, Elements of Law. 1871. Holland, Elements of Jurisprudence. 1880. 10th Edition. 1906. Pollock, Essays. 1882. *Passim.*

tory force of a contract is a fixed fact, a principle, an incontestable result. The philosopher, however, cannot pass over in silence the preliminary questions. Are contracts obligatory and if so what is the basis of their obligatory force? In the same way for private property, the philosopher asks to what point it agrees with the idea of law—and, above all, with the equal claim of all men to the means of satisfying their necessities. The lawyer and historian meet only by chance with such questions along their way. In the same way, as to the state, the philosophy of law asks these questions: Is the existence of the state a rational need or only a historical product? What form of government is best conformed to reason? Does government in essence rest upon contract?" etc.

But, even these examples are not satisfying proofs. Without being able to claim to give a complete solution to these questions, positive law, to the extent which it involves them, is compelled to find some solution for them. The lawyer must ask what are the conditions of the validity of contracts. It is impossible to explain these conditions without setting forth the basis of their obligatory force. On the other hand it is useless to ask such questions as what form of government conforms best to reason, for one cannot estimate the different forms of government without taking into consideration the historic conditions of the times. The fact appears that juridico-philosophical literature, so understood, is falling more and more into decadence, and is replaced by investigations upon general questions of law. These investigations bear upon the study of the historic and positive elements and make no claim to find the solution of deep legal problems in metaphysical science. So, we think ourselves authorized in considering as superannuated and abandoned the idea formerly held of the purpose of legal philosophy. The future belongs, in our opinion, to the philosophy of law considered only as general theory of law.

But if we identify philosophy of law with its general theory, how does it differ from encyclopedia of law? Are they to be confounded? What will the philosophers say to that? Thus, Friedlander in showing the scientific importance of the encyclopedia of law affirmed that legal philosophy could not exist by its side as a distinct science. In Russia, it was Prof. Karasevich who first asserted the necessity of identifying philosophy of law and its encyclopedia.

In Germany, this opinion is not generally admitted. The German jurists are so much in the habit of separating the two that Merkel himself, who demanded so resolutely that philosophy of law be replaced by its general theory, believed in the independent existence of an Encyclopedia of Law, meaning an abridgment of all branches of the law, embracing in it a general theory of the law. But, "Encyclopädie" thus understood has no longer the character of an independent science.

In Russian literature there are some jurists who pronounce for maintaining the distinction between philosophy and encyclopedia of law. Prof. Zveriov, notably, is of this opinion. According to him the encyclopedia of law has no subject of study of its own. It borrows nearly all its materials from philosophy. It is for him an incomplete repetition of the philosophy of law. It does not reproduce the whole of legal philosophy. It takes of it only what is strictly necessary to serve as an introduction to instruction in the law. The philosophy in his opinion is an independent science, while encyclopedia is only a form of instruction. It is the incomplete copy whose original is philosophy. Conceived as an introduction to the juridical sciences, composed of materials which the philosophy of law furnishes to it, encyclopedia presents to us throughout definite results so far as this is possible in the present situation of legal knowledge. Philosophy, on the contrary, makes of these same matters the object of its researches and studies juridical norms in the process of their formation.

"Encyclopädie" affirms and sets forth; philosophy discusses and studies. The one is dogmatic, the other critical. If encyclopedia proposes to prepare the beginner for the study of the special legal sciences, the philosophy of law seeks to be the conclusion of his studies. If the first serves to trace a plan for study, and show the route to be taken, the second is to give a general view of what has been done as a whole, to set in order the acquired knowledge and to take account of the work accomplished.

Zveriov's opinion does not fail to leave some difficulties. At the very start can we be satisfied to define encyclopedia as an object of instruction and to oppose it as such to philosophy as a science? Is not science, then, an object of instruction? Zveriov means, probably, that encyclopedia is only a special means of giving instruction in legal philosophy; but even with this correction his conclusion raises some doubts. He claims that encyclopedia gives a dogmatic exposition of some questions as to which philosophy presents a critical study. He adds even that encyclopedia exhibits results without showing the means which obtained them. We do not believe he means to say by this that it ought to proceed by simple affirmations. Such a bad method for any kind of instruction is especially so for university teaching.

We believe that he wished to say that encyclopedia, without insisting upon the differences which separate the schools, applies itself generally to setting forth fixed doctrines of systems as wholes. In this sense we can say that it prefers the dogmatic to the critical method. But even when so presented his observations raise objections. The choice of one or the other method is not left free. If for a given question there is as yet no theory accepted by the scientific world, we must be satisfied with expounding controversies.

So we cannot consider the philosophy of law as a science distinct from the encyclopedia of it. They are but one. They are only transition phases. They are but preliminary elements of one discipline, the general theory of law. The usefulness of a general theory of law was long ago recognized, but it was imagined that it could exist beside the encyclopedia without being absorbed by this last. Such is notably Falk's opinion. He proposed to replace natural law by a general theory of law, that is, by an exposition of the general principles resulting from analysis of positive law. But at the moment this conception was brought forth it could hardly survive. Only in our day does it begin to be admitted.

Müller develops it in considerable detail. He presents the general theory of the law as a system of principles of law,—*System der Rechtsgründe*. Without speaking of direct practical utility for legal science, it has a double task to perform. First, it studies the varieties of the facts, systematizing them and applying to them different methods,—speculative-idealistic, historical, and empirico-realistic. Second, from the material of law thus constituted it derives the general principles, combines them according to their intrinsic nature and makes of them a system which is the general theory of the law. Once the leading principles are isolated they are applied to the estimating of existing law, to show and clear up at the same time the path of evolution. The general theory of law evidently cannot have direct application to life, for it contains only general principles and not the distinct juridic rules which control the relations of daily life. Moreover, it is impossible to derive a science of practical law from the principles of general theory. The evolution of law has for its starting point natural elements,—the relations of life. The theorist draws his general notions from the study of these relations, and of the practical law to which they have given birth. He ought to conceive as a whole the system of practical rules and of legal relations of daily life, and then to decompose this general organism into its organs and distinct elements, to determine their relations and reciprocal influence, the norms and the purposes of their action, as well as the rôle of the whole and of each of the parts. The general theory of law verifies everywhere the positive law from the technical and logical point of view, shows the internal connection, the essence of the social organism, and refers them to the general principles of human activity in society and the state. It is thus the keystone of jurisprudence. It binds into a whole the separate parts and their diverse contents. To attain this object it ought to observe rigorously the objective method, and avoid all subjective construction. If in our day some general considerations precede the study of the different categories of legal training, it is because we have not yet a suitable theory of law, and each jurist finds the need of setting forth some of his own opinions concerning it.

In this way Albert Post believed that the development of law, conceived as one of the branches of positive social science, will have as a result the fusing of history and philosophy. Only the general study of law, *eine allgemeine Rechtswissenschaft*, can subsist at the side of the history of the law. It will have an empirical character when it is studying the phenomena of juridical life, a philosophic character when studying the causes of those phenomena. But the two parts of jurisprudence, history and theory, ought to be closely bound together.

Müller and Post in imagining the rôle of general theory of the law did not examine its relations to encyclopedia. The first German jurist who is pronouncedly in favor of their identification is Schütze. In his course on the encyclopedia of law he conformed to this idea, as his printed plan for the course shows. The lectures themselves were, unfortunately, not published.

In our day nearly all Russian encyclopedists recognize the necessity of identifying encyclopedia and general theory of law. At least, all the printed courses on "Encyclopädie," except those of Nivoline and of Rojestvensky, present only the general study of law. Kapoustine, even, replaces the name "Encyclopädie" with that of "General Dogmatics." But, as Karasevich rightly says, this terminology is not well chosen, for dogma is, as all the world agrees, opposed to history, and means an applied science of law.

This difference between the Russian encyclopedias and the German ones, the best and most systematic of which—for example, Falks's, Walter's, Ahrens', Warnkönig's and Merkel's—are only brief expositions of the separate juridical sciences preceded by a short general introduction; this difference, we say, is explained by the conditions of our legal instruction. In Germany, instruction in law consists simply, according to Stein's statement, in some studies in civil law in its different manifestations. The other branches, one may say, are not tolerated. There is no occasion to be astonished, then, that there is no general theory of the law, but only a brief exposition of civil law, Roman or German, and sometimes, as in Putter, Ahrens, and Warnkönig, the general history of law. Things do not go the same in our universities. The civil law has never predominated. Since Peter the Great, legal and political instruction have been combined. For this reason the Russian encyclopedist cannot put into his course a rapid exposition of all which is taught in the law faculties. The matters being very diverse, even a brief résumé of them would be something too complex. The conditions of our university instruction require of an encyclopedist not a résumé of the special sciences, but a general theory of the law.

BOOK I

THE CONCEPTION OF LAW

CHAPTER I

THE DEFINITION OF LAW

Section 5. *Technical and Ethical Norms*

Endowed with a faculty of generalization which belongs to us in our capacity as reasonable beings, we are guided in our conscious activity not only by concrete notions, but also by rules which indicate the line of conduct necessary to follow to attain such or such a desired end. These rules which depend upon the nature of the proposed end bear the general name of "norms." They vary with their ends, but all unite in two leading groups, technical and ethical norms.

Technical norms are rules which indicate the manner of acting in order to attain a determinate end. Such are rules of hygiene, of pedagogy, of grammar, of architecture, which teach us to preserve our health, to develop the faculties of an infant, to express our ideas in an intelligible manner, to build a house. There are as many technical norms as there are different ends sought by men. Observation of each of them brings only the realization of a single given end without assisting towards the other ends of human activity, and sometimes even hindering their realization. If the end pursued is vast and complex, its realization is naturally determined by a complicated system of rules bound together by the unity of the end. The systems of this kind form so many distinct arts. Thence comes the name,—technical norms.

Distinct technical norms correspond to the different objects of human activity; this is why men act always conformably to their ends. Each separate technical norm follows a single determinate end and leads to a realization of a single distinct purpose without entangling connections with others. At the same time, however, the different ends of human activity struggle together inevitably. The realization of one impedes often that of another. The man, limited in strength, in external forces, and in time, must give up the complete realization of his purposes. It is necessary for him to sacrifice secondary objects to attain leading ones. Obliged thus to choose between different ends man cannot do without a guiding principle to show the line of conduct to follow, the ends to sacrifice, and those to which the preference is to be given. The technical norms cannot answer this need. Showing the way to realize a given end, they do not give rules intended to introduce harmony into the realization of several ends. So there exist, besides the technical norms, some of a different kind, the ethical ones. Man cannot guide himself through life merely by technical norms suited only to the attaining of separate ends. He is guided necessarily by another principle which determines the choice of ends themselves. According as men are more or less capable of realizing this or that specific end we estimate their capacity in the given art. According to their manner of comprehending the mutual relations of these ends and by their choice of them we judge of their morals, of what the Greeks expressed by the word (ἦθος). So the rules which determine the correlation of the different ends of human activity are called "ethical."

According to what has been said the distinction between technical and ethical norms may be formulated thus. Technical norms are the rules directly applicable to the realization of the distinct ends of human activity, ethical norms to the realization simultaneously of all human ends.

Certainly we must conclude from this that ethical cannot replace technical norms. They have not the force of a general technical rule and cannot be applied directly towards the realization of a distinct and separate end. Observation of ethical rules does not lead directly to the accomplishment of any single practical purpose. That is always effected by conformity to technical rules. Ethical rules act only in the delimitation, so to speak, of separate ends, not their realization, only in determining their mutual correlation. They render possible the realization of several ends simultaneously by defining their "form," the formal side of their reciprocal connections, but these objects themselves are realized only in conformity with rules suited to their intrinsic nature. In this sense ethical norms are distinguished from technical ones as formal from material norms. Their observance only adds to the mutual correlation of ends a harmonious form, but does not advance the realization of their content.

Technical rules are as numerous as the ends which life assigns to us. The men who pursue distinct ends are guided by different technical norms. On the other hand, ethical norms, which preside not at the realization of separate ends, but over the determination of the relations constituting the combination of ends, do not vary with the nature of the end pursued at a given moment. The same person does not have different ethical rules for the different circumstances of his life. Ethical rules determine the connection of different ends. They are necessarily the same for all the manifestations of human activity, for all the circumstances of life. Thus, ethical norms are characterized by unity and technical norms by variety, by plurality. The same man at the same time may be controlled by the most diverse technical rules.

If technical rules are those indicating means for attaining determinate ends, their observance ought to be optional. All depends here upon the value assigned to the end pursued, whose realization is sought in accordance with a certain rule. Only he who counts his health important, will observe hygienic rules. No one would recommend them to a man who was seeking to put an end to his life or destroy, scientifically, his health. On the other hand, the man finds himself bound to yield to a rule which establishes the harmony, the desired unity, between the different objects which solicit his activity. If I have several ends to realize, it is impossible not to wish that there be harmony between them. Only the man attacked with mania concentrates himself upon a single one. The man enjoying normal health assigns always several ends for his activity. That the harmonious simultaneous realization of several ends is desired by most men, admits of no doubt, so there can be no doubt of the obligation to observe the rules of ethics. Therefore, technical norms are optional and ethical ones obligatory.

It is not simply their obligatory character which distinguishes ethical from technical norms. If a technical rule is not observed, there results only that a given end is not attained. That is all. This negligence has no influence upon the rest of the man's activity. I have cultivated my field badly, but perhaps I can build a house. A bad farmer may be a good pedagogue. Inobservance of ethical rules, however, disturbs our whole activity by destroying the harmony which guides it. The consequences of the violation of ethical norms are always felt. They have their counter stroke in all our affairs and prevent us, often, from attaining the most important ends. When we are conscious that the complete violation of ethical norms has placed us beyond the possibility of realizing for the future other human objects of the highest kind, we experience remorse, and recognize thereby the imperative character of these rules. To this interior sanction has been added another one outside. The violation of technical rules brings only the stopping of a given enterprise, and, consequently, touches only the persons interested in the affair. Whoever does not follow these rules, we call unskillful or imprudent, but the matter does not directly concern us. It does not matter to us whether the technical rule is observed or not. On the contrary, the violation of ethical rules brings into play the general interest. All human interests turn upon two main centres, the individual and society. Every ethical system, whatever be its characteristic principle, determines necessarily the connections of these two categories of human interests. Society cannot remain indifferent if ethical norms are violated, if the harmony of human ends does not exist, if personal and social interests conflict. Whatever violates ethical norms provokes, infallibly, the disapprobation of society, which is interested in the existence of a certain relation between the purposes of individual men and collective social purposes. Society wishes each member to observe moral rules; it condemns those violating them, and, in grave cases, even proceeds to punish them. Observance of moral rules is not then left to the subjective judgment of the individual. It has the character of an objective obligatory rule, of an imperative order.

But, if we consider the content of technical and moral norms, the connection between the two is going to appear under a different aspect. In their content technical norms are objective. In fact, to act conformably to a given end, is to employ the forces of nature to effectuate that end But the action of nature's forces is always rigorously constant. This is why if the law of a given group of phenomena is known, the corresponding technical rules will be the logically inevitable consequences of that law. For example, the rules of architecture are the logically inevitable consequences of the laws of mechanics. For technical norms, the choice once made of some determined end, are the rules of its realization, and are indicated of themselves, as inevitable consequences of the law of the corresponding phenomena. It results that the content of technical rules is determined by objective facts, except as to the connection between the man and these rules. If, sometimes, technical norms are insufficiently determined objectively,—for example, the rules of pedagogy,—it is only because the laws of the corresponding phenomena have not been ascertained with the needed precision,—in the case given, the laws of the mental life. The law of the phenomena being known, there can be no doubt as to the corresponding technical norm.

It is altogether different with ethical norms. They are never presented as inevitable consequences of a law. The rule to adopt for controlling the relations between different ends of human activity is conditioned by a series of absolutely subjective circumstances which are extremely variable. Each man has his objects, appreciates them subjectively, and settles according to his taste their reciprocal relations. What is secondary for one may constitute the chief end in life for another. Personal tendencies, theoretic ideas, religious beliefs, social customs, all these factors alter to infinity human interests and the relations among them. It is not logical consequences of a certain conception, but rather sentiments, which determine the relations which we establish between the different ends of our activity. The content of ethical norms has necessarily a subjective character. It is marked by the existence of many shades. It is always an object of controversy. We cannot base it upon rigorously logical arguments, carrying to all the evidence of incontestable truth.

Section 6. *Legal and Moral "Norms"*

We have just shown the difference between two leading categories of norms, the technical and the ethical. With which shall we rank legal ones? The answer is not doubtful. Juridical norms present all the characteristics of ethical norms. The observance of rules of law is not directly necessary to any material end. Law only outlines the frame for the various material interests and activities, forming the content of social life. At the same time, the observance of juridical norms is acknowledged as binding on all, independently of its desirability for this or that special end. In short, the content of law is not simply the inevitable logical consequence of natural laws, as is evident from the fact of the variety and even contradictoriness of legal rules existing in different times and countries. But juridical norms are not the sole ethical norms. By their side are moral ones. For the exact definition of legal rules they must be separated from moral ones. To that end, we shall try to show how it is generally possible to effect the combination and harmony of the various interests of human life. From this of itself will be obtained the main division of ethical norms, their separation into morality and law.

Full and unlimited realization of each of man's different aims is, in view of his limited strength and means, impossible. He is compelled to limit the accomplishment of some purposes, even to renounce some altogether. He must make a choice among his different ends, separate them one from the other, estimate one as more important, another as less so; in a word, the relative appraisal of interests is unavoidable. Without such moral appraisal one could not guide himself in the multiplicity of interests so varied and conflicting, could not recognize the importance of one aim over another. This appraisement of values determines their preference. But this appraisement of aims and interests belongs to morality. However different the moral principles advanced by different theories, all agree in proposing a criterion by the aid of which different interests in competition can be weighed.[1]

In this function of fixing the relative importance of interests centre all the moral theories. Whether we deduce moral rules from utility, truth, harmony, beauty, pity, love or innate feeling independent of all morality, matters little. The difference of foundations upon which moral theories rest produces divergences in the criteria which they use, but all the theories forever result in the elaboration of some criterion, which is the distinctive and indispensable mark of the theory producing it. The moral rules determine rigorously the distinction between good and evil, between what is to be done and what is not to be done, between moral and immoral ends. They present the higher principles which direct our whole activity, the criteria for all our actions.

The isolated man, outside of social life, may subordinate his activity to moral rules. Nothing, indeed, prevents his establishing a harmony between the different ends whose realization he seeks, after estimating their respective values. Good and evil appear in gradations. Good ends and bad are ranged in a definite order and thus there can be established a fixed relation between all human aims. When several conflict in their accomplishment, one can always by applying a moral test decide which should be placed highest in the moral scale, and, consequently, which are to be preferred.

[1] It goes without saying that this declaration relates not to mere material interests alone, but also includes the highest moral interests of man.

But reality does not show us isolated men, mutually independent. Each instant we must recognize our dependence upon our fellows. All our activity depends upon our relations with other men; without them the realization of our interests would be impossible. Those interests which are general subjects of human activity are not merely subjected to other individual existences, they are universally subordinated to general conditions of social life; for this reason many interests have not an individual but a social character. Man must act conformably not merely to his personal interests, but to those also of other men without whom he cannot exist.

When a man enters into relations with his fellows not only do his own interests contest together, but his own interests conflict with those of other members of society, the adoption of a common criterion, the establishment of the desired harmony, of a fixed order among the different interests in view, becomes more difficult. The interests of another against which our own are in conflict may be exactly equivalent or identical with ours. The moral criterion cannot then give such an indication as to settle the conflict. It is not merely when identical interests are in conflict that the moral criterion is insufficient. The application of a moral criterion to a multiplicity of interest at once can only be conceived as possible if the criterion is accepted by them all. Otherwise there will be under consideration some acts which will conform to a fixed moral rule, but which will not be the same for all the interests. The divergence will appear not only between the interests but also between the conditions which inspired them. Very rarely do men apply the same moral rules to the lesser details of their acts. In society only the more important requirements are recognized as obligatory. The details of our action are tried only by a subjective standard. The personal opinions of one man cannot be obligatory upon another. A common criterion may be lacking by which to test and compare the divergent interests of two men. Finally, even when the moral norms applied by the individuals are identical, the evaluation and comparison of the interests of different individuals may be impossible. The aims of human activity do not present themselves separately and in a distinct manner; they are mingled, interlaced, dependent one upon another, and subordinate one to another. When the question is as to the evaluation of the aims of a single man, there is no difficulty. The man himself can organize his individual aims and their reciprocal connections. But the aims of others are unknown to us except as manifested in external actions. Others' projects are known to us only by objective proofs, not in their subjective details. But without such knowledge a complete evaluation of different ends is impossible. Thus, the acquisition of a good is moral or immoral according to the intended use of it. This is why, when, proposing to acquire something, I establish that my acts injure another's interests, I cannot make upon these facts an accurate moral judgment. I cannot know certainly whether my own interest, or his, ought to be considered of most importance.

So, when the interests of people conflict, there cannot be established between them a fixed relation by comparing them and applying to them the same criterion. The interests are often identical. The many details upon which depends the judgment we apply remain ordinarily unknown. Finally, the complexity of our moral ideas complicates the question still further. It is only in their most intimate relations that men can understand each other and be led to apply the same moral rule with a view to reconcile the various interests under consideration. Many conditions must be fulfilled to establish such a state of things, absolute identity of moral ideas, entire freedom, perfect mutual confidence, and a love that mingles another's interest with one's own on equal terms. Such relations are not the rule in social life. Ordinarily men's relations are not marked by identity of opinions, by freedom, by confidence and by affection. As a result, it is difficult to find a rule readily accepted by all the world. It becomes necessary to recognize the infinite variety of situations and of personal preferences, to establish a fixed relation between others' interests and our own personal ones.

The mutual relations between men whose interests are in conflict may present two essentially different types. 1st. The interests of one may be wholly subordinated to the other's so that the former is only a means for effecting the latter's ends. In a case of absolute subordination of this kind, the master's relations with the subject are determined by the same principles as with other animals, and things which are considered merely as means for realizing ends. The accomplishment of these aims is guided by technical norms, choice among them by morality. There can be here no new peculiar norm to regulate the mutual relations established by hypothesis between master and subject. 2d. The persons whose interests conflict may present themselves clothed in the same legal capacity without bond of subordination between them. In such case the conflict cannot be settled by the complete subjection of one to the other. One ought under this hypothesis to establish a certain sphere in which each of the diverging interests can be realized fully, or in other terms, the simultaneous realization of these interests, to be free, can only proceed if their respective domains are set off to them beforehand; and thus the human conscience was obliged to work out some rule for securing a moral criterion for the evaluation of our acts and some other rules for fixing and marking off the respective domains wherein our interests and those of others can be realized. These different norms have the same function, the simultaneous realization of men's different aims. Consequently, the norms which delimit the field of action for our interests are ethical norms. But they do not give, differing in this from moral norms, a criterion for the evaluation of our interests, for the distinction of evil from good. They teach us only to fix limits, give the law for the realization of our interests when they trench upon those of others. Consequently, the norms for the delimitation of interests set the boundary between law and not law and constitute "juridical norms."

Thus, the distinction between morals and law can be formulated very simply: Morality furnishes the criterion for the proper evaluation of our interests; law marks out the limits within which they ought to be confined. To analyze out a criterion for the evaluation of our interests is the function of morality; to settle the principles of the reciprocal delimitation of one's own and other people's interests is the function of law. It is not difficult to show that from this fundamental distinction between law and morals result the other differences between juridical and moral norms. They are all explained by the capital distinction just stated.

Since law is the delimitation of the interests of different persons, juridical norms govern only our relations with others and not those with ourselves. Moral rules, on the contrary, determine our duties toward ourselves, for our acts have a moral quality even when they concern only ourselves.

The application of juridical norms is conditioned by the opposition between others' interests and our own, and by consequence, their observance is obligatory only when such interest of another exists. It is that interest which compels observance of juridical norms. If the person whose interests limit mine releases me from their observance they are no longer obligatory: *Volenti non fit injuria*. On the contrary, the obligation of moral rules does not depend upon the interest which other persons have in their fulfillment. Even if no one impose it upon me, moral duty keeps for me all its force; for the evaluation of interests, in a moral point of view, does not change even when they are no longer in conflict.

It results likewise from this, that moral norms impose an inflexible moral duty upon us. From juridical norms there results for us a right and a correlative duty. The right is precisely the "faculty" to which corresponds the obligation binding another person, the "faculty" of realizing a given interest within the limits fixed by juridical norms. The juridical obligation is the obligation to satisfy the requirements which flow from the right with which another is vested in regard to us, the obligation of observing the limits assigned to the different interests under consideration, as determined by the juridical norms. It is thus that, differing from moral duty, juridical obligation continues only while the interests exist for which it was established. Such, for example, is the idea of prescription which extinguishes obligations. Morality does not recognize this idea which has produced such juridical effects.

The moral evaluation of our interests arises from our conscience. Their delimitation depends upon exterior relations which are found established between the different persons under consideration subject to law. Morality, arising only from the conscience, admits of no constraint. Convictions are not created by the action of external force. Law, on the other hand, admits sometimes of constraint, precisely in the case of an encroachment upon the domain within whose limits it recognizes our right to act freely. Constraint cannot dictate to us our convictions, but can arrest and prevent an illegal act. The moral evaluation of interests can find its application when it is adopted by a single man, who constrains himself by it in his own acts. On the other hand, that there may be a place for the juridical delimitation of our interests all the persons whose interests are under consideration must realize the obligatory force of the norm employed. Morality is, then, rather a rule for the individual, law a social rule. All these secondary differences between law and morals are consequences of the fundamental distinction which we have indicated, that the one is the delimitation, the other the evaluation of interests.

From another point of view, it is not difficult to prove that every juridical norm is necessarily a norm for the delimitation of interests. This appears, first, from the fact that juridical norms find no application in our relations with our animals and slaves, who are considered as beings whose interests are inseparable from their master's and wholly absorbed by the latter; and, second, from the fact that every juridical norm supposes necessarily an existing relation between several interests, the norm serving to establish their respective limits. Civil law marks off the private interests of individuals who enter into relation with each other, those, for example, of husband and wife, parents and children, vendor and purchaser, landlord and tenant, debtor and creditor. In criminal proceedings, on one side, are observed the interests of the accused, and on the other those of society, represented by the government. In civil proceedings the interests of plaintiff and defendant; in constitutional law the interests of all the members of the state, from monarch to serving man; in international law the interest of states as members of the international community and of men as citizens of the different states.

Section 7. *Relationship of Law and Morals*

RENNENKAMPF. Law and Morals in their Reciprocal Relations. (Archives of practical and historical instruction, 1860.)

SCHTEGLOV. Law and Morals, 1883.

STAHL. Die Philosophie des Rechts, 1878. Vol. 2. s. 191.

AHRENS. Die Rechts-Philosophie. Vol. 1. s. 145.

ROEDER. Grundzuge des Naturrechts, 1860. Vol. 1. s. 110.

SCHAEFFLE. Bau und Leben des socialen Kõrpers, 1881. Vol. 1. s. 593.

LASSON. System der Rechtsphilosophie, 1880.

JELLINEK. Die Socialistische Bedeutung von Recht, Unrecht, und Strafe, 1878. s. 42.

WALLASCHEK. Studien zur Rechtsphilosophie, 1889. s. 52.

BALTS. Les fondements de la morale et de droit, 1890.

Law, then, in contradistinction to morals, does not present the ethical appraisal of our interests but their delimitation. How define, then, the relation between the two? Before fixing the proper domain exclusively assigned to some given interest do we first appraise its moral value? On the contrary, is not this last completely ignored in settling legally the status of many interests together? The extremely individualistic theories which were in favor in the XVII and XVIII centuries ended their development with the negation of all connection between law and morals. In order to explain social phenomena, these theories, as we know, take for a starting point the individual, absolutely isolated, enjoying unfettered liberty and without connection with his fellows. According to the theorists of that time, relations between individuals are caused by their voluntary and deliberate action. Their starting point was the full liberty of the natural man. The formation of society and constitution of a government, the establishment of a bond of mutual dependence, was regarded as the spontaneous work of the human will. Placing oneself at the point of view of this theory, the chief task of the legislator, called to the delimitation of the interests under consideration, consisted in preventing each person from encroaching upon the natural liberty of his neighbor. The legislator had not to ask himself in what this liberty consisted or for what purpose the man designed to use it.

The first author of the XVIII century to mark in an exact fashion the opposition between law and morals was Christian Thomasius. (*Fundamenta Juris naturæ et gentium ex sensi communi deducta in quibus ubique secernetur principia honesti, Justi ac decori*, 1718.) He gave to legal rules an absolutely negative character, which prescribed the doing of nothing, while fixing at the same time rules for discharging our full duty to our fellows. In accordance with this, he recognized as the chief principle of law the following rule: *Quod tibi non vis fieri, alteri ne feceris.* "Whatever you do not wish done to you, do not to another." Morals, on the contrary, according to him include all the rules determining duties towards ourselves. The fundamental rule of morality is the following: Do to yourself whatever you wish others to do to themselves. The rules of law and of morality distinct, for him, by their content, are so, likewise, in their application. Moral duties, being positive and regarding only ourselves, can be taught under the form of advice. Juridical duties, being only negative and regarding others, call for a command which if not observed brings punishment. No one can be left to the free determination of each observance of duty towards his fellows. The power of the state, armed with constraint, is called upon to oversee the observance of juridical duties and of them alone. The state's power ought not to extend to the sphere of moral duties.

The authors of that century who followed him, above all Kant, and Fichte, continued to accent the opposition between law and morals which Thomasius sketched. Kant considered as the fundamental principle of law, from which all legal norms flow by logical necessity, the following rule: "Act in such a way that your liberty accords with that of everyone else." Consequently, legal rules take effect only on the external side of actions and rest for their realization on constraint. With Fichte this idea receives more rigorous expression. For him, law is an absolutely mechanical result of the existence together of a number of persons, and the combination of external conditions produced by constraint and necessary for the common existence of them all.

The opposition between law and morality affirmed by the individualistic theories became a kind of watchword in the struggle for liberty of conscience and individual liberty generally against the system of exaggerated tutelage by the state. The religious persecutions, and the state interferences in the most intimate manifestations of personal life, resulted from the confusion of law and morals at this time. In this state of things legislation, called upon to establish juridical norms, naturally extended itself over questions of conscience and disregarded the moral dignity of human actions. On the other hand, the separation of law and morality brought on an application of the opposite rule which makes law indifferent to questions of morals. Its task was conceived as to set bounds to the external liberty of men without troubling itself as to how they would use that liberty, whether conformably to moral requirements or not.

As a reaction against the excessive oppression of individual liberty by the state's intervention, this theory has great importance. Moral ideas are always more or less subjective, touch always the most intimate and secret side of man's personal life. This is why legislation, which establishes as the foundation of its delimitation of interests a fixed moral evaluation, results infallibly in oppression to individual liberty. Indifference on the part of law with regard to morals agrees best with an extended liberty.

But, by the side of this advantage, the opposition between law and morals has also its weak points. If the law neglects moral rules, it necessarily results that it permits immoral actions on condition that the man does not actually pass the bounds to his liberty which it sets. The highest moral interests must, then, yield and be sacrificed to the formal exigencies of the law. The strict application of the law appears often in such cases as the height of injustice. "*Summum jus summa injuria.*" This is why as soon as the rigorous separation of law and morals has caused the triumph of individual liberty, and above all of the liberty of conscience, the extreme consequences of this doctrine attract attention and a reaction commences. Attempts are made to bring them together again. Fichte was of this opinion. In his first works he appears as a determined representative of the doctrine which separates law and morals. (Grundlage des Naturrechts. 1796.) In his last, he inclines to the contrary idea and recognizes in his System der Rechtslehre, 1812, the necessity of bringing law and morals together. At present the whole world is agreed upon this, thanks above all to the efforts of the organic school.

In reality law is never wholly separated from morality. The delimitation of interests cannot neglect their moral evaluation so as to base itself wholly on that negative norm which forbids assailing others' interests and others' wishes. The natural state of man is by no means that of isolation. The establishment of society is not the product of the conscious free will of the individuals who make it up, but depends upon the every-day conditions which establish their mutual relations quite involuntarily on their part. It does not suffice, then, for the delimitation of men's interests to prevent their interfering arbitrarily with each other. Humanity forms an aggregated whole, a solidarity is established among its members independently of their will. It results that many interests by their content have a character not individual but social. Their essence supposes relations among many men and a common solidified activity, tending towards the same end. Consequently, the delimitation of a man's interests viewed in connection with his relations to others' requires almost always not only that others' interests be not trenched upon, but also that man limit the realization of his own interests in order to permit the realization of higher ones of others. In these conditions it is clear that norms for the delimitation of our interests cannot be established without making a comparative moral evaluation of ends; in fact, in actual legislation moral principles, such as they were, have had a very great influence upon the manner of disposing of interests.

Moreover, law is not limited to regulating the exterior side of actions. It always takes more or less account of motives. Modern law goes much farther than primitive law in this respect. To establish obligations with regard to contracts, it requires that there be a real consent, a real meeting of wills. Moreover, the law makes this consent sufficient. It demands no observance of any special external form. Formerly, on the other hand, the obligation consisted solely in the observance of this form. It did not matter whether the consent was really voluntary. Now, the juridical character of an act is fixed not merely by the result to the injured, but by the intention of the doer.

A person who, having the intention to slay another,

causes only some severe wounds, is prosecuted for attempted assassination. He who has mortally injured another without intention to kill, is prosecuted for the blow or the wounding, but not for assassination. The severity of the punishment depends much more upon the intention than upon the injury which has resulted from carrying it out.

Moreover, morality requires us not only to have good intentions, but to act properly and, especially, properly towards others. Love for one's neighbor is the basis of christian morals; and modern ethical theories, while not resting entirely upon religious principles, have for the most part an altruistic character.

Because, at the present time, it is admitted that the individualistic theories are replaced by doctrines which, in explaining human relations, start, not with the principle of individual independence, but from the fact of the social dependence of men, no one longer seeks to resolve the question as to the relations of law and morals by opposing directly the one to the other. No one any longer thinks that law is absolutely independent of morals. On the contrary, law is placed in a relation of subordination. The end of law is now regarded as the realization of morality.

This change of tack with regard to the correlation of law and morals is observable already in Hegel. He regarded law, morals and morality, as successive steps in the dialectical development of liberty. He conceives law and morals as different aspects of morality. The very idea of morality has with him a quite original form. Morality (*Sittlichkeit*), according to him signifies a social order, the family, civil society, the state. The correlation of law and morals, he represented as an antithesis. Law in itself is deprived of all fixed content and is only the possibility of liberty. Morals, on the contrary, determine not the possible, but what ought to be. So law and morals are opposed to each other as the possible and the obligatory, and their opposition disappears in the highest unity, that of morality, which is the reality of that which in law appears only as the possible and in morals only as the obligatory.

The subordination of law to morality is still more complete in the doctrines of the organic school. Thus, Ahrens recognizes as the essential motive to human activity the tendency towards the realization of the human ideal, identical with the supreme good of humanity. This tendency is manifest in the desire to realize the different special aims which belong to human nature. As man is before all an independent, distinct creature, his aims spring before all from the needs of the personal life. Such are the preservation of his life, his health, of his honor. But man is a social being. For that reason he has also social needs, language, religion, science and art.

So we have two groups of goods which make up the ends of human activity. These two groups Ahrens calls material goods. By their side are, moreover, formal goods, which represent no special human interest, but only a fixed correlation between different elements of human life. Such are law and morality. Morality controls the motives and ends of human activity, and law determines what are the conditions for the realization of aims indicated by morality, conditions which depend upon the human will.

These opinions are likewise widely spread among the modern representatives of the positive tendency. The celebrated publicist, Jellinek, defines the correlation of law and morals thus: Law is a minimum ethics, that is to say the whole combined requirements of morals, whose observance, at a given stage of social development, is absolutely indispensable. By consequence, law is only a part of morals, the part which fixes the indispensable conditions of the given social order. All moral requirements beyond this indispensable minimum, constitute morals in the strict sense as distinguished from law The observance of these requirements is only desirable, not indispensable; they are in some sort an ethical luxury. Wallaschek expresses the same notion, modifying it a little and making it more precise. Law and morals according to him ought to be connected together as form and content. Morals show the ideal to be assigned to human activity and law seeks to effectively realize it. Every manifestation of morals must receive its envelope in the form of a juridical rule, and every law have its moral content. But since moral rules do not all impinge upon the mind with the force of objective truth, since they may be discussed and even denied, men ought be satisfied with the realization under the form of law of a certain number of moral truths, strictly indispensable that society may exist. To subordinate in this manner law to morals as means to an end, as form to contents, is to formulate a theory quite as extreme as that which before entirely separated them. We cannot see in law merely the realization of moral rules, for, first, the whole content of law is not determined by moral principles. There are juridical norms which absolutely leave out the moral point of view. Such are, for example, the rules of law which control the forms of juridical acts, provide for arrests and adjournments, the number of witnesses, etc. Second, the thing which demonstrates the inaccuracy of the theory we are combatting is the following fact: The law comprises a number of rules which have as their precise object the assuring to each one the liberty of his moral convictions. Since moral convictions are not identical among men, all law cannot be brought into the realization of moral ideals. Law can only fix limits within which the man, held to the realization of a certain moral order, should confine himself, within which he can move freely without getting in conflict with other moral conceptions perhaps absolutely opposed to his own and equally worthy of protection.

One cannot, then, draw out the relation of law and morals in a single formula equally applicable to all social phases and types of development. When in a society all moral opinions are alike they fix the delimitation of conflicting interests. When the matter in hand is the delimitation of interests as to which there is unanimity in assigning to them an unequal value, the highest in the moral point of view must be given preference. Interests less important which are opposed to it are necessarily restrained in their realization. This is why primitive society, in which were no differing moral opinions, where everybody lived in conformity to long established manners, fixed the delimitation of interests in accordance with such manners and the confusion of law with morals resulted. But when, with social development, long established manners lost their former stability and uniformity under the influence of more complex and variable social conditions, when new moral opinions began to penetrate the social consciousness, the law which ought to be recognized by all, based itself still upon the old moral principles; but the moral opinions were no longer the moral code upon which the former delimitation of interests established by law rested. Moral notions progress faster and develop quicker than law. The latter presents, so to speak, a lower step in development, a step which morals have already taken. This correlation, however, of law and morals is not necessary. When the law is fixed not only by ancient customs but also by the direction of a competent man, by a government which can free itself at least partially from the authority of custom, legislation can rest upon moral notions which rise much above the medium level of moral development of the given society. Finally, when with the ever-increasing complexity of social life several different general doctrines come to light in society, the delimitation of interests can only rest upon the fund of moral truth common to all these doctrines, upon what is admitted by all. Consequently, there is formed a sphere of moral activity outside of the sphere of the law, which latter can embrace only the moral truths held in common by the generality of individuals, not the divergences which separate extreme opinions. The limits of this sphere and the degree, so to speak, of the separation of law and morals are not constant and change in proportion to the number of moral rules recognized by everybody. It cannot be said that these limits vary exactly according to the advance of social development. This development certainly brings a more complex social life and more heterogeneous and probably more profound moral divergences. But in the most advanced phases of social development there may arise a general attraction towards some given religious or moral doctrine, and then the interpenetration of law by morals becomes closer and more intimate.

Section 8. *"Law" in the Legal and in the Scientific Sense*

MILL. System of Logic 1. p. 345.

EUCKEN. Geschichte und Kritik der Grundbegriffe der Gegenwart, 1878. s. 115.

MOUROMTZEV. Sketch of a General Theory of Private Law, 1887, p. 85.

Every general norm, juridic or moral, ethical or technical, is a rule conditioned by a determinate end; in other terms, it formulates that which is obligatory and imperative. By this peculiarity norms are distinguished from laws in the scientific sense. Law in the scientific sense is a general formula expressing an established uniformity of phenomena. It expresses not that which ought to be, but that which in reality is, not that which ought to come, but that which exists. The scientific "law" is only a generalized expression for reality.

It results that norms can be distinguished from the laws of science by saying that the former can be broken while the latter cannot. Norms show only how it is necessary to act to attain some given end; but action can easily be contrary to duty, and the observance of a norm neglected. The scientific law, on the other hand, does not depend upon men's wills, for it does not express what ought to be realized through a will, but what is independent of the human will and exists inevitably. There is yet another difference between norms and laws of science. Norms guide the activity of men and indicate to them the means of attaining their ends, fix the conditions of their actions, and thereby control the phenomena which they provoke. The laws of nature only display the uniformity of existing phenomena and cannot be the cause of them. They do not explain for us why phenomena are produced, but how they are produced. It is not "laws" which cause phenomena, but other phenomena, with which the first are in the relation of cause and effect. Thus, the law of gravitation does not explain why bodies gravitate toward each other, but merely in what way they do so. If we sometimes say that such or such a phenomenon is produced because there exists such or such a law, we mean not a connection of cause, but a logical connection. To sum up, it is agreed to call laws, the most general formulas as to the uniformity of phenomena, formulas which cannot be replaced with others still more general. This is why all partial generalizations appear as logical consequences of laws which are more comprehensive generalizations. For example, if we say that the movement of a falling body is accelerated because gravitation is inversely proportional to the square of the distance, the first proposition, which is particular, is a logical consequence of the second, which is general. There is here no causal connection.

So in opposition to norms which are imperative and obligatory rules, and may be broken, and which serve as causes for human action, law in the scientific sense is only the expression of actual uniformity in phenomena, admits of no violation, and, from that very fact, cannot be the cause of phenomena.

This definition of such "law," generally adopted in moral science, is recognized alike by positivists and by metaphysicians. Thus, Lewes[1] cautions us against the error of believing that natural laws direct phenomena, while in reality they only give formulas of the manifestation of those phenomena. In the same way, Eduard Hartmann says that "laws are not beings, which dwell in the air, but only abstractions for forces and sub-

[1] Lewes, Problems of Life and Mind. I. 105. Hartmann, Philosophie des Unbewussten.

stances"; it is not because the given forces or substances are such as they are that they act in such or such a manner; this constancy in a fixed action is what we call a law of nature.

Juridical norms express not what is, but what ought to be. They can be broken. At the same time they are causes of phenomena, and precisely of all those phenomena whose whole constitutes the juridical life of society. Moreover, they cannot be reduced to the notion of law in the scientific sense, a mere uniformity of action. But what is the relation between that "law," in the scientific sense, and juridical norms? Legal literature gives some widely different answers to this question.

Some authors affirm that juridical norms supply in the social life the action of laws in the scientific sense. While in nature regular and uniform order is established of itself as the result of the inevitable regularity of phenomena, in society it is established artificially by juridical norms which are enforced by human will. It is supposed that in social life, which is composed of conscious human actions, laws in the scientific sense can find no application. This theory is the result of the false opinion which regards laws as causes of phenomena, an error which proceeds from the fact that the word "law" is understood not only in its scientific meaning but also in that of norm. Thus, we talk of laws of art and of morals, of laws divine and constitutional. The primitive meaning of the word was exactly this—*Nomos-Lex*. By "law" was not meant the unfailing uniformity of phenomena, but a rule established by man's conscious will. In Aristotle there is no notion of scientific law. Roman writers first began to use the word "law" not only to designate rules for human activity but also to indicate the inevitably necessary order of natural phenomena. Lucretius talks of *Leges naturæ*. If we hold to its primitive meaning, if we understand law as the cause of phenomena and think phenomena are necessarily produced because there are in the world laws acting as special forces in producing phenomena, it will certainly be necessary to put back into a separate sphere the phenomena induced by our wills, for their causa is manifestly not law, but the will. In fact, however, laws in the scientific meaning as already recognized, ought not to be considered as the cause of phenomena. They are rather consequences than causes. Giving to these "laws" their correct signification, there is left no reason for refusing to extend their action over the field of human activity. Our actions are brought about by our conscious wills. That is incontestable. This proposition explains why we act; it is because there is in us a will which presses us to action; but it does not explain how we act. The nature of man presents certain qualities which are common to everything and this common character gives birth to a certain uniformity in men's actions. This uniformity, established and formulated, constitutes the (scientific) law of our activity. So law, considered as the expression for a fixed uniformity in phenomena, is applicable likewise to human activity. We cannot say that such laws have no control over such activity, that they must be replaced with something else. In truth modern science has succeeded in showing a certain regularity in social phenomena. Statistical research has shown the existence of constant laws for various phenomena of social life. So, too, we try to ascertain the laws of the coexistence and development of social phenomena by the historical and comparative study of human societies. If the laws of social phenomena are thus established, we cannot say that they are replaced for human society by juridical norms.

Contrary to the theory just examined, other authors

claim there is no essential difference between the rules of that which ought to be, and scientific laws; that what we call obligatory norms, morality laws, are but conjectures, hypotheses, which we make as to the laws which inevitably control our activity. With our imperfect means of investigation we cannot attain perfect knowledge, but approach it nearer and nearer by replacing the hypotheses which we make at first, with others more truthlike.

The idea just examined has the defect of mingling essentially distinct conceptions. Just as the preceding one is based upon the confusion between the (scientific) laws of phenomena, and their causes, this neglects a capital difference between norms and laws.

This difference, from which results the impossibility of seeing in law simply some hypotheses conceived by man's mind as to the laws designed to control his activity, appears chiefly under two connections. First, Law is not an existing fact outside of man's will and consciousness, a fact which he is restricted to ascertaining, as he is with regard to the laws of science. A rule, even if conceived as absolute and eternal, is so conceived only on condition of being considered as a norm whose observance is a duty to all. A legal rule is not a "law" which affirms the uniformity of a series of acts, of a group of phenomena. It is not in the repetition, the periodical and regular reproduction of these acts, that legal rules find their realization. Those who drew the celebrated declaration of the rights of man, in fully recognizing liberty, equality, and fraternity, as the immovable basis of enacted law, were compelled to recognize the fact that they had been forgotten by men, and for a very great while prevented from realization. Whether men know them or not, the laws of science none the less exist. When Newton found the laws of gravity, the order of phenomena did not change at all.

Before, as after him, the force of gravity was as the square of the distance. On the contrary, if we compare antique society which knew not the idea of equality, and modern society which has appropriated it, we see an essential difference between them, which appears, for example, in considering the question of slavery. Second, What distinguishes in a still more clear manner scientific laws from legal rules, is their infallible, inviolable action. The legal rule on the other hand is broken continually, even by those who know and acknowledge it. Consequently we cannot say that law is an unevadable order. That an order is obligatory does not mean that it is inevitable. We are under obligation to yield to duty, but we can repudiate it. We are powerless, however, against necessity. We must yield to it. Necessity may even release us from duty, *impossibilium nulla obligatio.*

So, whatever idea we form of law, we must conclude that it does not present the leading characteristics of scientific "laws."

Considering attentively juridical laws, it is not hard to see that they have as a whole a very relative character and one with which that of scientific laws cannot be compared. These last express the general uniformity of a given group of phenomena which admits of no exception. Its action does not change with time or place. Always, everywhere, and for every such case, it has absolute effect. Moreover, it is agreed to call a law of science not every general proposition, but only those which in the given conditions represent the utmost possible limit of generalization and cannot be reduced to formulas still more general and simple. Juridical norms have a very conventional general character. They are general rules, but applying only to relations which exist in a given society and for a given time, usually comparatively short. Consequently in different places, and in the same place at different times, we discover variations in the action of law. In such case the juridical norm does not represent the extreme limit of generalization. The juridical norm put out under the form of special custom or legislative enactments is only the combination of several different norms designed to regulate a given category of things. It can always be reduced to a more general and simple principle. For the same reason a juridical norm is not the expression of what is general or unchangeable even in juridical relations, but represents a variable and concrete element in the juridical order. Norms appear, change, disappear, act in a certain way upon the combinations of juridical relations, and cause these to take some other particular form. So they correspond not to laws in the scientific meaning, but to particular phenomena which are generalized by the formulas of scientific laws. If juridical norms, as we have shown, cannot be identified with scientific laws, nor recognized as capable of filling their place in the moral spheres, what can they be but phenomena? That juridical laws and scientific laws are absolutely heterogeneous notions, Gustave Hugo, the founder of the historic school of law, showed clearly at the beginning of the last century. Unfortunately, his idea was not sufficiently perceived by his disciples, and even now some jurists, misled by resemblance of names, still confuse juridical with scientific laws.

Section 9. *Relativity of Law*

To explain the actual relation of law to laws of nature, in the scientific sense, is an indispensable condition for determining the character of law in order to say whether it is absolute or relative. If juridical laws represent only a group of the phenomena of social life, law like all phenomena in general has naturally only a relative character. Being a phenomenon it is variable, depending upon conditions of time and place. The distinction between the just and the unjust, like that between the positive and negative quality of phenomena, between warm and cold, between heavy and light, arises from our personal feeling. The same delimitation of interests, appraised according to our personal impressions, may be found just or unjust. If this is so, the circle of phenomena which constitute the object of legal science is determined, not by the opposition of the just and the unjust, but by that between all the phenomena which admit of a juridical qualification positive or negative, no matter which, and those to which the opposition of just and unjust is not applicable because they do not admit of that quality.

The question is put quite differently if legal rules are to be regarded as the natural law of social phenomena, or as something that for such phenomena holds the place of it. In that case law is everything which conforms to such a natural law, prescribing their form of action to all the rest, a necessary order, constant and not to be disturbed, of their phenomena. By consequence law should not be relative but absolute, eternal and universal, independent of time and place. The distinction of just and of unjust from this point of view would be an absolutely objective distinction, not founded upon a subjective relation, but upon the immovable natural law expressing objective reality. As a result the task of the science would be determined altogether differently. The scientific explanation of law would need to begin by defining this natural law of right. Without having defined it we could not advance in the scientific study of law, for the simple reason that without it we would not know what is conformable to law and what is not; and these are precisely the points which are the very object of our research.

In truth, almost all the old juridical literature, which occupied itself with these general questions, followed this tendency. At the very beginning, for these authors it was necessary to find at any price a principle of law to serve as a measure, a criterion, to distinguish between the just and the unjust. This principle once discovered, would serve as a sort of philosopher's stone to make known to us the secret of the determination of the juridical order and be applicable everywhere and at all stages of the historic development of society. Sociability, fear, tendency to happiness, perfectibility, liberty, equality, harmonious development, and a series of such principles, have been successively proposed for this purpose; but none of them could answer the practical test. The actual life of peoples with its complex character could not be confined within the framework which this alchemy of law thought to trace out beforehand. If there were no surer method for the scientific study of law, it would be necessary to follow the opinion of those who, despairing of finding a basis more solid for the science in their ephemeral constructions, restricted the task of jurisprudence, and considered it simply as the art of interpreting the various systems of national law, an art which serves merely the immediate needs of practice.

But if we consider law as a whole made up of phenomena, the scientific study of its materials finds another opening. If we regard it as a whole made up of phenomena, then between lawful and unlawful there is no absolute opposition; there is only a relative difference. In the phenomenal world are no absolute differences. For example, the difference between hot and cold is purely relative. What is cold for Reaumur, is warm for Fahrenheit. All depends upon the measure chosen, and there is no absolute measure. When the physicist undertakes the investigation of the phenomena of heat and cold, he sets himself no task of discovering an absolute difference between them, but only of explaining the peculiarities of these phenomena compared with others, as for example, those of light or electricity. When juridical problems are to be passed on, it should be in the same way, if law is to be regarded simply as the *ensemble* of juridical phenomena. From this point of view, the distinction of just and unjust is relative and therefore variable. What is recognized as just among one people at a given epoch, is at another time or among another people considered unjust. Still further, if we place ourselves in a given phase of development of a particular people, the distinction is relative and cannot furnish an immutable criterion, since the concrete conditions in which the given fact is found must be taken into account. So the judge, placing himself at the point of view of actual law, declares to be just that which conforms to legislation and current customs. A publicist who has not the task of applying the law, who satisfies himself with fixing its value, may find the law itself unjust, and that to be just which opposes it. Another publicist standing at another point of view may express a contrary opinion and a third put forth a wholly new moral doctrine as to the point in controversy.

If this relativity in the distinction between just and unjust be granted, the task of law is not limited to the defining merely of the just. Just as the mechanician exhibits the identity of swift movement and slow, the physicist of the phenomena of heat and cold, so also a jurist, considering law as an assemblage of phenomena, must unite in his circle of phenomena both the just and the unjust. The distinction of just and unjust will not have for him capital value, but the distinction between what is related to the group of juridical phenomena and that which does not come within the juridical definition, no matter whether negative or positive, will do so.

To be sure, in drawing out mentally the distinctive points of a given group of phenomena to zero, or to infinity, we can image to ourselves law and not law as an absolute opposition. But this distribution of the phenomena will have value only as an hypothesis of our own imagining. It will have no value as reality. Where we establish a complete absence of law, the distinction of just and unjust would not be applicable and would have no meaning. The historic life of a people will certainly never present an example of such a state of things. In point of fact we have to do with an order of phenomena which has reached neither zero nor infinity.

In a word, for the science of law there is no need to mark an absolute distinction between just and unjust. It knows no such distinction. It takes under examination equally the just and the unjust, placing as the basis for the delimitation of the object of its researches not that distinction, but the one between what is and what is not law. To be sure, we can still find a good many people who think that to admit the relativity of law is to commit an unpardonable heresy. But in examining closely the development of the science of law commencing with the end of the XVIII century we may observe that this principle of relativity has been more and more recognized. The school of natural law which appears in the XVII century and marks the beginning of philosophic legal study, held a rigorously absolute theory. But this theory supposed the original qualities of human nature to be known. It broke in pieces upon the necessity of finding an objective criterion for distinguishing in man what is natural from what is not. The historic school which, at the beginning of the XIX century replaced that of natural law, undertook to show the relativity of law, and its national character, penetrated with the genius of the people who shaped it.

If each people has its special law, no one may talk of its absolute principles. But to determine the spirit of a people, and its qualities, together with their delimitation in relation to those of an individual, has seemed as impossible as the distinction in a man of what is natural from that which is not so. It is necessary either to adopt Puchta's mystic doctrine which personifies the mind of a people, or, placing oneself on more real ground, recognize that a people's mind is simply the manifestation, simultaneous and collective, of that of the individuals who compose the people. If this is true the popular mind can have no determinate character; consequently, law is not a product of the popular mind, producing itself and developing of its own accord, but on the contrary a result of the struggle of different interests which represent members of the people, a result which changes with the progress of the struggle. Ihering accepts this idea in his latest theory and proclaims the complete relativity of legal principles. There is only one point as to which, indeed, Ihering has not ventured to declare the relativity of law. Recognizing completely that the matter of legal principles cannot be rigorously determined, that it is relative and variable, he believes, nevertheless, that the source of these principles is always and necessarily the same, the state's authority. Consequently, from this point of view, he does not recognize the relativity of law. But there is left only one step to take, for under this condition it is admitted without reserve.

It is very important to show that the distinction of just and unjust is purely relative. First, It is only on this condition that one can establish a single idea of law, which can embrace all juridical phenomena. In the different opinions which are produced as to law, there is to be observed a certain duality. On one side different actions are examined with reference to their conformity to existing law or to their disagreement with it. On the other side the existing law in force is itself examined from the point of view of more general principles. When the just and the unjust are rigorously distinguished, no explanation of this can be found except in recognizing a double law, a positive and a natural one. But the doctrine of the relativity of law gives another explanation of the phenomenon just mentioned. It reconciles the variety of judgments as to the just and the unjust with the unity of law. It explains the diversity of judgments which we pass upon the different manifestations of law by that of the criteria applied to the definition of the just.

Second, The construction of the science itself gains in unity. According to the general opinion the science of law ought to study only law. But every jurist needs to occupy himself with what is not law, and there is a distinct juridical science, the criminal law, which occupies itself with the special study of violations of law. It is true that criminalists generally affirm that the true subject of their science is the sanction. Nevertheless, the determination of crime itself has a genuinely juridical character; punishment, on the contrary, is more political in its nature, and generally considerations of policy slip in. The center of gravity of the penal law is the definition of the constituent elements of the crime, and not the explanation of what is peculiar in the different systems of penal repression adopted by the legislator. In recognizing the relativity of the distinction between just and unjust and in connecting both of them with the object of legal science there is removed at the same time the necessity of any artificial reasoning to explain the juridical character of criminal law.

Third, If one admits that law is relative, it is impossible to restrict the science of it to any particular form of the delimitation of interests. If law in its entirety is relative, there is no reason to exclude from the circle of phenomena, which the science of it studies, any norms for the delimitation of interests, whatever their form of construction, whether they are norms established by representatives of social authority, or by custom, or by reason of subjective ideas which individuals have of their rights. Certainly the subjective notion of law is relative, and in this relativity there is a reason for not admitting the existence of any "natural" law by the side of the positive law which is the true object of the science. But if law in its entirety is relative, nothing prevents placing among the notions of it even the norms for the delimitation of interests elaborated by the individual conscience. This gives to legal science a greater breadth, a greater unity, even a more solid base; for the ideas of law which are manifested in customs and in legislation are elaborated first of all by the individual conscience. The juridical theory, which neglects this source, cannot explain the origin or the development of law.

In defining law as the delimitation of interests, I admit the complex relativity of it. This definition embraces all the delimitations of interests, whatever they may be, whether from the subjective point of view just or unjust, and in whatsoever manner these delimitations may be established, by customs, legislation, judicial procedure, or by the subjective notion of law.

CHAPTER II

THE LEADING DIFFERENT CONCEPTIONS OF LAW

Section 10. *The Definition of Law by What it Embraces*

To define legal norms as "norms for the delimitation of interests" is to give a definition of law which is not recognized by all the world. None, however, which has obtained universal assent can be found in legal literature. Those actually in use are very diverse, and several among them find partisans among the most distinguished jurists. It is necessary then to make a choice, and to do this with full knowledge, it is indispensable to study them all, in order to show their respective bases and values. It would be aside from the purpose to make here a detailed analysis of all the definitions of law which have been produced up to our time. It is the task of the history of legal philosophy to set out all the definitions of law in their historic order. For us it will suffice to examine the most typical definitions, the ones most widely received and which lie at the base of the modern tendencies in legal science.

If we compare our definition with others, we shall observe first of all that it does not contain certain features which play a leading part in others. Our definition does not in any way determine the substance (*materiam*) itself of legal norms, the manner in which they delimit conflicting interests, or the principles which form the basis of the delimitation. The questions as to how legal rules are formed, by whom they are established, are equally left open. Finally, in our definition nothing is said of the coercive character of law which is often considered as its fundamental, distinctive attribute. Meanwhile, the very terms of our definition may raise doubts and controversies. Some authors, partisans of the formal tendency, would say that law delimits not merely interests, but also wills. Partisans of the utilitarian tendency, on the contrary, would assert that instead of delimiting interests, law protects them. It is consequently necessary to explain why we have chosen this intermediary formula which passes by in silence the matter and the sources of legal rules as well as the means of enforcing them.

To define law according to the matter, the content, of its rules, it would be necessary that such matter be identical and common in all laws so that they could appear as the result of the same general principle. In reality, however, the legal conceptions of different countries and of different epochs of history, and even those of a given people at a given historical period, do not present such a single system of logical consequences derived from some sole general principle. The law of each people is the result of a continuous evolution throughout its history. Every historic epoch, however, brings its own moral notions, its own conditions of life, which determine the matter of its laws. So the law of a people is built up in a series of historical layers. It is necessary, also, to take into consideration the borrowings from foreign legislation. In this manner there enters into the composition of the law's substance some ancient principles, and some new ones resulting from more recent evolution, principles peculiar to the genius of the country, along with borrowed ones.

The material of every system of law is therefore very complex. When one seeks to define law by its matter there inevitably result formulas which determine not what the law actually is, but what in the author's view it ought to be. Instead of a scientific, objective, definition of law, we have only a subjective judgment. It is impossible to bring into one general common formula the heterogeneous materials of all laws existing and which have existed; and for this reason, to define law according to its matter one must commence by choosing between different legal principles. This choice can be based upon no objective fact. It depends on the subjective judgment of the author. The result is a great variety of formulas. The perfecting of human society (Leibnitz); the harmonious development of the person (Ahrens); the maintenance and development of the moral order (Trendelenburg); the realization of well-being (Kapoustine); the combining of liberty and equality (Soloviov); these and a whole series of others are presented by their authors as the distinctive matter of legal rules. In point of fact we find a good many laws which do not have for their end the harmonious development of the person (laws organizing social classes) or the combining of liberty and equality (laws establishing slavery), etc.

Such definitions do not show the characters common to all law, but merely determine the ideal for the development of law in the future, an ideal entirely subjective. Meanwhile, among the different proposed definitions there has been one which has enjoyed great favor among the learned. It is found among partisans of the most different tendencies. It is the definition of legal rules as "norms of liberty."[1]

[1] Hobbes. "Neque enim jus aliud significatur quam libertas quam quisque habet facultatibus naturalibus secundum rectam rationem utendi."

Kant. "Das Recht ist der Inbegriff der Bedingungen unter denen die Willkür des einen mit der Willkür des andern nache einem allgemeinen Gesetze der Freiheit zusammen vereinigt werden kann."

Krause. "Das Recht ist ein Lebensgesetz für die Freiheit vernünftiger Wesen."

Fridländer. "Das Recht ist die Gestaltung der Lebensverhältnisse zum zwecke der Freiheit."

Bauman. "Das Recht ist der Inbegriff derjenigen Forderungen vom Mensch zum Mensch welche für einen auf Freiheit Aller gegründeten Verkehr unerloslich sind."

Pachman. "Law is the measure of freedom in the community."

Binding. "Das Recht ist eine Ordnung menschlicher Freiheit."

It is the ambiguity of the formula which explains its success. If one recognizes in the definition of law as "norms of liberty" a definition founded upon the matter they contain, he must mean by it that the principle of liberty is the basis of all legal rules; this principle must furnish the essential substance of them all. They would consist, then, merely in the application of the principle of liberty to the regulation of human relations.

Such, indeed, was Kant's opinion. For him, law is merely a combination of special logical consequences resulting from the fundamental rule, "Act in such a way that your liberty shall accord with that of all and of each one." But it is impossible to bring under such a formula the mass of legal rules as we see they are. The oriental states by their legislation establish castes. The states of antiquity recognized slavery. Those of the middle ages with their feudal aristocracy show how difficult it is to see in legal rules merely logical applications of the principle of liberty. Kant himself in propounding the principle had in view not the actual law of which historic reality shows us the spectacle, but only that of reason, *Vernunftrecht*.

When this definition is applied to positive law in its historic development a different meaning is given to it. Legal rules are then considered as logical consequences of the principle of liberty because they are all in one fashion or another delimitations of human liberty, establishing its boundaries, measure, and restrictions, and in this sense forming "norms of liberty."

Undoubtedly, in delimiting interests the law limits their realization, and consequently from this point of view is a restraint upon human freedom. But even so, the substance of legal rules is not determined by the formula we are examining. This definition affirms merely that legal rules restrain, regulate liberty; but the formula does not explain in what way this regulation is accomplished. It results that this formula like the one proposed in this book, leaves at one side the subject matter of laws.

It must not, however, be supposed that the two definitions are identical. If every delimitation of interests is considered as a norm of liberty, this definition will appear altogether too broad. Every rule establishes necessarily a limitation of liberty whether it be a rule of law or of morals. So the definition of law as norms of liberty will not answer by itself. It leaves no room to distinguish between delimitations of liberty by rules of law and by rules of morals.

Moreover, the Kantian definition of law as "norms of liberty" has the further defect of supposing a rigorous contradiction, a complete separation between the interests of the persons under consideration, and consequently suffers from attributing to law merely the function of separating and dividing, and not that of unifying and grouping the persons subject to it. In truth, liberty as an object of conscious volition may be merely a property of an individual; but it presents itself, also, as a purely negative idea in so far as it puts the individual in opposition to the rest of the world. On the other hand the notion of an interest, of a need, is a positive one, and the needs, the interests of an individual, are precisely the bonds connecting him with the world, and especially to the other persons around him. Our interests are by no means exclusively personal, still less individual. Most of them are common either to all humanity, or at least to a more or less extensive special group of men. In realizing these interests we may encounter those of other men; this possible contact makes their delimitation necessary. In delimiting, however, these common interests, the law does not delimit the liberty of each individual. It combines the liberty of all by the unity of law with a view to facilitating the common realization. The rules of international law, for example, which delimit the common interests for all humanity and for each nation, cannot be defined as "norms of liberty." The basis of this delimitation is not the opposition of one individual and his interests to another, but that of a private person to a commonwealth and of one nation to the community of nations. But these two groups of interests belong to every man when regarded at the same time in his quality as a man and also as a member of some particular nation. This is why in delimiting these interests we do not delimit the liberty of one in relation to that of another, but merely locate the two interests which are equally a part of the liberty of each individual. To take another example, the state is concerned that the excessive exploitation of labor shall not bring on in the future destructive consequences by reason of the physical and moral degeneration of the workers which might result, and the state, therefore, limits the length of the working day, protects pregnant women, and little children, etc. Such regulations do not limit the liberty of the workman in relation to that of the employer. They affect equally that of both. They may be more vexatious for the workman than for the manufacturer; but they assure for the future the health and morals of the workers. There is no opposition of one private interest to another, but the opposition is between the present and the future, the temporary and the eternal. Each of us lives in the future as well as in the present. To feel entirely safe in the present, one must be sure of the future. So in this example we must recognize not a limitation of one person's liberty in respect to another person, but care of an interest which makes a part of the freedom of each.

The definition of law as "norms of liberty" is a manifestation of the individualistic tendency in legal science.

So long as one sees in society only a combination of independent individuals bound together by a social compact, it was entirely correct. But with the change of ideas as to society and as to the relations of individuals to it, the definition has become quite inapplicable. Today the individual is not considered as the chief factor, determining the whole social order. On the contrary he is himself considered as a product of society, and we are rather inclined to make him depend upon society. Legislation is not confined merely to the task of delimiting individual interests, but is occupied more and more with realizing common interests which cannot be considered as the exclusive property of any one. Consequently, law cannot be defined as "norms of liberty."

Section 11. *Definition of Law by its Source*

MOUROMTZEV. Definition and Fundamental Division of Law, 1879.

THON. Der Rechtsbegriff. (Zeitschrift für Privat und Oeffentliches Recht. B. VII, 1888. s. 245.)

SCHAEFFLE. Bau und Leben des socialen Kõrpers. B. I., 1881. s. 623.

SCHEIN. Unsere Rechtsphilosophie und Jurisprudenz. 1889.

The definitions of juridical norms according to their source are more objective than those which are based upon the matter of law. They do not contain a judgment upon law as it ought to be. They propose to determine the distinctive character of actually existing legal norms. This certainly explains their favor with the jurists who are partisans of a tendency which is a reaction against the idealist conceptions which preceded it. Widely spread in later times in Germany, it has penetrated into Russia. The definitions of this kind present, one may say, two varieties. Those of one kind define legal norms as those established by the state's organs of authority; the other recognizes in a more general way that society as a whole is the source of law.

In the first case juridical norms are regarded as orders emanating from the organs of state power. From this point of view, law presents itself as the *ensemble* of state legislation. All which is not founded upon some state enactment is not law. Therefore, there is no law where there is no state. Law finds birth only in a state, is an exclusively state product. Customary law is not true law. There can be no law acting outside of a state's boundaries. In other words, international law is not conceivable. From another point of view, since legislation (*lex*) is here recognized as the sole source of law, no juridical principles from any other source can oppose the will of the legislator, whether it be customs, science, or the individual conscience. So law and legislation are identified.

The popularity which this theory enjoys is explained chiefly by the necessities of judicial practice. In daily life legal contests centre in fact, most of the time, upon the question whether or not such a precise question is provided for by legislation. Customary law in most modern states does not play anything like such a rôle, having been almost effaced by written legislation. Very few persons are compelled to occupy themselves with mere theoretic questions of law, with its evaluation, with legislation. The great majority are accustomed by life itself to confuse the notion of law with that of legislation. Accustomed to see in the latter the measure for the delimitation of interests, we forget that to the interest of legality, to the interest favoring invariable action according to legislation, other interests may be opposed which sometimes compel authority itself to give up the absolute enforcement of its legal powers which happens, for example, when an amnesty is granted.

But aside from this practical foundation, the positive notion of law finds still another one in theoretical tendencies altogether different. The partisans of the old school, who admit the existence of an absolute idea of justice, see in the identification of law and legislation a means of reconciling their doctrine with fact. The diversity and variability, in a word, the relativity of law, is a too evident fact. By consequence, to save the dogma of an absolute justice, a rigid dividing line is traced between law and justice, and the first is considered as an accidental and variable form of the second. In demonstrating the relativity of law it is thought, at the same time, the absolute character of justice can be better defended. Such was Stahl's method. Even in the modern literature we meet still with partisans of this theory. It will suffice to cite Lasson (System der Rechtsphilosophie von Adolf Lasson, 1882). The law, said he, is an exterior order having an historic form more or less accidental. Therefore all law is positive law. It can only exist in a state. It is a product of the authority of that state. Justice is an absolute principle. It has its source in equality. It is the ideal which the law ought to pursue (*ideale Anforderung*), but which nevertheless can never be completely realized. This manner of looking at the question is no doubt compatible with the theory of the existence of an absolute principle of justice, for in this case its most objective, palpable and just form, the positive law, is considered as something absolutely distinct from this justice. Consequently, to discover justice properly so called, it would be necessary to have recourse to the more subjective, and less determinate ideas, which our consciousness gives. The phenomena which we are examining, being inexact and not seizable by the senses, it is naturally difficult for us to reach a precise result.

But partisans of the realistic tendency who make no pretensions to demonstrate an absolute principle of justice admit equally the identity of law and legislation. The realists think in that way to be able to apply to legal study the positive method which was created for the natural sciences. In comparing the science of law with the natural sciences we take account first of the objective and, so to say, palpable character of the very subject of the natural sciences. In applying to jurisprudence this positive method which has brought such progress to the physical sciences, the realists think to reach results as precise and palpable. The palpable form of law being legislation, the identification of them is considered a requirement of the positive method.

Behold the reasons because of which we admit very

often the identity of law and legislation, understanding it as an order coming from the supreme organ of the state's authority. This opinion has received its most vigorous expression from the pen of Schein. Law, according to him, is a norm established by the state and not by individuals. At the same time, it is not an order compelling the state to act conformably to certain principles. The norm indicates only how the state itself acts ordinarily. The law is for the state as for the individual the *ensemble* of principles which it follows in its actions, which it imposes upon itself, or observes voluntarily. Schein means by the state not the whole society but only the government, the organs of authority. Private law itself he considers a collection of rules promulgated by the state. All the rules of civil law exist only to serve as norms for the acts of judicial power. By the enacted laws the state only announces that it intends to follow in the future certain principles.

This definition brings up at bottom in the negation of law. The actions of the state are at bottom the actions of men who are considered as organs of the state's authority. Man to no purpose undertakes the function of an organ of authority; his psychic nature is not thereby changed. He still guides himself by ethical and technical rules. Consequently, if we accept Schein's definition and develop its logical consequences, we must then go so far as to say that every technical rule, every rule of architecture, for example, acquires the character of a rule of law when the organs of state authority are led to apply it in their acts. Meanwhile, the rules which govern the line of conduct of the state cannot all be considered as juridical norms. Thus, among the acts of governmental activity we place apart always its political acts of government. It is the same when the government, charged with the administration of the country, applies hygienic rules or other technical norms. It cannot act her by "law."

Generally, writers do not go as far as Schein. Norms are considered as juridical only when imposed by state authority for observance and declared obligatory by the government.[1]

In this case it is the imperative character of these dispositions which constitutes the distinctive trait of law. If it becomes thus possible to distinguish between juridical, technical, and moral norms, it is always true to say that, on the other hand, this conception restricts beyond measure the domain of law. According to this system, in fact, only promulgations of the legislator constitute law. Customary rules are excluded. But the study of juridical phenomena shows us every day that positive legislation is not the sole source of law.

The jurist who identifies law and legislation ought not to neglect the examination of the question as to the formation of legal enactments. He ought to examine the conditions of their first formation, and those of the latest ones. These researches will inevitably lead to the conclusion that law in its entirety cannot be referred to legislation. History shows us that the first enactments were only customs thus registered after having been established and preserved by the judicial proceedings of that time. All primitive legislation bears the character of a supplement to existing customary law. The making of special additions to and changes in it, of course necessarily presupposes its existence. So we see that legislation is separated from custom only by the wholly exterior process of enactment through state authority. The conditions of legislation at the beginning, therefore, do not allow of the general identification of law with its mere

[1] Jellinek. Die Rechtliche Natur der Staatenverträge. 1880. s. 31. Thon. Cited above.

special form of enacted legislation, and compel the recognition of juridically sanctioned customs as law. We reach the same conclusion if we turn to the formation of modern legislation. Here the opinions as to just and unjust, which have had birth in society, are enacted into law as a result of an external formal act; for example, the taking of a vote in Parliament. But the matter of the law existed already before its publication, having been furnished either by public opinion or by ordinary judicial procedure.

If law and legislation (*jus et lex*) were identical conceptions, the existence of juridical theories would be hard to conceive. Every theory which did not result in enacted law could not be qualified as juridical, and meanwhile it is known there are upon each question, no matter how insignificant, numerous theories which are not admitted in official law and have not found expression in positive legislation. If we recognize a juridical character in these theories formulated outside of all state authority by some savant, we shall find ourselves in the presence of juridical norms not coming from the state. If norms become juridical only in taking the official form (*lex*) the theory of their derivation from enactment or recognition would be the only one possible. The doctrines having the same content, which develop the same matter from juridical norms, as well as from enacted laws, could not exist. But it will suffice to open any treatise on civil or criminal law to be convinced of the existence of such doctrines as to the matter of law. They may serve the material of legislation, but they have a juridical character even before their transformation into it. It is true there are writers who do not admit the existence of a theoretic law. They say that the idea of a theoretic law, of a law which does not act, is as absurd as that of a wind which does not blow.[1]

[1] Bergbohm. Jurisprudenz und Rechtsphilosophie. s. 437.

Meanwhile, it must be admitted that man conceives the existence of enacted laws which do not act, where, for instance, they are abrogated. Juridical norms, replaced by others, do not become thereby rules of art or moral principles. They remain juridical norms despite all, quite as if still acting. The laws of the XII tables are in our time regarded by everybody as forming part of the law of the world as much as at the time they were in force. In the same way men always conceive of a law which is no longer acting; but as it exists in consciousness, it has a necessary effect upon relations, usages, judicial procedure, and legislation.

Other writers while completely recognizing the source of law as its distinctive trait and the true ground for its definition, yet do not identify it with state legislation. They define juridical norms as social norms, opposing them to moral ones which they style individual norms.[1]

This is not so defective a definition as the one just previously examined. We might even say, in general, that it sensibly nears the truth, but is extremely vague. What is individual in human life is so closely connected with what is social that it is impossible to draw a separating line between them. Norms established by an individual cannot be distinguished from those established by society. In truth norms, as in general everything in life and human consciousness, are the joint product of individual and social factors. Man is born into society, inherits from his parents a collection of customs and social habits. He is educated in society,

[1] Brocher de la Flehère, Les révolutions du droit, I. p. 29. Le droit n'est pas autre chose qu'une éspèce de conscience sociale. Schäffle. Bau und Leben, 2 Ausg. II. s. 80. Das Recht eine durch den Trieb der Selbsterhaltung geschaffene und den entwickelungsgeschichtlichen Bedingungen der Gesammt erhaltung angemessene gesellschaftliche Ordnung der Anpassungen und Organisationen, der Vererbungen Streitführungen, streitentscheidungen und Streiterfolge darstellt. Kashnitsa. Essence of Law. P. 152. Law is the conformity of social relations to the essence, the life, the destiny, of society as a whole, or conformity of the individual life to the social life.

acts in society, belongs to it by every side of his existence. How can he believe that there is any precise limit between the social and the individual spheres so that certain ethical norms are created by the individual activity and others, which we call legal, by the social activity?

We must then disavow all these definitions of law by its source because of their common defect. They presuppose as determined one of the most difficult of questions, the one most discussed in the science of law, that of its origin. Does law spring up as a result of individual activity? Is it created by the conditions of social life? Does its existence depend, or does it not, upon that of the state? All these questions are still widely discussed. Until these questions as to the origin of law are settled, it will remain impossible to define law by means of its source.

Section 12. *Definition of Law as Coercive Norms*

IHERING. Zweck im Recht. B. 1. 2d Edition, 1884. s. 320.
MERKEL. Recht und Macht. (Schmoller's Jahrbuch für Gesetzgebung B. V.)
BIERLING. Zur Kritik der Juristischen Grundbegriff. B. I., 1877.

Already in the middle ages it was quite generally admitted that constraint was the essential, distinctive characteristic of law. This opinion was everywhere adopted from the beginning of the last century. Law as a system of rules enforced by constraint was then opposed to morals which admit of no constraint, which require a voluntary submission. Thomasius, Kant, and above all Fichte, pushed this distinction even to the complete opposition of law and morals which they considered respectively as rules for the outer and inner life of man. The basis of this contrast was certainly the dualistic conception of the universe. If conformably to Descartes' doctrine mind and matter are recognized as two independent substances, the external and the internal life are two absolutely separate and distinct spheres. There is between them no mutual bond, no reciprocal influence. Each of them exists by itself, each has its peculiar laws and in each, equally, its own peculiar forces act. The exterior and interior life would be opposite poles. Consequently the exterior order, law, could not be upheld by internal agents. It rests exclusively upon external force, upon constraint. Between constraint and the forces of interior life, there is nothing in common. There is nothing which by transition unites them. Therefore constraint can have no internal psychic foundation. It constitutes the independent external base of law's action.[1]

[1] Doppel proposes this scholastic argument: "Quidam volunt Jus dictum esse per metathesin, ut sit jus quasi vis conversis literis."

Such is the necessary consequence of the rigorous and absolute separation of the internal and external spheres of human activity. This separation, as we know, is completely rejected by modern science. We know that our moral life depends upon our physical vigor, that even physiological phenomena change constantly into psychic ones and the latter into physiological ones again. Their rigorous delimitation is often impossible. In a word, the moral and physical sides of our existence are not two sedulously separated parts; on the contrary, they interpenetrate, so to say, each other and touch at every moment. From this point of view it would seem that the theory which claims that law being only an external order ought to be based solely upon constraint should fall of itself. If the moral and the physical life depend upon one another, external constraint necessarily provokes internal movements and the theory that law is an external order ought to be allowed no value. This theory, as has been first stated, has at the present time no meaning, for we no longer, as in the past, oppose external and internal phenomena. In fact, the organic school, which starts, as has been said, with assuming the mutual dependence of all phenomena of the universe and of all the manifestations of human life, no longer considers law as a system of external conditions and constraint as its essential attribute. It would seem that the realists who extend the application of the principle of causality to all phenomena without exception ought to be the first to rally to the support of this conclusion. They ought to reject that limitation of law and of morals which makes of the first an external rule resting upon constraint, and of the second a moral law supported by internal moral agencies. But the phenomenon, which always occurs in such cases, appears here. Realism which appeared as a natural reaction against the idealism previously all-powerful in the science of law has fallen into the contrary excess. Just as formerly the gross materialism, which referred everything to external experience, was opposed to the theory of innate ideas, so modern realism declines to admit into the domain of law any rule which has not the sanction of external constraint for its enforcement.

This theory, widely received among the learned who occupy themselves with positive law, has found much support and a general theoretic base in the celebrated work of Ihering, Zweck im Recht.[1]

This doctrine contains a very grave error, as I shall endeavor to prove. Constraint is neither a fundamental, nor even a general, attribute of juridical phenomena. First of all, it is not a fundamental attribute. One calls fundamental, an attribute which is presupposed by all the others from which they all flow in such sort that without it the phenomenon could not be conceived to exist. All the other characteristics depend upon the fundamental one. By it alone can we conceive a phenomenon, since it carries in itself, so to speak, all the rest.

But constraint is not connected with law in this manner. We can conceive of law without this attribute. If society were composed only of perfect men, constraint would be superfluous and unknown. Each one without stimulation by it would respect the right of another and fulfill his own duties. Law would exist none the less, for in order to fulfill my duties and render to each what is his, I must know wherein my duties consist and what is owed to each one. Even in the real society of men with all their weaknesses it is recognized that

[1] Zweck im Recht. 1. 318. "Die gangbare definition lautet: Recht ist der Inbegriff der in einem Staat geltenden Zwangsnormen und sie in meinen Augen vollkommen das Richtige getroffen. Die beiden momente welche sie in sich schliesst sind die der Norm und die der Verwirklichung durch den Zwang."

society is the more normal the more rarely constraint is used.[1]

Inadmissible is the law which is supported completely and exclusively by constraint alone; inadmissible a state of things where no one fulfills voluntarily his juridical duty, where it is necessary to constrain everybody to obedience of the law. It is inadmissible because what power is there to be charged in such case with exercising the right of constraint?[2]

All these facts are so clear and evident that those who think constraint the essential attribute of law dare not affirm that it suffices for its enforcement.[3] Commonly they put the question a little differently. They are satisfied to affirm that if the force of law, its power, is not based on constraint alone, constraint is nevertheless an indispensable supposition, preceding all the other foundations on which the predominance of law might be left to rest; and that if law had not constraint behind it, all the other bases of its power, religious sentiments, utility, etc., would lose their effect.[4] To sum up, they say law supposes reciprocity. I am obliged to respect the rights of another if he respects mine. If one attacks me unjustly, I am not bound to respect his rights while doing so, *vim vi repellere licet*. This is why, to fulfill completely our juridical duties, it is necessary to be sure that they are observed by everybody. For the same reason juridical norms are just or useful only

[1] Ziller. Allgemeine philosophische Ethik. 1880. s. 221. Man ist auch wenigstens allgemein überzeugt, dass Rechtsleben um so gesünder sei, jeweniger zwang angewendet zu werden brauche.

[2] Ahrens. Encyclopädie, 1857. s. 43. Trendelenburg. Naturrecht, s. 19. 89. Jellinek. Recht, Unrecht, Strafe, s. 50. Bierling. Zur Kritik der juristischen grundbegriffe, I. 1877. s. 51. Thilo. Die theologisirende Rechts und Staatslehre. 1861. s. 330.

[3] Ihering. Zweck im Recht, I. s. 556. Schäffle. Bau und Leben des socialen Körpers, I. 1881. s. 663.

[4] See especially Fichte. "Grundlage des Naturrechts." 1796. I. s. 163–179. Among contemporary writers, Lasson, "System der Rechtsphilosophie." 1882. s. 205–207.

if they are generally observed. If laws were observed only by reasonable men and it was granted to others to break their requirements, the most righteous law would become absurd. That law, for example, is very just which directs the killing of an animal attacked, or suspected of being so, with a contagious malady. But it is just only if everybody observes it. If some evil-minded persons neglect it all the losses sustained by the upright will be useless, since the sick animals kept by their selfish owners will suffice to spread the malady.

At first sight these arguments appear irrefutable. But on examining them it is not difficult to show that they go too far and either prove nothing or too much. In fact, if law can really be observed at all, only on condition of being absolutely and rigorously so by all the world, then it never will be observed. When the law in force has a coercive sanction it may still be broken. There is not in the world any power which can constrain every one to obey it. Moreover, men in general do not guide their conduct by certainty since it is hardly ever to be had; but they act upon probability, which answers practically to show us the line of conduct to follow. So far as concerns law, men are satisfied with a probability of its observance in the great mass of cases. Whether law has a coercive sanction or not, there never is assurance that it will be observed by everybody under all circumstances. Under no conditions is it certain that all animals attacked by contagious maladies will be destroyed as quickly as possible; but that this requirement may be reasonable it answers that it is likely that most of them will be, for thus we may hope that the disease will not spread as readily as before. But if it is probable, even before its publication, that the law will be observed in most cases, constraint does not go for nothing. Thus it is almost certain that, even when coercive measures are taken with a view to assuring the completest application of the measure, a law for the destruction of diseased animals will be observed only if everybody thinks it useful.

So constraint is not the fundamental attribute of the law. Neither is it an attribute common to legal phenomena. The theory that constraint is the essential characteristic of law has been able to take form and spread, owing to a special fact. As Bierling has already shown, general questions of law have been studied hitherto by jurists who were concerned mainly with the civil law. General dogmatic instruction is ordinarily given in civil law studies.[1] Moreover, even the system of natural law arose chiefly from analysis of civil law institutions. But it is only necessary to turn to public law institutions to be satisfied that constraint cannot be accounted a common characteristic of all law. To begin with political laws, they may be violated by the government's organs themselves. It may be asked how, in this case, can constraint be used to sanction the violated rights.[2] But, perhaps we shall be told that a preliminary question belongs here, Is public law really law? Does not Rennenkampf claim that public law has not a rigorously juridical character?[3] Does not Gumplowicz affirm, for his part, that if private law is law, then public law ought not to be so called, but ought to be designated by some other term, for it differs qualitatively?[4]

Leaving aside for the moment public law, even in the domain of civil law can all be realized by constraint? Are not the parties often without possibility of real-

[1] Bierling. L. C. s. 11. Die Lehre von den allgemeinen Grundbegriffen gehörte gewissermasen zur Domaine des Privatrechts.

[2] Thon. Rechtsnorm und subjektives Recht. 1878. s. 6.

[3] Sketch of Legal Encyclopedia. 1868. p. 159.

[4] Gumplowicz. Rechts-staat und Socialismus. s. 13.

izing their juridical claims because the judges are too indulgent to the defendant, or because he has for the time concealed all his goods in some secure place?[1]

The opinion which we are setting forth may be otherwise expressed. In considering constraint as an essential attribute of law, it cannot be affirmed thereby that every concrete juridical claim is realized by constraint, but only that all laws in general and in the normal order of things are capable of being realized in that way. Therefore, the discussion is not as to the real concrete possibility of restraint, but as to an ideal supposed possibility. If this is so it cannot be said that every law can be enforced by constraint. It must be said only that such a possibility ought to exist. The question thus put becomes exceedingly vague. In every case the question as to what are the attributes of law turns into "what ought to be its attributes." Admitting, moreover, this manner of stating the question, the theory we are combatting gains nothing. To begin with, there are norms which do not suppose constraint. Those whose violation brings coercion are only a part of juridical norms. If they are considered as the only juridical norms, it will be necessary to exclude those whose violation is followed by punishment, for to punish is not to compel the observance of the rule for whose violation the punishment is inflicted.[2]

It is not difficult to show that the observance of a good many laws cannot possibly be fully enforced through constraint.[3] Those to whom this condition

[1] Geyer. Phil. Eint. Holtzendorf's Encyclopädie. 4 Aufl. 1882. s. 5.

[2] Thon. Rechtsbegriff. Grunhut's Zeitschrift. 1880. VII. B. Heft 2. s. 245.

[3] Kuhnast. Ihering's Definition des Rechts (Beiträge zur Erläuterung des deutschen Rechts, herausgbn. von Rassow und Küntzel? 1880. No. 2-4?) s. 155. Es scheint aber auch, als ob die Frage wohl aufgeworfen werden darf ob überhaupt die Erfullung irgend einer Rechtspflicht und insbesondere die Leistungsabischt erzwingbar ist.

is applicable are, strictly speaking, norms which carry the obligation of not doing something, those imposing obligation to give up something or its profit. But laws requiring of a person an act, especially a personal act, cannot be enforced by constraint. A man cannot be compelled by force to do a particular task. There may be cases, and are such in fact, where the man will prefer to submit to capital punishment rather than to an act contrary to his conscience or even his interest.

In all this discussion in speaking of constraint physical constraint is meant. The whole argument relates to that. Constraint can, certainly, be understood differently. Thus, Ihering in making constraint the fundamental attribute of law, has in view not only physical but also moral constraint. Why not give it this large meaning? If it is taken thus, the idea of constraint is enlarged so as to make the discussion useless. If constraint is regarded as including both physical and moral pressure, it certainly does accompany all juridical phenomena. But when so understood, it serves as the sanction not only of juridical norms, but also of moral principles, religious dogmas, and even the "laws" of logic and æsthetics. The conscious violation of moral duty is inseparable from ideas of repentance, of fear and of contempt. Sin evokes the idea of wrath and chastisement from God. The violation of the rules of logic brings error and uncertainty in results obtained.

The violation of the laws of beauty, themselves, finds a sanction in the discomfort produced by ugly spectacles. All these ideas produce the same moral constraint as does the threat of legal exaction, or punishment. In this broad meaning the degree and character of the constraint is very variable; but the constraint applied for juridical ends is far from being the severest. Fear of God's wrath or infamy may be vastly greater than that of a pecuniary loss or a few days in prison. Moral constraint thus cannot be regarded as the essential attribute of law. It forms a part of everything that has to do with human consciousness. Consequently in saying that law is supported by moral constraint we mean only that the orders in juridical norms are addressed to the human conscience and nothing more.

Thus, there cannot be recognized in constraint the essential and distinctive mark of law. Doubtless, and we freely admit it, constraint, and above all moral constraint, plays a very vital part in law. Its importance comes from the fact that the development of juridical order has always for a result the prevention of all violence. However undeveloped a society may be, juridically, constraint is always recognized as a means of social authority. In our day the organs of authority ought to use constraint only to compel observance of legal requirements. Consequently the moral order of things in modern society is such that physical constraint is employed only in the law's service. It is only in this sense that we can say that it is the distinctive attribute of law. This surely does not mean that it is the general characteristic, or indispensable basis, of law. We say only that with the progress of social life law tends to put itself above force and to use it only so far as it is a valuable means for enforcing legal requirements. It is very important that public powers have in general monopolized in their own hands the use of force. It serves not only to guarantee social peace; it consolidates the rights to which it can give effect, and which do not thereby lose their nature. For the same reason it strengthens all other rights. The realization of a right by constraint impresses men's minds necessarily. In the minds of the great mass, who know not how to fix limits for the possible application of constraint, the notion of law becomes involuntarily associated with its coercive enforcement.

When a rudimentary idea, one made without the aid of critical analysis, is formed of law, it always carries the persuasion that all laws without exception can be made respected by force. This elementary notion may have its social value, but has none in science, since, as we have seen, it cannot withstand a rigorous analysis.

Section 13. *Formal and Utilitarian Conceptions*

As we have said, our conception of law as rules for the delimitation of interests conflicts with two contrary opinions. The partisans of the formal tendency object that without doubt the function of law consists in delimitation: but that what it delimits is not interests, but individual wills. The partisans of the utilitarian tendency, on the other hand, think that law is not the delimitation, but the protection of interests. Let us see what is the meaning of each of these different formulas, and try to show that each is contaminated with an exclusiveness which prevents our accepting either.

The formal theory of law is the older. It found its birth at the same time as the school of natural law, and is characterized by individualism and by its mechanical theory of society. It reached its highest development in the XVIII century in the doctrines of Thomasius, of Kant, and of Fichte. These authors entirely separated law from morality, and gave a character rigorously formal to law. They saw in law the exterior order of human relations. Its function was to assign to each individual an inviolable sphere where he could freely realize his own will. But they did not seek to know in what the will consisted and the interests which cause it to act.

The predominating influence of the formal theory at the beginning of the XIX century and during the preceding one, had a double cause, historical and theoretical. This formal theory, which considered law as having for its sole task the assigning to each one a certain sphere for the free realization of his will, and did not concern itself about the use which the individual might make of his liberty, was a reaction against excessive development of government tutelage. The administration at this time thought itself called upon to meddle in all the details of personal activity. Legislation undertook to impose upon each one his residence, his costume, what he should do, and how to do it.

This excessive development of state control completely destroyed individual initiative, that chief agent of social progress. The state legislated as to matters of conscience, prescribed religious beliefs and persecuted those who departed from rigorous orthodoxy. Under such conditions it was necessary to set limits to the state's interference in the sphere of individuality by giving to the individual himself a sphere of autonomous activity. Such was the historical basis of the formal theory of law. Its theoretical basis rested on the historic notion of human society which was dominant at that time.

When we consider society as a simple and mechanical aggregate, composed of a certain number of individuals, when we do not see in the individual a product of social life, but when society itself appeared as the result of a social contract; when, in a word, the mechanical theory of society was accepted, at such a time the individual with his conscious will might be regarded as the one activity in social life. The social order according to this theory consists in the delimitation of different spheres assigned for the activity of the different individuals making up society. The sphere, so assigned to each one, and in which his will is all powerful, is considered as constituting his right in the subjective sense. The rules which control the individual wills constitute the objective law.

Once formulated, this idea of law has been admitted even by authors who have abandoned the mechanical theories of society. Hegel, who thinks that the interests of the individual ought to be subordinated to the social order, whose end is the realization of morality, understands law, nevertheless, in a purely formal manner. The theory of the will receives, too, in him a peculiar development. With Kant the individual will is limited by ourselves; with Hegel by will, itself, but by the objective, general will, which is expressed in the state's organization. So the notion of law for Hegel comes altogether from that of will; law for him is a delimitation of the individual subjective will, by a general objective one.

The doctrines of Kant and of Hegel exercised a very great influence over legal literature in the first half of the XIX century. It is not astonishing that the formal theory which considers law as the delimitation of the will has maintained until now its importance. We find it very often in the definitions of current manuals.[1] But historical conditions having changed and the organic doctrine having taken the place of the mechanical theory of society, this view has been somewhat abandoned.

Intervention of the state with the sphere of the individual is actually limited in all countries, and in certain ones even too much so. Individual liberty is almost universally recognized. To the old preoccupations which gave birth to the formal theory of law, have succeeded new ones inspiring other tendencies. The individual man freed from state tutelage has not been found to be as free as was expected. When intervention of the state was suppressed it was perceived for the first time in what dependence individuals find themselves with respect to society, in what degree the disinherited are subject to the wealthy.

But the state, so far as it represents the conception of morality, cannot admit that the highest interests, for

[1] Windscheids Pandekten 1. sec. 37. Kuntz. Wendepunkt der Jurisprudentz 32.

example public health and safety, should be subjected to lower interests, simply because these last have force on their side. A new appeal is made for its intervention, which is necessary in order that the liberty of the weaker be protected against the strong, and so it becomes necessary to enlarge the sphere of legislation. The law may not content itself with delimiting the spheres for the realization of individual wills. It is obliged to take into consideration the different interests, which make up those spheres themselves. All these questions, set by life itself, have had as a result a new manner of understanding the law. The first school to oppose itself to the formalism of the old legal theories was the organic school represented by Krause, Ahrens and Röder.[1]

Having rejected the mechanical theory of society this school naturally could not continue to understand law as a combination of rules directing individual wills. The notion of law which it has developed is much wider. According to it, law is the combination of conditions necessary for the harmonious development of the individual. It also defines subjective right, as individual will limited by legal rule.

The first writer who separated completely the definition of law from that of will is Ihering, in the third volume of his Geist des Römischen Rechts. For him subjective right is not a will which can be limited. He replaces the will by interests. The social work of law is the protection of interests, not the delimitation of wills.[2]

Ihering's conception of the social functions of law offers doubtless advantages over the theories which define law as the delimitation of wills. In the old theories legal science maintained a strictly formal char-

[1] Ahrens. Encyclopädie 51.

[2] Geist des Römischen Rechts, III. sec. 60.

acter which took no consideration of the subjects of human activity, the aspirations, the needs, the necessities, which guide it, but only of its external forms. So understood, jurisprudence cannot show the social value of legal institutions, nor the conditions which have caused them, nor the ends to whose realization they lead.

On the contrary a jurist, who considers law as the juridical protection of interests, is led involuntarily to a more complete study of existing institutions. In examining the interests which direct human activity and which are protected by the law to which they gave birth it is possible for him to pass beyond the limit of a simple study of legal forms of protection. He explains the reasons for this protection, its influence upon the progress and development of social life, how it contributes to progress, and how hinders it. He becomes able to understand the historic alteration in legal forms by applying himself to the study of the changes in the character and tendency of the interests protected by them. With respect to the legal forms in force, especially the newly established ones, he reaches the possibility of exhibiting them clearly, and developing fully their beginning before him in scarcely recognized embryo, so that by recognizing the alteration of interests we can predict also the changes in the forms of their legal protection, or at least foretell their tendency.

These changed notions of law have necessarily exercised, and are exercising each in its turn, their influence upon the legislator. The first separates him from life and the other brings him in contact with it. The will, regarded apart from its material manifestation, appeared the same in all the world as one of the general forms of life. Hence the idea that law is independent of conditions of time and place, and that it is possible to justify oneself in promulgating law upon considerations wholly abstract.[1] On the other hand, interests vary indefinitely with different persons, times and places.

The legislator who takes into consideration the material of law has to study the manners of the society for which his laws are designed. With our conception of it, it is impossible to write laws without previously studying the interests of society. The conditions of social life with which the legislator has to do are local and concrete, and not abstract ones.

So that following the idea just given of law we assign to the legislator a function very extensive and complex. If we protect the will without concerning ourselves with the use which the subjects are going to make of such a right, of course only very general conditions, under which the protecting help shall be extended, can be established. These conditions, moreover, are generally negative, and are limited to protecting the individual against direct infringement of his right. On the contrary, if the legislator proposes to protect interests, the conditions of protection have in view the peculiarities of each interest, and, consequently, can be of a positive kind.

The comparison of these contrasting theories leads to the preference of Ihering's, but other arguments can be found to show that the theory, which assigns to law only the function of delimiting wills, does not conform to the real phenomena of juridical life and that among these phenomena are several which it leaves without explanation.

[1] Stein, himself, despite the essentially historical character of his theories, is led by his manner of understanding law, which he borrowed from Hegel, to affirm that law in its fundamental principle is quite opposed to its own matter, that it does not arise from the activities of life but by means of the simple idea of it (Gegenwart 94), and still further he affirmed that law by itself has no history and that what we are accustomed to call its history is the history of life in those relations in which it turns to legal ideas. *Id.*, page 100.

In the different legislative rules in force one can find institutions which do not simply protect the will, but protect it only as it is applied to the realization of an interest which is thought worthy of protection. Of this fact a very general example, which the whole world recognizes, can be cited. Justice does not enforce all contracts, but only those pertaining to an interest of some importance. No tribunal would attempt to compel performance of an agreement to dance the waltz at a party with a particular person. No one would think the interest resulting from such an agreement enough for the law to be applied to vindicate it.[1]

Besides those interests which are not essential, those which are contrary to morals are not protected, and the law refuses its protection to contracts concerning them. So, contracts having protection as their object are not sanctioned by any tribunal.

One can also show the inconsistency of the old theory by demonstrating that persons who have no wills are nevertheless invested with certain rights. For example, the law protects the interests of unborn infants, idiots and the insane.

Finally, the protection of interests takes place sometimes at the instance of the individual, and sometimes contrary to it. We find examples of such protection in the institution of guardianship of minors and spendthrifts, in compulsory instruction and compulsory vaccination.

[1] By Am. Translator. The explanation of this in our manuals of the law of contracts, *viz.*, that the parties themselves make such agreements with the understanding that they are not binding, either offers no explanation, or is an instance of the illegitimate use of fiction for that purpose, like that of corporate personality mentioned below in this section. Such understanding either arises from the nonenforcement, which is sought to be explained, or is a pure fiction. Usually it is the latter, and the matter of nonenforcement is not at the time adverted to by either party. The *vera causa*, unquestionably, is the insignificance of the interest in question. *De minimis non curat lex.*

So that if we make the will the subject-matter of law, it is impossible to explain its institutions because there are laws whose object is not the protection of any individual will. On the contrary, no law can be cited which does not protect some interest, if the law is actually in force. Without doubt many legal institutions find a rational and sufficing explanation in the theory which sees in the law only a delimitation of wills. This does not prevent the defining it as a protection of interests, for the fact that a definite sphere is guaranteed to the individual for the free realization of his will, establishes also an interest; consequently, in defining law as the protection of interests, we regard it from a more general point of view. This definition embraces the preceding one, which looks only to a particular case of the protection of interest.

It is necessary to add also that in understanding law, as the delimitation of wills, one necessarily shows himself a partisan of the individualistic conception. The will is always individual. Each one has his will; and this is why, in admitting this theory, it becomes necessary to oppose the individual and his rights to society. Meanwhile, the real legal order presents a good many rights which cannot be connected with any particular individual. The theory based upon the will can explain a good many phenomena only by an appeal to the theory of legal persons, to whom are accorded rights analogous to those conferred upon individuals. But the judicial person is a fiction by means of which some group of persons, or some undetermined one, is considered as a distinct person, and, like an individual, is endowed with rights and obligations. There may be cited as belonging to this class of ideas the loan societies, the various corporations, benevolent societies, etc. For the purposes of legal construction this kind of fiction is perfectly legitimate, it simplifies the explanation of certain acts. But it loses all value when resorted to for a philosophical explanation of the existence of rights which do not belong to any individual. In such a case fictions ought not to be employed. However, by replacing "will" with "interests" we can explain the phenomena without employing fictions. The will is an attribute of human personality. Men's interests, on the contrary, are very little determined by their individual organization. For the most part interests are products of social conditions and have therefore a social character. The interests of mankind cannot, like man's will, be opposed to those of society. Most interests are common to all men, others are at least common to some distinct groups of persons, and it is only a very few which have a strictly individual character. So in understanding law as the legal protection of interests we are led to replace the individualist's with the social theory. Law is not considered as something which the individual opposes to society, but something that society has created and which it gives to the individual. In fact, the theory of Ihering and his partisans presents itself to us under this aspect as the social theory of law.

Nevertheless, despite its value, Ihering's conception cannot be accepted without submitting it to extensive modifications. His point of view, that law is a protection of interests, cannot be accepted. If one holds to this definition of law he is compelled to recognize that if in society a single interest alone was protected to the exclusion of all others, this protected interest would nevertheless have a legal right, and that consequently the relations which the man, possessing it, would have with his fellows would be legal relations. Such, for example, would be the relations of a despot with an oppressed people; those of a father with the rest of his family who do not enjoy legal rights; those of citizens with foreigners at a time when these latter had no legal rights; those of a master with a slave. But all this contradicts the truth that one can exercise a legal right only in connection with persons who are also subjects of law, that juridical relations are only possible between persons who enjoy legal rights. One can have a right "over" a slave but not "with" him. The interest protected by the law which consists in disposing at pleasure of the slave's life is restrained and limited in its realization not by the slave's interests, which are not taken into consideration or protected, but by those of other persons who do possess legal rights; by those, for instance, of the true owner who has given me the right to employ the slave's services. It is the interests of this man which, like my own, are protected by the law. On the other hand, we cannot have a right "over" persons who possess their legal rights. So, when you make a contract of hiring with a domestic, you have a right in connection with the person whom you take into your service, but not "over" him. Your right is only to his labor.

Our Professor Mouromtzev thought he avoided this difficulty by adding to his definition of law, that law is protection given by society to an individual, having for its end only the guaranteeing of him against obstacles coming from other members of the society. He regarded the law as a peculiar form of society's influence over human relations. Men's relations are made complex generally by the effect of the special situations in which they are worked out, of the society in which men live. Society is naturally disposed to assist men when they seek to establish relations with each other. This social assistance may come in two ways. First, It may be employed with a view to removing obstacles thrown in the way by men not belonging to the local society. Mouromtzev calls this the first "modality" of protection. Second, Society protects the relations which some of its members have with each other against attacks by persons who are equally parts of its organization. It appears under two forms, organized and unorganized. Organized protection is distinguished from the other by following a course of procedure settled beforehand, and by means specially designed to do this. This form of protection, determined beforehand, is the law, according to Prof. Mouromtzev's definition. Consequently, the law is, for him, not the whole means of protection, but only socially organized protection directed against the dangers that come from within the society itself. This rectification of Ihering's formula presents no advantage. It comes necessarily to the denial of all international law whose subjects are precisely members of different societies. Besides Mouromtzev, to be consistent with himself, must deny the validity of some parts of international law whose juridical character is incontestible. To be sure, while holding to his theory one can still attribute a juridical character to that protection of interests which is brought about by the aid of collective measures, with the co-operation merely of the international community, because under this hypothesis we have a protection given by the international community to one of its members; but it is impossible on this theory to affirm the juridical character of the prohibition against a foreigner's reprinting a book without the author's permission. In this case, and in other analogous ones, the protection having for object to prevent a fact from taking place on territory not subject to the legal group, could not be regarded as juridical protection according to Mouromtzev's definition. Too narrow in this hypothesis, the definition on analysis is found to be too large in other cases. It extends, in fact, to the attributing of a juridical character to the protection which is given against the act of an individual who is a part of the local group, but who enjoys no legal rights and has no interests guaranteed by law. The relations of a master with a slave deprived of all rights, and, in general, our relations with individuals outside of the pale of the law would have to be recognized as juridical.

All these consequences resulting from the formula which we are combatting are avoided if our definition is accepted. The function of law consists, in our view, not in the protection but in the delimitation of interests. Consequently, juridical relations can exist only with persons who have legal rights, and whose interests are placed under the protection of the law. Where the protected interest exists only on one side there can be no delimitation of interests. In such a case the protected interest absorbs completely what is not protected. It is necessary to observe that the utilitarian definition, according to which it is the function of law to protect interests, leads in its logical consequences to an excessive intervention on the part of the state. The protection of interests supposes naturally the choice of the best means for their realization. It results that if the task of the law is to protect interests, it ought to compel the citizens to adopt in the realization of their interests the means which are considered the best and, consequently, might stifle completely the personal initiative, that capital agent in social development. The delimitation of interests, on the contrary, checks only their collision without mingling itself with the choice of means for realizing them. To the degree that realization of the given interest does not prevent that of others it is determined only by the extent of opportunity and the requirements of morals without being regulated by legal rules. If we assign to the law as its function the delimitation of interests it stands thus between these two extremes, between the indifference to individual action which the formal conception of law requires, and the suppression of individual independence which would seem to be the logical consequence of the utilitarian theory of law.

CHAPTER III

HYPOTHESIS OF NATURAL LAW

Section 14. *General Characteristics*

The matter constituting juridical norms is extremely variable according to time and place. The same interests are differently delimitated by law in different states and at different historical epochs. From this fact it seems to result that the matter making up juridical norms depends wholly upon the free choice of men, that law is the voluntary and intended work of humanity. But by the side of variable and temporary elements of law, can be found elements imposed by objective necessity. Although the judgments of man vary in the course of society's historic evolution, we find, nevertheless, that the conceptions of law and non-law which are formed in us in one way or another cannot be modified at will; so that in the history of almost all legislatures, we can find cases where attempts to borrow foreign legislation, or to put in force unsuitable theoretical principles of law, have wholly failed. The will of the legislature encounters obstacles in social conditions and the law, after being promulgated, remains a dead letter and is not applied.

We are forced to recognize in the law, by the side of this variety and diversity, elements imposed by objective necessity. The presence of these elements has been observed by the very earliest savants who attempted a scientific explanation of legal phenomena. It was necessary to fix that element of law which appeared to arise without the action of man. As there was not until the XVIII century any accurate notion of regular historical evolution, following certain laws, they found themselves in the alternative of considering law as instituted by man, entirely arbitrary, governed by no necessity, or else as something immediately provided by nature and, consequently, unchangeable and independent of men's wills. The first of these points of view is superficial, contrary to the inevitable character of law, and did not satisfy even minds which were not prepared to appreciate the problem of law's origin. The second point of view resulted in the theory of natural law unchangeable, eternal, and universal, resulting necessarily from man's nature and independently of his will.

It is a seductive hypothesis. It assimilates legal norms to laws of nature. Instead of subjecting man to arbitrary orders from his fellows, it subjects him to unchangeable orders of nature. Instead of an artificial and conventional law it sets up a natural and necessary one; but this hypothesis finds in the fact of variety and inconsistency of law an irrefutable objection. If there exists a natural law which is unchangeable and eternal, how can a positive law which is imperfect find a place beside it? Despite all this, the manner in which the question was put being granted, and granted that it was necessary to choose between arbitrary man-made law and it, the hypothesis of natural law becomes the only possible explanation for that character of necessity and generality which belongs to law.

Despite the sure manifestation of variable elements, which seemed to contradict its necessary character, every reflective mind was compelled to recognize in law an objective necessity and not a purely human creation only. Practicing lawyers alone could be brought to deny the hypothesis of natural law. It appeared incontestable as soon as the question was examined, from the philosophic point of view. For several centuries this hypothesis ruled without division, and was almost unanimously accepted as the scientific explanation of law.

Appearing for the first time in Greece, with Socrates, it was strongly developed by the Roman jurists. They considered natural law as a common and indispensable element of all law in opposition to the vagaries of national legislation. In the philosophy of the middle ages, conformably to the religious tendencies of that time, natural law was identified with divine law, eternal and unchangeable, to which were opposed variable human laws. In the XVII and XVIII centuries, under the influence of the dominant rationalism the theory of natural law wholly separated again from all religious basis, and natural law once more was considered as an abstract system which was derived by logical necessity from man's reasonable nature and which existed by the side of the positive law.

It is only the historical school, represented by Hugo and Savigny, which has refuted for the first time in a philosophical way the hypothesis of natural law. This was not the result of chance, but of the logical tendency of the school, which applied to the explanation of law the historical conception. The historic study of law existed previously, but the historic conception appeared only with this school. In the XVI century the French jurists, with Cujas as their chief, studied the history of Roman law; but their labors were only historic researches. They sought to reconstitute the old Roman juridical life and nothing more. There was no question of the process of historic development. It could not be otherwise, for the idea of historic evolution had not yet been formulated. It appeared only in the XVIII century, thanks to the labors of Vico, Montesquieu, and Herder. The historic school has great value, especially because it applied to the study of law the new conception of a regular historic evolution. This conception led it to deny the hypothesis of natural law. The regular character, and by consequence the necessity, of the development of law historically being ascertained, this hypothesis was no longer indispensable. Doubtless, law is in part necessary and independent of man's will, but the regularity of its development best explains its necessity. This explanation has the advantage of harmonizing at the same time with the idea of the variety and of the variability of legal institutions. The doctrine of the historic school easily overcame the theory of natural law. Neither Hugo nor Savigny saw any need to spend much time upon its refutation. These authors simply opposed to that theory the idea of historic evolution. This theory, when put forward, took away at once the main foundation for the old one; that is to say, the legal philosopher was no longer in the alternative of choosing between the natural law theory and the arbitrary character of law. The historic school showed that it was possible to solve the problem while avoiding this alternative. Law is not formed directly by nature, nor is it, either, an arbitrary creation by man. Law, according to the doctrine of the historic school, is a product of social life which follows in its evolution a regular advance, and to that extent is necessary. It is not created by the arbitrary will of individuals, but by the steady inevitable advance of human development. Being neither arbitrary nor natural, law is a historic necessity.

However, the historic school did not give to this idea of regular historic development, a formula so general. It saw in law a product not of human society, but of each separate people. Law, for it, is exclusively national and ought to be defined as a product of the conscious spirit of a people, whose qualities determine the content of each national legal system. At the same time, the national mind is not conceived as forming, developing, and gradually changing itself. On the contrary, they believed that each people at its appearance on the arena of history had already its popular genius definitely established and containing in itself all the historic life of the people. In other terms, this school comprehended the historic development as an organic and not a progressive one, not as an evolution. This was not meant to affirm that the development of law is the creation of some new factor, but only that it is the production of what from the beginning was already in embryo in the popular genius. This doctrine does not explain how the genius itself of the people is formed, containing in itself the peculiarities of each national legal system. It does not determine the connections between what is national and what is universal. But it is precisely in the development of law that one observes some common characteristics in spite of the complexity of national legal systems. Legal development, in the most different peoples, presents always a certain uniformity.

To give such a narrow formula to the historic evolution of law was to explain law in an incomplete way. The theory of natural law reappeared, but this time under a new form. Hegel and his partisans commenced to oppose natural law not to arbitrary law (*Jus Voluntarium*) but to historic and national law. At this point of view, natural law reappeared as the general and immovable base upon which historic systems arose and were regularly developed. In changing a little the way of putting the question, the organic school sees in natural law a general unchangeable ideal whose realization determines the meaning of the historic development of law. On the other hand it is necessary to admit, according to this school, that if the lines of the development of law are invariable and identical for all human societies, the results of this development ought necessarily to present common characteristics. This resemblance in the result of the historic evolution of national systems might be otherwise exhibited as a consequence of the analogy, or of the uniformity of the principles, which control the formation and the evolution of each system of law. The latest theories of natural law go much farther and claim that this law presents itself not only as the general foundation for the historic development of law, but also as its ideal end, prior to all history. They do not admit that this general foundation which constitutes the subject-matter of natural law was created by history, like the special concrete elements of law. According to these latter theories natural law was given to us without conscious intervention of the human will and independently of our activity. It existed before any historic development, whose very possibility depends upon its existence. Consequently, these theories do not have merely the name of theories of natural law; they affirm the actual existence in natural law of a prehistoric element which has not arisen in the course of historic evolution and which in this sense is eternal.

The appearance of these theories after that of the doctrine of the historic school is explained, as we have already said, by the fact that the historic school understood historic development in too narrow a way, and defined it as an organic development of a type determined beforehand, and not as a progressive and creative development. The connection of different systems of law with universal principles thus remained without explanation. The partisans of Hegel and the organic school sought to explain it by saying that historic forms of law are only special manifestations of a sole and eternal principle of law, and in that way they went back to the old theory of natural law. Nevertheless, it is not difficult to show that the idea of a regular evolution, relieved of the too narrow formula which the historic school gave to it and expressed under the more general one of a progressive and not simply an organic development, explains with sufficing clearness the existence in law of necessary and universal elements.

The inevitable uniformity in natural phenomena has for a result, that identical conditions produce always identical consequences. The conditions for the existence and development of different human societies, various as they are in their special elements, are nevertheless entirely identical in certain general ones. Always and everywhere there are found certain conditions of human life on earth. The actors and the stage in the historical development of humanity are always the same. There is much more resemblance than difference among men. The surface of the earth, diversified as it is, remains always a whole. This is why human life wherever developed presents universally the same general leading characteristics, despite the difference in individual ones. Human law, whatever the complexity of its contents, possesses inevitably some general qualities. But this does not prove that there is outside of the historic process a general unchangeable principle which marks out the course of legal development. The generality is only the result of the action of general conditions, nothing more.

We cannot limit ourselves on this subject to these general remarks. Given the extensive importance of the hypothesis of natural law, and its profound influence upon legislation and legal science, it is necessary to examine in greater detail the different phases of its development.

Section 15. *The Natural Law of the Roman Jurists*

VOIGT. Die Lehre von Jus naturale, æquum et bonum und Jus gentium der Romer. 1856. B. I. s. 267–336.

LEIST. Die realen Grundlagen und die Stoffe des Rechts.

BOGOLIEPOV. Importance of Private International Law. 1876, p. 26.

MOUROMTZEV. Sketch of a General Theory of Private Law. 1877, p. 241.

According to the doctrine of the Roman jurists natural law is a part of positive law. According to them, the positive law of each country is made up of two essentially distinct elements. Some rules are established by men's wills and can be changed at their pleasure; others are unchangeable, existing of necessity always and everywhere, because they depend upon nature itself. Natural law is distinguished from positive law by this necessity, unchangeableness and independence of human will. But they recognize a positive law, also, as acting at the same time and in the same way as natural law. They placed the latter in the sphere of concrete phenomena. They attributed to its action as genuine a force as to that of positive law.

Under this form the hypothesis of natural law can be subjected to a critical verification by which it can be ascertained whether it is true that those legal rules regarded as natural are always and everywhere necessary elements of positive law. If it is established that all these legal rules, apparently natural, depend upon conditions of time and place and are necessary elements of positive law, the hypothesis as set forward by the Roman jurists must be rejected.

The Roman jurists give in their works a good many reasons tending to show that legal rules do not depend upon the human will, but are created by nature itself. They attribute to them as a basis, either human nature, or the nature of the things which are the subjects of rights, or the nature of the legal relations themselves. So, basing them upon human nature, they affirm that it is necessary to admit that minors cannot undertake binding obligations and that the institution of guardianship is indispensable. Since in its nature humanity remains always the same, whether slave or free, the Pompeian law which punishes the murder of parents and patrons and which in its strict meaning applies only to free men, ought to be applied also to slaves. In its own nature humanity cannot be likened to a fruit. Hence a slave's infant born at the time when its mother was under the control of a master, who had in her only a "*usufruct*," ought, notwithstanding the general rule, to be restored with the mother to her general owner. (*Ulpianus. Vetus fuit quæstio an partus ad fructuarium pertinet, sed Bruti sententia obtinuit; fructuarium in eo loco non habere; ne que enim in fructu hominis homo esse potèst, hoc ratione nec usumfructum in eo fructuarius habebit.*)

In his own nature man can be instructed indefinitely; then, if in a will mention is made of slaves who have learned the art of hair dressing, it must be held to include those who have studied this calling only two months. (*Martianus. Ornatricibus legatis, Celsus scripsit, eos quæ duos tantum menses apud magistrum fuerint, legato non cedere; alii et has cedere; ne necesse sit, nullam cedere, quum omnes ad huc discere possint et omne artificium incrementum recipiat. Quod magis obtinere debet, quia humanæ naturæ congruum est.*)

The Roman jurist deduced another category of legal norms from the nature of things. "Perhaps someone will ask," said the jurist Paul, "why by silver we mean also things made of silver, while by marble we mean only the mere material." This rule rests upon the following proposition: all which from its own nature can be several times transformed without losing identity, because of such a power in the material, is regarded as never subject to such action. (*Illud fortasse quæriturus sit aliquis, cur argenti appelatione etiam factum argentum comprehendatur, quum si marmor legatum esset, nihil præter rudem materiam demonstratum videri posset. Cujus hæc ratio traditur, quippe ea, quæ talis naturæ sint, ut sæpius in sua redigi possint initia, ea materiæ potentia victa, nunquam vires ejus effugiant.*)

All the world, according to natural law, can but make use of the sea, of running water, and the air. (*Martianus. Et quidem naturali jure omnium communia sunt illa: aër, aqua profluens et mare.*) Gaius thinks that natural reason requires that a contiguous wall be the common property of the neighbors. When certain things by their very nature are consumed in use, they may not be made subjects of "*usufruct.*" (*Rebus exceptis his qui ipso usu consumuntur: nam eæ neque naturali ratione neque civili recipiunt usumfructum.*)

Finally, the nature of the relations themselves can be also considered as a source of legal institutions. The Sabinian School, starting with the notion that the law of property is the most absolute part of law and least subject to arbitrary adjustment, affirmed that, according to natural reason, in a case of specification, the right of property over a thing must always remain in its owner. It is contrary to nature that one man should possess the same object as another. (*Paul. Contra naturam est, ut, cum ego aliquid teneam tu quoque id tenere videaris . . . non magis enim eadem possessio apud duos esse potest, quam ut stare videaris in loco eo, in quo ego sto, vel in quo ego sedeo tu sedere videaris.*) Conformably to nature relations cease to exist in the same way that they are created. (*Ulpianus. Nihil tam naturale, est, quam eo genere quidquam dissolvere quo colligatum est.*)

If, then, an exchange provided for by a contract is impossible, the agreement itself becomes so. It is a determination required by natural law. (*Si id quo dari stipulemur, tale sit, ut dari non possit, palam est naturali ratione inutilem esse stipulationem.*)

The examples just cited differ decidedly from each other. First, Several of them have no connection with "nature" and are only necessary consequences of experiences and ideas historically established. The explanation, for example, given by Paul of the difference between the expressions "silver" and "marble," rests entirely on the way in which the Romans understood these words. With us the meaning which they gave them would have no force; because sculptors call with us "marble," not only the block of marble but also objects cut from this material, just as they call "bronze," a work in bronze, and "canvas," the picture painted upon canvas. So the rule, according to which things consumed by their use cannot be subjects of "*usufruct*," or of lease, is a logical consequence of certain exclusively Roman notions which are absolutely conventional. In the Russian language there are no corresponding expressions.

Second, Another group of the examples is formed where the term "nature" is taken in a moral sense, as for example, where it is recognized as contrary to nature for a man to be assimilated to a fruit. It is certainly contrary to man's nature that he be considered as the fruit of anything. It is also quite as contrary to his nature to consider him in any way as a "thing." Notwithstanding this, in Roman law, itself, slaves were counted as things.

And lastly, third, Among the cited examples, some in truth have a connection with objective natural conditions; but this does not mean that they contain legal rules established by nature. In this class of ideas are all cases where a limit, fixed by the conditions of physical possibility, is regarded as a legal rule. Thus, it is impossible to take the air into one's exclusive possession. This element, therefore, cannot be a subject of ownership. This indicates only that our actions are limited by natural laws; that we cannot do that which is physically impossible. But this limit is set by the physical nature of matter, and is no legal rule. It determines no legal obligation. To the same order of ideas belong, also, a good many examples in which legal rules, which are established by human will, are regarded as natural ones but only in connection with some natural distinction among men or things. These are precisely the legal rules most commonly recognized as those of natural law. In fact, what is due here to "nature," is the distinction between the qualities of the man or of the things, a distinction which causes a variation in human interests, from which results a necessity for using special rules for their delimitation. These rules are established not by nature but by man, and are, consequently, not always and everywhere the same.

Such, for example, is the legal distinction among men according to their age. The distinctions are certainly natural, and exist independently of any legislator's will. But the fact of our attributing to them legal importance is neither universal nor necessary. On the contrary, it results from history, existing at one place, and one epoch, and not existing under other conditions. For example, in Russia and France, infants under ten years old cannot for lack of discretion be subjected to legal penalties. But in Russia there is a formal law according to which no criminal prosecution can be commenced against children under ten, while in France there is no such rule.

Nevertheless, there have been cases of prosecution in

this country of children of three and five years. This proves that if the distinction according to age is really a natural one, it nevertheless has in itself no legal effect. This effect can be given it only by a law, and such a law may not exist.

It is the same with the legal distinction between personal and real property. As a natural fact, this distinction always exists, but a legal effect to it can be given only under historic conditions which are quite variable. In modern law, and generally in that of the middle ages, it has great legal importance, for from it result numerous consequences in regard to the means of acquiring and of protecting such property afforded by law, especially in the matter of succession. But in the Roman law, for example, it had very little weight. In distinguishing *res mancipi* and *res nec mancipi* the distinction between movables and immovables was not observed.

To sum up, we are unable to recognize in these examples any necessary natural rules. They are all variable, and established historically by positive law.

Section 16. *The New Theories of Natural Law*

LASSON. System der Rechtsphilosophie, 1882.
STAHL. Die Philosophie des Rechts, 4 Aufl., 1870. B. I.

The school of natural law, which appeared in the XVII century, considered it not as an integral part of positive law, but as an unchangeable independent law existing by the side of the positive. In determining the value of this idea, we cannot use the process which served for refuting the Roman doctrine as to natural law. If we oppose natural to positive law there is no longer need to show in this last the existence of elements of natural law. Consequently, the complete absence in positive law of absolute and unchangeable principles can no longer serve us as an argument against the correctness of the doctrine we are setting forth. Positive law can be variable and heterogeneous, if above it rises always the eternal law of nature. To refute this theory no longer requires, merely, insistence upon the variety and divergence of fundamental principles. It is impossible to say that if natural law really existed there would be no question as to the nature of its fundamental principle. The movements of the heavenly bodies are fixed by an unchangeable law, but how many different opinions arose as to them before mankind succeeded in understanding the law!

For the refutation of the natural law doctrines of modern times, other means must be employed and other aids depended on. It is, before all, a hypothesis and, at the same time, one founded upon the supposed existence of a factor whose reality is exhibited by no empirical demonstration. Similar hypotheses exist in the natural sciences; for example, that of ether; but these hypotheses, although they cannot be directly verified by experiment, nevertheless must not contradict the results of experience, or lead to consequences not in harmony with its results. It is only on such condition that an hypothesis can be scientific in character. This is why, if the new doctrine of natural law leads invariably to the negation of positive law, whose existence is an undoubted fact, it must be regarded as false. There is no difficulty in showing that this doctrine, so far as it is a system of special absolute rules, leads in truth to this conclusion.

The theories of the XVII and XVIII centuries saw in natural law a complete system of juridical norms. All the relations of man without exception can in their view be regulated by the principles of natural law. But how is it possible that there exists, in addition, by its side a positive law? How can this latter arise if there has long been a system of natural juridical norms, sufficient by themselves? Natural law is a collection of rules dictated by reason and in conformity with nature. It contains, they say, in itself the absolute, unchangeable, principles of justice. Consequently, every institution of positive law which contradicts natural law necessarily violates the eternal and absolute principles of right and justice. Why, then, despite this, call these principles, which contradict right and justice, law? If in the natural we have an absolute test of what is law and what is not, how can we bring under the conception of law all the institutions of the positive law?

To say the truth, the early authors of the school of natural law sought to reconcile the fact of the existence of positive law with the supposition of the natural law, but they only reached such reconciliation by contradicting themselves. According to the doctrines of Grotius, and the representatives of the rationalist tendency in the school of natural law (Puffendorf, Thomasius, Leibnitz, Wolfe), natural law is inborn in man, and is that upon which positive law is based. Thus, for them, the obligatory observance of contracts is one of the rules prescribed by natural law. Consequently, if men agree to set up a political power with a view to establish order in society, and give to it the right to make laws, these laws are obligatory upon everybody. But these contracts, these rules, can they contradict the requirements of natural law, or on the contrary, have they force only so far as they conform to its principles? If we admit that positive law, to be obligatory, must not contradict natural law, the extreme diversity of positive legal rules is not explainable. If we examine simultaneously several contradictory institutions of positive law, only one among them can conform to natural law; all the others must contradict it. But if we admit that the institutions of positive law based upon contract are obligatory even if they contradict the principles of natural law, this does not harmonize with the rigorously obligatory character of the latter. Natural law is eternal and unchangeable, not only by man, but by God himself, as Grotius affirms. How, then, can man replace its laws by others in contradiction with it? Rousseau, infinitely more logical, derives the inalienability of natural rights from the freedom, innate and absolute, of natural law. But in revenge, Rousseau comes thus to a denial of the obligatory character of positive law, that is to say, to contesting an absolute fact in order to justify the hypothesis he adopts.

The representatives of the empirical tendency (Hobbes, Locke, Hume) have sought another explanation. They do not admit that the natural law is innate. There is such a law, but we must learn it by experience. The variety and diversity of positive law systems comes from the imperfection of human knowledge. If natural law were fully known, it alone would govern men's mutual relations. Further, if natural law is the only one in conformity with nature, then positive law is contrary to nature. How, then, can it exist? Is that which is contrary to nature possible? The representatives of the empirical tendency cannot affirm such a proposition, especially as they do not admit the dualism which opposes spirit to matter and since they subject psychical phenomena to the law of causality. If our psychical life is subject to the law of causality there can be nothing in it contrary to nature. On this supposition there cannot exist rules which are not in harmony with nature. Consequently, the variable norms of positive law are also in harmony with nature, and in this sense natural. We cannot oppose to them the famous "natural law" as the only one in harmony with nature.

In the XIX century, in place of the doctrine of the school of natural law, appeared a theory which understands natural law as an eternal idea manifesting itself in the historic development of positive law. Such is the opinion of Hegel and his school. But this new way of understanding natural law leads in reality to its negation. In fact, the idea which serves as a basis for historic development cannot be a law practicably applicable and capable of regulating the legal relations of men. This idea determines the development of law but not the rights of man. In thus understanding natural law the coexistence of the two, natural and positive law, is not admitted. Hegel recognized only positive law, but sees in it a manifestation of the absolute idea of law. The pre-existence of the absolute idea of law, before its historic development, does not agree with historic facts; if the historic development took place in this fashion there would be found in the law in all the phases of its development, common and identical characteristics; but we can only establish such common characteristics by comparing corresponding stages of legal development.

This proves that the common characteristics in the law do not precede its historic development, but are products of its history.

Section 17. *General Criticisms of the Natural Law Idea*

We have examined the principal forms which the natural law hypothesis has taken in the course of its development and have criticised each of them, but natural law does not give birth merely to scientific hypothesis. It is not mere scientific theory, unconnected with practical life. On the contrary, the idea of natural law has played a very important rôle in practical life as well as in the scientific theory of law. For many persons it is not a mere supposition, but a fervent belief. Its existence has been deemed self-evident and necessary. How shall we explain the origin of this idea of natural law and its influence?

The appearance of the idea is explained by the following fact. Our conceptions are not produced solely by the generalization of notions derived from experience, but also by the contrast, or opposition to these notions which they generate in the mind. We can directly observe only what is conditional, limited, temporal, only what exists. But by the aid of direct contrast with these immediate results of experience we form notions of the absolute, the unlimited, and the eternal, and even reach the conception of the non-existent. So, recognizing by direct observation a variable, complex and conditional positive law, we form in our minds, by an antithesis such as has been mentioned, the notion of a single, unchangeable, absolute law.

In this way is the appearance of the conception of natural law explained; but how does the conviction arise that there is an actual law corresponding to this conception?

We constantly meet with such a conviction, the cause of which is in the *a priori* errors to which the human mind is subject. "Mankind," says Mill, "in all ages have had a strong propensity to conclude that wherever there is a name there must be a distinct separate entity corresponding to the name, and every complex idea which the mind has formed for itself by operating upon its conceptions of individual things was considered to have an outward objective reality answering to it."[1]

This tendency to attribute reality to all our conceptions is found not only in the ordinary judgments of men, it serves as the basis for philosophic systems. This error was at the base of the platonic doctrine of ideas, and is the basis of mediæval realism which began with Scotus' teaching. On this error rests, still, the anti-Kantian or dogmatic rationalism. The time when dogmatic rationalism had a predominating influence was precisely that of the greatest development of the natural law hypothesis.

Thus, the notion of natural law springs from the simple antithesis to variable law which we recognize in our experience, and from the tendency of the mind to attribute external reality to all our notions. It still remains to explain how certain principles of positive law, in reality variable, have been taken for immutable principles of natural law. Here again the judgment was deceived by *a priori* error, but of a little different kind.

Men in general are inclined to regard the habitual and the simple as identical with the necessary, and the natural. Almost always the quite simple and the familiar seem to us necessary. Thus, Lactantius thought he found an argument against the doctrine of the earth's spherical form in the impossibility of imagining antipodes, where it would be necessary, to use his expression, that one's feet be higher than his head. Today no one finds any difficulty in imagining antipodes. His trouble

[1] Logic, Book 5. Chapter 3, Par. 4.

was because his mind was not accustomed to this idea. Aristotle thought a descending motion in liquids and solids was the most natural, and that ascending motion was an artificial one, produced by force; and, consequently, he thought the first had an increasing, and the latter a decreasing, rate of speed. Modern mechanics regard both alike as equally natural. Every one is surprised to observe the Roman jurist affirming in the Pandects that the adulterer is blameworthy only from the point of view of natural law; but that the violation of the trust of guardianship is condemned because of custom; that poisons cannot be used as remedies, and cannot, because of their nature, be objects of commerce.

The influence of custom is insufficient to explain by itself all cases wherein juridical rules appear to us as natural, for there have been some principles regarded as natural which are not more frequently applied in the law than others and have no general legal force. Thus, for the Roman jurists it seemed natural that a legal relation be ended by the same procedure by which it was established. This correlation between formation and extinction of the legal rule had not in Roman law the force of a general rule. In our day equality is announced as a rule of natural justice. Meanwhile, it is only in modern life that the inequality is disappearing which has heretofore prevailed. So, several representatives of the school of natural law have made unrestricted liberty the basis of it, but such liberty has never found an effective realization. To explain the origin of this kind of doctrines it is necessary again to take into consideration our tendency to prefer in everything the simple to the complex. What the mind grasps most easily, thanks to its simplicity, we are inclined to consider as most regular and truth-like or even as an indisputable proposition. Thus, for a great while, the orbits of the heavenly bodies were supposed to be circles because it was thought the circle represents the most perfect line. In the same way, the proposition that nature acts always by the simplest means, was recognized as an axiom. The same reasons explain the widely received opinion which attributes a natural character to the simplest legal forms and principles.

All these explanations as to the origin of the belief in the natural character of different principles of law, despite their apparent difference, are based upon and lead back to the common one of *a priori* errors. In other words, the belief in natural law owes its origin to the logical error of wrongly recognizing as evident and necessary, institutions which in fact are not so.

But how comes it that this error has played so considerable a rôle in human history and has been in the past a factor of progress? To understand this phenomenon it is necessary to recall the fact that the idea of progress is a recent one, and dates only from the XVIII century. Till then, the golden age was regarded not as in the future but in the past. All change was thought to remove man farther and farther from the happy past, and to bring with it increase of evil. A prudent statesman could have only one ambition, that of keeping society in *statu quo*. There could be no question of improvement. The golden age was gone beyond return. The only thing possible was not to remove it too far. When this general idea prevailed, new ideas and new principles could have no success. The new, because of its novelty, appeared dangerous; to be received it must take on an appearance of antiquity. But what could present itself with such a genuine seal of the antiquity of the remote past as that nature which existed always even when the oldest customs were forming?

The natural law, then, was the oldest part of law that belonged to the remotest past. It appeared with the first man, and preceded all other law. It was sufficient, then, to present a new idea as a principle of natural law to get it received. This gave it all the prestige of antiquity which belongs to the most archaic positive law. In this way the Roman jurists took up the moral doctrines of the stoics in proposing them as a manifestation of natural law taught men by nature itself. So, in the XVIII century the new principles of liberty were opposed to the law of the middle ages, whose force was exhausted, as new principles of natural law, eternal and unchangeable.

CHAPTER IV

ORIGIN OF LAW

Section 18. *Theory of the Arbitrary Formation of Law*

MOUROMTZEV. The Formation of Law as conceived in German Legal Science, 1886.

If the hypothesis of natural law ought to be rejected in its entirety, if the whole law ought to be considered as a product of historic development, the question as to its origin acquires a special importance. In admitting the existence of natural law, we are compelled to hold that law is innate in man. On this supposition men in creating variable institutions of positive law, start with the notion of a ready-made natural law which they find in the minds of their fellow men. But if we do not admit the existence of natural law, we must recognize that there has been a time when human consciousness contained no notion of law. How, then, could it make its appearance and how could a conception of law take its rise? It would appear somewhat difficult to settle this question. In all legal literature there has not been up to the present time any one received explanation of the genesis of law.

Before the historic school, law was presented in all its parts as an institution formed by man. It was looked upon as something men had fashioned for their own convenience. At first sight this explanation may seem the simplest, but if we look at the matter carefully, there is no difficulty in recognizing that it has no value. This explanation may have, and has in fact had, two different forms. The origin of law can be connected either with an order from the state or with contract.

The doctrine, which sees the origin ot law in an order from the government, rests upon the fact that law established by the political power of the state forms the principal part of law in modern life. The conclusion has been drawn from this that it has always been so, and that law owes its origin to governmental authority. To this are to be added some psychological considerations. It is claimed that force and power inspire an instinctive fear in men, and that they are always inclined to attribute an eminently obligatory character to that which the state ordains. There is certainly something of truth in this assertion. The fear of authority, and its prestige, certainly play a great rôle in the formation of law. But this is not sufficient to explain its origin. Respect for authority brings men to obedience, but obedience is not law. Obedience may take different forms, and that which depends upon the sentiment of law presupposes that one recognizes in the government the right to establish legal rules, otherwise this obedience would have no juridical character. One would obey from fear, blindly, instinctively, unconsciously. Besides, law was primitively regarded as something necessary and independent of human will. It was attributed to a divine author and in general assigned to celestial origin. According to this, the contents of legal rules were not dependent on the wills of men. Men ought to find the substance of these rules all prepared and ready-made without the action of their own will or consciousness. But by whom was this matter furnished? Evidently the theory which explains the origin of law, by the state's order, can give no satisfactory answer to this question. The authority of the hypothesis we are discussing, having existed only in men's imagination, cannot be the real source of legal rules. But even in cases where the governing will is an actual will of men, there rises a new question. How comes it that other men recognize in these persons the right to establish obligatory rules for the whole society? The establishment of the earliest obligatory rules must be preceded by recognition of a certain right in the government. Moreover, even in despotic states we never see arbitrary power raised to the height of a principle. Even the despot is regarded as acting according to the requirements of justice. His actions may be regarded as unjust. If this is so, the standard of justice is not in his sole will.

Another opinion, also inspired by the theory which makes the conscious and creative will of man the author of law, connects itself with the theory of contract. It is asserted that law was originally established by agreement between all the members of the given society. Here we are led to observe again, that from the existing state of things conclusions are drawn as to the conditions of the original formation of law. In our actual society the rules which control the present relations of man are often established by contract. But for such a creation of legal rules to be possible, we must admit the obligatory character of contract; but this is not a self-evident axiom. The obligatory force of contract, on the contrary, is a legal principle historically elaborated, and by no means considered to be the general rule. In modern law the obligatory character of contracts is generally recognized, but not without exception. Agreements touching very slight interests and immoral agreements have no obligatory force. It was not, then, the agreement which made the obligation, but its particular form. Without the latter it had no force. It was in this way that the obligatory character of contracts actually came about. This is why if we attempt to explain the origin of law by contract we fall into a vicious circle. It is to say that the origin of legal rules is in contract, and then admit that the obligatory force of contract results from a legal rule established only in the course of history. But this legal rule sanctifying contract, is it, too, founded on contract? An affirmative response leads to an absurdity and a negative one shows the impossibility of explaining the origin by a contract.

It is quite as impossible to explain by a contract the origin of law as it is that of language. When language exists, we can by agreement introduce new words into use, as, for example, new technical terms are brought in. But it is impossible to explain in this way the first origin of the language, for if it did not exist it could not thus be extended. The institution of legal rules by contract presupposes, therefore, the existence of a law as a necessary basis upon which to rest the validity of the contract.

Section 19. *The Doctrine of the Historical School*

LABOULAYE. Essai sur la vie et les doctrines de F. C. de Savigny, 1842.
LENTZ. Ueber geschichtliche Entstehung des Rechts, 1854.

The question of the origin of law was treated in a more detailed and scientific way by the historic school. Before this school, the search for rational principles of law absorbed the efforts of the learned. The historical school placed the question of the origin of law upon different ground. They placed it upon the plane of positive law; they thought it impossible to derive a theory of law from speculative efforts of human reason, and proposed to turn scientific effort towards the study of historic reality. Consequently, it became necessary to ask the question, not "what is law?" but "how came it to be?"

The founder of the historic school, Gustave Hugo (1768–1844), formulated the question in these terms. His Lehrbuch des Naturrechts als einer Philosophie des positiven Rechts, 1809, consists of two parts. The first studies man, regarding him as an animal, as a reasonable being, and as a member of the state. In the second he sets forth the principles of civil and public law. In this second part he begins by examining how law is formed. He assails the opinion, then current, that it is simply a result of legislation. His paragraph 130, though quite short, contains the germs of the historic school's doctrine. He shows that law is formed outside of legislation, that in all states, and especially in England, as at Rome, we find parts of the law developing independently of legislative authority. Such, for example, is customary and pretorian law. He returns with more detail to the subject of this theory in his criticism upon Schlosser's book in an article in the *Göttinger gelehrte Anzeiger* of 1789, and in an article entitled, "Is Legislation the Sole Source of Legal Rules," published in *Civilistiches Magazin* in 1814. The positive law of a people, said he, is a part of its language. We may say the same of all science, that it is only a well-made language. Mathematics, even, is no exception. We do not *a priori* call angle all that enters into that term; numeration is not founded *a priori* upon the decimal system; the circle is not divided *a priori* into three hundred and sixty degrees. It is still more true in sciences where the signification of words varies, and consequently in all that connects itself with manners, in whatever is positive, and so in law. The Roman contract, for example, was not by any means the same thing as that of today.

How is our language formed? Formerly, it was thought that God himself invented and had taught it to men. Thus, language was thought to have been made by an enactment. Other authors supposed it was made by an agreement among men, through which names were given to things. Such explanations no longer get any credence. Everybody knows our language forms itself, and that the example of those who speak well, or are thought to do so, has a great influence over our development. It is the same with manners; no administrator, no combination of men ever decided that respect should be shown in Europe by uncovering the head, and in Asia by veiling it.

It is the same with law; like language and manners, it develops itself without aid of enactments or prescriptions, according as circumstances present themselves, according as our fellows act in this way or that, according as the rules so established best suit the given cases.

In this way positive law can shape itself independently of the legislator's intervention. But when the government thinks it useful to establish a new rule for the future, this rule belongs naturally to positive law, and is taken into consideration like all government orders. This is not to say, however, that everything prescribed is always actually observed. At Göttingen, the streets to which the authorities wished to give new names continued in spite of all ordinances to be called by the old ones. Many laws and agreements are never observed. Nobody dreams that each enactment will be rigorously observed. Legislators themselves expect no precise execution of their enactments. Laws are violated, not only by the ill-disposed, but by perfectly well-meaning persons. Nobody can deny this fact. He may regard it as a defective condition of things. Nevertheless, he must not forget that it has always been so everywhere; and this observation has its value. He must not forget at the same time that the object sought by the positive written law is to determine and make exact the legal order of things, to make its observance more certain by giving fixity to its principles. But what is the factor which co-operates most effectively to the knowledge and observance of a rule; is it a printed enactment which few have ever seen, or a permanent practice with which all competent people are in harmony? Suppose a group of people recognize wills having six witnesses, as valid; and, relying on this, each will is made with six witnesses. Suppose afterwards it is found that a statute absolutely requires seven witnesses. Which rule ought to be the law, the statute of which no one was informed or the custom familiar to all? Although the government is the representative of all the people, the people also can well do something directly for itself. It is probable that the rules so derived suit the interests of the people better than those proposed by the government.

The best explanation is in comparing the formation of law with that of games. Every game, billiards, cards, etc., is a contest according to fixed rules, according to "laws." Some details are agreed upon in advance, such as the first play, etc. There is a category of rules governing the playing; but the game has its own rules independent of all agreement. How are they formed? Some games, to be sure, for example Boston, have been invented all complete by some single man. But most games are of a different kind, like whist, whose rules have been established little by little by the successive resolution of doubtful questions in the particular cases. A large number of determinations of this kind result in fixed rules of the game which thus form themselves without enactment or agreement. (Civilistisches Magazin von Prof. Ritter Hugo in Göttingen. B. IV. Berlin, 1811. Secs. 117–134.)

In Hugo we thus find already indicated the characteristic traits of the historical school's doctrine. The comparison he proposes between law and language is notable, for the representatives of this school constantly use it. It is in Savigny's (1779–1861) works that it is completely set forth. He is counted even outside of Germany as the greatest jurist of the XIX century. He was not a pupil of Hugo, but, as he himself recognized, Hugo's work had great influence over him. The first work of Savigny which attracted attention to its author was a study upon possession. It placed him at once in the first rank of contemporary jurists. Already there can be observed in it quite distinctly the peculiar characters of the new tendency. But the general idea of law and its development, Savigny has particularly set forth in his two works, Vom Beruf unser Zeit für Gesetzgebung und Rechtswissenschaft, Heidelberg, 1814; and also the first volume of his System des Heutigen Römischen Rechts, Berlin, 1840. The political events, then marking the course of German history, impelled him to write the first of these works, a little pamphlet. Germany had just been relieved of French domination during which there had been applied in some places the French code, a system quite preferable to the old German law. This introduction of French law offended the national sentiment of the Germans, but showed them the inefficiency of their own law. When the French domination was thrown off they began to ask what was to be done in the way of legislation. Some declared for returning to the old condition of things. Others demanded a single code for all Germany. The chief representative of this latter tendency was Thibaut (1771–1840). His Ueber die Nothwendigkeit eines allgemeinen bürgerlichen Rechts für Deutschland was published in 1814, and again the same year in a second edition in the Civilistische Abhandlungen, Heidelberg. He proposed to assemble a congress of theoretical and practical jurists to prepare a general code for all Germany. He thought local legislatures passing laws for each separate state could not reach the desired result; first, because there might not be in some particular state men of learning equal to the task; second, because local legislation with the political subdivision then prevailing would lead to the complete breaking to pieces of Germany—a total failure of national unity.

As to the object, properly speaking, of this common code and of the reform, Thibaut justifies this by showing the defects in German legislation of that time. According to him the codes were superannuated and defective in form. All legislation consisted in a series of separate enactments, which, established by emperors and princes, remained separated and appeared so antiquated that the most conservative jurists themselves would not urge the cause of their maintenance. Roman law was generally employed; but it was a foreign law and its dominant ideas did not, as Thibaut considered, answer to the legal ideas of the German people, the less so because introduced into Germany under the form given them during the final decadence of the Roman empire.

Moreover, said Thibaut, the main part of the contents of these Roman laws does not answer to the requirements of modern conditions; and he cited as examples the law of *paterfamilias*, of guardianship, and of hypothecation. To the many inconveniences resulting from the use of Roman law, Thibaut added that the Roman law was not known because the authentic text has not come down to us. We have several different editions, so that in Gebauer's, for instance, the variations, taken together, constitute a fourth of the text, and their number augments constantly with the finding of new ones. If they were all harmonized this would not prevent jurists from having opposite opinions upon various questions, for a conscientious jurist never accepts another's opinion without first examining it. If this is so, practicing lawyers would be greatly embarrassed by having to choose between equally authoritative conclusions supported by equally authoritative persons who have devoted themselves to the study of Roman institutions. Convinced of the insufficiency of existing law, Thibaut demanded the enactment of a new code which should fulfill the requirements of modern life in general, and of German life in particular.

In developing this thesis, however, Thibaut did not anticipate the objections which Savigny was to bring forward. Savigny did not inquire whether the existing law was good or bad, perfect or imperfect. He put the question on another ground. In the introduction to his Vom Beruf, he attempted to show that the work of Thibaut could not be taken separately, but must connect itself with the historic conditions of its time. In Thibaut's project of reform, says Savigny, you will not fail to find traces of that contempt for the past which characterized the XVIII century and an exaggeration of the rôle of the present, which expects nothing less from the latter than the realization of absolute perfection. This had its influence on law. New codes were demanded which could by their improved operation give to justice the precision of mechanics. At the same time these codes were not to be submitted to historic conditions, were to set forth the law as a pure abstraction applicable to all people and all times. Moreover, he continues, these views as to making over the codes are inspired by one's theory as to the formation of law. They think that law is created by the simple act of the legislator and the material in legislation is an absolutely accidental phenomenon which can be altered to suit the legislator's taste. Savigny sets himself to the task of showing that both the ideas on which Thibaut's proposition rested, the exaggerated hope he had of his own time and the dependence of law upon the legislator, are equally false, that law cannot be fashioned to suit the legislator's fancy, and, in particular, that it could not be admitted that at the beginning of a new age a codification should be attempted while German jurisprudence was admittedly so far behind.

Passing over this last consideration we shall limit ourselves to a résumé here of Savigny's ideas upon the origin of law.

According to Savigny, it cannot be admitted that law in its origin depends either upon chance or human choice. Fact contradicts this. Every time a legal problem is solved we find ourselves in the presence of completely formed legal rules. So, it is impossible to say that law was created by the will of the separate individuals who compose a people. On the contrary, it must be considered as a product of the people's genius manifesting itself in all the members of the people and leading them thus to the notion of law. We cannot prove the soundness of this opinion by direct historic proofs. History finds in all peoples law already established, having a positive character with an original national imprint like their language, manners and political organizations. But we find indirect proofs to support the hypothesis. The fact that in our consciousness the notion of positive law is always connected with that of necessity, which would be impossible if law were a creation of our free will, testifies in favor of a formation of law in which the will has no part. Another argument can be given furnished by the analogy with certain other manifestations of popular life, especially with language, which is also by no means a product of man's free will.

The law exists in the general consciousness of the people evidently not under the form of an abstract idea, but under that of a living comprehension of legal institutions in their organic combination. Generally at the beginning of their formation people are not rich in ideas. But they have then a consciousness of their state—of their vital conditions, and of the law, which is not then complex in its matter, and would appear to them as an object of immediate belief. A material form is, then, needed for every manifestation of spiritual function. In the case of language this material form is its continual use; in that of political organizations its material representative is the existing legal institutions. In our time, when the mind is trained to abstraction, the main leading principles contained in the current legal formulas play the same part.

But this supposes already a good many abstract ideas which are not to be found in primitive law. We find in this phase of legal development a series of symbolic actions which accompany the creation and cessation of legal relations and which, thanks to their external manifestation, tend to keep the law to a fixed form. These symbolic actions were a sort of grammar of the law which answered the necessities of their time. This solidarity of the law with the popular genius persists into later epochs, and in this respect again law may be compared to language. Just like our language and all other manifestations of popular life, law develops uninterruptedly and its evolution like its first appearance is under the law of internal necessity. But in a civilized society this internal development is complicated, and the study of law becomes exceedingly difficult.

Law has its source, no doubt, in the general consciousness of the people. If we take, for example, Roman law, we might well admit that its chief foundations, the law of family, of property, etc., existed in the general consciousness of the people; but hardly so as to the complex matter which the pandects offer. This observation leads us to examine the question under another aspect. With the progress of social life the different sides of national activity individualize and separate from one another. What was before done by all the world becomes the function of a special class. The jurists form thus a special class, and their legal studies replace the immediate activity of the people as a whole. Thereafter the law becomes more complex, more technical. There is, so to speak, a double existence: on the one side a general national life, on the other the distinct science of the jurists. The relation of law to the general life of the people might be called its political element; its connection with juristic science, its technical element. The correlation of these two elements varies with the elements of the life of a people, but both participate more or less in the development of law.

If law is thus considered as a product of a people's life, as a manifestation of its spirit, it is clearly of much importance to define just what Savigny means by "the people." In his Vom Beruf he leaves this question aside. It is only in the System which appeared when the principles of the historical school had received their full development that we find a paragraph devoted to explaining the notion of a "people."

If we abstract the matter, the contents of law, in order to examine only the general essence of all law, it appears to us as a norm determining in a certain manner the community life of a collectivity. An accidental aggregate forming an indeterminate collection of men is an arbitrary notion destitute of all reality. If such an aggregate really existed, it would surely be incapable of making a law. But wherever we see men live together, we see them forming a spiritual unity. This unity manifests and declares itself in the use of a common language. Law forms a part of this spiritual unity since in the popular spirit with which everybody is permeated there is manifest a force capable of satisfying the need for regulation of this common life of men. In conceiving the people as a unity, we must not only think of living numbers of the existing generation; the spiritual unity embraces also successive generations, the future and the past. Law is preserved in the people by force of tradition which establishes and maintains itself because the succession of generations does not take place rapidly and at a stroke, but regularly and insensibly.

It might appear too narrow a view that law is a product of the life of a people; perhaps one might say that the source of law should be sought not in the genius of a people, but in that of humanity.

The formation of law is marked by a character of solidarity; it is possible only where solidarity of thought and action are to be found. These conditions are only found within the limits of distinct nations. Naturally in the life of each people there appear also universal tendencies and qualities.

Savigny is the most typical representative of the historical school. Puchta, the first of his disciples (1798–1846), in his Encyclopädie als Einleitung zu Institutionen, 1825, and in the first volume of his Institutes, 1844, a work which was translated into Russian, yielded to the influence of the philosophic doctrines of his contemporary, Schelling. Puchta makes objective, personifies, the popular mind. He considers it as a force acting in the organism of popular life and existing independently of the consciousness of the individuals who make up the people. The popular mind, like the soul in the organism, produces all, including the law. Individuals take no active part in its formation. It is upon the nature of a people's genius that the development of its law depends; not upon its consciousness. This is why if Savigny speaks still of the formation of law as a result of the common life (*eine gemeinschaftliche That*) Puchta on the contrary considers the development of law as natural and independent (*Naturwüchsigkeit*). According to this doctrine, law proceeds from the popular spirit as the plant from the germ; its form as well as its evolution is fixed in advance. Individuals are only passive bearers of the law which they have had no part in making.

Puchta has developed with a good deal of detail his idea as to the origin of law in his celebrated monograph on customary law. (*Gewohnheitsrecht*, 1828.) Here is his demonstration: Holy Scripture, said he, explains the origin of mankind in this manner. There was first one individual, then two, a man and a woman, then their descendants. The first individuals formed from the start a determinate group, the family group. The first family multiplying, divided into several and became a tribe, a people, who, continuing to multiply, divided into new tribes to become in their turn new people. This explanation is so natural that we find it in the pagan legends. The important thing it establishes is that at no moment did men ever live without forming some organic unity. The unity of a people is founded upon unity of origin not only physical but spiritual. Common parentage, however, does not alone suffice to form a people. There would then be only one. The separation between one people and another is marked by the delimitation of their territories, and thus, to their natural unity is added another, which is expressed in the political organization (*Verfassung*), thanks to which the people forms a state.

The state is not a natural group. It is established by will. The political organization is the expression of the general will as to that which makes the essence of the state. This general will could have originally and immediately no other source than natural agreement and unanimity (*Naturliche Uebereinstimmung*). The state, then, is created by the immediate action of will, but this will, and consequently the state itself, has its root in the natural society. The people should be conceived as a natural group. Consequently, the possibility of its acting ought to be abandoned, for only an individual can act. A mere grouping, a unity, so far as it is only a mere idea—a body wholly uncertain, cannot act. The action of the people in the natural meaning of the term can be considered only as an indefinite influence over its members, an influence depending upon the nature of the "people," that is to say, its parentage. Law is connected with these manifestations of popular life. (*Thätigkeiten der Volk.*) Climate, etc., does not influence men directly; it determines the qualities of the nation and these later act upon its members. The individual can reflect the law in his consciousness, not in his capacity as an individual, or as member of a family, but only as a member of a people. This characteristic distinguishes law from matter of individual consciousness. The existence of juridical liberty supposes that to the man's will is opposed another, which is considered as partly foreign and exterior, and partly the individual's own will, based upon his personal convictions. Man becomes a legal person and subject to law only so far as his will is at the same time individual and general, is at the same time absolutely independent, and meanwhile is based upon a general conviction that it is acting in harmony with others.

Puchta proves in the following manner that law can only arise out of the life of a people: As long as there was only one man there was opposed to his will only that of God which would wholly overcome his. When there was only one family and not a people, the husband was master of his wife, who had no distinct will. So, it is only in a people that there arises that opposition of wills necessary to the formation of law. By this process, however, one can only prove that the people is *causa instrumentalis* of law. It is necessary also to prove what is *causa principalis*. Two phases in law can be distinguished; first, the conviction as to what is law; second, the realization, the application of that conviction. Law which cannot be realized is no law. Still further, an accidental realization, as by war, for example, does not answer, for a force purely natural serves law only accidentally, since it could as well enforce what is not law. The law's protection, strictly corresponding to law itself, can only be applied by a special organ of the "general will," that is to say, by the political organization. The source of law is nothing else than that will which directs the formation of the state, the general will of the people. The state cannot be considered as the creator of law.

The state is only an organ of expression for the general will which exists before it and which created the law. But before the creation of the state there is no law because there is no organ which expresses the general will. In considering the people as the creator of law there is no need of opposing "people" to "government." It is not necessary to believe in anything more than an activity of the people, either composed of individual activity, or derived from this last.

Here Puchta enters into a discussion with Schlegel. He calls the latter's opinion upon this point trivial and superficial. The conviction of an individual he declares cannot transform itself into that of a people. Thus, according to Puchta the popular mind is a distinct, independent force. It is not a product of the historic life of a people, it exists from the beginning of the people's historic evolution and determines both the customs and history of the people. It carries in itself its own notion of law which is manifested in the consciousness of each member of the people. The popular idea as to law is its primitive source. But Puchta stops here. He does not explain how this general idea of the people as to law is formed. He supposes it simply given and existing. Therefore, his explanation stops midway, incomplete.

Section 20. *The Origin of Law*

In order to explain the origin of law we must not limit ourselves to explaining its evolution. The main and most difficult question arises in the explanation of its primordial origin, in explaining the way in which the conception of it first appeared. In modern life its activity is conscious. We start with the idea that existing law is incomplete. But whence came the first conception of law? The determination of this question is by so much the more difficult as the idea supposes always an object and materials already existing. Ordinarily the object of a conscious act is given by another conscious act which precedes. But when the question relates to the prime origin of the conception of something this mode of explanation cannot be used. We can only suppose either that the conception of law is innate or that the object of this conception was originally given by unconscious act.

The idea of law might be innate. This proposition can be understood in two ways. First, The material of law, its subject-matter, can be regarded as innate, but this necessitates admitting the hypothesis of natural law which we have just shown is incorrect. Second, The consciousness of the necessity of legal rules might be regarded as innate independently of their possible substance. If this were so, the notion of law must appear from the beginning in human consciousness under its general form, separated in a distinct manner from other ideas, such as morality, and religion, for example. But in reality we discover the contrary. The idea of law appears primitively under a concrete form; the general idea of law, which embraces all of its concrete elements, is relatively late in forming. An uncultivated man recognizes only separate laws; he has not reached the idea of law in general. In the same way the separation between law, on the one side, and morality and religion, on the other, is a thing which appears relatively late. In the beginning, law, morals, religion and customs form a single whole. Therefore, from this point of view we cannot admit that the conception of law is innate.

There remains the possibility of supposing that primitively the conception of law acquires its materials unconsciously. But how explain this fact? How can legal rules be unconsciously established?

To give an explanation of it, the manner in which the primary origin of conscious activity is understood must be considered. Modern psychology does not admit that conscious will is innate in us. Thus Bain (The Emotions and the Will) explains the phenomena of will by the general psychological law of association. According to him the will is not inborn as a primitive faculty of the mind; it is a product of our psychic development. Primitively, we act unconsciously; it is the spontaneous activity of our organization that presses us to action. This activity depends upon the nervous energy which accumulates in us, thanks to the vital phenomena which produce it. So are explained the movements of the fœtus; it is thus that children act, cry and run; it is thus that we ourselves act without any reason after a long, fatiguing inaction. But all acts which we perform unconsciously leave behind them in consciousness two ideas, that of the action itself, and that of its consequences, agreeable or otherwise. The oftener this experience is repeated, the closer the association in our mind of the two ideas, so that when we recall the action this idea brings up the associate one, that is to say, that of the consequences agreeable or disagreeable; and it is thus that the given action seems to us good or bad, desirable or not. The more perfect the association of these ideas the more fixed are our desires; the weaker the association the more vague are our desires. But even when conscious desires arise by the reproduction of the idea of a given action and of its consequences, this does not suffice to produce the given action. Many things appear desirable which we never reach. "*Video meliora, proboque, deteriora sequor.*" This explains that the idea alone cannot arouse activity. There must be a certain tension of energy in the nervous system for action to follow. The same desires, according to the state of the nervous system, according as it is depressed or excited, may transform themselves into actions, or may not do so.

Steinthal (Abriss der Sprachwissenschaft) explains in the same way the origin of language: Influenced by emotion man makes involuntarily certain sounds; these sounds make on him and on his fellows a certain impression. With a return of the same circumstances there is formed little by little a closer and closer association between the idea of the sound and that of the impression which led to it. The idea of this impression arouses in the mind, thanks to the association, an idea of the sound, and if the impression is agreeable the sound is pronounced consciously. This association explains the transformation of involuntary sounds in consciously pronounced words. The idea of the impression, associated with the sound, constitutes the meaning of the word.

It seems to me we can explain, also, in the same way the origin of law.

Given the identity of conditions and the simplicity of relations in primitive society, the individuals who make it up must live in an identical fashion. The weak development of the conscious idea, the repetition and narrowness of experienced impressions, a very strong tendency to imitation, cause the primitive man to act in most cases just like his fellows, like his father and his early ancestors. Consequently, each man is persuaded that under the same conditions everybody will act the same way. He expects this habitually invariable conduct; he counts upon it and with this expectation arranges his own affairs. If as result on some particular occasion he is disappointed in his expectations, if some one does not act towards him as he anticipated, as others usually act in such circumstances, he experiences a feeling of dissatisfaction and anger; he utters reproaches against the betrayer of his expectations and seeks to avenge himself. The oftener collisions of this kind occur, the more the idea of violation of the conduct which custom has established is associated with that of reproaches, with anger, and revenge on the part of the sufferer from such violation. And so the observation of customs, first instinctive and unconscious, establishes itself and is transformed into a conscious idea. At length the custom is observed not merely because of habit and unconscious propensity, but also because of the idea of disagreeable results which the violation of custom brings. Consequently, the consciousness of an obligatory character in custom has then appeared. The custom is observed, even when there is some interest and some tendency to violate it, in order to avoid unpleasant consequences of its violation. The appearance of this idea of necessity, *opinio necessitatis*, transforms a simple habit unconsciously and instinctively observed into juridical custom, consciously observed, and recognized as obligatory. This custom is the primitive form of juridical norms. Thus, the origin of law depends upon the conscious observance of certain rules recognized as obligatory, but the matter in these primitive juridical norms is not consciously formed; it is given unconsciously by established customs.

This explanation of the origin of law makes comprehensible the reason why, primitively, law is considered as an order independent of will, why a divine origin is assigned to it. Human consciousness finds law already established and set up as the result of customs unconsciously established. As he is unable to explain in a natural manner the origin of these customs, man regards law as a divine institution. Law has thus, in men's eyes, the guise of objective order, independent of human will, and of the free choice of man.

In considering as obligatory the long established customs, man makes no distinction between the primitive form and the matter of these customs. He regards as absolutely obligatory an observance of the form as well as of the matter which it carries. For this reason the first phases of development of law are characterized by rigorous formalism.

If ancient customs were looked upon as obligatory, whatever their matter, this explains the complete confusion in primitive society of morality, religion and rules of convenience.

Section 21. *Development of Law*

IHERING. Kampf um's Recht, 7. Aufl. 1884.

In the preceding paragraph it was sought to explain the origin of law. It remains to show how it develops. We find very different opinions as to this in legal literature. They can all be brought under three categories. According to some, law does not develop regularly, and the changes produced by time are accidental or arbitrary. This is the point of view of the old theories which preceded the historical school. These theories have been definitely abandoned. The idea of legal historic evolution is so universally admitted, that the doctrine of the arbitrary, or accidental character, of historic changes in the law does not even find adversaries in modern literature.

Another theory as to the character of the development of law, which has held up till now its vogue, is that of the historical school. One can characterize it by saying that it is the doctrine of the natural formation of law (Naturwüchsigkeit). The historic evolution of law appeared as the successive development of the principles of law conceived by the popular mind; it was conceived as a development taking place without any struggle, as pacific as that of the plant springing from a germ. Just as in the germ the qualities of the plant which comes from it are naturally and necessarily already fixed, so in the popular mind, from the people's appearance on the historic arena, the principles which determine the matter of its national system of law are settled in advance. In this respect, law is completely analogous to language. Juridical norms like rules of grammar develop of themselves without the intervention of the individual will.

This doctrine of the historical school evidently exaggerates the idea of the regularity of historical development of law. In resisting the theory which conceives the law as a product of individual choice, the historic school came naturally to deny to the individual will any part in the law's development. Besides, the conservative tendency of the school helped to render still more negative the part of human will in legal development. The historic school appeared at the commencement of the XIX century as a formal reaction against the revolutionary doctrines which rested upon the rationalistic system of the XVIII century. The doctrine of a legal development, independent of human will, took away all field for revolutionary attempts towards changing old organizations.

This idea as to the development of law was not a necessary consequence of the historical tendency. Pressed too far, it would contradict the notion of historic evolution of law. History is not a progress taking place of itself, where human beings are only uninterested spectators; it is made up precisely of human actions; it is created by man. If history in general has this character, the history of law in particular can have no other. Human actions constitute the chief immediately acting factor in it. Legal rules are not indifferent to men like those of grammar, as, for instance, the employment of this or that preposition following such a case, or of conjunctions after such a mode. They touch directly upon the vital interests of man. Therefore, the establishment or removal of a legal rule provokes necessarily a struggle.

Thus, the natural development of law cannot go on without stirring up strife. In fact, law springs up as the fruit of a strife, sometimes a lasting and obstinate one. But this does not prevent the regularity of its development. The question is only to know what are the forces acting upon this development which lead to it. Is it the struggle of human interests, or is it some mysterious popular spirit sprung from no one knows where? The regularity of the action of the forces which form law remains outside of this consideration.

This new theory that the development of law is a product of the struggle between social interests was brought forward by Ihering in opposition to the doctrine of the historical school as to the natural growth of law. Ihering made this theory the subject of a small but substantial pamphlet: The Struggle for Law.

The idea of a "struggle for law" expresses, much more simply than does that of its "natural growth," its historic development and the manner of its production. The theory of natural development considers as an absurdity the revolutionary changes which we meet with so often in history. It is incapable of expressing in a satisfactory manner the heterogeneous character of a natural system of law, some parts of which, after their dissimilarity is recognized, cannot be considered as the result of natural development of eternal and unchangeable principles in the popular mind.

The idea of the "struggle for law" has still another advantage over that of its natural growth. This latter considers law exclusively as a product of the popular life. The historical school was compelled, for example, to deny the existence of international law because it cannot be recognized as a product of a single people's life. The representatives of the historical school ignored completely any universal character in law, attaching importance only to its national peculiarities. On the contrary, according to the theory of the "struggle for law" the development of law does not connect itself with any special form of social life. Therefore it can show why law may be elaborated not only within the confines of a single people's life, but in those of the whole social collectivity.

Notwithstanding all this, Ihering's doctrine cannot be adopted without some reserves. We cannot admit that in its entirety law is a product of conscious activity, of conscious strife. On the contrary, it must be admitted that, primitively, customs are established unconsciously, and that with the lapse of time they become legal institutions. These ancient customs have the advantage of being very precise. Being old and in constant use and known to all the world they are more stable, more fixed, than any mere legal rule. Therefore, in the interests of public order it is desirable that they be maintained. But at the same time they are very formal. Being old, they never correspond to the latest conditions of social life, and when social relations change, these old customs become very inconvenient and embarrassing. It becomes more and more necessary to replace them, using new legal rules consciously established and corresponding to actual vital conditions. In contrast with the old law, rigorous and troublesome, these new legal rules seem to us more just. Whence it follows that legal development as a whole is a struggle of old law unconsciously established against new law consciously adopted. The Roman jurists had already observed this duality in the law; the difference which they make between *jus strictum et æquitas* has precisely this meaning.

BOOK II

LAW FROM THE OBJECTIVE AND THE SUBJECTIVE POINTS OF VIEW

CHAPTER I

LAW OBJECTIVELY CONSIDERED

THON. Rechtsnorm und subjektives Recht.
BIERLING. Zur Kritik der Juristischen Grundbegriffen. B. II., 1883.
THOEL. Einleitung in das Deutsche Privatrecht.
BINDING. Die Normen und ihre Uebertretungen. B. II., 1872.

Section 22. *The Objective and the Subjective Points of View in Law*

In regulating human activity, legal rules give to men's relations with each other a special character. From relations of fact they transform them into relations of law. Every man regulates his own activity according to legal rules. His relations with his fellows are not determined in each case of conflicting interest, according to the facts which present themselves, but according to the delimitation of those interests by law. Men's mutual relations controlled by legal rules are made up of rights and obligations which correspond to and depend upon each other. In delimiting the interests in conflict the legal rule sets, first, the limits within which a given interest may be realized. This is the right. Second, it sets at the same time corresponding limits excluding other contemporary interests. This is the obligation. The relation thus established between right and obligation is a juridical one.

In this way law comprehends at the same time rules and relations. These legal rules and legal relations are two quite distinct, if inseparable sides of law, the objective and the subjective sides.

Legal relations are called law (right) in the subjective sense because the right and the obligation alike pertain to the "subject," their bearer.[1] Without him they could not exist. Rights and obligations must necessarily pertain to some one. On the other hand, legal rules do not necessarily imply any one's presence. They have a general and abstract character, and are not designed for any particular person (subject). This law is in a sense objective.

As we are proceeding now to examine the distinctive characteristics of legal rules and relations, we will commence with objective law, which from its abstract character submits itself more readily to analysis. We must observe meanwhile that objective law did not precede subjective right; quite the contrary. Historical development begins with the particular, not with the general. So, at the beginning, rights (subjective law) first spring up. Then come the general rules which regulate these rights.

Before the appearance of a single general themis, there was a belief in a plurality of such deities, applying themselves to the determination of individual cases. The primitive judge did not apply pre-existing general rules of law to particular cases, but for each new case affirmed a new law, and only by the method of successive and gradual generalization of the particular decisions in time reached general rules, rules not yet presenting at first a high degree of generality, but comparatively narrow casuistical rules.

Of whatever sort they are, general legal rules once accepted, necessarily control subjective rights. The formula for determining every such right takes the form of a syllogism. The legal rule serves as major premise, the different interests controlled by it as the minor one, and the statement of rights and obligations which results forms the conclusion.

[1] "*Pravo*" (law) in Russian, like *droit* in French and *jus* in Latin, and *Recht* in German, has the double meaning of "law" and "right."

Section 23. *Juridical Norms. Orders*

SAVIGNY. System. 81. §25.
THOEL. Einleitung, §34–39.
THON. Rechtsnorm und subjektives Recht, §345.
BIERLING. Zur Kritik der Grundbegriffe II, 307.
ZITELMANN. Irrthum und Rechtsgeschäft, 1879. s. 200–229.

Juridical norms, as in general all others, are requirements to do something, and in this sense, orders. Being orders, they are not permissions, enunciations, or indications. They always command. They indicate what is to be done and in what way it is necessary to proceed for the accomplishment of an act in order to avoid a clash of interests.

It is by no means necessary to conclude from this, as is sometimes done, that all juridical norms are the work of a conscious will or of the authority of some man. The rule as to what is to be done contains, certainly, a command, but it is not an order emanating from an individual will. Thus, we know that technical rules are not the work of any man, but the natural consequences of the existence of certain natural laws, just as moral rules, to the extent that they are not divinely revealed, are not established by any one's will, but result from a moral sentiment. This is equally the case with juridical laws. To the degree that they present themselves at first under the form of customs, they are not acts of any ordaining will.

Zitelmann, who contests the imperative character of legal rules, as dispositions established by volition, is clearly right on this point, but he goes too far when he affirms that these legal rules, even in their content, are not commands, but only judgments, as to relations of cause and effect between juridical facts. He himself acknowledges, however, that a legal rule is a hypothetic judgment as to what is to be done; but every judgment of this sort constitutes in itself naturally a command. Moreover, the relation of juridical acts, determined by juridical norms, is not one of fact and necessity. Such a relation will only be recognized by those men who consider it as obligatory.

Legal rules do not carry permission, definition, nor enumeration. Sometimes the articles of a law take such a form as to lead to the belief that there are other than ordaining rules and such as to produce a belief in the existence of rules which authorize or which define. This opinion has had followers even amongst Roman jurists, as Modestinus, who distinguished four categories of law. *Legis virtus*, said he, *est imperare, vetare, permittere, punire.* But even then his definition was questioned and Cicero, for example, admitted the existence only of ordaining and prohibiting laws. *Legem esse æternam* (De legibus, II, c. 4).

Modestinus' classification is evidently wrong. We cannot, indeed, put *imperare, vetare, permittere* and *punire* in the same rank. Penal laws which indicate punishment do not in truth contain the order for punishing the criminals. That belongs to the tribunal. For a long time, however, Modestinus' definition prevailed. Savigny gave it a decisive blow and showed the impossibility of setting in a separate group the rules for punishment. On the contrary, a good many jurists have always admitted the existence of rules which authorize, and even of those which define, as was done by Thöl.

It is in the meanwhile difficult to recognize, in the form of these different rules, anything which modifies them essentially. If in a legislative act we find an article exhibiting the form of a definition, nevertheless, in its actual application this act is nothing but a command.

So, if law gives the definition of a contract or a crime, there is here only an order for connecting with human actions constituting a contract or a crime, the juridical consequences of such contract or crime.

It is important to observe here that the juridical rule is not expressed by a single article but in several. One defines, the others indicate the juridical consequences connected with the acts previously defined.

Sometimes it happens that the legislator employs the descriptive form instead of the imperative one. Instead, for example, of saying that some person ought to do this, he says that the person does do it. So, for example, article 47 of the Fundamental Laws declares that "The government of the Russian Empire rests upon the solid basis of laws." This means undoubtedly that it ought to be so. Otherwise the legislator would appear to go so far as to deny the possibility, even, of failure of compliance with his rule. When the law describes the personnel and the organization of institutions and state services, it says that these subdivisions of the administration have at their head certain persons, that they possess a certain organization. This means, in fact, that there ought to be such persons and that such an organization is fixed by law. The replacing of the imperative form by the descriptive is explained either simply by greater convenience of expression, or by a briefer turn of phrase; sometimes, also, by the desire of impressing upon the disposition created by law a more absolute character. The imperative form, in fact, would appear to suppose the possibility of a reality not corresponding to that required. The descriptive form, on the contrary, which sets forth that which ought to be, as already existing, excludes even the idea of a reality different from that indicated in the legal formula.

The existence of rules carrying a permission is warmly disputed. The partisans of this category of rules assert the existence of articles of this nature in all legislation. They add some considerations of a more general theoretic character. In all legislation we meet, in fact, quite frequently with articles having the character of permission which may be divided into four distinct groups. The first group of articles of this kind is explained historically. They are those which indicate the suppression of a prohibitive rule formerly existing. The suppression of a prohibition is naturally a permission, but we must observe that it institutes no new rule, only suppresses an older one.

Then there are some articles in which the authorization is the consequence of the terms of the formula. They serve in general as an introduction to distinct prohibitions, limiting the scope of these latter by certain permissions.

After an article like this, "All the world is authorized to, or may," follows a series of articles enumerating the exceptions to this general permission. Evidently the juridical rule is contained in the special prohibition and not in the general authorization. If we suppose the authorization suppressed, there would be no change in the legal rule; only its form would require some modification. To say that an act is permitted except in some particular case or to say that in that case it is forbidden, is absolutely the same thing.

The character of the articles which compose the third group is more disputable. In the laws which organize the public service of a state we meet frequently with articles providing that "there can be taken such a measure or such other one."[1] In reality these articles are not rules carrying permissions. Legislation in organizing a public service, that of justice for example,

[1] The character of these provisions raises the more doubt because they are generally intercalated between others which contain unquestionable commands.

imposes upon it usually the absolute duty of doing some certain act if certain facts are presented. The tribunal cannot set aside such a rule. It is not permitted to inquire whether the application of this rule in the given circumstances is indispensable or even useful. Sometimes, on the contrary, the law leaves to the tribunal itself the duty of ascertaining according to the circumstances the necessity for applying the measure. Does this mean that the tribunal can according to its liking apply it or not? By no means, for if the necessity or utility of the measure is recognized, the tribunal is bound to apply it.

Such a law, then, is not an authorization to the tribunal; on the contrary, it imposes a double duty, the estimating of the need of the measure, and the applying of it, if such need is recognized.

If the law says that in certain cases the police may call the army to assistance, this means merely that if the police recognize the utility of such a measure, its duty is to employ it.

The fourth group is made up of rules by which alternative obligations are created, when no direct command is given, but the choice is left of doing some one of several given acts.

Here, then, it is a matter of course that the alternative order keeps its character of a command and the alternative rules are distinctly imperative ones. The permission consists wholly in the fact that choice between the performing of several obligations is authorized. The juridical force of these rules consists not in the permitting of a choice, but in forbidding the making of a choice outside of the established alternative.

So all the examples given of rules asserted to carry permissions are without force. It remains still to examine one proof furnished to support the existence of these rules of permission. It is of a more general character than those just examined. Some have gone so far as to deny the general rule that that which is not forbidden is permitted. They have set forth that not to forbid is not the same thing as to permit. The absence of prohibition does not give a right to perform the unforbidden action. Permission given by law to perform an act establishes, on the other hand, a right.

To answer this it is necessary to establish first clearly the meaning of the maxim, "Everything not forbidden is permitted." If we consider permission as equivalent to the creation of a right, man has a right to do every permitted act and undoubtedly what is not forbidden cannot on that account be considered as permitted. In making no prohibition, no right was created, because a right, as we shall see later, supposes always a corresponding obligation, and merely from the fact that the law does not forbid an act, we should not conclude that any obligation is imposed by such fact. The law does not forbid anybody to look at the setting sun, but this does not mean that I am compelled to place my house so as not to interfere with another's view of the west. Permission to one does not mean obligation upon another. A permitted act can become a right only when everything is forbidden which might interfere with that permitted action, because it is only on this condition that any corresponding obligation arises. So a right can find birth only in a prohibition and not in a mere permission.[1]

We conclude, then, that all legal rules are commands, but commands may take various forms. Every limitation upon the realization of interests which are in conflict may be of two kinds. We can reduce them either to the prohibition of acts which prevent the performance of some act, or to the requirement of the per-

[1] A legal right, then, is not merely capacity to do an act, but capacity aided by law through establishing an obligation.—*Translator.*

formance of the acts necessary to the realization of such interests. So one may say that the command in a legal rule may be either positive or negative, an order properly so called, or a prohibition. It is true that every command may be expressed under the form of a prohibition and every prohibition under the form of a command. To direct the performance of an action is the same thing as to forbid its non-accomplishment. This does not destroy, however, the importance of the distinction between positive and negative rules, between commands and prohibitions.

This difference is manifested especially in the obligations which each creates. Orders produce obligations to do, positive obligations; prohibitions engender obligations to abstain, or negative ones. From this distinction among obligations depends, as we have already seen, the coercive effectuation of commands, and all prohibitive rules admit of coercive realization. Rules which contain the injunction to perform a positive act are susceptible of coercive realization only when they create no personal obligation.

Section 24. *Elements of the Legal Norm*

TSITOVICH. Course in Civil Law. I. p. 45.
BINDING. Normen. I. p. 74.

Juridical norms are not simply commands, they are at the same time conditional commands. The limits given for the realization of an act are variable, and the rules arising from the realization of this act vary according as this or that interest, more or less important, opposes such realization.

So the explanation of a legal norm depends upon the presence of certain facts. There are no absolute juridical norms. Even the rule absolute from the moral point of view, like the provision against attacking a human life, is not absolute as a legal norm. The greater number of human interests ought, it is true, to yield to the interest of preserving life, but not all. In the case of lawful defense, war, and in the application of penal laws, to kill is permitted by law. Legal rules, then, are conditional rules. Each one consists naturally in the definition of the conditions for applying the rule and in the exposition of the rule itself. The first of these two elements is styled hypothesis or supposition, and the second, disposition or order. Such a legal rule can be expressed in the following fashion: "If . . . then . . ." Example: "If the deceased has several sons, then his goods shall be divided into equal parts." "If any one commits a theft, then he is punishable by imprisonment."

Each article of the law does not always necessarily contain these two elements. The rule may be set out in several articles. One article may contain the hypothesis and another the disposition. So it happens that the law may not contain an express declaration of its conditionality. Instead of: "If . . . then . . ." we can use another formula, "He who does this or that is punishable by . . ."; or, better, "In such case the goods which . . . shall return to . . ."

But all these formulas come finally to, "If . . . then . . ." That is the fundamental formula to which the others can be reduced, while the other formulas cannot be applied in every case. Thus, the laws which regulate the descent of estates cannot be expressed by the formula, "He who shall do such act shall have the right . . ." The command being the form common to all juridical norms, the hypothesis and disposition are their universal elements.

These two elements may take different forms. The hypothesis can in effect be expressed under a general and abstract form, or under a concrete, casuistical, one. The circumstances on which the application of the norm depends may be the result of general principles and the hypothesis will be under an abstract form, or on the other hand, they may have their origin in individual instances and the hypothesis will take a casuistical form. The thought in all primitive peoples assumes the concrete form. Their legal rules, consequently, are clothed at first in concrete forms applied to each particular case and it is only little by little, in generalizing themselves, that these concrete forms become abstract and general definitions.

The casuistical form is defective, for it causes a multiplicity of rules and does not adapt itself to the generality of legal definitions.

With casuistical rules each case demands for itself a separate rule and meanwhile, as the diversity of possible cases is infinite, the casuistical rules, however great their number, cannot always include every case which life presents.

The abstract form, on the contrary, has great advantages. In a single definition all the homogeneous cases are indicated and combined. It requires, then, only a quite moderate number of rules, which at the same time are fully comprehensive.

It presents, however, some inconveniences. In the first place, the abstract form, because of its too general character, leads to a certain vagueness in the application. There is no embarrassment as to the casuistical rule in knowing whether or not it is to be applied to a given case. With the abstract form it is not always so, and a large field is sometimes opened for contradictory interpretations.

Besides the differences which we have just indicated among the hypotheses, sometimes casuistical and sometimes abstract, there are others which arise from different degrees of definiteness in the hypotheses. These hypotheses may be, indeed, absolutely determined or undetermined or may be relatively determined.

A hypothesis is said to be absolutely determined when the facts on which it depends are distinctly indicated in its own form, when we indicate, for example, that every contract involving an amount greater than five rubles must be upon stamped paper.

There is an absolutely indeterminate hypothesis when the rule comprises no mention of the facts on which its application depends, but places upon each agent of authority the necessity of stating them. For example, if the law permits "in case of necessity" the taking of such or such a measure. Here the hypothesis is absolutely indeterminate.

When will the condition arise? On what terms? The law does not say; in this last case the agent charged with accomplishing the rule has a power which is called discretionary. He can act, taking for a guide certain considerations, but he is only bound by the formal restrictions of the law.

Lastly, we say that the hypothesis is relatively determined when the application of the law is subjected to certain conditions; for example, if certain measures are prescribed only in case of an epidemic, and in such case not absolutely, but only under condition that these measures shall be recognized as necessary by competent authority. The rule may then, under this hypothesis, not be applied at all, and if an epidemic supervenes, it will be applied only if it is recognized as necessary.

Rules with the hypothesis relatively or absolutely undetermined are found often in administrative law and also in procedure. The courts have, in fact, a quite extensive discretionary power.

The necessity for the application of these rules depends on circumstances so varied that it is unavoidable to give to administrations and courts of justice some discretionary power.

Concrete restrictions, unchangeable at law, must be replaced by definitions which are elastic, so to speak, adapting themselves readily to the multiplicity and variability of facts. These definitions are given by judges and administrators.

The distinction between casuistical and abstract forms is not applicable to the disposition. This latter contains, in fact, a rule, a command, and contains nothing else.

We distinguish several kinds of "dispositions" according to the degree of determination of the commands which they contain.

Like the hypothesis, the disposition may be absolutely determined, absolutely indeterminate, or relatively determined.

In the disposition absolutely determined, the command is a categorical rule. No discretion or latitude is given to him who executes it. Such, for example, are dispositions of the kind which indicate the date when a bill of exchange is outlawed, or those which indicate the eldest son as the successor to a throne. These are categorical commands, leaving no option to the one charged with their execution.

Dispositions of an indeterminate form are, on the contrary, those which leave to the one who is to apply them a discretion to moderate their application or even not apply them at all. For examples we will cite the texts which authorize the police to take some measure deemed necessary in case of a riot for the re-establishment of order, or again, in case of epidemic, all the useful measures for arresting the spread of contagion. All the dispositions of the criminal code are indeterminate. Criminal laws, in fact, are applied by tribunals which have the right to choose between laws.

We observe in all our examples that the exact and immediate application of the rule is confided to some organ of government, or of the police, or of the court. These agencies are bound to fulfill this function and at need can be constrained to do so. There are rules also which require some given individual to enforce them. Ranged in this class should be the rule which requires that goods of a defunct shall belong to a devisee indicated in the will of the deceased, or that which in a contract leaves to parties the privilege of arranging details. Doubtless there are fixed limits to the rights of the devisee or parties to the contract, but there is, none the less, a large share in the application of the rule confided to them.

Experience has shown that parties to a contract do not employ very freely the authority which the law gives them of arranging their mutual relations, and the law usually fixes some general rules which operate by the side of those which the contracting persons establish for themselves. If these last do not indicate in the contract all the details of its application, it will be necessary to refer to those which the law has established. These rules, which apply only in cases where the interested persons have fixed none themselves, might be called dispositive rules and the others which apply in every case, prescriptive rules. Rennenkampf has recently proposed the name "ordinative" instead of dispositive, and "imperative" instead of prescriptive, respectively, for such rules; but his names have not prevailed.

The relatively determinate disposition may have two forms. It can fix merely the extreme limits within which the competent authority, or the persons interested, may choose. For instance, when the maximum or the minimum of a reparation is fixed, or the maximum of delay in a contract of hiring, leaving to the parties the right of stipulating for a shorter one. It can also take an alternative form, limiting itself to indicating several measures between which choice must be made in applying the rule. For example, the court has often the choice between requiring a reparation to be made or the imprisonment of the guilty party. The trial judge may have a discretion to order an imprisonment or to satisfy himself with a reprimand.

Individuals themselves have quite frequently to apply dispositions of this kind. The victim of a crime, for example, can institute proceedings for damages before a civil tribunal or a prosecution before the criminal jurisdiction, just as, also, one who has to complain of a violation of a contract with the treasury can take his demands before the administrative, or before the judicial, tribunals.

All which has just been said as to juridical norms and the elements which compose them is absolutely general. The hypothesis and the disposition are indispensable elements in every legal norm. They are, of course, in every penal law; but they take then some particular names because of the special situation occupied by penal laws in the general system. Each penal law is composed of two parts; in the first are indicated the acts, the facts which constitute the crime or delict, and in the second are the punishments.

All the formulas for penal laws can be reduced to this one: "If any one commits such or such an action, he shall suffer such or such a penalty."

In our modern legislation we do not usually indicate that all forbidden action is to be punished. This is understood. It is the natural conclusion resulting from the penalty incurred by the doer of the act.

Also, in a penal law the first part contains, besides the indication of the facts constituting the offense, the disposition of another rule which forbids the criminal action, and this is why criminalists reserve this word "disposition" for that first part, while they denominate as "sanction" the second part of the penal rule. The penalty constitutes the sanction for the observance of the legal rule, since it can be incurred only as that law is violated.

Section 25. *The Matter of Juridical Norms*

Because of the great diversity of interests at play and also of the numerous juridical principles by which they are controlled, the matter of legal rules is extremely varied. The detailed knowledge of them is nothing less than that of all branches of positive law, of law studied in its historical evolution and in comparative legislation. We shall limit ourselves here to some general rules and to the summary indication of the fundamental categories into which all the matter of juridical norms may be reduced. Such a generalization is possible, because all human interests, despite their great diversity, are on the whole subjected to identical conditions.

To reach a proposed end, man employs forces. Thanks to these, he produces changes in the conditions of his existence, of his individual well-being. The forces which man employs for the satisfaction of his needs and pleasures are limited. Meanwhile, the man cannot attain his ends without a certain exhaustion of these forces. The struggle between individuals thus appears to us as a struggle for the possession of those forces which alone can assure to individuals the realization of their projects. Legal rules have precisely for their end the regulation of the human struggle for the control of these forces.

Laws, in fact, enjoin upon the man, first, not to employ for the realization of his interests other forces than those which the law recognizes as good; second, the performing only of acts leaving possible for other men the utilization of forces corresponding in their limits with those assigned by law.

Legal rules, then, have for their end the avoiding of

the shock of the collision of individual interests; they are established with a view to order.

As the relations between the different interests under consideration are not the same, the content of legal rules, while keeping certain general traits, varies also. We can bring into three groups these different conflicts of interest: first, the conflict of interests absolutely equal belonging to different persons; second, the conflict of equivalent but unequal interests; and third, the conflict of interests which are not equivalent.

The first group presents some interests offering this peculiarity, that it is quite difficult to assign to them an exact limit. Since the two interests in view are absolutely equal, there is no reason to prefer one to the other. Their realization, therefore, should be admitted in an exactly equal degree. If, on the other hand, the realization of only one of them is possible, then the choice between the two is left absolutely to chance. We find frequent application of this rule. Thus we accord the use of a thing to the party who first takes possession, according to the rule, *Qui, prior tempore, potior est jure.* In the same way in case of danger incurred by two persons, if the safety of one can be obtained only by the destruction of the other, the issue is left to brute force as between the two. Sometimes the law is used to decide between the interests in conflict.

The unequal but equivalent interests may be compatible or may not. Compatible interests are delimited as in the case we have just examined, by applying the rule of perfect equality.

We must observe always a difference. If in the case of absolutely equal interests we were to apply perfect equality, it would be arithmetical equality. In the case we are now concerned with, however, it is proportional, geometric equality which is required. The forces are distributed between the interests which ought to be delimited in a fashion proportional to the quantity which is necessary for their realization as regards each other.

In the case of incompatible equivalent interests the choice can be left merely to chance. These interests being different, it is easy, as a matter of fact, to find reasons for a choice between them. It will be, for example, the interest of the majority or that of the minority, or the one will be older than the other and already recognized by usage, and will be preferred for this reason.

This difference between the interests may arise, either from the subjects, that is, the bearers of the interests, or from their matter, of what sort they are. The organization of society into classes is an application of this difference of interests, as to the subject. It happens also that general interests are naturally preferred to individual ones. Interests of the state, for example, are estimated higher than those of a province, or of a commune, and these latter are given consideration before those of an individual. Even in this last case it may happen that the interests of one should be preferred to those of another. Thus, in the case of violation of a law, the interests of the just are preferred to those of the wrongdoer. When it is necessary to choose between the interests of the mother and those of an unborn infant, the mother's are preferred. The mother exists already; the infant has only a problematic existence. It is plain that the importance attached to a certain interest depends upon the moral ideas dominant in society.

Let us observe besides, that in the application of legal norms, general interests, even for a particular case which concerns only a conflict between individuals, are taken into consideration merely for the reason that, as we have alreadv seen, laws are established with a view to order. Peace being a very important general interest, it is in the interest of peace for the most part that the interests in play will be regulated. Hobbes was not wrong in considering as a fundamental law the Roman rule, "*Pax quærenda est,*" and Herbart gave as the origin of all law the necessity of settling conflict. However it is obtained, peace is always an advantage. It procures an economy of force which in its absence would be absorbed in the conflict. It permits the regarding of the future with confidence, while on the other hand, the issue of a struggle is always uncertain.

So, in view of the great advantages which peace offers, when we are controlling the interests under consideration, whatever they may be, we give preference to the adjustment which contributes most to the establishment of peace. For this reason law in general is disposed to preserve interests already existing and applies the rule "*Beati possidentes.*" For this reason, too, effective possession if it lasts long enough, assures to the possessor property in the object and turns into a right in him. Property can be acquired even by unlawful possession, provided it be old enough.

Besides this very general interest, which precedes the others and which peace offers in regulating the interests at play, there are others which, without having so general a value, are also applied, as the interest of individual liberty which plays such a great rôle in modern law. Because of it, modern law gives preference to the solutions best compatible with individual liberty. It is needless to say that other collective interests are set in play by the conflicts between individuals. Their greater or less importance affects the solution adopted by the legislator.

Section 26. *The Sanction of Legal Rules*

Legal rules as orders addressed to the conscious wills of men are not always observed; so they have need of special guaranties for their enforcement.

It is necessary to constrain the man to the observance of legal rules; without such constraint the rules would remain a dead letter. These means of constraint are "sanctions." In what do these sanctions consist? Each violation of a legal rule gives birth to a new clash of contradictory interests. On the one side we find the interest of him who is injured by the violation of law. He wants compensation. On the other side is found the interest of the wrongdoer, the author of the harm. Frequently, too, he can invoke some rights for his defence.

We can say that the general consequence of violation of any legal norm is the birth of a new rule created to regulate the interests brought into presence as a result of the violation of law. Let us examine how these interests are regulated.

Law is violated generally because it interferes with us in the accomplishment of some act, because it prevents the realization of some of our interests.

The first means for producing observance of legal rules is to prevent the actions which violate those rules from attaining their end. Such acts are to be recognized as void. For example, the sale of immovable goods by a secret act is considered as void, without value to any one. Property sold in this manner is considered as unsold. The purchaser gets no rights of property. The law requires every sale of this kind to be made before a notary. The object is thus attained, and if by private act the sale cannot take place, there is no motive for individuals to proceed in that fashion.

The laws which have as their sanction the inefficacy of acts which violate them are called perfect, for they come the nearest to a law of nature. This inefficacy may have two forms. The acts may be absolutely null at law, or they may be only voidable, that is, such as may be annulled. They are absolutely null when that is the result decreed as a consequence of non-observance of the law. Such, for instance, is the result of a sale of real property by a private act, although the parties were agreed as to the intention to transfer the property. It is, on the other hand, only voidable, when rescission can be demanded by one of the parties interested in the contract. Thus a contract produced by duress can be annulled only on the application of the party subjected to the violence.

It is necessary to distinguish farther, absolute from relative nullities. The act violating the law and considered as totally non-existent is stricken with absolute nullity, as for example, the sale of real estate by a private act. When the act is only relatively void, it is because some clauses of the contract may be upheld. A bill of exchange, for example, given by a married woman without her husband's consent is void as a bill of exchange. It has, however, a certain value. It is that of an ordinary obligation.

Sometimes a void act has already produced its result. It will not suffice then to proclaim or demand the nullity of the act. The annulment of the act must be followed by one which re-establishes the violated right. Such a re-establishment of the violated right may be accomplished by the agents of authority and may consist either, first, in the cessation, if necessary by force, of an unlawful condition, the expulsion, for example, of a renter from a house which does not belong to him; or it may consist, second, in the accomplishment of a violated obligation and this at the expense of the one who has violated it, as the repairing of a pavement of a torn-up street.

There are also some cases where the act which violates a right contains in itself the realization of the object with which the wrong was done,—robbery for example; some cases where the right violated cannot be re-established,—murder for example. To acknowledge the crime is not sufficient in such a case to repair the injury done, so law has established other sanctions. These acts, which violate law, bring with them consequences indicated in the law, as in the laws which the Romans called *leges plus quam perfectæ*. These consequences may be of two kinds, civil damages for the benefit of the injured, and punishments set up by public authority in the general interest.

We might say that to a certain extent every violation of law works an irreparable injury.

This harm is from one point of view that offense which every injured person experiences and from another point of view is the violation of the law itself, all whose prescriptions are meant to be scrupulously followed. These harms are of so great a variety that it is impossible to classify them. They depend usually upon the conditions under which they are wrought.

We know only that private damages are the oldest. As to penalties denounced for the general interest, we may say that they depart farther and farther from private damages in the degree that governmental authority is augmented; and in our modern law the sphere of application of these punishments is not fixed by any general principle, but by different considerations which are set forth in the penal code.

These consequences attached by the law to the

criminal act which it punishes do not render unnecessary the re-establishment, so far as possible, of the violated right. Thus in the case of forgery, besides the penalty to which the guilty one is subjected, the writing is void. So in a case of robbery, besides the punishment involved of the robber, he is required to restore the stolen things. It may happen meanwhile that the re-establishment of a violated right may bring on forbidden consequences to those absolutely strangers to the doing of the acts. The annulment of a marriage, for example, may bring upon children the consequence of becoming illegitimate. So the nullity of a marriage results only from a very grave violation of law. Any less important act may bring about the punishment of the parties, but leaves the marriage valid.

It is the same when a contract has not been made upon stamped paper. The wrongdoers pay a penalty. The validity of the contract as to third parties remains.

Such laws, whose violation brings penalties upon those who violate them while preserving the legal force of the act, are called "*leges minus quam perfectæ.*"

Besides these laws, classed so by the sanction which they carry, the existence must be recognized of a whole category of laws which offer no sanction, the consequences for whose violation have not been fixed. These laws deserve some attention. They are for the most part laws fixing the rights of the organs of authority.

The organization of a service charged with the execution of the laws is considered by itself, as a preventive measure against action contrary to the law, and for this reason it is in public law that the *leges imperfectæ* are the most numerous.

But the organization of a service is always weakened by such imperfection, since the agents who have it to do are men. If a certain liberty, however, is not given them in the performance of their task, such an organization will become stiff and dead. It will by no means satisfy the numerous requirements of the development of life and movement of society. If you make an organization more vital, more mobile, better applicable to concrete conditions, to the necessities of the times, you give necessarily to individual tendencies the possibility of manifesting themselves. The organizations employed for the development of the state consequently explain, but without justifying them, the *leges imperfectæ*. The vice of such a system commences to show itself.

We must consider as inapplicable the theories of the constitutional school which boasted above all of the organization of its governmental machine.

There is general agreement today in recognizing the necessity of attributing a sanction to the rules of public law. The prosecutions which can be instituted in our day against acts of administration have transformed a good part of them from imperfect laws into *leges perfectæ*.

There are, however, some laws which necessarily will remain always without sanction. These will be the ones which establish the supreme power. This supreme power, which is not subjected here below to any authority, which is controlled only by its own moral dignity, can in fact possess only in itself the guaranty for the accomplishment of all the duties which devolve upon it.

CHAPTER II

THE SUBJECTIVE RIGHT

SAVIGNY. System d. heut. röm. Rechts B. I.
IHERING. Geist. d. röm. Rechts. B. III.
IHERING. Zweck im Recht B. I. s. 72.
MUELLER. Die Elemente des Rechts und der Rechtsbildung, 1878.
BIERLING. Zur Kritik der juristischen Grundbegriffe. Jh. II. 53, 47–148.
REGELSBERGER. Pandekten I, 1893, §§57–82; 195–233.

Section 27. *Legal Relations*

NEUNER. Wesen und Arten der Privatrechtsverhältnisse, 1886.
PLOSZ. Beiträge zur Theorie des Klagerechts, 1880. §§65–76.
PUNTSCHART. Die moderne Theorie des Privatrechts und ihre grundbegriffischen Mängel, 1893.
MOUROMTZEV. Fundamental Definitions and Divisions in Law, 1879, pp. 53–122.

Since legal relations are also social relations, but governed by a legal rule, it is necessary in order to explain them satisfactorily to treat first of the relations in general.

Every relation supposes a "lien," a dependence, and a capacity of influence by means of this "lien." Where there is no dependence there is no relation. If between several trigonometrical quantities, for instance, it is said that there exists a given relation, this means that they depend one upon the other and that changes in one of them provoke corresponding changes in the others. So, then, if between given phenomena there exists a causal relation, this means that the consequences depend upon the cause and that the presence of the cause produces that of the consequence. On the other hand, if between several things there is no dependence, we assume that there is no relation between them.

So, human relations consist in some sort of a dependence, in the power which certain individuals have over others.

Men's mutual dependence is caused by several conditions which may be placed in three groups: physiological, economical, moral.

The physiological distinctions of sex and age introduce mutual dependence among men. Because of their sexual inclinations, human individuals experience the necessity of uniting. The child from its birth requires the care of the parents and these last become old and require in their turn the aid of their children. We might add to this the influence of the laws of heredity, which are also physiological laws. By their means men of a common origin present strong physiological and moral resemblances and form natural groups according to race, independently of their wills. To this group also, must be added the propagation of maladies among men by contagion or by heredity. From the point of view of their health men are thus dependent upon one another.

In the same way man's necessity for protecting himself against external forces of nature, which is the basis of economical activity, brings also mutual dependence. The forces of one isolated man are too weak for the struggle with the elements around him. Men find themselves compelled to mutual aid in two ways; there is simple collaboration in regard to a labor performed by united forces, and the complex collaboration which we call the division of labor. In this latter each man does something special and each for all and all for each.

The moral life of man increases still more the mutual dependence of one upon another, since the necessity of exchanging thoughts is one of the very strongest, and mankind support isolation only with great difficulty. The mutual dependence of men from the moral point of view, indeed, is so much stronger that in the psychical development of man the social factor plays, perhaps, the chief rôle. Our turn of mind is not, for the most part, our own work, but the product of the social life to which we belong. It is necessary only to recall the important rôle played in the development of mind by language, which by its essence is necessarily a product of the social life, common to all, and cannot be an attribute of any single person. The dependence of men with regard to each other, springing from society, increases in direct proportion to the development of social life, and even the physiological conditions of such dependence act with greater and greater force. Thanks to the development of social culture the time during which the man lives under relations of dependence on his parents grows longer and longer. The bonds which unite the spouses become stronger since their relations with each other include those necessary for education of their descendants. To the influence of heredity is added that of education which gives the child traits of character not possessed by his ancestry.

The increasing density of population, and the lack of space, introduces among men a dependence in increasing degree which we might call hygienic. The force, and action, and economic demands of these dependences increase unceasingly. On the one side economic necessities augment, and on the other the division of labor grows. Social development is inseparably bound up with the development of man's moral faculties. It increases these latter, augments their moral interests in extending the moral solidarity of ever enlarging groups. Because, also, of these conditions human life is made up of many different relations among men. These relations have doubtless an artificial character, but men are combined by their means, and through them exercise influence over one another.

Men, so far as they aid themselves by legal rules, transform their social relations into legal ones, social dependence into a legal obligation, and the power of influence which they have over each other into rights. The legal rules fixing human interests delimit necessarily the realization of those interests and impose upon each man some obligation of guaranteeing the realization of others' interests. So the law adds to the existing bases of mutual dependence a new one, a legal base. If my relations with other men are fixed by law, the realization of my interests depends not only upon social conditions, but also upon my legal rights and my legal duties. At the same time, conformably to these obligations there is created for others a possibility of influencing me in a particular way under the form of legal claims.

Legal relations suppose, then, a dependence under the form of rights and duties, and suppose also a legal claim, that is to say, an enforceable right, which is the consequence of this dependence.

Among Roman jurists these relations, established by law, were designated by the expression *juris vinculum*. The characteristic peculiarity of these legal relations consisted for them precisely in the dependence upon objective law. The active side of the legal relation, that is to say, the legal claim occupied their attention so little that the conception of a subjective right in the sense of a capacity had not even taken birth.[1]

The jurists of western Europe, on the other hand, and in the very beginning, the glossators, attributed a particular value to the active side of the relation, to the assertion of the legal claim. They do not assign the origin

[1] Bekker. Pandekten. I. 1886, p. 46.

of the legal claim to the legal relation, but, on the contrary, consider the relation as a consequence of the assertion of the claim.

The explanation of the difference between the schools is readily accounted for by the "subjectivism" peculiar to the Germanic peoples in opposition to the "objectivism" of antiquity, and also by this second reason that Christianity developed the rôle of the will with peculiar force.

The law, as it is concerned in western Europe, does not consider its subjective side as an element of legal rules, but as a free and individual will, recognized and protected by law.

Since in law this individual will is recognized, there results the altogether natural consequence, that the duty of other men is not to encroach upon the domain of this will, and thus are established the relations between two wills.

The logical development of this conception leads naturally to the complete negation of legal relation and to its replacing by the simple conception of subjective right in the sense of a legal assertion as Brinz exhibits it.[1] But the exclusive importance given to the legal claim is not compatible with the real character of legal phenomena. In public law especially, it is impossible to consider the legal claim as the formative principle, the fundamental base of the manifestation of law.

The obligations in public law are indicated in an extremely clear fashion. The subjects of such obligations are always exactly determined, while, on the contrary, rights are scarcely more than the consequences of these obligations and it is an indeterminate body of persons who enjoy them. Nearly all constitutional law reduces itself to the study of the duties of the organs of authority, and the rights which are given them are so many

[1] Brinz. Archiv. f. civil. Praxis. Bd. LXX. s. 379.

conditions, guaranteeing their assurance of the possibility of accomplishing their duties. Judges, for example, are bound to render justice and it is with this view only, that of accomplishing this function, that they are accorded certain rights.

So, too, all the relations of private law cannot be explained as consequences of the legal pretensions of the owner of some right. The relations of passive action of right, as Ihering defines it, cannot be thus explained. We find such action only where there is an obligation without a corresponding assertion of claim. Such are the obligations which the law imposes for the protection of the interests of unborn children. Such are the duties of a debtor with regard to an unknown creditor, a debt whose proprietor is anonymous or unknown, and such the duties of the owner of a servient tenement where the dominant one is *res nullius*.

These different examples show clearly that the obligation can exist without there being a corresponding right in any definite person to assert it, and that it is, consequently, impossible to derive all legal relations from the assertion of right.

A legal claim, on the contrary, cannot exist without a corresponding duty. If nobody is bound to yield to my assertion of a legal right, if it is not obligatory upon anybody, it has no legal validity. This is why in legal relations as generally in all others, it is the passive side, the obligation, which has most importance. This importance is recognized today even by the civilists. It is thus that Puntschart thought it necessary to replace the conception of juridical relation by the conception of juridical dependence (*Rechtsverband*), translating by this term the Roman expression *juris vinculum*.

This new conception is scarcely practical. The juridical connection is a term recognized by all, and which offers this advantage, that it embraces the idea of the realization in the active rôle and at the same time in the passive one, of the action, as well as of the dependence.

Every relation is defined by circumstances of fact as well as by legal rules. There is no relation completely and exclusively determined merely by the law. Rights and obligations exclusively fixed by the law do not exist. The relations, for example, of husband and wife, lessor and lessee, master and servant, are governed by the law and also by the social situation, by their practicability, the character of the parties, their mutual dispositions, their moral and religious convictions, etc. It is by the diversity of these social conditions that the individual and peculiar physiognomy of each concrete and peculiar relation is created, but the juridical form of all these identical relations, all marriages, for example, all contracts for leasing, remains absolutely the same because the same legal rule is applied to all. Since it is precisely the juridical form of relations which concerns a jurist, we comprehend readily how important it is for the juridical critic to distinguish this legal form from the variety of facts.

So the jurists have imagined the conception of legal relations which should be completely and exclusively determined by legal rules. In these relations there is only one legal form common to all the identical ones. These relations are called juridical institutions. They are a legal abstraction from the concrete, actual matter, and if this legal form is common to all the relations of a certain kind, it serves as the common type for all the relations of that sort.

The different interests which make up our social life are so closely bound up that the legal relations, which have the struggle between these interests for a base, are not isolated, but on the contrary form an inseparable whole. This combination of legal relations forms what we call the juridical state. It is the same with legal institutions considered as the common type of legal relations. They form a whole which we will call the juridical order.

Every legal relation, as we have seen, is composed of a right and a duty. Neither can exist separately. They are necessarily attributes of some subject. So the indispensable element in every legal relation is the subject. This element is not always single. The right is the possibility of realizing an interest and the realization of my interests supposes necessarily the use of some sort of means. Every right requires, then, necessarily to be exercised on an object whose use leads to the realization of the sought-for interest; so every legal relation supposes a subject of right, a subject of obligation, and object. It is by the examination of these elements that we reach the determination of legal relations.

This examination, meanwhile, is not all. Legal relations do not stand immovable; they change, they evolve without ceasing. It is then necessary, besides studying their form, to regard also their conditions and changes.

Section 28. *The Subject of Juridical Relations*

KIERULT. Theories des Civilrechts B. I. s. 82.
ROEDER. Naturrecht B. I. §52 und ff.
TRENDELENBURG. Naturrecht. §§85–88.
LASSON. Naturrecht. §46.
BEKKER. Iherings Jahrbücher für Dogmatik. B. XII. Rechtssubjekten.
WALLASCHEK. Studien zur Rechtsphilosophie, 1889. ss. 144–181.

Juridical rules, being rules for the delimitation of human interests, are applicable only to relations between men. Moral rules are absolute duties. They do not depend upon the interest which other persons may have in their accomplishment. There can, therefore, be moral duties towards oneself and these duties have for each man an obligatory force. Law, on the other hand, having for its end the delimitation of interests in conflict, presupposes a relation between these interests and therefore between persons.

We cannot in this matter subscribe to the opinion of Dernburg,[1] Regelsberger, Mouromtzev and some others who recognize the existence of juridical relations with regard to things. The relation of the proprietor of a thing with that thing is not distinguishable from the relation of that thing towards one who has no right over it. The proprietor, just like one who has no ownership but uses it, employs the object according to fixed technical rules and according to personal taste. The only difference between the one and the other is in relation to other persons. When a relation is established with respect to the thing by another person, then a legal claim would appear. Legal relations exist then, not between an

[1] Dernburg, Pandekten, I. §22.

individual and a thing, but only between several individuals on account of the use of a thing.

Legal relations, it is readily seen, are possible, then, only between individuals. Only individuals can be subjects of juridical relations. They alone are capable of them. This faculty of being subjects of legal relations we shall call "capacity."

Law in its modern conception recognizes in fact the existence of legal capacity only in man. It was not always so. Primitive man, assimilating natural phenomena to human acts, considered them as the manifestations of some conscious will. Legal rules were not limited to their action upon human relations, and were recognized as to things and animals, giving them rights and duties. Even in the middle ages animals were brought to judgment and punished; but at present only men are recognized as accountable for their acts.

The punishments inflicted upon those who mistreat animals do not contradict this principle. It is not in the animal's interest that the punishment has been fixed, but with a view to protecting the sentiment of humanity in those who would be offended at the purposeless torture of an animal. The proof of this is that if the harm to the animal has some reasonable object, whether in the interest of science, or to supply the table, there is no punishment.

A quite recent German opinion, specially advanced by Bekker, maintains, however, that animals can also be subjects of legal relations. If, for example, someone leaves by will certain goods under this condition, that they shall serve after his death for the maintenance of his dog or his horse, these animals become proprietors of the goods and are subjects of certain rights.

Some years later, however, in the Pandects, Bekker recognized that it is better to restrict the conception of subject of a right to persons alone. Such a limitation is necessary not only in the interest of convenience, but also in that of truth.

We can in truth assign goods to any use we please, but as a matter of fact these goods are assured of their destination only so long as there is a man interested in some way in its accomplishment, whether by esteem for the memory of the deceased or for some other cause; so, after the disappearance of the interested person, the interests of the dog or horse are no longer guaranteed. Then, even in this case the interests of the animals do not constitute by themselves directly the basis of the legal relation, but only in a conditional, indirect fashion, and to the degree in which they serve some human advantage or interest. The real subject of the legal relation even here is one or more persons interested in the accomplishment of the devise made for the animal's profit.

As much, also must be said as to what concerns supernatural beings and physical forces. The repression of religious crimes does not have for its purpose the interest of the divinity, for the divinity has no need of such protection, but only the religious sentiment of the believers. The goods of which the church is the proprietary assure the satisfaction of religious needs, those of the ministers of the cult, and consequently of men.

We come thus to another question. To recognize only men as subjects of legal relations, does not this contradict the conception of the legal personality of moral persons? This conception is based, we know, upon the fact that certain rights and certain duties exist for the advantage, not of individuals, but of a class of individuals,—corporations, for example, or establishments. We distinguish, for example, the goods and the duties of the actionaries from those of the society which they serve, those of individuals from those of the state, those of the administration of a hospital and of the sick who are found there, from those of the hospital itself considered as a public establishment.

As Savigny, who is an authority in this whole matter, urges, such juridical persons are not genuine subjects of legal relations but are only a fiction. Brinz goes farther yet and rejects absolutely the whole idea of fiction; this whole conception of legal persons is, as he says, entirely unnecessary.

The writers, on the other hand, like Beseler, Gierke, Dernburg, Regelsberger, defend the existence of legal persons, and recognize them as real subjects of legal relations and not as pure fictions. Regelsberger formulates thus his opinion: The object of the laws, says he, is the guaranteeing of human interests, but a good many of these interests cannot be realized in whole or in part except by the combined powers of several individuals. This is why there exist other subjects of legal relations than individuals. There are these moral juridical persons. While possessing no corporal individuality, they are real subjects of rights; they constitute social organisms. Their vivifying element comes from man, but in so far as they are members of the organism and act conformably to its purpose these men give birth to a particular force (*verbandsleben*), and to a collective will distinct from their individual wills. In the view, then, of the defenders of the real existence of moral juridical persons as distinct subjects of right, the purpose is always the same; it is some human interest, but an interest common to a whole group of individuals. The force of this moral person is the product of the activity of all the members or representatives of this group; its will is that of the individuals who compose it. All the juridical relations of a moral person can, then, be reduced to relations of individuals, but these relations are very complex, greatly mingled, and it is for this reason that they are considered for the advantage of legal analysis as the relations of a single subject artificially constructed, and this subject is the moral person.

It is in this way that Ihering explains his conception of a juridical moral person. The conception of juridical person is for him only a particular process in the juridical construction of the actual relations of physical persons.

Here, also, are some men who are the real bearers of interests delimited by law, but these interests are common to the whole group of individuals whose composition can be varied without changing its identity; so the legal rules, instead of delimiting separately the identical interests of a throng of individuals, consider these identical interests as a single one and the group itself as a single subject of legal relations, as a single juridical person.

It is only a special process for reaching a simplification of the mutual relations of men. It would be very difficult, for example, to determine the relation existing between the person who buys something of a stock company and each stockholder of the society, or again, the relation which exists between every holder of a state's obligation and each citizen of the state. It is much simpler to consider the relation only between the purchaser and the society, or between the citizen and the state.

Our conception of legal personality might be compared to that of the parentheses in algebra. Just as in algebra we place within the parentheses the quantities united by signs plus and minus to simplify the calculation, so in law we place together all the identical interests of a certain group of persons by the conception of juridical personality, and determine afterwards the relations between the group and each member.

It is, as we have seen, only men who can be subjects of legal relations. This does not mean that all would always be "capable."

The history of modern law, on the other hand, offers us a good many examples to support this idea. For a long time slaves were considered only as things, goods, which could not be subjects of legal relations, and were without any juridical capacity. In modern civilized states slavery has been abolished under all its forms, but in the barbarous states like those in central Africa it still exists.

Modern law, then, recognizes all men as "capable" but each one does not possess equal capacity for all rights. This capacity can be more or less extended. All the incapacitated can be brought, however, into four different categories: those who are smitten with natural restrictions, or with social restrictions, those which have their source in incompatibility with certain legal relations, and finally, those which result from penal restrictions.

By natural restrictions we mean restrictions which have for cause age, sex, race. It is thus that in a general way women are recognized as incapable of exercising political rights. Individuals under sixteen years of age cannot serve as administrators. Deaf-mutes cannot be members of a jury.

Social restrictions depend upon social situations, as the inequality between classes, between professions, and between religions. Members of religious bodies, for example, cannot own land. Innkeepers are sometimes denied the right of being electors in the towns. The Jews are not allowed to live outside the territory assigned to them.

The restrictions which have their source in certain incompatibilities with legal relations arise from the fact that the possession of certain rights precludes others. A married person cannot marry again so long as the preceding marriage is not dissolved. High functionaries in the state cannot at the same time hold private employments.

Finally there is, we have said, a class of penal restrictions. These are the consequences of an arrest or a judgment. They are an integral part of the penalty involved upon one condemned.

Capacity means that the person can have certain rights, but does not necessarily mean that the person actually possesses them. To have ability to acquire a right, and to exercise it, are not the same thing. If one is capable of possessing an ownership of real property, this does not mean that everybody has it. Capacity and possession are two quite different things.

Certain rights require, besides capacity, the presence of particular facts, certain events, as, for example, the death of a testator, or certain acts, an acquisition, for example, by which the connection between the person and the right is created.

The appropriation of rights by their subject is called the acquisition of right, and the rights are rights acquired. There are rights which have an exclusive character and which cannot be exercised at the same time by several persons, and as an example of such rights we cite the right of property, but if the right is not exclusive and may belong at the same time to an indefinite number of persons, the presence of the conditions necessary for capacity suffices for their possession; for example, the electoral right.

Capacity commences at birth, to end only at death. It is only living persons who have it. The child born dead cannot be the subject of legal relations. It is considered by the law as if it had never existed. However, certain rights exist for the advantage of the infant not yet born, but under the condition that it shall be born alive, and thus certain duties are imposed upon persons who have, so to say, charge of the birth and life of the infant. They cannot, for example, during pregnancy divide the father's estate if he is already dead.

Man is recognized as capable of rights from the instant of his birth; from the complete detachment of his body from that of his mother. This capacity lasts until his death, that is to say, until the final disappearance of the last signs of life, the beat of the heart and the respiration.

A prolonged absence, if the dwelling place is unknown, is equivalent to death and brings to the absent a loss of capacity. Some legislative enactments, that of the Baltic, for example, recognize as dead one who in his absence has attained the average age of mankind,—that is to say, seventy years of age. Other legislators, Russian for example, recognize as dead one who has been absent a certain length of time independently of his age.

With death, capacity completely disappears. A dead body has no rights. If the law has proclaimed penalties against the desecrater of tombs, it is with a view to the protection of those persons whom such conduct would offend owing to their relations to the deceased.

Section 29. *Rights and Duties*

IHERING. Geist des rôm. Rechts. B. III.
THON. Rechtsnorm und subjektives Recht, 1878, 223 und ff.
BIERLING. Kritik der jurist. Begriffe, II. 49, ff.
BEKKER. System, I. s. 46.
SCHUPPE. Der begriff des subjektiven Rechts, 1888.
ZENTHOEFER. Das subjektives Recht, 1891.
SCHLOSSMANN. Der Vertrag, 1876. ss. 213, ff.

The explanation of the conception of right in the subjective sense, of right-power, is the most difficult and controverted question in the study of legal relations.

The influence of legal rules over the conditions for realization of our interests is so varied and these different forms of influence interpenetrate so closely that it is very difficult to proceed to a special examination of each of them and to separate with clearness the "right-power" from other consequences which the legal rule draws with it into the sphere of the realization of our interests.

Legal rules first of all forbid the use of certain means for realizing human interests and so make a distinction between what is permitted by the law and what is forbidden by it.

The prohibition limits the possibility of actual realization of an interest, restricts it. Permission, on the other hand, brings no change in the conditions of the realization of an interest. What is not forbidden may within the limits of possibility be done. Where the law does not forbid the doing of a thing, only the lack of material means serves to prevent its accomplishment under this permission.

It is permitted to all the world to ride in a carriage, but he only can do it who has the necessary means. The legal rule here neither creates nor guarantees the possibility, but authorizes it as it in fact exists.

The influence of legal rules over the conditions for the realization of human interests is not limited solely to negative action. It is shown also under a positive form, and may have as a result an extension of the actual possibility.

In forbidding the employment of certain means for the realization of human interests, it enlarges by this very fact the possibility of the realization of other interests. The other interest may reach its realization not only within the limits of actual possibility but its owner can demand also that the prohibition in the law be observed and the obligation imposed, of not doing some particular act, obeyed. In this case the legal rule adds a new force and increases the favored person's power for the realization of his interests. It is this direct and positive influence of legal rules, this influence which confers an enlarged possibility of realization, which we call "subjective right" or "right-power." In other terms, this right is a possibility of the realization of an interest to which corresponds a legal obligation.

By this fact, that the law creates a corresponding obligation, it is distinguished from a simple permission. When one has a right to anything, all is permitted to him, but he has no right over all which is permitted, but only over the things guaranteed by the creation of a corresponding obligation. These rights can exist only between individuals and not in our relations to the phenomena of the outer world.

We must distinguish, then, the simple permission to do something which is only an absence of restrictions, from the right created by the increased possibility of accomplishment resulting from the extension of a corresponding capacity.

The influence of the legal rule can also take another form, a form which holds the mean at the same time between the simple absence of interdiction and the creation of a new right. Human interests are, in general, so closely bound together that any change produced in the conditions for the realization of one of them brings always some consequences for other interests which are bound up with it more or less complexly.

So the creation by a legal rule of a duty to guarantee the realization of any interest brings always consequences as to the realization of other connected interests. So, for example, the creation of a higher tariff upon imports brings advantages, not only to the producers of the commodity in the interior of the country, but also to smugglers. The obligation on the proprietor's part, as the result of a contract with his tenant, to maintain a stairway to the rented story, and cover it with a carpet, gives to the tenants on the lower stories the possibility of using each.

But neither the smuggler nor the tenant have rights because of the advantages which they draw from the existing legal obligation. They can make use of it only under the circumstances of fact which the contract points out. If the circumstances change and they can no longer use these advantages, they have no right to ask of anybody the re-establishment of the former state of things, so as to use the carpet or to draw greater profits from smuggling. The person, on the other hand, who has a right, if circumstances intervene which interfere with its exercise, can demand its restoration and this by virtue of a legal rule.

We should, then, distinguish right from mere power, as a possibility to which directly corresponds a legal obligation, as distinguished from the possibility which we have of using accidental consequences of others' rights for the realization of our interests. The action of legal rules here exhibited is called by Ihering reflex action of law. The obligation corresponding to a right can be imposed upon all those whose situation would lead to resistance to its use. In this case the subject of the obligation is not determined by his personal character, but by an objective character, from the opposition which arises as a result of the use of the given thing.

The rights to which such an obligation, which is common to all, corresponds are called rights over things. They are called also rights against all, or again, real rights. Opposed to them are rights against persons. The obligation corresponding to these last rests only upon a determinate individual or individuals. It is only by connection with this obligation that rights as against persons can be realized.

The right of property might serve as an example of the "real right" (*in rem*). The owner of the thing can require of everybody that he do not stand in the way of the owner's right of property. As an example of rights against persons, *in personam* may be cited in hiring for service.

Every right supposes, necessarily, a corresponding obligation. If the obligation does not exist, there will be only a permission and not a "right." But an obligation may sometimes exist without a corresponding right. This happens when the interest which constitutes the subject-matter of the corresponding right arises subsequently to it or is temporarily suspended. Thus the obligation not to assail the right of an unborn child corresponds to no right, since the fœtus is not yet a subject of right. The obligation is here created in expectation and by way of protection of the life of the infant to be born.

In the same way when a bill of exchange is lost and is temporarily out of possession of anybody, the obligation of the acceptor has not for the time being any corresponding right. The obligation meanwhile does not disappear on this account, because the instrument may be found by some person and this person acquire the rights given by the bill of exchange. The action in such a case Ihering calls passive action of law.

We have defined subjective right (right-power, *droit-pouvoir*, *pravomochia*) as the possibility of the realization of an interest to which corresponds directly an obligation. The definition assumes the formal and material point of view of legal right. On the external and formal side this right is a claim (*Rechtsanspruch*) of an individual for the performance of the obligation by the one subject to it. On the internal and material side it is the possibility of the realization of an interest, and as this realization supposes always the use of some natural forces the "matter" of the legal right is, in general, the use of such forces. Their use supposes only the presence of needs. The assertion of a claim supposes necessarily a conscious will. Our will can be set in movement not only to satisfy our personal needs, but also those of others.

Man can act in the interest of another, but the use he makes of goods is inseparable from the need which he has of them. The claim which he has for the performance of an obligation, guaranteeing the satisfaction of his needs, can be realized by other persons. This clearly happens when the subject who has the need has no conscious will or not enough. To guarantee the realization of his interests it is, then, necessary that there be the will of another person who directs him. Guardians act thus for the demented and for minors.

The same effect is reproduced with a view to convenience when a regulation of interests common to a whole group of individuals is attempted. Instead of all the wills acting together in the common interest, one of these wills acts for the whole, and so arises what we call the legal person. Meanwhile, even when such a distinction is under consideration as that between the subjects of a will, serving a given interest, and that interest itself, one ought to separate the bearer of the interest, the beneficiary, from the bearer of the will, the director. When the will acts for the advantage of another there results, not a right, but an obligation. He for whose advantage the right exists which produces a legal rule is not always the bearer of the right. Sometimes, owing to the reflex action of law, he enjoys the advantage of a right which he could not have independently. He would become the subject of a right only if the possibility of the use of it is guaranteed to him by a corresponding title, even if that title is realized by another's voluntary action.[1]

Most jurists, on the contrary, in defining the notion of the subject of a right, attach importance only to the right, or to the claim, or rather, to its employment, and they reach in this way some radically false consequences.

It is thus that we must explain Bekker's paradoxical doctrine, System I, s. 56. According to him, the owner of the right over given goods is the party whose bills, drawn against them, are guaranteed by these goods; as if it were possible to decide what bills are secured by the goods if one does not know to whom the goods belong.

[1] It is in this precise way that Bernatzik, Kritische Studien über Begriff für juristischen Person (Archiv für öff. R. B. V., 1890. s. 223) defines the subject of a right. "Rechtssubjekt ist der Träger eines jeden menschlichen Zweckes, den die herrschende Rechtsordnung als Selbstzweck dadurch anerkennt, dass sie dem zu seiner Realisirung erfordlichen Willen rechtliche Kraft verleiht."

The "matter," the content, of the right over things, we have said, is the employment of those things by the bearer of the right. Such is the general definition of the matter of a right, but the usage of the right may be extremely various. It may be, first, a simple use with no necessity of excluding others from the use of the same object nor the possibility of varying the means of such usage. This use consists in the right to employ a thing in common with other persons and conformably to its predetermined organization. Such a usage is a fundamental element of the matter of an obligation in this sense, that it is absolutely indispensable to the exercise of any right; but, it is the most restricted form of a right. The use which each of us makes of public roads is an example of such a right.

There is for every right not only a fundamental element like this usage, but a natural element which depends upon the very nature of our needs and not upon the complexity of social relations. Simple usage serves for the immediate satisfaction of human needs, so only physical persons can make use of things. Legal persons cannot of themselves, and without an intermediary, make use of objects.

A second fundamental element of the matter of a right is possession. It consists in the possibility of excluding other persons from the usage of the object over which we have rights. For example, the lessor of an immovable thing cannot only use that thing to satisfy his needs, but he has, besides, the right of excluding all other persons from its use, even when he is not employing it.

From its nature, then, possession is a condition which facilitates and guarantees the use of goods, but possession has at the same time a more independent scope. It augments use, enlarges, so to speak, its natural limits. Man has the use of goods which he employs to satisfy personal wants. Possession gives him the added possibility of exploiting for his own profit the needs of others. If a man has the right by possession to prevent others from making use of the object, he has also the right to authorize its usage under certain conditions, notably under the form of compensation. We see appear thus the advantage of acquiring in this way possession of things of which we have no immediate need, but from which we may draw in the meanwhile a profit by letting them to others.

The third element in the content of a right is that of disposing of the object, the *jus disponendi*. Ihering defines it as the right of changing or modifying the manner of using the object. Neither usage nor possession quite embraces this power of disposition of the object. The possessor of an object ought to keep unchanged its original organization and purpose. The lessor of a house, for example, can neither remodel nor destroy it.

The right of disposing of an object is made up of three different elements. It includes, first, the right of modifying the usage without destroying the object and without turning it over to another person. This is the *jus abutendi*. It includes also the right to transmit the object to another person, the *jus alienandi*, for this is one way of using the object. Finally, the third element is the right of destroying the object, of annihilating it. This is the *jus disponendi de substantia*. This third element exists only if the right of usage is applied to things.

Section 30. *The Objects of Rights*

REGELSBERGER. Pandekten I. s. 357.
BEKKER. System. I. s. 81.
KIERULF. Théorie, I. s. 129.
IHERING. Zweck im Recht, I. s. 70.
GOLMSTEIN. The Principle of Identity, p. 49.

Since the "matter" of a right is the use of something and there can be no such use if there is no object to which it applies, every right has, therefore, an object. Every actual right is over some particular thing. Some, as Bekker for example, admit, however, the existence of rights without objects. This comes from their taking into consideration only a particular element of right, the legal claim or title, but the "matter" of the right is always the use guaranteed by this legal title, a use which necessarily supposes an object. The object of a right may be anything which serves as a means for the realization of interests delimited by law. All our interests are realized by the aid of some force, and so it may be said in a general way that forces are the objects of right.

The employment of the forces which serve as means for the realization of our interests exhibits itself most frequently in the way of acts. For this reason some jurists have considered acts as the sole objects of right. It is, however, a conception which we cannot admit, for, if we examine it closely, it results in some consequences impossible to sustain.

Take the case, first, where rights belong to persons who cannot legally perform any act, for example an infant or a demented person. In such case it is another person, a guardian, who does for them the acts necessary for the preservation of their estates. Consequently in recognizing acts as the sole object of right it would become necessary to admit that the object of certain rights, rights of property for example, may vary according to their subject. If the holder of a right of property carrying with it a certain obligation is a person of full capacity, the object of the right corresponding to this obligation is certainly the personal action of the owner, but if he is not a person of full capacity, the object of this same right is no longer his personal action, but only that of another, his guardian for example.

We see that there are two altogether different objects in the same right. If we do not consider the acts of the guardian as the object of the right, then this right, as long as it relates to one without legal capacity, is without an object, for an infant at the breast can of himself do nothing in the way of acts necessary for realizing the use of the goods belonging to him.

The forces which are the objects of rights are exceedingly various, both in their own nature and according to the persons who are the subjects of such right. In the legal point of view the distinction of the nature of the forces has no importance, but the connection between the forces and the bearer of the right has some effect over the character even of the right. The objects of the right are classified according to this connection.

We distinguish four categories of objects: first, the personal forces of the subject; second, the forces of nature; third, the powers of some other person; fourth, the forces of society.

Each of these objects has a different connection with the subject of the right. Personal forces are the inalienable property of the bearer of the right. They are created at the time of his birth, and their division among men is the work of nature herself. The law does not give to man the use of these forces, but limits and protects them. The powers of other men are not created for our use and bestowed upon us by nature herself, for our profit, but to obtain their use we must employ the means set at our disposal by the law. These forces, being intimately connected with human personality, this very connection makes necessary a limitation of each one's rights over their object, for if the right was unlimited by hypothesis, it might result in a right not only over another man's power, but over his very person.

Man can make use of nature's forces so far as they are exhibited in things. These things are not equally distributed among men by nature; they possess no direct connection with the human person. This is why legal rules not only fix the usage of these things, but also fix the principles of their distribution amongst men. These rights over things are the most complete and absolute of all rights.

The forces of society belong to no individual, but to society as a whole and present this characteristic peculiarity, that each individual as a member of society is subject necessarily to the action of its forces.

The use of personal powers, physical and moral, is the prime necessary condition for the realization of our interests, but this usage may at the very start have for consequence the preventing of the realization of the interests of another. It is necessary, then, to apply certain restrictions to the use of these personal powers, and, as this usage is manifested always by some act of the man, these restrictions cannot be other than restrictions upon the liberty of human actions.

In the second place, the activity of other men may also cause hindrances to the use of our own personal powers. There is need, then, of guaranteeing by legal rules the use of personal power, in imposing upon others a corresponding obligation.

According to a rule common to all juridical restrictions, it is only those actions which bring about an external realization of our thoughts and our desires, which produce changes in the external environment, that are subjected to such restrictions, for only such actions can bring about any hindrance to the realization of other men's interests. An action amounting only to a manifestation of thought without tending towards its realization would not be subjected to such a restriction. The simple manifestation of the intention to commit a crime is not punishable, excepting always the case where the form of manifestation is itself an assault upon the interests of others. Thus, it is forbidden to express an opinion as to another having an offensive form. It is forbidden, also, to show under the form of menace a desire to do that which the law forbids. The manifestation of ideas by the press or the public tribune is subjected to special regulation, since in these particular cases the manifestation takes a very general scope.

The reader cannot know in advance what is the question treated in a pamphlet or a newspaper article, and after reading it he cannot rid himself of the impression which such reading has produced. It is the same with what has taken place in the casual passer's hearing of a public discourse.

The conception of liberty of thought is in a general way a relatively recent one. In the ancient law, on the contrary, even the simple manifestation of the thought was sought to be controlled. In former times it was believed there was possibility of doing harm by the simple thought, by the evil eye, as they said, or at least by words to which were attributed some of the force of acts designed to put them into execution.

The employment of our own personal forces is, then, guaranteed. This guarantee has for its purpose the protecting of our life, our health, that of body as well as that of mind. It happens often that individual powers do not suffice for the realization of an interest and that the collaboration of a number of individuals is necessary, and thus arise rights over the forces of other men. The modern idea of right does not, however, admit the existence of rights over the very person of a man. It admits only the existence of rights to his services, and even these rights have very frequently no absolute character.

If he who is employed to do an act, to perform some particular service, refuses to do it, he may not be constrained. These rights have a special character. The employee is permitted either to perform the act or to indemnify by a sum of money his employer. Only the right of the state over the services due from its citizens has an absolute character, such as the obligation to military service.

As to different parts of the human body, distinction must be made between those which are separated from it and those not so. Thus, the hair once cut, a tooth once extracted, may be compared to any other object because this hair or this tooth have no force, no means of action by themselves, once they are separated from the man's body.

On the other hand, the parts which are not detached cannot be subject to legal rights of others, can be subjected to no power of another, for no rights can be held over the human body or its members. We cannot acquire a right of property in another's hair not yet cut off, or in another's teeth still undetached. No right can be acquired to the use of the body of another individual, of a monster, a dwarf or a giant for example, with a view of exhibition. Rights can be acquired only over the action of the man, the promise to use his body or some parts of it, but if he refuses this usage, he cannot be constrained to it; he can only be required to find an indemnity for damages resulting from his refusal.

Besides these individual powers, the general human ones, the powers of nature serve also as means for the realization of human interests. The action of natural forces appears always in some form of physical phenomena and man can utilize this action for the realization of his interests only if he possesses the matter showing these phenomena. The different parts of matter are things; it is these things and not the natural forces which are the direct objects of right.

All things cannot be objects of right, but those only can fill this rôle which are subject to human influence. For this reason the stars, the firmament, cannot be objects of right. There are some things which can be objects of right only in connection with particular persons. There are others whose use by all is authorized by nature, like air, running water, the high sea. These are *res communes omnium*.

Certain things which by their nature are capable of becoming objects of private possession are, however, not left by positive legislation in the domain of private things. These are public things, the *res publicæ quæ extra commercium sunt*, for example, roads and highways. Physically, they are susceptible to private ownership, but such a situation is regarded as incompatible with their design. Among these public things we should distinguish those which are outside of the private domain only accidentally. These are such as belong to nobody, *res nullius quæ extra patrimonium nostrum sunt*.

In the same thing may appear the action of not merely one, but of several forces. The law may permit to a man the use of all the powers in a given thing, or only of a part of its manifestations. In the first case, as is readily seen, the power of the person over the thing is at its fullest extent. It is the complete right of property, its *dominium*.

The owner may employ all the powers of a thing which belongs to him, at least so far as these powers have not been excluded from the permitted use of the thing. On the contrary, a person who has only the right of enjoyment, who has not over the thing the right of property, can use the thing only within the limits which this right of usage confers upon him. The same thing, therefore, may be at the same time susceptible of a right of ownership and of other less complete rights than this, right of usage, rights of enjoyment, *jura in re aliena*.

To the distinctions between the different physical properties of things it is necessary to add the different legal properties of those things. In legal language, for example, a great difference is established between movable goods and immovable goods.

Immovable goods are the soil and everything which is completely adherent to it, as trees and houses. All others are movable goods. Here is a distinction which has serious consequences in acts of division, for example, in rules of inheritance and in the guarantees furnished by law.

The thing, being a portion of matter, is in its turn divided into portions. This notion of portions of matter has only a very relative force. The part can be considered at the same time as dependent upon the whole object, or as itself forming a distinct whole. One readily acquires an idea of things composed of parts and forming a whole, *universitas rerum*, which, formed out of many things, serves, however, only for the realization of a single interest. Legally, this whole is considered as one single thing, as in the case of shops and stores and their merchandise, flocks, etc. The connection of these different things with each other is sometimes a relation of subordination, and it results that one thing is an attribute of another; the door, for example, may be considered as an attribute of the house. We call attributes certain things without which the principal thing could not answer its purpose, the design for which it was organized; as for example, a carriage deprived of its wheels. The attributes are always subject to the same disposition as the principal object.

The final category of objects of right which we have enumerated is that formed by the forces of society. We must distinguish them from the powers of the individual. In reality this force of society is not, as one might suppose, the sum of the forces of each of the members who compose it; it is a much greater force than that. The explanation is found in the organization of the society, which unites the individual forces in the habit of each one's submitting himself to the requirements of the social life and in the moral authority which every society has with regard to its own members.

The relations between men have multiple forms. The smaller society is subject to the greater and the weaker of two powers can be very often regarded as a force dependent upon the greater.

Finally, all human associations are reducible to one, to the greater society *par excellence*, to humanity. Humanity embraces all societies and absorbs them into itself. But all societies have not an evident external influence. Only those which are organized possess this. The force of those societies which act directly upon each of their members can be the object of right. The most important of these societies are the church, the state, and the family.

Section 31. *Juridical Facts*

IHERING. Geist, III. §53.
ZITELMANN. Irrthum und Rechtsgeschäft. s. 200 ff.
THON. Rechtsnorm und subjektives Recht. ss. 71 ff. ss. 325 ff.

Juridical relations are not unchangeable. They arise, evolve, and disappear. On what do these different changes depend?

Every legal relation supposes necessarily a right and an obligation resulting from the application of legal rules. We have already seen that this application depends upon certain facts fixed generally by the hypothesis under consideration.

Legal relations, then, depend upon these "juridical facts." Generally, indeed, the application of a legal rule gives birth to several of them and not to one. To acquire, for example, a right to property by possession there is necessary, first, the intention of holding the thing by proprietary title; second, a given duration of such possession; third, an uninterrupted possession; and fourth, an uncontested possession. It is only when these four conditions combine that possession gives birth to a right of property.

A combination of all the circumstances necessary for the application of a legal rule may be called the "content of the suppositions of fact," in German, *Thatbestand.* The different conditions which form the suppositions of fact may pertain either to external facts or to the mind and will of an individual. In the last supposition they can exist only so far as they are relations between human actions, for it is only in such actions that the human will is manifest.

It is necessary, then, to distinguish between the "objective" and the "subjective" content of suppositions of fact. So, for a will to be valid there are necessary besides certain conditions of outward form, writing, presence of a certain number of witnesses, etc., certain subjective conditions on the part of the testator, sound mind, sufficient memory, freedom, etc. The combination of conditions of form, external conditions, constitutes the objective side of the testament. The moral conditions of the validity of the testament form, on the other hand, its subjective side.

The application of the legal rule may depend merely upon objective conditions. This happens when the juridical facts are not human actions. An inheritance, for example, is declared open by the simple fact of the death of the former holder, and is opened for the advantage of all the heirs by the simple fact of their existence. There is no subjective condition. The law does not interfere with regard to facts which embrace only subjective conditions. Indeed, the law has only to do with ideas which have already received their application. These alone have legal importance. We easily recognize, then, in every application of law two elements,— the subjective one, which is the thought, and the objective one, which is the external manifestation of that thought.

Here, then, is a primary distinction to be made among juridical facts; facts which are exclusively objective, and actions which are essentially at the same time objective and subjective.

There is commonly a harmony between juridical facts and the law. It may happen, however, that certain of these facts are opposed to it, and we have, then, facts which are legal and others which are illegal. Hence, a new distinction between legal facts conformable to law, and others opposed to it.

To look a little closer at the distinctions to be made

between facts and acts and between legal and illegal facts we may class them in four categories: first, legal facts; second, legal acts; third, illegal facts; and fourth, illegal acts. Such a classification presents, however, some inconveniences.

It is the truth that certain of the legal acts are juridically considered as facts because their objective side is of little importance. These acts, whether conscious or not, have always an absolutely identical legal weight; for example, the destruction of a thing does away with all right over it; whether this destruction was voluntary or not, the result is always the same.

So, actions whose legal consequences are not affected by their subjective side ought to be classed with facts and are most commonly called so, juridical facts properly so called. Illegal acts alone form a distinct group, whose juridical importance depends specially upon the intention with which they are performed. It is necessary, moreover, to observe that illegal acts have juridical importance only so far as they give rise to a durable illegal situation, a situation requiring the re-establishment of a violated right. For the rest, usually instead of saying illegal facts we say illegal condition, and more commonly designate illegal acts under the name of violations of right.

We distinguish, then, four categories among juridical facts: first, juridical facts, properly so called; second, juridical acts; third, illegal states or conditions; fourth, violations of right. Juridical facts, properly so called, comprise all those which embrace nothing contrary to legal rules, nothing anti-legal, and whose accomplishment does not bring with it any creation of new rights or, rather, any change or extinction of rights or obligations already existing. Rights and obligations never have importance except as they serve to delimit the contending interests; it is only facts bringing forward new interests which will be determined by new laws. So, on the birth within the state's territory of a man whose father was a citizen of that state, it is presumed that the individual takes the nationality of the country of his birth.

The fact of not using a right for a long while generally indicates that an interest formerly in existence exists no longer, and that in disappearing it has taken with it the right. All extinctive prescriptions are established upon this idea.

In other cases, the juridical fact constitutes the cause which puts an end to the existence of an interest or modifies it. Thus, a person's death deprives him of all interest and all right. All interests in the meanwhile are not bound up thus closely with specific facts. We can even say that more frequently interests do not present through facts specific indications of the birth, the modification, or the extinction of a right. In these cases the hypothesis of the rule does not contain its index, and the application of the rule is subordinated to the presence of certain interests. The work of adaptation of the rule to the interest is performed by those of whom duty or their own personal interest requires it. The interests, which call most frequently for the performance of a juridical act, usually exhibit themselves in the specific act, especially when it has for its purpose the maintenance of the existence of the interest. These interests are difficult to recognize in fortuitous acts and in those compelled by overwhelming force. Consequently, the application of rules delimiting interests depends either upon external signs, which reveal themselves readily, or upon special acts having its purpose; that is to say, upon acts performed with a view to bring about their application.

These juridical acts are of two kinds. If their accomplishment is left to private persons with an object simply personal, they are contracts; in the Roman law, *negotia juris;* if, on the contrary, their accomplishment depends upon functionaries charged with this care by their duty or their functions, they are orders, decrees, *Verfügungen*. Both may be unilateral or bilateral. The first are those which contain the manifestation of the will of but one of the parties to the agreement; the second, those which contain the manifestation of the will of two or of several parties.

A unilateral contract relates only to the rights of the executing parties because it is those rights alone which such a contract can regulate. We cite as examples of this category of contracts the testament and the contracting of ourself for service. The unilateral order of administration acting as authority can affect the rights of individuals, can restrain or even suppress them.

A bilateral contract is one having for its base an agreement of independent persons one with the other and not connected by any bond of subordination. The bilateral order, on the contrary, has not the same character. Of the two wills forming it the one is the master and the other the subject. The two wills are brought into connection, the one in order to demand, to solicit, the other to authorize, agree and ratify.

The performance of every contract, just as of every order, requires certain relative conditions; some as to the subject who shall perform the contract or the order, others as to the form which the contract or order should assume. The capacity of forming a contract we call capacity to contract. Minors, the insane, those who have lost their civil rights, do not possess this contractual capacity.

It is necessary also to indicate certain acts for which there exist special restrictions and which require a special capacity, the act if performed by an incapable individual being void.

Capacity to give authority to orders or decrees constitutes competency. General competency is impossible, and the order performed outside of its assigned limits, determined by the rules of administration, has no more validity than the contract of an incapable.

For some juridical actions special forms have been established. Sometimes these forms are not closely obligatory and serve only to give greater force to the contract or to establish the proof for the future of its due execution. These forms are established not only with a view to proof, *corroboration*, but sometimes such forms are necessary attributes of the act itself. Without them the act has no juridical value. It is considered as void and as never having existed. These are necessary forms to the act itself, *corpus negotii*.

The written form of a bill of exchange may serve as an example for forms of the first category. A loan of money may exist without written proof; if the debtor acknowledges his duty there is no need of any writing. As example of form which makes an integral part of the act itself, that required for a purchase or sale of real property may be cited. This sale or purchase must be evidenced by writing, without which it is not recognized as valid even when nobody contests its existence. With regard to the orders of government or administration this distinction applies also. Some forms are imposed only with a view to convenience and their omission may bring disciplinary penalties, but the order be none the less valid. Other formalities, on the contrary, are absolutely necessary that the order may be valid and obligatory upon the citizens.

By juridical representation certain acts can be performed by one person instead of another. The representative performs the act in the name of his principal and under the condition that all the juridical consequences of the act shall belong to the party represented. Juridical representation may be forced or voluntary. The representation is said to be forced when it is on behalf of persons who cannot themselves do legal acts, who, as we have already stated, have no contractual capacity. It is said to be voluntary when a perfectly capable person instead of doing an act himself charges some other person with doing it in his place.

The illegal situation and the violation of right have this in common, that both are in opposition to the legal rule. They present always an important difference as follows: The requirements of legal rules address themselves to the deliberate will of man. Law cannot in fact control the actions, the unconscious forces of nature, so only man's will can violate a right. Nothing which is the work of other forces can amount to a violation of right.

The unconscious forces of nature may meanwhile cause a condition of things in open opposition to the requirements of a legal rule. The wind, for example, may displace an object and carry it over into another's domain. We can class with these cases, those where the man acts unconsciously,—in an attack of insanity, for example. In all these cases there is no violation of right; there is only an illegal condition. The illegal condition requires always the re-establishment of a disturbed right, the restoration of a condition which existed before and which conforms to the requirements of the legal rule. This right exists always for the advantage of the one whose right has been disturbed.

The violation of right brings, besides, other consequences. It is a great danger indeed for a legal rule that by non-compliance its authority is seriously assailed and with it that of law in general. Hence, the necessity of the sanction to avoid the recurrence of wrongful acts.

A conscious violation of law supposes always fault on the part of the author of the wrong and requires an indemnity. Finally, the author of the wrong may exhibit a condition of mind which requires to be corrected.

Punishment inflicted on the author of the wrong serves to realize three ends,—to prevent the wrong; to furnish indemnity by the delinquent to the injured party; to correct the delinquent. But all violations of law are not punishable. Only those violations which involve features of a general interest ought to be punished; the others, those which comprise only an assault upon rights of individuals, upon rights of private interest, require only an indemnity to repair the damage caused.

Violations of law which result in punishment are called crimes. To constitute a crime there must be a conscious, intended act violating the law, and one ought to distinguish between premeditated crime, which is one having for its purpose the violation of a right, and the infraction committed by imprudence, which ought, however, to be punished also because it results in consequences contrary to law.

CHAPTER III

PUBLIC AND PRIVATE LAW

Section 32. *Classification of Rights According to their Matter*

SAVIGNY. System I. s. 23.
STAHL. Die Philosophie des Rechts, II. s. 300.
AHRENS. Encyclopädie. s. 117.

Juridical relations are extremely various. The detailed study of their groups constitutes the very science of law.

The general study of law cannot do without a profound examination of the fundamental peculiarities of each group of special rights, and for this purpose a general classification of juridical relations is necessary: A fundamental division universally recognized is that into public and private law.[1] There are numerous discussions, however, as to the exact point of distinction between them. The Romans placed it in the character of the interests protected by law; the ensemble, the totality, of public interests protected, constituted public law, and that of private interests formed private law. "*Publicum jus est* [*Inst. Ulpian. II.* §2, *De Justitia et Jure*,] *quod ad statum rei Romanæ spectat, privatum, quod ad singulorum utilitatem pertinet, sunt enim quædam publice utilia quædam privatim.*"

Down to our times this definition has found partisans. Bruns (Holzendorff's Encyclopädie 3 Auf. s. 340) and Neuner (Privatrechtsverhältnisse, s. 1) have adopted it.

[1] By the side of public and private law are recognized ecclesiastical (Walter), international (Warnkönig), and social (Mohl, Rösler) law.

It has been resisted, however, for a long time by a good many jurists. This Roman definition does not define anything at all. It does not delimit or determine in any way the different regions of law. Interests cannot be opposed to one another as being public or private. They can exist nowhere except in the man, and every general interest is nothing but a combination of individual interests. We can say in a certain sense that the whole law is created for the protection of the interests of individuals, that is to say, private interests. Moreover, legal protection is only extended to those interests of individuals which have a more or less general scope, which relate, for example, to a whole group of individuals, as physicians, or to a person whose interest, like that of a monarch, by reason of his important position, is of a general order. In this sense we might say that the law protects only general interests.

We can distinguish again between public interests, and divide them in their turn; but, without insisting upon the altogether relative character which such a distinction presents, it may be said that it does not correspond with any actually existing. It cannot be established, as a rule, that public law is concerned with more general interests and private law with those which are less so.

Faults committed in the course of a campaign by a furnisher of supplies, faults which may lead to a famine in a whole army corps and bring about its defeat, have a much more general interest than the election of a member of some municipal council; and, meanwhile, in the first case, the market for supplies is under the control of the civil law, and in the second, the nomination and election of the functionary under that of public law. So again, the organization of a ministry presents an interest incomparably less important and less general than the regulation of the conveyance of real estate or of hiring for service, and yet in the first case we are in the domain of public law and in the second that of private law. The insufficiency of Ulpian's definition, its lack of precision, has induced many attempts to reach a more precise one.

We will examine first the classification proposed by Savigny. His system, accepted by Stahl, might be called the teleological system. It is a definition borrowed partly from that of Ulpian, but distinguished from it radically, however, by certain points.

Ulpian defined the law according to the interests which it regulated. Savigny and Stahl, on the other hand, distinguish legal relations according to their purpose. In public law, according to Savigny, the state is the purpose, the individual holds only a secondary place. The contrary is the fact in the civil law. The individual is the end, and the state only a means.

Stahl says almost the same: "Certain legal relations have as their end the satisfaction of individual needs; others seek to establish a combination of men under a single authority and to cause them to live in that unity."

This distinction between legal relations according to their purpose has been quite recently developed by Ihering in his work Das Zweck im Recht (Bd. I, 1877? s. 452). He indicates its real meaning, and distinguishes the relations by their purpose into three classes, according as the beneficiary in view is the individual, society, or the state.

But this distinction is not for Ihering a fundamental one in law, and he shows that each juridical institution may have as its beneficiary the individual, the society, or the state. For example, property can be private, social or public. This distinction, then, cannot be a fundamental one in a legal system. We seek, in fact, a classification of institutions, and not a classification of forms which the same institution may take in succession.

Savigny and Stahl have tried in their classification to group together two schemes of classification, up to that time distinct, the one established according to the interest regulated by the law, and the other according to the position of the subject, regarded sometimes as an independent individual, sometimes as a member of a social organization. Ahrens has equally tried the same combination of these different processes of classification, and opposes the immediate purpose to the final one. The final end of all law is the human personality, but the human personality can be at the same time the immediate end of a juridical relation, and this immediate end is a relation of private law. If it is, on the other hand, society or the state which is the immediate object of the legal relation, we find ourselves then in the presence of a relation of public law.

So, then, the purpose, the final function of public and private legal relations, is the same. It is only the means employed for the accomplishment of this purpose, for its realization, which is varied. In private law this purpose is realized by the individual determination; in public, by the collective act of the entire society.

Ahrens' classification is insufficient. His theory, like Stahl's as well as Savigny's, does not explain how it happens that the state is so frequently the subject of relations of a purely civil and private character.

When the state buys, sells, exchanges, or hires, it is itself the object and not the means (Savigny); the furnishing of boots for the army does not have for its end, evidently, the satisfaction of an individual (Stahl); and the end sought is not attained by individual volition, but by the activity of the entire state, which pays the expense of furnishing them (Ahrens).

Finally, Ahrens seems to forget that juridical protection, whatever be the interest which it concerns, supposes the collaboration of the whole society and not the mere determination of an individual.

These unfortunate attempts to adapt the definition left us by the Romans have urged several modern jurists, especially Russians, to wholly abandon the Roman conception. Some have sought the basis for the distinction between public and private law in the distinction of interests according as they have or do not have a patrimonial character. Others have seen especially in private law a right of disposition. The partisans of the first opinion are Mayer, Oumov, and especially Kaveline; the second opinion has been maintained by Zitovich.

Kaveline[1] thinks that the distinction ordinarily made between public law and private law rests upon no theoretical foundation. Private law comprehends some parts totally different from each other, and this can be explained only because it is transmitted to us thus combined by the Romans. The one of these different parts presenting a certain degree of unity, having some rules from pretty much the same source, has been combined under the name of civil law, that is, the *jus civile* of the Romans, a term which they gave to their whole law.

In our day, in Russia particularly, there is no reason to keep this group intact and apply to it the same name as in the ancient classification, since today civil relations are no longer determined by the Roman law. Instead of this classification, with its at present purely historic importance, Kaveline proposes a classification which he thinks more rational and at the same time more simple. His classification has for its base the distinction which he establishes between patrimonial rights and all other rights. The modern civil law, says

[1] "What the Civil Law?" 1864. "What is Private Law's Place in the System of Law in General?" (Journal of Civil and Penal Law, 1880.)

he, is the mass of laws affecting our patrimony. It is necessary to exclude from it all the legal relations which have no patrimonial character, as for example, the family relations.

The civil law thus understood according to Kaveline ought to embrace the totality of relations affecting any title to the patrimony. A good many legal relations which are classed nowadays in the public law ought, he thinks, to be put into the private law, as for example the laws as to taxes, penalties, and the privileges and compensations of functionaries.

Such a classification has in its favor an apparent simplicity and clearness. A careful examination shows us, however, that it is scarcely admissible. It is not possible to conclude with Kaveline that the modern conception of law is due simply to chance, that it rests upon no rational basis. Even if it were true, as Kaveline affirms, that the civil law in its actual condition offers only an agglomeration of parts of law more or less distinct, combined together by the Roman law, this agglomeration, we are convinced, is not the work of chance.

It is because these different laws continued always to answer to the requirements of social life that they have been preserved, and it is only that which is indispensable in all legislation which has been transmitted to us by the Roman law.

The private civil law is precisely that part of it which exhibits the greatest unity. It is in the civil law that the least trace is left of the vanished years and the numerous differences between races. This suffices to require us to make of the rules which constitute it, and of the relations which it governs, a group apart, a distinct category. Moreover, as Mouromtzev has already shown, it is wrong to pretend that the actual civil law is identical with that which we have received from the Romans.

Moreover, it is only starting with the XVI century that the bringing together of the *jus privatum* and the *jus gentium* has been attempted.

There are institutions, the bill of exchange, for example, which were quite unknown to the Roman law. It is not, then, precisely correct to say that it is merely because it is derived from a common source that the civil and private law has been classified as it actually is.

We should observe, besides, that the simplicity and clearness in Kaveline's classification are only apparent. In reality to separate patrimonial rights from rights which are not so, is no easy thing. All rights, personal ones as well as others, have an economic scope and touch in some sort material interests affecting our patrimony. Kaveline places in the private civil law some relations, considered till that time as relations of public law; for example, the penalties inflicted by law. But who does not see that other penalties, for example that of deportation, might also have an economic effect bearing upon our patrimony and sometimes do have this, as their chief scope?

Even if we classify in the private civil law some relations like those existing between the state and its functionaries [1] from the point of view of their powers, or those between the state and the citizens [2] from the point of view of the military system, and of taxes, there is no reason for not also placing in the private civil law some relations which are incontestably relations of public law; for example, the rights resulting from the organization of the government, and from the organization of political representation as established in the country.

Do not these relations offer an economic side at the point of view, for example, of indemnities to which deputies and senators are entitled, or if the function of

[1] Rights over Goods, p. 326.
[2] *Ibidem*, p. 228.

these representatives of the people is gratuitous, at the point of view of the expenses which are caused necessarily in the performance of their duty?

If we connect with private civil law the different relations which control the sustenance of the poor, it is necessary to place there also the combination of dispositions with regard to gratuitous primary instructions, and so on. We shall come by this method easily to place in private civil law all the social relations.

The classification of Kaveline, besides, lacks precision in not defining the "material value" of patrimonial right, which is the juridical relation which serves as the basis of this whole classification. What does he mean by it? He gives evidently to these words the meaning which the economists attribute to them, but these latter employ the words in two essentially different meanings, value in use, and value in exchange.

To the idea of value in use one attaches the whole idea of the importance of that which serves in one fashion or another for the satisfaction of man's needs. Wagner, for example, considers the political organization as susceptible of being measured by its economic value. Evidently a classification based upon value in use cannot be applied to legal relations. Every right, in so far as it serves as a means for the realization of human interests, can be considered as having value in this sense.

The conception of value in exchange is more limited. To define it, savants themselves appeal to the idea of law. Everything which may be the object of a private right has value in exchange. When slavery existed, man himself had such value. When offices and employments were subjects of commerce under the system of selling offices, these charges and employments had also their value in exchange. If land by any chance became incapable of private ownership, on that day it would no longer have value in exchange. The distinction between public and private law cannot, then, rest upon the conception of value in exchange since this value depends upon that very distinction.

Kaveline's system offers serious inconveniences for the study of law. It leads necessarily to arbitrary distinctions. It results in separations between those things which constitute naturally part of the same branch of law. It is in this way that he goes on to separate the recovery of a ruler's taxes from the imposition of them; to treat in two different parts of the law the privileges assigned to functionaries, and the theory as to the legal situation of such functionaries in the state. It is impossible, meanwhile, to give a clear explanation of this theory without speaking of the privileges of functionaries and their rights and duties.

Finally, let us observe that in his definition Kaveline gives us no idea of what the public law is, out of what materials he composes it, or what are its relations with private law.

Zitovich [1] thinks also to find the fundamental distinction between public and private law in the economic nature of these rights, but he reaches this result by a quite different route from that followed by Kaveline. According to him private, or civil law, is the ensemble of institutions, of rules of positive right, which fix the distribution of economic wealth at a given time or among a given people, or, more briefly, the civil law is the law of distribution (*Verkehrsrecht*). It must be observed that his definition does not exclude from the civil law thus understood the relations of family rights. These relations, he says, are in reality rights of distribution. They indicate in a precise fashion the causes which lead to the distribution of wealth, the principal of these causes being inheritance. Finally, the individual who very often

[1] Course in Russian Civil Law, I. 1878. pp. 4-7.

is at the same time the author and the subject of the division is regarded under different aspects. His situation as a member of a family may have a great importance. Finally, the subdivision, here under consideration, is not exactly an economic distribution; it is a distribution which has at its base the moral unity, the internal solidarity, of each family.

We may, once for all, observe that what Zitovich says in speaking of the family applies equally to the state. The relations of the state with the citizens give rise, also, to distribution. The state allots privileges, distributes gratifications, makes loans, pays debts. In all these operations the individual appears as the author and the subject of distribution, and it is of importance for the law to consider him under this relation and observe what his situation is, not now as a member of a family, but as a member of the state. The distinctions between classes have had great importance in this point of view.

All the wealth which the state accumulates by means of taxes which are imposed upon the nation, and also by means of revenues derived from domainal goods,—all this wealth is not distributed according to the laws of economic distribution, but rather according to political reasons In a general way we can say that the organization of the state has as extensive an influence over the distribution of wealth as has that of the family.

Reasoning in this fashion, Zitovich ought to come to the conclusion that all juridical relations, being relations of distribution, should be placed in the private law. Public law, for him, also, results necessarily in the deplacement of wealth in the economic order, and then can we assert that there is in the civil law nothing but relations of distribution? Evidently not. Family rights, for example, comprehend quite a different thing and contain dispositions which do not all affect the patrimony. On the contrary, in the public law certain branches, like financial legislation, deal exclusively with relations of economic distribution.

We see, then, that all the attempts to establish distinctions between private and public law have remained unfruitful. The distinctions among interests which constitute the matter of juridical relations do not suffice as a basis for the classification of those juridical relations

Since juridical norms determine, not the interests themselves, but only the different limits which exist between them, the forms which they affect, let us seek, then, to distinguish the juridical relations, not in accordance with those interests which are the same in all the phenomena of social life, but in accordance with the manner in which those interests are delimited, according to their form.

This impossibility, which we have just recognized, of finding in the matter of juridical relations the basis for a distinction between public and private law is further confirmed by the examples furnished by the history of law, by the different forms in which relations absolutely identical, so far as their matter is concerned, have been clothed.

In the middle ages, for example, certain powers, certain prerogatives of public power, were only accessory rights attached to the possession of the soil.

Section 33. *Formal Classifications*

KANT. Metaphysische Anfangsgründe der Rechtslehre, 1797. s. 161 ff.

PUCHTA. Vorlesungen über das heutige röm. Recht. I. s. 75 ff.

JELLINEK. System der öffentlichen subjektiven Rechten, 1892. ss. 40–65.

THON. Rechtsnorm und subjektives Recht. ss. 108–146.

MOUROMTZEV. Definition and fundamental divisions of law, pp. 185–217.

The insufficiency of classifications founded upon the matter and content of the juridical relations has led savants to seek a classification of public rights and private rights from external signs, from the forms of juridical relations. Several formal classifications have been tried. We may group them under two categories. Some think to find the basis of a distinction between public rights and private rights in the different situations in which the subjects of juridical relations find themselves; the objects, for example, which rights give to a man are given him either as a member of society or as a human individual. Others recognize a distinction in the character of the protections which the law gives to defend injured individuals and look to see if these protections are granted on the initiative of the individual injured or on the intervention of public authority.

The first of these two conceptions owes its origin to the influence asserted by the school of natural law, the school of the state of nature, which is conceived as having preceded the formation of society.

Law at its origin by the formation of society is exclusively private law. This law continues to exist when the society is formed, but it is then surrounded and completed by institutions which have for their end the organization of the state and of its organs and of its functions. This additional law is public law. The relations it has with private law are those of support and protection.

All public law has been created to serve as a support for the sanction of private law. This is an opinion adopted by Kant, amongst others, to serve as a distinction between public and private rights.

This classification, due to the theory of the natural state, has had meanwhile the same fate as the theory from which it came. This theory lost its favor some time ago, and nobody today defends it. The classification, however, to which it gave birth, is still admitted by a good many authors and has even been somewhat expanded.

It is to the historical school, which was one of reaction against the school of natural law, that we owe the author who has best defended this classification. Puchta in his works appears as its determined partisan. Puchta distinguishes rights according to whether the man holds them as an individual or as a member of an organized society. In the first division are the rights of property and rights of family; in the second, public and ecclesiastical rights. The rights of property and rights of family constitute private rights, hence his division of rights into three great classes, private rights, public rights, and ecclesiastical rights.

We observe at once an incoherence in this classification. In fact, if it has for its basis the distinction of rights which belong to a man according as he appears as an individual or as a member of a society, it is necessary to oppose the right of property to all other rights. But Puchta combines rights of property with rights of family.

Other writers have brought modifications of Puchta's

theory and have corrected his definition to this extent, that they have divided all law into two categories only, public and private. Public rights, they have said, include only rights which necessarily presuppose the existence of an organized society among men and which cannot exist without such a society. Private rights are those which suppose only a simple coherence of men. Rights of family in this new theory will be considered as private rights, since they can exist outside of society and independently of the state.

While this theory seems more logical and more complete, it presents, nevertheless, a grave defect. It has for a basis this idea, that men can live without being organized in society and that one can admit among these men, living outside of all society, the existence of rights. This is an altogether false conception. We are more and more convinced that right exists only in society; no society, no right. There are, it is true, a good many degrees in the organization of a society, but even a crowd assembled by chance is not without some bonds of connection, without some relations between the individuals who make it up.

Let us look at some of the developments of this last theory. The relations of private right, marriage, exchange, gifts, say the partisans of this doctrine, are possible even where there is no state and no organized society. They can exist even amongst a band of brigands, amongst individuals gathered together by accident in a desert.

But the relations of a public character, for example election to parliament, are possible only in an organized state. It is easy, however, to use these very examples to refute this theory.

Without doubt we can elect a member of parliament only where there is a parliament. That is very true, but we can also form certain agreements, perform certain acts of exchange only where there are notaries and by consequence, an organized society.

Moreover, even a crowd assembled by chance can hold discussions over their common affairs and give directions in the general interest. Let us suppose a ship which suffers wreck and over which the captain does not exercise, as he might do, his right of commanding the passengers; these latter may discuss together their present situation and take necessary measures for the common safety. Among them the more energetic will speedily become dominant. Doubtless it might be said that there is here nothing organized, that there can be no question of a vote, of a right to vote, but nevertheless the vote exists in the throng under such circumstances. The sexual union itself will be only a fact, nothing else; the exchange or the gift also will be only facts and not the result of the exercise of a right. The thing may be transmitted, but no right, for there is none.

Another defect resulting from a classification so extended is that it results logically in introducing into the public law the relations between members of any association, any society, that of the stockholders in an incorporated company, for example, or even the relations of the family group.

The partisans of the system go so far without recoiling from the overthrow which they are giving to the current conception which rules as to the matter.

Bahr, for example (Rechtstaat, 1865), would divide all law into private law (*Privatrecht*) and the law of societies (*Genossenschaftsrecht*). The first includes the relations of men considered as members of an organism, state, society, church. Public law thus considered is only a subdivision of the law of associations.

Gierke holds equally to this same opinion; but such a classification does not answer at all to the historic grouping of the relations men hold to each other.

Jellinek, under a form a little different, accepts this distinction of rights into public and private rights. He distinguishes rights into two categories,—there are bearers of rights who can exercise choice and others who can only hold (*dürfen und können*). The law, said he, can only recognize as permitted those relations which existed before it, and independently of it, to which it brings no new element, unless it be that individuals who previously had power to act can now act legally (*dürfen*). The consequences of the recognition of this power to act appear very clearly when it is attempted to study the effects of legal prohibitions. Every prohibition can be reduced to this formula,—you may not, you cannot legally (*du darfst nicht*). In every case the prohibition does not render an act impossible to do, it merely declares the doing of it illegal. The prohibition can always be violated. But the action of the law is not limited merely to permissions and prohibitions. The law can add to the individual's capacity a new element. It can give to acts and contracts a juridical force which brings with it some new consequences quite different from those attached by nature to the same act or contract. It has, then, that which is called juridical force (*rechtliches Können*).

These two elements, power and force, are so closely connected that the first never exists without the second. What I may do legally is only the sum of my power over actual facts, recognized and assented to by the law; but juridical force may exist meanwhile without such "power"; in the case, for example, where the law does not merely protect the natural capacity of the person, but gives to him a new capacity.

Jellinek's distinction between public and private law has its foundation exactly in this correlation of juridical power and juridical force. In private law the first element, the power, exists always; in public law one requires always the presence of the second, the state's force, and public rights are all based on a force resulting from the law. They are no part of the natural liberty regulated by law, but constitute an enlargement of this natural liberty.

This distinction is purely artificial, and if examined closely loses all its value. *Dürfen und können, pouvoir et puissance,* "power and force," are not essential elements of the matter of subjective right. Such a distinction between these two elements depends not upon the matter of the right, but upon consequences brought on by the violation of a right. If the violation of a legal rule results only in a liability on the part of him who violates the law (*lex minus quam perfecta*), it may result that one cannot violate this law, but he finds that he has had the force to do so. If such a violation brings about the legal nullity of the act forbidden by the law (*lex perfecta*), the power to perform such act does not exist. If, finally, the violation of the rule brings at the same time a liability upon the doer of the act and the legal nullity of the act (*lex plus quam perfecta*) there is neither power nor force to violate such a rule.

On the other side, it is necessary to observe that the element of "*Dürfen*," of permission, is not at all a stranger to public law.

The individual who does not possess the needed legal capacity not only has not "*Können*," ability, to accept a given function, but neither has he "*Dürfen*," permission, since the usurpation of this function is a punishable act.

A classification having for a base the distinction of consequences which the violation of the law involves, has been proposed by Thon. If the violation of law brings to him who has suffered by its violation the right of an indemnity, the right in this case is a private one; if, on the contrary, this violation brings about the intervention of public authority, then it is a public right.

More briefly, private rights are those which are specially protected by the initiative of the person who has suffered damage; public rights are those protected by society, the state, independently of the intervention of the injured individual. This classification of Thon has found a good many partisans amongst Russian jurists, among others Mouromtzev, Gambaroff and Duvernoi. It is, however, not very accurate.

First, the distinction between public and private rights would appear only when they are violated, but even when they are not violated, we distinguish quite clearly between public rights and private ones. Thus all the world, for example, knows that one can transfer family rights, while public rights are not subject to alienation.

Then, it is not precise to claim that private rights are the only ones protected by private initiative. There are also crimes or offenses pursued only upon the complaint of the one who has been the victim. When there is a system of administrative justice the right of pursuit is left to private persons the more frequently even if the public rights have suffered some injury as to their protection by the administration.

Finally, and this is the most important point, the right of pursuit given to individuals who have suffered injury and the action of authority are not two pursuits which exclude each other. They can very readily take place simultaneous y as the consequence of a single act violating some single right. Let us take as examples the case of robbery and assassination. There is a criminal proceeding inst tuted, but there is also a civil pursuit on the part of the victims or the successors. These two prosecutions to be sure, are quite distinct, but they cannot serve to establish a criterion, a mark of distinction between public and private rights. Otherwise, we would be compelled to admit that the same right can be at the same time a public and a private one.

Section 34. *The Distinction Between Public Rights and Private Rights*

All the theories which we have just examined have furnished no satisfactory explanation of the distinction between public and private law. They give, however, some characteristic indications of this distinction. They have shown us that it is necessary to avoid seeking the basis of this distinction in the different interests in view of which public and private rights are created. The basis of the whole distinction should be sought in the form with which juridical relations clothe themselves. Such a distinction ought by no means to have as its principal foundation merely the subject of the right or the consequences which the violation of the right brings. This distinction ought to be more general and ought to be applicable even when there has been no violation of the right.

All rights being appendant to human beings regarded as members of society, it is necessary to seek the explanation of the distinction between public and private right in the diversity which the legal forms of all the relations established among men present.

The right, as we have seen, is in general the power to make use of something. This faculty can be guaranteed to an individual under a double form. The simplest form is that of dividing the object into several parts, and each of these parts being assigned to an owner. Thus, we establish the difference between *tuum* and *meum*. The whole conception of private property is founded on such a division. It is again this same principle of division which serves as a basis of the institution of the family, excluding the intervention of outside persons, the law having assigned the family a proper sphere of action.

This distribution is often taken for the fundamental idea in law because all questions of law are connected with property. Some consider the idea of communism as the negation of all rights because it excludes this division, together with the idea of property.

However, the simplest form of distribution is not the only one, nor the oldest, nor the most perfect for assuring the use of an object. By the side of this form which depends entirely upon the distinction between *tuum* and *meum*, there is another form, that of the adaptation of the object to the joint realization of certain interests.

The insufficiency of the first form of which we have just spoken, that of division, appears readily. There are objects which it is impossible to divide; for example, the different parts of a navigable river, of a public highway, cannot be apportioned. If one should proceed with the attempt, he would destroy at a stroke the public utility of these objects. Other objects, although divisible, require an adaptation, some sort of a change, for the realization of the interests concerned. With money, for example, it is not sufficient merely to divide up the gold and silver among individuals; it is necessary to give it a form, to coin it, to preserve the gold and silver from counterfeiting and deceit.

Consequently alongside the distinction of *tuum* and *meum* there must exist another form of delimitation of interests, another mode of distribution and division. This second form we will call "adaptation," and we will distinguish it thus from the first, from "distribution." The portions of land, highways, for example, left for the use of all, the money whose coinage guarantees the value of the metal employed, are "adaptations." Each of these forms, taken alone, is insufficient. Even if private property is not recognized, private possession has need to be protected. We can imagine the state of things in which there would be no such protection. Suppose, for example, the soil, the other objects which we use here, to be for the use of the whole world and without individual appropriation. It would be necessary, none the less, to establish some security for that portion of the soil, for that object, which we are employing at the very moment when we are serving ourselves with it.

If there were no right of property to be protected, there would be at least a temporary possession which would require to be guaranteed.

This right to the possession of an object, the same as ownership of an object, supposes a preliminary distribution of objects, placing them at the disposition of individuals. This is the division, as we have seen, between *tuum* and *meum; meum* is not only what I have acquired by lawful means, but what I find really in my own possession.

So these two forms of the guarantee of legal possibility are equally necessary. They cannot be replaced, the one by the other. Always and everywhere their coexistence is indispensable. So, and very advantageously, they can be regarded as the basis of all classification of legal phenomena. But the grouping which has its principal foundation in the distribution of objects among individuals, or in their adaptation to common needs, does it correspond to public rights on the one side, and to private rights on the other, as their historic development has exhibited them? I think the answer should be in the affirmative.

We can explain all the differences between public rights and private rights by the distinction between distribution and adaptation as above explained.

The most remarkable differences existing between public and private rights are those which connect themselves with the acquisition of rights and their loss, with their content and with the relations between rights and obligations.

Private rights are acquired as a result of special circumstances having a distinctly individual character and connecting directly or indirectly with some particular individual. And this individual character of the acquisition is strengthened constantly by the special bond which arises between the thing assigned and the person receiving it. Also, in private right we distinguish, always vigorously, between capacity and possession, between possibility of acquiring a right and actually getting it. All those who have capacity may in general possess a thing, but it is only those who have received the right of possessing a thing who have really a control over it.

When an object adapted only to common usage is under consideration, it cannot be in the same way. An act of acquisition, of individual appropriation, even temporary, cannot intervene, since it is a group of persons whose interests are served by the object. It suffices to be one of the group in order to have over this thing a right of use. Here the capacity and right come together. This is what happens in the exercise of all public rights. All those who satisfy the required conditions for electoral capacity have the right to vote. For the exercise of this right there is no need of any special individual qualification.

It is quite otherwise with the private right. If, for example, I am capable of participating in the issuance of a bill of exchange, this does not by any means require that I shall be the owner of the rights and obligations resulting from a bill of exchange.

The loss of a public right results from a loss of capacity, independently of the will of the bearer of the right. Private rights, on the contrary, can be lost without any change whatever in the juridical capacity of the person and by the mere fact of his will. He can renounce a right, can alienate it, can grant it to another to be exercised in his place. We see here, further, an application of our distinction between the distribution and the adaptation of the object.

The right possessed by the member of any society to the collective use of an object is lost when this member ceases to be a part of the society. He cannot grant the usage of his right to another individual who does not belong to this society. Alienation is not applicable to public rights. It could not have as a result any transfer of the right, the other members of the group having already a right to the use of the thing.

As to the object over which a right extends, if as a result of distribution it is assigned to a particular person, its adaptation, if any, is made by the owner and according to his will. He makes the object conform to the purpose which he proposes and in the way he wishes. A sovereign power of disposition belongs to him, for his own personal interest. Such is the matter of all private rights. They are absolute rights, including at once use and disposition.

In the public right, on the contrary, the power of disposition does not exist. This power takes the form of an obligation. The administration of the railroads, for example, has the right to control their iron roads, but this is at the same time only an obligation. The administration cannot use this power for alienation. It will make use of the iron roads, not in its own interest, but in the interest of all.

It is the same with common roads and highways. It is impossible to give to each of those who use them the right of disposition, and those who have them in charge have equally no right of disposing of them except in the general interest.

From this distinction between distribution and adaptation result, also, the differences which exist in the correlation between right and obligation, differences which we recognize in the public and private right. When the object belongs to an individual, the personality of the bearer of the right is always exactly determined. On the contrary, when the object is adapted to a collective usage, it is society considered as a whole which possesses it. The determination is here general, and persons who form the society are not specific individuals. On the other hand, the subject of the obligation is exactly determined.

All the peculiarities of public and private law, we see by the foregoing, are explained, then, in a satisfactory manner by the distinctions between distribution and adaptation.

We can by the same criterion furnish the explanation for the existence of private rights in the state for its own profit.

If the power given by the state is attributed to it with a view to the adaptation of a thing to the general use, we find ourselves in the presence of a public right. Such is the right of the state over its means of communication. If, on the contrary, the object which the state possesses has been given that it may serve itself with it in order to get therefrom the necessary means for the adaptation of other objects, this is a private right. Such is the right which the state possesses over its own goods. The revenues from such property serve for the maintenance of this or that grand division of administration.

It remains still to explain the numerous classifications which we have examined above. We shall do so by further use of the distinctions established between "distribution" and "adaptation." The preceding classifications derive their foundation from a secondary point, from one of the accessory consequences of the leading idea which we have just set forth.

Let us observe first of all that if we divide an object amongst several individuals, the will of each of these individuals plays a preponderant rôle in the application of the thing to some given use. How or in what fashion shall each one employ the object? This will depend upon the bearer of the right. The answer is altogether different if the object is applied to the collective use of all. In this case the manner in which each one shall use the thing, and the adaptation to be made of it for the common interest of all, is according to a rule fixed by the legislature. Here the liberty of disposing of the object no longer exists. Each person, who has a right of use over the object, finds himself bound by exact limits, can modify neither the object nor its value, because an identical right exists for the advantage of every other member of the society.

For this reason, the first form of these two actions of law, the distribution, results in consequences presenting a more individual character; the second, on the other hand, in consequences of a more social character.

The predominance of patrimonial rights among private rights, the facility with which these rights are transformed into a value which is the price of the object, can also very easily be explained upon our theory. When we proceed to a distribution of certain objects among individuals it happens frequently that the object assigned to an individual does not correspond to any need he has. Exchange is the only means to be employed in such a case.

The facility with which a thing can be exchanged or alienated has, then, a great importance. It is a quality of things of a general order which has even more value than the other. This capacity which things possess of being exchanged makes them applicable to all needs without exception, and, if the capacity of exchange is expressed always by price, it is evident that all efforts tend everywhere to transform the right over an object into a right over its price.

In the individual distribution of objects, private law leaves to each the necessity of determining what means he shall employ for the satisfaction of his own wants and for the production of other values. Public law, on the other hand, adapts the object to a given public use and regulates at the same time the use of the object and the means of its production. Private law in economic matters does not attempt to regulate either the employment or the production of wealth, but merely its distribution. It is this which permits Zitovich to define civil law as a law of distribution.

The assigning of an object does not take place without an individualization of the thing as well as of him who has a right over it. The application of an object to a common use combines several individuals together and brings about their association by this community of use. Hence the notion that private rights belong to man, considered individually, and public rights to man, considered as a member of an organized society.

The right to dispose of the thing of which one is the owner makes him the one upon whom depends the protection accorded to this object. If the object is applied to a common usage, on the contrary, this protection will depend no longer upon the will of any individual.

In this secondary consequence of the distinction between rights over things accorded to a collectivity of individua's and those granted to an individual, Thon and his disciples have sought to find the sole basis of the distinction between public and private law.

BOOK III

SOCIAL CONDITIONS FOR THE DEVELOPMENT OF LAW

CHAPTER I

SOCIETY

SPENCER. "Principles of Sociology," 1876–1877.

LILIENFELD. "Gedanken über die Socialwissenschaft der Zukunft," 1879.

SCHAEFFLE. "Bau und Leben des socialen Körpers," 2d edition, 1881.

FOUILLÉE. "La science sociale contemporaine," 1880.

KAREIEV. "Fundamental Questions in the History of Philosophy," Vol. II, 1883.

GUMPLOWICZ. "Grundriss der Sociologie," 1884.

Section 35. *The Mechanical Theory*

So far we have considered law wholly aside from the medium of its application. This medium is society. It is only in the bosom of society that law is formed or acts, because its task is precisely to fix and to limit human interests in relations to each other. Wherever there is no society, wherever man shows himself merely as an isolated individual there is no place for law.

Every phenomenon depends upon the medium in which it is produced. Law does not escape this general rule. It depends upon the social medium in which it is applied.

Let us see what is the nature of society's influence over law and over the state, which is the form of social life most closely connected with law. The explanation of society has been often attempted, and many theories still divide the field. Most of these theories can be reduced to two groups if one classifies them according to the conception they hold of nature and of society.

For some, society is a wholly artificial creation, man's work, produced by his will; this is the mechanical conception. For others, society is a natural fact, arising and developing outside of human will, in obedience to inexorable laws, like all other natural organisms; this is the organic conception.

The first conception was especially that of the XVII and XVIII centuries. The idea that society was a creation, the product of human activity, was at that time generally admitted. It was the consequence of other philosophical and psychological ideas.

Philosophy, at that time, indeed, did not consider the universe as a living whole. The universe was divided into two quite distinct parts, spirit and matter, the two combined by a mechanical juxtaposition. According to this philosophic conception we must reduce everything to a mechanism, to forces. Beings were, in the eyes of the philosophers of that time, only organisms acting automatically.

Social phenomena naturally could not, under such theories, be explained otherwise than by a mechanical conception.

Psychological theories, then, of course, resulted in the same conclusions. Both the theories then held, that of innate ideas and that of sensationalism, despite the opposition between them, agreed in this, the denial of the existence of any transmission of psychological development from one generation to another.

Some admitted that man at all epochs possessed from his birth an intellectual outfit, a world of innate ideas, but this outfit remained always the same; this world was not augmented among his descendants. Others thought that man at birth knew nothing, was an absolute void, ignorance complete, that man acquires ideas only by personal experience. For the believers in innate ideas, as well as for the sensationalists, the development of the man's intelligence was limited, then, to the life of an individual. Each carried his own intellectual baggage; the point of departure was always the same. Some denied the existence of any connection between two generations. Each generation was subject to no influence except what it created, was moved only by itself and usually for itself.

Social life was regarded as the necessary consequence of the ideas just set forth and not as the result of a successive development of humanity; it was only an arbitrary, artificial institution of men.

Society supposes necessarily the combination of individuals. It cannot be the result of a single will. Several wills are necessary for its formation. The mechanical theory, therefore, explained the formation of society as the result of an agreement amongst men, a social contract. The cause of this contract was merely the necessity of combining separate individual forces which were too weak for the combat with external nature. The power confided to society had no other end than the guaranteeing of external security and internal order.

The organization of social power and its relations with the liberty guaranteed to each individual took the form of a contract. The creators and organizers of society freely consented. The conception to be formed of a social life established thus was a wholly individualistic one. The personality of the individual was regarded as the dominating principle and controller of social life. Nobody imagined that the individual depended upon the medium in which he lived; for the whole world, on the other hand, the medium, the social order, was fixed and guided only by the free will of individuals.

There was no difference, then, between the conception of man living before the existence of all society and that of man living in the midst of an organized society. One part of a mechanical aggregate suffers no change from being detached, nor does it alter its nature by being incorporated. A part of a living organism, on the other hand, is radically changed by separation from that organism. Sometimes it dies; sometimes, if it continues to live its own independent life, it is profoundly modified.

In the mechanical conception of society man was in this respect like a portion of a mechanical aggregate, and, even out of the pale of society, was considered as endowed with the same qualities, sentiments, and needs, as if he were a member of society. Further, it was believed that the development of man in his natural state was more advanced than it was in society. Otherwise, it was said, man could not form so complete and abstract an idea as that of society, of social power, of individual liberty, because in the state of nature man had only the method of analogy for forming such a conception. Meanwhile, all those who have written with regard to man in a state of nature have asserted that society was not created, that social power was not established otherwise than with the conscious purpose of realizing human interests; and, in the different proposed outlines of the social contract, the relations between social power and individual liberty have always been clearly indicated.

This purely mechanical theory of the formation of society is today wholly abandoned, as being in absolute contradiction with received history and psychology. Everywhere history shows us, even in the most remote times, man existing in a state of society. There is no reason to suppose that the famous pre-social, natural state out of which men emerged by means of a social contract, ever had any existence. In the mind of the people social order never appeared as an arbitrary institution, but as the act of a will other than human, as an objective order. History compels us to recognize the social state as the true natural state of man. On the other hand, psychology teaches us that the intellectual development of man is specially due to the influence of his social environment. Our intellectual development, our sentiments, our moral principles, all depend upon the social life, upon the environment into which we are born and in which we live.

If we admit the existence of a pre-social state, we must recognize necessarily that from it men would never develop in any way; their minds would always have remained so simple that it would have been impossible for them ever to rise to general and abstract conceptions of society, to conceptions different from all the ideas suggested by their surroundings, ideas such as those of contract, society, public power, individual liberty, etc. Even among men living in society such ideas remain, with many of them, unrecognized. If society were not "natural" how could such ideas have become familiar to those who had never experienced even the fact of the combination of a few men?

Sociological researches have shown and explained that social development followed in its progress exact rules. If the form of social organization is not an arbitrary and artificial fact, then society itself cannot be a human invention; if the development of society takes place according to fixed and inviolable laws, then the existence of society does not depend upon our free will.

This whole doctrine of the natural state, and of the formation of society by a voluntary and conscious combination of men, is now given up by the entire world.

We turn aside, now, from the whole notion of such a pre-social state and of a social contract which followed it. Historic observation shows us that such a state never existed; even the utility of such a fiction for the scientific explanation of social phenomena is contested. The celebrated publicist, Karl Salomo Zachariä,[1] for example, expressed himself in the following terms on this subject: "In opposing the state of nature to the social state it is not meant to say that men really lived at any given time in a state of nature. Granted, then, that men have always lived together in society, it would be still necessary to distinguish the political and organized life from the so-called state of nature, which does not present the same features. Man cannot form an idea of anything except by comparing it with an object having contrary, or at least distinct, qualities." The man of our day is not only a member, but a product of society. Outside of society we cannot imagine him, at least such as he is in society. Outside of society all the development of sentiment is impossible, at least so far as relates to sympathetic sentiments, altruistic ones. Speech is an impossibility; man outside of society could not attain to that degree of intellectual development which so profoundly separates him from the animals. The conception of this famous state of nature is no more necessary to psychology than for physiology is the conception of a wholly separate existence, distinct and unconnected, of the different organs of a living being.

The purely mechanical theory ought, then, to be absolutely given up. It is necessary always to recognize that it has played a great rôle in history. It is in a certain way the first of the attempts to give a scientific explanation of social phenomena. Prior to it the social life was considered as the product of an outside force, independent of society and its elements. It was not thought social life could be determined by the nature of society or the different elements of which it was composed, but by some force remaining wholly foreign to the society.

[1] Zachariä. Vierzig. Bücher von Staate. 2 Ausg. 1838, Bd. I. s. 49.

The society was considered only as passive and inert matter subjected to the action of this foreign and supernatural force.

The mechanical theory, on the contrary, presented society as a product of the action of its own elements. Social life was not a result of phenomena produced and directed by external and supernatural powers, but a result of the actions of social elements; that is to say, of men. The character of the society is not determined by an extraneous will, but by the nature of its elements. Such a conception was doubtless an advance over the opinion held up to that time. The error of this new conception was in the fact that it did not recognize that the elements composing society are themselves social products. They themselves have their history, their evolution, do not come fully formed from celestial regions, take their birth from men, from those men who have already lived the social life and have acquired a certain body of social habits by transmission, imitation and the establishment of usages and customs.

The mechanical conception of society, in our day, has a historic value in this sense that it is a conception in direct opposition to the organic conception now held, which is a reaction against the mechanical one. In these last times the extreme consequences to which the organic conception has been drawn have led certain choice spirits to turn back towards the old theory, the previous mechanical explanation of society, only modifying a little its form.

This modification recently[1] applied to the old mechanical conception consists in the fact that it is admitted that society in its outlines is established independently of the human will, but affirms at the same time that its progressive development has resulted more and more from the interposition of human wills. It is only in the advanced state of its evolution that it can be said that society is really a product of human volition. The representatives of this last opinion are, in France, M. Fouillée, and in Russia, Kareiev.

M. Fouillée considers society as an organism contractual in this sense: that its organic character, a character predominant in society at its origin, gives place more and more to relations freely established among men. Kareiev admits, equally, this same opinion, but under another form. According to him society in its evolution is compelled to become a natural fact, a combination of voluntary facts produced by the political art of man. Consequently, here is the point which distinguishes this new theory from the old mechanical one,—the authors whom we have just cited do not consider the agreement, the formation of society by way of contract, as the starting point of social life, but, on the contrary, as the result of a long social evolution, as the purpose of social progress. All civilization, looked at in this relation, is only the gradual subordination of social life to human ideals.

The opinions of M. Fouillée and Kareiev have their origin in an undoubted fact, that of the influence of opinions and human tendencies over social life. Man, as the member of a society which does not answer to the ideal he has formed, is moved to get rid of this contradiction and to modify social relations in accordance with his ideals. The generations, one after the other, continue unceasingly this same labor and elaborate slowly a conscious reorganization of society. This work cannot fail of a result. Little by little human ideas take form and are realized in the social environment. More and more society moves towards an end which is sought for it, which is wished by all the men who have labored at its reorganization. There is here a product of their agreements and it is in this sense we may say that society has a contractual character. In other terms, society becomes more and more the incarnation of human ideas and the product of human art and effort.

We cannot accept meanwhile this opinion without making some reservations. First of all, the notion of a conventional organism carries in itself an invincible contradiction. Organism and contract are two conceptions which exclude each other. If we keep to the usual meaning of words, that which is organized is always in opposition to that which is artificial, arbitrary, produced by the conscious will of man.

All contract is impossible without the agreement of conscious wills. One cannot in a general way affirm that in the course of time society will take on a contractual character. Contract, as we find, supposes, necessarily, the harmony of several wills, and the social life, which is the result of desire and aspirations of a long course of generations, is not the expression of any single will common to all these generations. Social aspirations change, in fact, with each generation. The order which we assert in social relations, that succession which history shows us, does not correspond to any ideal traced in advance by the successive generations. There can be no question of contract between generations. Even in a single one the ideal does not manifest itself fairly by contract. There exist in each generation parts which are not in agreement. The influence of these parts on the social life is determined only with great difficulty, according to objective social conditions.

The form in which Kareiev expressed his opinion as to the origin and development of society is more fortunate. It does not contain such an evident contradiction as that of M. Fouillée with his conception of a contractual organism, but it raises, however, several serious objections.

The product of art is solely the product of the conscious will of man. An unexpected, an accidental, result of a human act is not a product of art. Well, the ideas which have marked most strongly the work of the centuries, those which have left the deepest imprint, the history is there to prove it, have resulted in consequences which failed to answer the provisions of their producers.

Let us look, for example, at what took place under the French revolution. The constitutions of 1791 and of 1793 are, it is true, reproductions more or less complete of the theories of Rousseau and Montesquieu, but these constitutions never reached their application. Most of their dispositions have remained a dead letter. In fact, the general progress of the revolution, and the social state which has followed, are not consequences of those constitutions. The revolution has not been that which its producers themselves wished; it has disappointed its organizers.

If anyone is shown merely the facts which have developed themselves up to this time, the organization of the state under Napoleon and under the restoration, it will be impossible by the recital alone of these facts to form even a proximate conception of Rousseau's social theories. But if we put the same person, on the other hand, before a work of art he will recognize at once the idea of the artist who did the work. There will be no need of explanation. It will itself express the idea which produced it better than can any other demonstration.

We might compare humanity to a work of art if humanity possessed only one idea or combination of ideas common to all men, realizing itself under different forms of social life and of which the ideas of different generations and of separate men would be only partial manifestations; but the existence of such an idea of combination, sole, common to all humanity, is quite problematic.

Independently of these conceptions, the opinion of Kareiev raises still another objection. His conception supposes that the influence of human aspirations is always growing stronger and that the action of objective factors upon the social development is always diminishing. As a matter of fact, such objective factors like the influence of nature, of famine, of new discoveries, continue to act in a most powerful fashion even in our times. Some inventions of a purely technical character, without any connection with the men's social ideal, as, for example, the invention of gunpowder, or that of the steam engine, have had a greater influence over social life than any number of theories. It would be strange to believe that modern social life is an incorporation of the ideas of Schwartz and Watt, and there is no good reason to assume that in the future such factors will have ceased to have their influence over the social development. We cannot, then, declare that society becomes more and more exclusively the work of man, and of his will.

Section 36. *The Organic Theory*

The organic conception of society is a quite modern idea, and hardly appeared before the end of the XVIII century. To be sure, even in the most remote antiquity, we meet with something like it, with comparisons between society and the man or the animal. Plato's dialogue, Politicus, rests entirely upon such a resemblance; and Hobbes himself, the originator of the state of nature, compares the state to a leviathan. But the conception of an organism in the particular sense which we give it today was then unknown.[1] In Aristotle the word *organicus* is by no means the term opposed to *mechanicus*, and the use of this word in the sense meant by Aristotle lasted down to the end of the XVIII century. *Organicus* and *instrumentalis* are synonymous expressions. The leviathan state of Hobbes is only an immense machine. It is not a living organism but an automaton. Hobbes, convinced materialist as he was, naturally did not recognize some essential distinctions between machine and animal. Such is also the view of the Cartesians. For Descartes and his successors, as for the materialists, animals were only machines moved in an automatic fashion. It was the same with the human body. The soul in connection with the body played the part of an indifferent spectator. Spinoza and Leibnitz had also the same opinion as regards the relation of the soul and body, but evidently this was not the opinion of the whole world. To this mechanical conception of life in man and the animal is opposed that of spiritism, whose representatives in antiquity were Pythagoras, Plato, Aristotle, Hippocrates, and in the middle ages

[1] Claude Bernard, "La Science Experimentale," 1878, pp. 149–212. Definitions de la vie: Les Theories anciennes et la science moderne.

Paracelsus, Van Helmont, and the scholastics. It is above all in the doctrine of the celebrated physician Stahl who lived in the XVIII century that this last theory has been most completely set forth.

According to Stahl, the body is only an inert instrument, the puppet of some immaterial force and having no activity of its own. We find in Paracelsus and Van Helmont such a doctrine as to the existence in our organism of such immaterial forces which have all power over the different bodily organs. In Stahl all these forces are replaced by a single one,—by the soul, the invisible time marker, who controls the movements of all the functions of the organism.

So in the partisans of the mechanical, as in those of the spiritistic theory, while the explanation of life is different, in the one as in the other the body is equally understood as a mechanism. In both theories it is only a machine. The difference consists in that the machine is in one case considered as acting automatically, in the other as the passive instrument of the soul, as without independent activity.

Out of these theories there could scarcely arise any clear opposition between the organic and the mechanical conceptions. It was only after the appearance of the vital theory, due to Bichat,[1] that such an explanation was offered. Bichat, who lived at the end of the XVIII century, affirmed that it was necessary to seek the cause of vital phenomena, not in some immaterial principle, but, on the contrary, in qualities possessed by the matter producing these phenomena. According to him the phenomena of life are explained by special vital properties innate in the living matter which constitutes the living organism. These vital properties are not only distinct ones, but it may be said that they

[1] Died 1802. His General Anatomy appeared the year before.

are opposed to the general physical and chemical properties of matter. Physical properties are eternal and inseparable from matter; vital properties, on the contrary, are transmissible.

The inert matter which enters into the formation of every organism is thoroughly interpenetrated with these vital properties, but for a time only, since by their essential character these vital properties are in time consumed and exhausted. At the beginning of life they are in the phases of growth, stationary during mature existence, they decrease in later life to disappear with death. This is the whole development of living beings. All life is only a long struggle between physical and vital properties. Health and disease are merely different phases of it. Recovery is a victory of the vital properties and death of the physical ones.

The doctrine of vitalism was destined, as we easily see, to produce a complete revolution in the notions as to the connection between mechanical and organic phenomena which had till then prevailed. It created at once a complete opposition between living and dead matter, between a mechanism and an organism, between physical and biological sciences. Moreover, vitalism permitted the showing of the connection between the different parts of the organism and of those parts with the whole, and attributing to the organism an independent activity of its own whose principle was in the properties of the organism and of each of its parts.

It was at the end of the XVIII century that there appeared for the first time in philosophy a clear opposition between the ideas of organism and mechanism, first in Kant and after him in Schelling. The philosophic system of this last author is a profound organic conception logically developed of the entire world. He explains all the phenomena of the universe by their analogy to the organic life.

To the influence of these new theories must be added the historical tendencies which had then already manifested themselves. The mechanical conception of the world was the negation of the idea of development. A mechanism in its essence is an unchangeable thing. It ignores development, for mechanisms, apart from each other, are connected by no succession or evolution. The mechanical theory, therefore, is from its nature anti-historical. It explains social organization not as the result of a long evolution, but as an artificial institution of man's, which may vary according to men's tastes and without relation to the past. The will of the present generation, behold in it the explanation of social phenomena. It sees no connection between past and present. For it the latter does not require the explanation which the former furnishes.

The historical conception, however, emphasizes this connection. In seeking to establish its analogy, the historical doctrine naturally turns to the organic side. It is in such a medium that the past and heredity play an important part. For all these reasons the organic conception of social phenomena rapidly became very popular and the prevailing one of the XIX century. It found partisans among thinkers of the most diverse schools. The sociologists as well as the positivists adopted it. The sociological doctrine of Comte harmonizes well with the organic conception, and the connections between his theory and the vitalist one are many.

In his biological doctrine Comte takes as his point of departure the vital properties of Bichat. He rejects, it is true, the idea of an antagonism between physical and vital properties and admits the harmony of the organism with its surroundings as a necessary condition of life. He emphasizes, too, the influence which metaphysical doctrines had had over Bichat, and even proposes in respect to this some rectifications of detail. This influence, said he, is an extraneous addition which Bichat himself has attenuated in his later books. Comte[1] appropriated the fundamental idea of vitalism and rejected the notion that the phenomena of life can be drawn from those of physics and chemistry.

Sharing in Bichat's ideas and admitting with him the opposition there is between vital phenomena and all others, Comte naturally recognizes society as an organism, being unable to deny the resemblance between vital and social phenomena.

The organic sociologic doctrine took very different forms. In Schelling and Krause's organic school the vital point is this,—in social as in organic life all the phenomena are dependent upon one another, are reciprocally conditioned.[2]

Others, like Bluntschli, for example, content themselves with establishing an analogy between social institutions and external forms of the human body. Thus he assimilates government to the head, as it is the head of the state, the ministry of the interior to the ears, and that of foreign affairs to the nose. For him the distinction between state and church is that which separates man and wife.[3]

But of all the forms which the organic theory takes, the most accepted was that which agreeing with positivism identifies the laws of life with those of society. This form finds partisans in all modern literatures. It is in Spencer, Schäffle and Lilienfeld that it has received its completest development. I shall develop especially

[1] Cours de Philosophie, 4th ed., vol. III. 14th Leçon, p. 187.

[2] "*Bedingheit.*" Krause distinguishes it from "*Bedingtheil,*" which means a passive state. *Bedingheit*, on the other hand, means a mutual relation at the same time passive and active. System der Rechtsphilosophie, s. 48–50.

[3] Bluntschli. Psychologie Studien über Staat und Kirche, 1841.

Spencer's conception, as he is the best authorized representative of the doctrine.

If we observe first of all the general character of the organic theory of society, we ought to recognize that the identification of the laws of life with the laws of society does not rest upon a sound foundation. The observed resemblances between social phenomena and those of organic life do not allow the combining of them to oppose both to inorganic phenomena. To establish such a classification we must show that the resemblance between social phenomena and those of organic life is much greater than that between those of organic life and those of inorganic matter. It would be necessary to show, moreover, and this is a very important point, that the differences between social phenomena and vital phenomena are not so numerous or important as those between the phenomena of the organic and those of the inorganic world.

As long as such proof is not exhibited there is no reason for opposing life and society to the inorganic world. It would be necessary, on the contrary, to adopt a triple classification, into inorganic, organic and social phenomena.

But the partisans of the organic theory of society do not admit this classification, and address all their arguments to the incontestable points of resemblance between the society and the organism, and to the analogous processes to which both owe their birth.

Thus do both Lilienfeld and Spencer. They set forth the correlation which there really is between the phenomena of life and those of society. Like a living organism, they say, society grows, differentiates its structure, develops special functions and separates from its own substance parts capable of an independent life. Hence, these authors conclude that society is only an organism. Such a broad comparison already is of a kind to throw doubt over the accuracy of their theory.

Even when we admit the undoubted analogy at some points between the organism and society, the complete analogy between them can be established only under one condition whose absence reduces the importance of the concessions which the organic school has attained. The analogies are possible only as we compare the phenomena of a highly developed society; not to a highly complete, but to a very primitive organism. Without this it would be impossible to find analogies between all the organic phenomena and all social ones. So, if it is true that there is a correlation between the details of an organic life and those of a social unit, it is equally true to say that this correlation exists only so far as the whole is under consideration.

It cannot be said that the most advanced forms of society correspond to the most advanced forms of organic life or that the least perfect forms of the latter correspond to the most rudimentary forms of the former. Quite often, on the contrary, the most advanced forms of social life resemble much more the rudimentary than they do the advanced forms of organic life. If only this general correlation exists, doubt rises immediately, and we ask if it is quite certain that social life presents us an organism, if it is not rather a combination of phenomena in some respects like those of organic life.

Another defect in this theory of the equivalence of society and organism is its vagueness and arbitrariness. A comparison of Spencer's and Lilienfeld's doctrines from this point of view is particularly interesting. According to Spencer the individuals who form a society may, according to their social position, be compared to different cells of the organism, the working classes corresponding to the digestive organs, the ruling classes, to nerves, etc.

Lilienfeld, on the contrary, believes that the men can be compared only to the nerve cells. The nervous system of the social organism would, according to him, include not only the governing organs of society, as Spencer thought, but quite all the persons composing the society. The nervous system of a social group would be its entire population. The other elements are not made up of men. The distributive system is formed, for example, by the network of the means of communication.

The difference between Spencer's theories and those of Lilienfeld, I think, is a very important one. Both, however, establish, though in different ways, with equal success a parallel even in the lowest details between society and the living organism.

The same uncertainty may be found in the conclusions reached by the organic theories. Most of the partisans of this theory conclude, indeed, that the state's field of action ought necessarily to be extended and the individual's restricted; that the individual ought to be subjected to society. Thus Schäffle in his organic doctrines ends with the conclusions of academic socialism. Spencer, resting, too, upon his doctrine that the state is nothing else than an organism, reaches the precisely opposite conclusion, the individualistic doctrines of free competition, and an extreme limitation of the state's social action.

The third defect of this organic conception of society is that it does not answer to the general object sought in scientific hypotheses. Every such hypothesis has for its end the facilitating and advancing the application of the deductive method to some branch of science. But if there is no exact correlation of the forms of organic life with social ones, and if their comparison leaves the field open to arbitrary and contradictory conclusions, then the organic theory evidently cannot serve as a solid basis for scientific deductions.

Up to the present time, in fact, the organic doctrine has led to no distinct conclusion; has not to its credit a single previously unknown principle. It has given to matter which already existed only a novel form; has only furnished a new system of exposition, a fresh rubric, a changed terminology. It has brought nothing new into the matter. It is, therefore, at least useless. We might even affirm with proofs to support us, that it has been harmful. All these comparisons of the social state and organic life inflame the mind, open up a vast horizon to the imagination and appear very attractive; but they are of a nature to turn the student away from less easy and agreeable but more fruitful labor, the gathering up of new materials for the explanation of the different peculiarities presented by social phenomena.

Such are the defects of the organic theory as a theory. Let us look at some of its details. Spencer at the beginning of his argument tries to prove the impossibility of seeing in society only a mechanical aggregate. This seems for him to follow from society's being made up of living parts; but that which is made up of separately living parts cannot form a single living whole.

Then examining the question as to whether society ought to be considered as a peculiar aggregate distinct equally from mechanical and from organic ones, Spencer answers in the negative and finds that in all their essential properties organic and social aggregates present complete resemblances. The characteristic peculiarities of a living organism are, according to Spencer, its growth, differentiation of its structure, the specialization of functions, its multiplication by birth and its mortality. He affirms that social life presents also such peculiarities. The development of society is always accompanied by its extension which constitutes its growth. The phenomena of growth in the social order arise under forms analogous to those of growth in the organic world; by the interior multiplication of cells within the human society which is already an aggregate, and by the annexation of new cells from without, as in states by conquest and annexation of new provinces.

The development of society is expressed, moreover, not merely by its extension, but also by the transition from a condition in which its composition and structure are uniform towards one where the same elements become more varied, by the formation of castes, of different social classes, by the creation of social establishments and a constantly increasing specialization in each one's functions.

Spencer shows that there is still at this point of view a resemblance not only in the whole, but even in the different forms of the differentiation and specialization. So the gradual advance of differentiation of governing bodies in a state corresponds in all points to the differentiation of the nervous system.

Among the lower animals there is but one system, in higher ones, two: the nervous system that governs external connections of the organism, and the sympathetic which controls the internal functions. In the same way in primitive states there is only one system. In the beginning the military and civil administrations are compounded together; but little by little, by the incessant development of society, they are separated into two distinct systems.

The phenomena of multiplication among inferior beings, segmentation and budding, are compared by Spencer to phenomena which rise when a state is divided up into independent ones or when colonies detach themselves from it. According to Spencer the death of a society might be difficult to establish in such a way. The natural death of societies, however, is only hard to exhibit because the international order is so ill assured that the dominant states crush the weaker ones before it happens.

But when durable and solid peace shall be established in the international relations of states, their artificial death will disappear and we shall have only the natural death of societies. So, according to Spencer, it is with the society absolutely as with the organism; it grows, multiplies, is differentiated, specialized and dies.

But alongside these resemblances are there not also distinguishing differences? Spencer says not. It is objected most frequently that society is marked by the characteristic that there is no material bond between the human particles that make it up to consolidate its different social elements into a single whole; it has not continuity.

This is only an apparent difference, says Spencer. Just as in the animal the parts which compose it are each of a different degree of vitality, so in the composition of society men are not alone in forming it. Territory plays an important part, and by its intermediation forms a material bond between individuals.

The only difference which Spencer recognizes between society and the organism is that in the latter the whole is the sole end in view, while each part is only a means, whereas in society the contrary is true. The individuals constitute the end in the case of society, and the latter is only a means for realizing human purposes.

Such in outline is Spencer's theory. Does it advance really the proof of the organic nature of society? As a matter of fact if we do find the resemblances which he shows, there are established alongside of them some essential differences. The two forms of growth observed in living organisms ought to be compared, says Spencer, to those revealed in the developments of social groupings. Society grows, also, either by annexing new social groups come from without, or by the multiplication of its own numbers. But growth by annexing new groups from without is something wholly impossible for the organism; or at least such growth is possible only for organisms presenting the very lowest degree of differentiation in their structure. Organisms having a complex and developed structure cannot grow by this process.

In social life, on the contrary, we meet with this form of growth in the most complex social organizations. The history of human societies, also, shows us numerous examples of societies annexing some organ having a highly special function which it kept after such annexation, after entering into a new social aggregate. The history of modern states is full of examples of the annexation of agricultural districts, of industrial centres, of commercial parts, fortresses, etc., according to Spencer distinct organs and social differentiations of the social body. The same phenomenon appears in the emigrations of individuals from one country to another where they continue to follow their profession. An analogous fact appears when a member of a foreign dynasty becomes sovereign of a state; when artists, professors, capitalists and others migrate into another country.

Spencer's view of the rôle played by emigrations of peoples is that it is an insignificant fact without weight. It is sufficient to recall the coming of the negroes into America, and in our day the beginning of Chinese immigration into the same country. The whole history of America gives the lie direct to Spencer's theory.

The specialization of function though equally present in social life presents some distinct differences from that found in living organisms. Specialization in society is necessarily a mark of a certain degree of development. The army, for instance, once consisting of all the males in the society, specializes with time into permanent military organizations, mercenary or otherwise, forming a distinct social element.

But, while in the organism the succession of such steps

of specialization follows in all its phases the same invariable advance, it is quite otherwise in social life. In society the specialization is not without limits; when it reaches a certain degree, an inverse development commences. So in the universal military service which has been introduced into almost all the modern states, the barrier which separates the army from the rest of society is reduced, and there is something of a return to the ancient times when the whole people and not a fraction of them make up the army.

This consideration leads us naturally to another essential difference. In the organism each cell participates in a sole rigorously determined function. The same cell cannot be by turns a bone and a nerve cell. In society, on the other hand, we find this diversity in the functions of a single individual. The same person may be successively a laborer on the soil, a corporation's secretary, member of a jury, or of a city council, of a legislative assembly or even president of the republic; and this accumulation of functions in themselves very different, does not diminish but, on the contrary, augments with the development of society. The same thing might be said as to the phenomena of multiplication.

The separation of parts in a state presents in reality only a superficial and wholly exterior resemblance to the multiplication of organisms. In both cases there is an element which separates out and continues an independent existence. But in the organic life the multiplication of organisms operates to maintain the existence of the species. The individual is of the same type as his progenitor, and with them he forms a single species. Multiplication is above all the production of like beings.

In social life, on the contrary, the separation of parts gives results quite different. If a province separates from the state, that separation is the consequence of a distinction, of some peculiarity which provokes the rupture of the two political groups. Ordinarily in such cases there is a national, religious, or political antagonism. The part which cleaves from the other presents naturally in its new independent organization these essential differences.

The examples of North America and of the Balkan Principalities confirm what has just been said,—every separate state has a very distinct individuality. For this reason the notion of species is not applicable to states.

With the subject of multiplication is closely bound up that of the death of societies. Death, limiting the existence of the individual, is an indispensable condition for the progress of the species. The law of death for the individual is thus counterbalanced by the absence of any fixed limits for the duration of the species. The species, it is true, may disappear from the earth, but it cannot be said to be mortal in the same sense as is the individual. The individual is foredoomed to die, not merely when he finds himself in unfavorable conditions, but even when he is best situated to live. Death comes naturally with old age. This is why we meet with natural death wherever we are dealing with individuals and not with species. These observations indicate clearly enough why society regarded as a unity does not really either multiply or suffer natural death.

Spencer's theory, according to which the absence of natural death among societies is only a passing phenomenon, caused by the insufficient development of international law, is a gross sophism. If the savage freely attributes death or accidents to some breach of religious duty, this is naturally explained by the peculiar conception he forms through his superstitions of the world. The conception is of a purely subjective order. Ferocious beasts have instincts still fiercer than those of primitive man, but cases of natural death are not unknown among them, as is well ascertained. Spencer's explanation of the phenomena of natural death is insufficient, and it is impossible to conclude with him that its absence in social life is unimportant. On the contrary, if we take into consideration the connection just indicated between the individual's death and the life of the species, this trait as distinguishing society from the organism finds an altogether natural explanation.

We cannot fully assent, either, to Spencer's attempt to minimize the other differences between the organism and society, growing out of the absence which he admits of a material union between the latter's members, the discontinuity in every society of the whole and of its several parts. Spencer seeks to show that this lack of continuity, this absence of material union between the parts is only apparent. In this effort he brings in the territory, the goods, the domestic animals as benumbed members of the social organism less alive than the other parts, like an animal's bones, hair or skin. But these latter are integral parts of the organism resulting from its own natural activity and essentially different from foreign bodies attached to it.

Such a theory does not at all explain the existence, for instance, of the church, whose establishments are often wholly separated into the remote parts of distant countries. Groupings having a territorial basis, moreover, may see their territorial continuity broken by an intervening foreign province or may consist of colonies wholly separate from the parent country.

As regards the relations of the whole to its parts in the society and the organism, Spencer asks only the question, "Which is the end and which the means used to reach it?" This question seems wholly idle. Every conscious being regards itself as the end, and all else as only a means. The man regards as a means both cells of which he is made up and the society into which he enters as an integral element. Such a conception of purpose is entirely subjective, and if the cells could comprehend and think, they would infallibly consider themselves as the end, and the rest as only a means to their existence. A scientific conclusion resting upon such an entirely subjective premise cannot be admitted.

If we set aside all teleological notions, we can adopt a quite different method for proposing and determining the question as to the relations of parts to the whole in society. Whether we consider the man as the end and society as the means, or inversely, we cannot fail to observe the essential difference between man's relation to society and the cell's relation to its organism. Man in society enjoys a far greater independence than does the cell in the organism. The cell is always simply and exclusively an attribute of a single organism. It has no power to participate at the same time in the life of several organisms. It cannot temporarily quit its organism for another. In social life, on the contrary, participation by foreigners in local social functions is a very frequent occurrence. It is not only possible, but becomes increasingly frequent and necessary with social evolution.

Man can be simultaneously a member of several societies whose characteristics and functions differ. Subjects of the Russian state, for example, may be of Germanic nationality and belong at the same time to the Catholic Church. In such a situation it is not the weak, isolated individual who is set before the political society's influence, but, on the contrary, the individual supported and strengthened by other societies.

A still more important point is that each individual is not the product exclusively of one given grouping, but of the united influence of several social combinations.

As the individuals belong at the same time to several of these groupings, there arises a diversity, an extreme multiplicity among the populations of modern states; there even sometimes results discord, and the struggle of the individual against his social environment.

Section 37. *Of the Nature of Society*

Having thus followed step by step Spencer's parallel between the organism and society, we have found at the side of indubitable resemblances, some essential differences at the points indicated. Let us try to group these differences and see the connection between them.

In studying sciences relating to the inorganic world, we see that all conceptions are invariably based upon existing facts; all phenomena are determined by present conditions.

To study the chemical properties of any substance or the laws of its motion there is no need of going back to the origin of the substance or of its motion, and of knowing in what way the body was formed or by what shock its motion imparted. We can study the motion in absolute ignorance of its source. In the inorganic world, then, everything can be determined by the study of actual facts.

In mechanics, in physics, in chemistry, the doctrine of development, the history, the embryology, if we may so call it, of the science, does not exist. A mechanical aggregate, a pile of stones, for example, can exist indefinitely if its equilibrium is not disturbed. Whenever it is, the aggregate will fall in pieces, for it cannot adapt itself to varying external conditions.

The existence of a mechanical aggregate is conditioned by the present situation. The past has given it no energy to provide for a new one. For this reason it can experience no natural death. A pile of stones may last eternally, or fall quickly to pieces if external conditions alter. The past, in a word, has no influence over its fate.

If we look now at the phenomena of organic life, we

observe something entirely different; the study of isolated phenomena without examining their successive development is impossible. If we take out of the sciences of organic life the study of the genesis of phenomena, there will remain only the nomenclature. To study living beings it is necessary to learn the history of their formation; it is necessary to indicate their place in the scale of all living beings and to show even its intra-uterine history. The study of the individual's origin is in the natural sciences an indispensable thing. A zoölogist who should make no embryological investigations could not explain in a truly scientific manner any phenomenon of organic life.

So, too, the study of the conditions of the existence of mechanical aggregates and that of organic bodies presents some important differences between the two groups of phenomena. A mass of stones will fall apart at any time, as has been said, if its conditions of equilibrium are disturbed; while every animal possesses vitality from its birth and thereby can adapt itself to a certain amount of variation in external conditions. The being offers a certain amount of resistance to unfavorable conditions. Spencer defines life as the capacity to adapt oneself to external conditions. This means that every animal can adapt itself to conditions because its existence is to that extent determined by its past, by the vital force received at birth. The organism can also in some degree change and adapt external conditions. So, the inorganic world is determined by present conditions, the organic one by both the present and the past.

The laws of heredity show that upon the past of all mankind and perhaps upon that of the whole organic world, depends to a certain degree the character and life of each individual. Each fœtus receives a certain degree of energy which is employed afterwards for the adaptation of the individual to the external conditions of his life. If those conditions are unfavorable, the expenditure of energy is greater. If they are favorable, it is expended more slowly; but, however favorable the conditions, there will come a time when it will be all gone. Individuals do not normally perish by chance, but because they have used up their stock of energy in the struggle with the external conditions of life.

If now we pass from the study of organic and inorganic phenomena to that of social ones, we should ask first if these latter are determined by the present or the past, or by both, or by some new element. Doubtless, the general laws which govern the organic and the inorganic world apply equally to the phenomena of social life. The present plays a great rôle in all societies. Such, for example, is the situation in which a state finds itself by reason of international conditions. To take, for example, Belgium and Switzerland, their existence is before all else the result of the present conditions of international life and of their geographic situation, which is such that no neighboring state can afford to assent to the taking of any part of their territory by any other state.

By the side always of the present, the past meanwhile has always in social affairs an important part. Each generation has a certain influence upon the development of future generations' social life; and, moreover, our inheritance from our fathers is of overwhelming importance.

The life and organization of a society yield the more to the influence of the past, the richer that past is in historic events, and thus a society actually weak may nevertheless subsist a long while merely from the prestige of a glorious past. Take, for example, the Roman empire. It continued a long time after contemporary circumstances had wrought its decadence. Its past was so rich that the barbarians, themselves, who had overthrown its political power, bowed before its civilization.

By the side of the historic life which thus helps determine social life, and with its present conditions favorable or otherwise, there is, besides, a third very important element, which constitutes the characteristic trait of social phenomena; it is that man endowed with memory and consciousness passes easily in thought from the past into the future. Memory and desire are two sides of the same phenomenon. What man by his experience has gathered and accumulated in the past, he transfers under one form or another into the future. He is capable, in a word, of forming a conception of the future, an ideal.

The existence of an ideal, or on the other hand, its absence, are the most important points in the social development. We have seen that the animal after expending all its energy dies; society, on the other hand, does not perish, however unfavorable its conditions, provided its ideal is strongly enough traced. There may come, it is true, circumstances such that the creation and maintenance of any such ideal becomes impossible and the death of the society results inevitably, but this is a very rare case.

Society, therefore, is controlled by these three distinct elements:

1st. The present conditions under which it acts.

2d. Its past.

3d. The ideal drawn from that past.

The effect upon social phenomena not merely of past and present facts, but also of conceptions as to the future on the part of the society's numbers, has produced necessarily an extreme complexity and independence in social phenomena. This complexity and independence has still another explanation.

According to the true saying of Claude Bernard, the complexity of organic life depends also upon the fact that besides its external environment each organism has, so to say, an internal environment consisting in its own liquid element. Thanks to this interior environment, the organism can keep a high temperature and a moist condition amid cold and dry surroundings. To this is due the relative independence of the organism from its surroundings at any particular moment of its life. By this means is established its relation to the past; since this internal environment is a product of past activity.

If we apply this comparison to what takes place in the social order, we may say that society has a triple environment: first, an external one, formed at any given moment by its existing physical and geographic conditions and those of the other societies then existing; second, an interior environment, composed of the customs and institutions bequeathed by the past; and, finally, a special ideal intellectual environment made up of conceptions born in the heads of the individual members of the society which form a perspective of the future.

This triple connection of social phenomena with present, past and future time or, in other words, with the external, physical, and the interior and intellectual environment, causes all the differences we are compelled to recognize between society and the organism.

In affirming that society is affected by a special ideal and intellectual environment, we recognize that the bond connecting the different members of society has a moral, psychical character, and explain thus the absence of any physical connection in human societies. Psychical phenomena, in fact, are distinguished before all from material ones in that they do not rest upon any local base; the spiritual connection between the members of the same society does not require physical contact.

In the same way, we explain the possibility of a man's belonging to different societies at the same time, and of his belonging to different organs of the same society at the same time. Ideas, differing in that respect from matter, are not impenetrable to each other. The possibility of augmenting a society by annexation is explained by the same means. Moreover, the dependence of social phenomena upon ideas of the future explains why societies know no natural death.

In organic life vital energy necessarily exhausts itself with time, and the more rapidly the more active the life. In society, on the contrary, although there is an equal expenditure of energy, there is no exhaustion because the expenditure is replaced by new force drawn in by the ideal which guides and inspires the whole society. Ancient customs disappear, old institutions become useless, but this does not bring about the death of the society.

If this society still keeps its capacity for psychical creation, if it continues able to fashion a new ideal, the old and feeble customs will be replaced by new legislation, new beliefs will arise and society draw from them a new source of life. So there is no limit to the social life. Societies doubtless can and have perished, but differing in this respect from mechanical aggregates, they know no natural death, and this same absence of death as we have seen, explains the absence of reproduction and multiplication, the one depending upon the other.

The organic notion of society, since it does not serve to explain all social phenomena, must give place to the psychical conception of it, which recognizes the ideal that guides all human society as a factor distinct from the social aggregates, and which places the phenomena of social life side by side with these of the organic and inorganic world as an independent group, and one wholly apart from the phenomena of the world.[1]

[1] In the second edition of his book, Schäffle reaches the same conclusion. Die menschliche Gesellschaft ist eine rein geistliche (psychiche) bewirkte durch ideenzeichen und durch Kunsthandlungen vollzogene untheilbare Lebensgemeinschaft organischer Individuen. "Bau und Leben," I, p. 1.

In setting aside the organic theory, however, we cannot fail to recognize the services which it has rendered to sociology. If the mechanical conception of society has had a great historical rôle, we must recognize the same fact as to the organic conception.

The mechanical theory denied history and its influence over social phenomena. The organic theory, on the contrary, has always recognized the existence of a connection among social phenomena and affirmed the influence of the past in producing the facts of the present. The organic theory, too, has given a new impulse to the scientific explanation of social phenomena. But that theory stops half way. How strange it appears on Spencer's part, the representative of evolutionism, that he found it necessary to support himself upon the facts of the past, but did not at all observe, or did not regard the future, and never believed in the important part in the development of society played by this conception of the future.

The evolutionist theory ought not to stop with the study of actual facts, unless man's present conception of the future be included among them. It ought not to draw its conditions of individual and social development from the present; it ought to establish the existence of a continuous progress. Therefore, Spencer ought not to have limited himself to the study of the past. He ought to have shown us how society is controlled in its development by the conception of the future.

We ourselves insist upon numerous resemblances between the organism and society, but we believe that society is an organism presenting important peculiarities arising out of its power of forming an ideal of the future. Our explanation answers completely the most varied hypotheses.

A hypothesis, in truth, to be established, requires that the causes to which one or another group of phenomena is traced be true causes; that is to say, that they be truly a force producing the phenomena of the group, that their existence be demonstrated and verified.

The verification of a hypothesis consists in the fact that the results drawn from it by way of deduction must conform to actual phenomena. So, if the capacity to form an ideal is a characteristic sign of all social phenomena, we must conclude that this capacity is in direct proportion with the development of social life. The reality is there to prove for us how far such an assertion is well founded.

If we compare in fact a civilized society, one in which the association is for each of its members the highest of needs, with an embryo people living still in the savage state, we observe a very great difference, and convince ourselves of the comparative ease with which the savage gives up all such connection. The intelligence of the savage peoples is, too, far inferior to that of the civilized. The weaker social bonds are among people, the weaker their intellectual development and the greater their carelessness of the future.

The savage man, as has been often enough shown, lives wholly for the present moment without concern as to the future; he accumulates neither goods nor knowledge by way of providing for it.

A second conclusion to draw from the theory which we indicate is that if the notion of the future, the capacity to create an ideal, is proportional to the development of social life, the conditions necessary for the development of the psychic faculty, creatress of the ideal, ought at the same time to serve for the development of social life. This is what in fact happens. The conditions for the development of the psychic life of the individual, and those of the development of social life, are identical.

If in the organism the independence of the distinct cells

is in inverse proportion to the development of the organism as an entirety, we cannot establish on the other hand in the social life that the independence of the members of the same society diminishes as the development of the society augments. Quite the contrary, individual independence is one of the prime conditions of social development. Where the development of individual thought is stifled, the growth of the social ideal is impossible; society retrogrades, finds its development paralyzed, its internal as well as external relations less active. If such a state persists, the very existence of society may be put in peril.

If the conditions of psychic and those of social development are identical, we ought to understand why a human group in which the conception of the future plays an important rôle is very strongly united and capable of maintaining itself against unfavorable external conditions.

The whole national life of the Jews, for example, could be controlled by a conception of the future, by the expectation of the Messiah, despite all the unfavorable conditions of their existence. Meanwhile, the national bond which unites this scattered people is such as the other nations may well envy.

If the social relations are determined by the degree of the development of the ideal formed by individuals, it must be admitted that in actual social life the conditions of existence can be modified according to the ideal traced by the members of the same society, and false notions may have a great influence upon the social development. For example, notwithstanding the unquestionable error of its dogmas, the era when the Mahometan world was most prosperous was precisely the time when its erroneous ideas were most widespread.

No possible limit can be assigned to the social ideal, and therefore no possible limit can be assigned to social growth and there is no model type which can be set up beyond which it is impossible to go.

Such limits, such model types, on the contrary, exist in the organic world. Living beings do not surpass them, and having reached them exist for no further end except multiplication and the maintenance of the species. In society, too, we observe one entirely different phenomenon. A change of ideas can bring about a complete change in social life.

The ideal of themselves which men may form is so immense that it may embrace all the groupings formed by similarity of occupation, by habitation, nationality, etc. So we must reject for society that doctrine of the historical school which admits for society as for the organism a type determined *a priori* from which insignificant deviations are scarcely possible.

According to this doctrine, there exists in each people a quite settled natural genius and some peculiarities and functions equally settled and not subject to alteration in the course of historic evolution. This doctrine appeared in the political field as a protest against the tendencies towards revolution at the end of the XVIII century, and against the attempts made to bring into our country (Russia) the political institutions of England.

According to the historical school the political organization of England is good for England alone, for it corresponds to a national genius very peculiar. France, Germany, and the other countries ought, on the contrary, to develop themselves by other means more conformed to their national genius. Just as a bird cannot become a mammifer, and reciprocally, so no state can change its institutions, its organization which is conformed to the national spirit. This doctrine of the historical school is false, since we have already seen that a change produced in the social ideal may bring about a change in the whole social development.

The influence of one people upon the life of another is a proof of this. The ideal is a force supporting the social life and this ideal may be the result not merely of our own special experience, but also of the experience of neighboring peoples.

By the study of another people's organization, of its political development, the members of a political society can form a political ideal like to that of such people. In this way the relations between peoples may bring in a new element which may determine social relations.

Section 38. *Man's Psychical Nature*

TROITZKY. Contemporary German Psychology, 1867.
RIBOT. La psychologie anglaise contemporaine, 1875.
SPENCER, H. Principles of Psychology, 1876.

If we explain the peculiarities of social life by the psychical character of the bond which combines men into society, the understanding of man's psychical nature and of the conditions of his moral development becomes for us of the highest importance.

We cannot, of course, enter here into a detailed analysis of psychological theories. Such a study would carry us too far. It is necessary, in order to explain the nature of society and the connection between the individual and society, to outline some ideas derived from contemporary psychology.

Psychology, up to very recent times, was divided between two extreme tendencies, both going wrong through their exclusiveness,—intuitionism and perceptualism. The one admits the existence in us of ideas born with us. For those holding to this side, the individual is born with a lot of ready-made ideas antedating all personal experience. These ideas were held to be the same in all individuals.

The others, on the contrary, considered man as a being at birth absolutely destitute of any semblance of an idea, a mere *tabula rasa* which the experience of life was to garnish by filling the void with a more or less rich mass of contents.

According to this second theory each individual is a being wholly different from all others. He owes everything to his personal experience, and all that he is comes to him from without. From this point of view the man, consequently, depends upon external influences; incapable of autonomous activity, he was a skillfully constructed automaton.

In spite of the radical differences and the different starting point of the two theories they have common defects. First of all, both are equally remote from the whole idea of psychic evolution and so are both equally incapable of furnishing an explanation of the relative independence of the individual and of the principle of his relatively autonomous activity.

The idea of psychical development in the individual is not very old. For a long time there has been recognized the transmission from generation to generation of a certain amount of knowledge, fruit of the preceding generation's experience. This was as far as it went. Only science was regarded as transmissible. The sentiments and the will were not. In any case the mind was deemed unchangeable, and as identical in all classes of humanity. To the partisans of intuitionism the man at all stages of his life was the same. There was no way of modifying his fund of innate ideas.

Under the opposite theory, also, the man had in him something unchangeable and identical in all individuals, the *tabula rasa*. The psychic development was limited, then, to that of the individual. One generation had no influence upon another.

This negation of all psychic transmission from one generation to another prevents either theory from furnishing any explanation of the relative independence of the *milieu* in which he lives on the part of each individual. For the sensationist, the man was a machine reacting in an automatic way against external influences. If you should take away all these influences you would deprive him of his principle of action. Of himself, he has no active capacity.

The partisans of the intuitive theory recognize clearly enough in man a certain activity of his own, but they explain this activity only by isolating the man from the *ensemble* of connected phenomena united together by a natural bond, and by attributing to him a free will, entirely independent of all determinate law.

Modern psychology, which has especially developed itself in England, rejects alike both theories as we have set them forth. It does not admit the existence of innate ideas, at least not in the absolute sense in which the intuitionists assert them. Neither does it believe like the sensationists that our whole psychic life results only from our personal experience and is the product of external facts.

Modern psychology holds to the mean between these two conceptions. It recognizes that the whole psychic life can be explained by the entire experience, external and internal, by the individual's personal experience, and by that of all humanity,—the collective experience. The moral life is no longer recognized as simply the result of external influences, of the individual's environment. What the man gets from the external world, is completed and modified in him by the concepts of the inward experience. So, too, our ideas which are by connection with the entire development of mankind derived from universal experience, are as regards particular individuals innate ideas, bequeathed by the preceding generation. Such a theory has not the faults indicated in the preceding theories.

Under this theory man is no longer an automaton guided solely by external phenomena. The movements of his soul may be due to conceptions furnished to him by his own inner experience. Physiological or even pathological facts, special dispositions of our own organisms, may produce in us, independently of any external experience, some special activity of the mind. We must add to these those actions produced by sentiments, tendencies and tastes bequeathed to us by our ancestors, and we can easily explain the relative independence of the individual as regards his external environment. There will be no need to interpose the opposition between human actions and physical phenomena, no need to appeal to any special freedom of the human will.

Modern psychological theory rejects, also, the ancient opinion which denied the psychic influence of one generation over another. If our ideas and sentiments are a product of the entire secular experience of humanity, individuals and generations ought to be connected not only in space but also in time.

The psychic life of each generation is only a link connecting former generations with those to come. The unbroken bond of psychic development through succeeding generations has its source in psychic heredity, and this theory in fact gives to the laws of heredity an important place. They have great importance in all social sciences because they establish a connection between each individual and all mankind, past and future, or at least connection with some particular nation.

All aptitudes and tendencies, physical and psychical, are, thanks to the laws of heredity, not a product of individual life but of man's collective life. The modern psychological theory recognizes, then, a connected transmissibility in the psychic development of generations and sees in the individual in a pre-eminent degree a product of historic and social life. The psychical character of this social bond which combines men into communities does not prevent the hereditary social influence from having a regular and continuous advance. Human ideas, although they are a distinct factor in social life, are themselves the result of a regular successive development; they develop along with the social life itself.

An objection has been made to this last idea,—that our wills are not subject to any definite law, not even that of causation. This opinion has its importance. It has played so great a part in the history of philosophic theories and has exercised so great an influence that an attentive examination of the doctrine of free will is necessary.

Section 39. *The Freedom of the Will*

SCHOPENHAUER. Ueber die Freiheit des menschlichen Willens (in Die Beide Grund-Probleme der Ethik). 2d ed., 1860.

FOUILLÉE. La liberté et de déterminisme.

BINDING. Die Normen und ihre Uebertretung. Vol. II, Sec. 32.

HERTZ. Das Unrecht, 1880. Sec. II.

It is necessary in order to get an accurate solution, to state the problem clearly. The freedom of the will is set in opposition to the idea of conformity to law. But what do we mean by "law"? We have examined already what is meant in science by the word. Law, there, is not some one's order which is the producing cause of certain phenomena; it is merely that uniformity of phenomena which men agree in observing.

In fixing this definition of scientific law we avoid all confusion. If we recognize in law a force causing phenomena, and the will as a force acting by the side of law, we shall involve ourselves in the question as to whether or not the will can also be the cause of phenomena.

The will can be the cause of phenomena only in a case when the phenomena are not subject to any given law, if we assume that the law is the cause of phenomena. With such a notion of law, to say the will can be the cause of phenomena is to say that it is free, because it is to say that as *vera causa* it is not controlled by others. But to accept such a definition of law would of course be inconsistent with the definition of a scientific law just given.

If law is not regarded as a cause of phenomena, but merely as a formula for an observed uniformity in their recurrence, to see in the will the determining cause of an act, is not, necessarily, to admit a separation between the spheres of application of law and those of the will. If we admit that law, scientifically, is only a formula expressing the uniform march of phenomena, the question as to the freedom of the will assumes a very different form.

Experience, drawn from external facts, does not show us any which can be considered as absolute principles of phenomena which are to follow. External facts show us a continual succession of causes and effects and each phenomenon, while the cause of following ones, is the effect of those which precede. Absolute principles which should make certain phenomena result from others without themselves being the cause of still others in the future can have, then, no existence. Every observed phenomenon must be considered, then, as merely a link in the uninterrupted chain of causes and effects. All phenomena are uniform in this sense, that each is a cause of future phenomena and a result of preceding ones. This property of phenomena is the law or principle of causality.

That this law is an actual one of all phenomena of the external world admits of no doubt. The question of the freedom of the will reduces itself to ascertaining if our internal experience, differing from external experience, does not give us a different principle from the one just stated. Does our internal experience testify of desires and acts within us which are themselves the cause of phenomena without being at the same time themselves the effect of preceding ones?

If the acts of our wills have no cause, are themselves absolute principles, creators of a series of independent phenomena, then we must say that our wills are not subject to the law of causality, and while themselves the cause of phenomena, they are themselves without cause; that is, they are free. If, on the other hand, the acts of our wills are the result of preceding impressions, or desires, or of character, then the will is not free. It is subject, also, like external facts, to the principle of causality.

There is here no question as to whether or not the will serves as a cause of phenomena, but merely of knowing whether or not it has, itself, a cause. Most authors have unluckily mixed these two questions which have nothing in common. Nobody even among the warmest defenders of the will's freedom would recognize any such freedom in an idiot, but undoubtedly the will of an idiot can also be the cause of phenomena.

In stating the question thus clearly we have wished to avoid the two most frequent errors on this subject,—the recognizing, first, that fatalism is equivalent to a negation of the will's freedom; and second, that a formula can be found which will serve to reconcile freedom of the will and the principle of causality.

Fatalism answers only the question whether or not the will is, itself, a cause of phenomena. It replies no, without troubling itself to ascertain whether or not the will has itself a cause. Fatalism admitted that every phenomenon is determined by a supreme will; that fate rests over all men; that every event must take place logically, unavoidably and independently of men's wills or acts. However great men's efforts to avoid the accomplishment of any result, fatal necessity none the less brings it about because of predestination. Death supervenes, if fate has so ordered, despite all man's efforts. It even comes more late only if the hour has not yet struck.

The whole fatalistic doctrine, consequently, comes back to this, that neither external events nor human actions depend upon the will, and generally that phenomena take place not by reason of any interdependence between them, but from some external force. Man does not control external events and cannot modify them, whatever he may do with that in view.

This theory reorganized, then, the existence of some force outside of the uninterrupted chain of phenomena. It denies the bond of causality between those phenomena and introduces the idea of a perpetual miracle. This fatalistic conception, however, denies not the will's freedom, but merely the existence of any law of causality. The fatalist's position is sometimes admitted, strange as it may appear, by those partisans of the universal sway of the law of causality who rely in their arguments upon statistics. These last show us that certain spontaneous human actions in given social conditions are invariably renewed from year to year always in the same identical way. The annual figures for assassinations, marriages, suicides, etc., are repeated again and again, often more uniformly than the facts of birth and death. This proves, say the fatalists, that men's spontaneous acts are subject to scientific law as clearly as their involuntary ones.

A false notion of scientific law and an erroneous conception of the question as to the freedom of the will unite to produce this false affirmation that statistics prove the existence of laws requiring annually a given number of crimes, marriages, etc. Statistics do not in any manner justify such deductions.

If the uniformity in human actions constitutes the law, that law is not the cause of the phenomena. It cannot be said that there is an annual fixed figure for suicides because there is a statistical law which says so. If there is such an observed uniformity, it is because the conditions leading to suicide remain from year to year almost the same. Change these conditions, and at once a corresponding change occurs in the figures for suicides. The figures do not prove that any statistical law is the cause of suicides. They merely indicate uniformity in the causes on which suicides depend, and that they remain uniform from year to year. If the suicide depended upon an absolutely free will, no such uniformity could appear. It is necessary to have always in mind this idea that the uniformity is the product of a combination, a series of forces, which engender these social phenomena.

It cannot be admitted, as true, that the laws of statistics express orders of a certain kind, not depending upon men, which force to the contracting of marriages and the perpetrating of crimes or suicides; that the modifications which control the facts of statistics are the consequences of the resistance of the free will of the individual to laws leading to these phenomena. The laws of statistics cannot be so personified. They are not forces engaged in a struggle with the human will.

The explanation above given of the essential distinction between fatalism and the free will subjected to the general law of causation goes far to permit the easy solution of the entire question as we have stated it. If, in fact, in denying altogether the existence of any freedom of the will from the law of causation we are not thereby forced to accept the doctrine of fatalism, we have no longer the principal motive for clinging to the doctrine of the will's freedom. So that we do not accept the fatalist doctrine, there follow no terrible consequences, and the question can be put on a wholly scientific plane.

Another widely spread error, based like the preceding one upon false logic, consists in admitting the existence of a half-free will. It is again because of confounding the fatalist doctrine with the negation of the free will that such a mixed solution results.

The theory is manifestly false. It is clearly impossible that the will should be by turns free and not free. But the partisans of the theory do not state it in such a clear form. They present it under a much more complex one and one requiring an attentive analysis. I will examine here three very ingenious attempts to gain admittance for such a theory.

The first is Fouillée's. He seeks to prove that even if we do not accept as a starting point the existence of the will's freedom, yet by a logical reasoning a certain degree of freedom of the will can be shown to exist. Let us admit, says he, that our wills are not free, that all our actions are necessarily determined by our sentiments and ideas. If this is so, nevertheless we must admit that the idea of liberty of the will, like every other, may serve as a stimulant for our voluntary energy. We can, in fact, see that the men who are convinced of the freedom of their own wills act in just about the same way as if they were really free. The stronger this conviction is in a man and the more accustomed he is to guiding himself in accordance with it in all his acts, the more nearly his conduct approximates to that of a man whose will should actually be free. Therefore, though by no means free, the man can by controlling his acts in accordance with this idea of liberty act nevertheless as a free man and approximate more and more to the ideal of liberty. He cannot completely reach this ideal, but he can tend to come always nearer and nearer to it.

It is not doubtful that the man in guiding himself in accordance with this false notion of the freedom of his will can in many cases act as if he were really free. Under the necessary conditions the idea of liberty may become the dominating motive of all his activity. In seeking to show himself and prove to others that he has a free will, the man may stifle the more natural appeals to his nature, but he has constrained himself in vain. Because he has been carried away by this idea of liberty, he has become no freer on that account. He has only become a blind and miserable slave of an idea, a passion. Such a man is like a maniac who imagines himself King of Spain. To affirm, as Fouillée has done, that the belief in his own freedom makes the man free, is as if one were to say that the maniac's delusion can really create him King of Spain.

Reid's theory is more profound. According to him, it is impossible to explain all the phenomena of the will under the principle of causation. If the will did not have at least some portion of freedom, it would be impossible for it to reach a conclusion when in the presence of two equal motives. For example, if we found before us when thirsty two glasses of water precisely alike in all respects, and if there was no freedom of choice, we would have precisely an equal desire for each and would undergo the fate of the ass in the legend, which died between two bundles of hay. We never reach such a situation, however, but always find ourselves able to make a choice even between two absolutely identical objects.

In this possibility of choosing despite the perfect equality of the things presented to our desires our freedom consists. When the motives support each other we cannot resist them, but if they are equal we can choose one or the other.

In this manner Reid outlines the frames within which our freedom can act. The cases in which our opposing inclinations are absolutely equal are rare enough so that a liberty, so restrained, would have little practical value. In most cases the man would not act freely. Reid's doctrine, however, cannot be accepted. First of all, it cannot be said that when the motives are equal the man can make a choice. Cases of hesitation and utter irresolution are not rare. Quite frequently it happens to a man as to the bride in Gogal's "Marriage," that he can make no choice. Moreover, when a man, in spite of a precise equality of motives, does make a choice, it is not difficult to explain it without resorting for that purpose to the "freedom of the will." It is explained simply and completely by the law of the association of ideas. If the man has ever experienced the painful consequences of indecision, this idea quickly comes back to his mind, and he at once takes some resolution in order to avoid such troublesome results.

In Russia, especially, there has spread in these latter times, the idea that man is in his acts subject to the law of causation; but not in the same manner as are the phenomena of the outer world. Human actions are distinguished from others by the fact that they are determined not merely by preceding external phenomena, but also in part by those which are to follow. Man's conduct is not merely the result of impressions received from without, but also of his moral state, of his own character. It might be said with regard to the fall of a stone, that its fall is not caused alone by the movement of the arm which started it, but also by its own properties. If instead of throwing a stone, a bit of down had been thrown, it would have remained in the air instead of falling to the earth. Consequently, the resulting phenomena are not merely the result of the preceding action of the arm, but also of the still earlier interior movements in the stone which brought about its own conformation.

The properties of the human being are certainly more complex, but there are presented merely considerations of more and less.

Our Russian conception evidently mixes two essentially distinct questions. Does freedom of the will merely mean independence of external conditions? Evidently not. Spinoza, for example, agreeing with Descartes, declares that matter can have absolutely no effect on spirit, but none the less denies the freedom of the will. Wherefore, even if our acts are the result only of previous external conditions, it is impossible to affirm the freedom of the will. If internal conditions are the cause of actions, they are not produced by any free will.

So, all attempts to solve in this manner the problem of freedom of the will are vain. We must put the question categorically, "Is the will free or not free?" It cannot be considered as halfway free. It comes under the principle of causation or it does not. When the question is thus put it is very simple, and the answer by no means doubtful. To maintain that the will is absolutely free, is in such formal contradiction to the best known facts that it today hardly finds any longer a serious defender. Let us resume briefly the reasons which forbid the recognition of a free will's existence.

First of all, the law of causation is an absolute principle applicable equally without exception to all phenomena in the world. Therefore, there is need of positive scientifically verified reasons for supposing that the will is the one force not subject to this law. We shall see later that such reasons have not been found.

Then we know that phenomena universally have as a basis the law of the conservation of force. Freedom of the will is not compatible with this theory. A free movement of the will is one which is undetermined by preceding movements and so does not depend upon the expenditure of energy to produce it.

Finally, let us add to this the further consideration that freedom of the will is a logical absurdity. Everything in order to exist must do so in a given manner regulated in advance. This is an indispensable condition for the maintaining of its own identity. But the free will is something which does not exist in any determinate manner, that is to say, it is a contradiction in terms. If we take into view the conditions of human life, we observe that the dependence of the moral life upon the organism is today an uncontested fact admitted by all the world, even by the metaphysicians, as for example, Hartmann. But if psychic phenomena depend upon the organism and it is subject to the law of causation, how can they escape that principle. Still further, the doctrine of the will's freedom is possible only if we admit the existence of many independent forces in our souls, and that is a psychological theory which the whole modern world rejects.

Observation of the facts also shows that the essential freedom of the will cannot be accepted. Quite frequently it happens that we are not masters of ourselves. The man accustomed to analyze his own actions can say in advance for what reasons he will do or not do some particular act under given circumstances. When we are not satisfied with ourselves, when we wish to bring about some change in our manner of acting, to correct ourselves in some respect, we commence with the proposition that the will is not free; we avoid malign influences; we seek circumstances which incline us away from old habits and tastes; we change the *milieu;* we remove to new surroundings. By reading and conversation we compel ourselves to establish the new way of life.

All this is entirely incompatible with freedom of the will. If the will were free, what would matter the men with whom we might consort, the books we might read, our own thoughts or our surroundings, if all this could not in the least affect our desires and our free will were in no way determined by outer things? Observation of ourselves leads to the conclusion that our wills are not free.

Observation of others leads to the same conclusion, and here the demonstration is still more decisive. All our relations with others are based upon the proposition that their wills are not free. We mark their character, study the influences to which they are more or less subject and guide our own action by the results thus obtained, relying upon them in dealings with such persons. Supposing the will to be free, we should very quickly find that durable relations are impossible among men. We would not know what they are going to do, and we could not in any way get any influence over them which could be relied upon. It is, too, only because we assume that the will is not free that we attempt to teach the child. If the will were not determined in any way there would be no such thing as educating youth.

Observation of oneself and even of oneself in relations to others and of those others cannot be considered as rigorously objective observation. The subjective relation holds too large a place.

But the results of statistics furnish very strong proofs in support of the doctrine we are maintaining. They show that human actions which seem the most spontaneous and independent are reproduced in precisely the same number from year to year; whence this consequence is to be drawn, that these acts, altogether spontaneous as they seem, are themselves, also determined, even as all the others.

It has been thought that serious objection was raised to this latter proof, in urging that the regularity of the figures furnished by statistics is easily explained by the law of averages. These are, it is said, average figures obtained by very numerous observations and have no value to determine what will take place in any given instance, and therefore no relation to the problem as to the free will of the individual.

This objection has no importance. There is in truth no doubt that the regularity of the statistics is explained by the law of averages, but the conformity of human actions to the same law has already proven the regularity of those actions. The law of averages itself, of course, presupposes a regularity in the phenomena subject to it.

If the savant makes his experiments numerous enough to set aside the peculiarities of the individual bodies he employs, this necessarily supposes that these bodies themselves have a certain regularity, and that this depends upon the law of causation. Where some agency may have supervened which is not subject to the effect of law, a miracle for example, in such a case the law of averages would be inapplicable. The influence of a supernatural force cannot be set aside by any augumentation of the number of observations, and it is precisely because any such influence may be disregarded that the law of averages may be used. It would be the same with the will if it were free. Freedom, if genuine, would make the law of averages inapplicable to human actions.

The partisans of free will cannot bring to the support of their thesis a single argument which is truly sound. They allege that we are sometimes conscious of freedom. Does it not happen, in fact, that under certain circumstances, we are sometimes conscious of such freedom, and sometimes, on the contrary, we are perfectly conscious that we are not free?

Quite often it happens that we are in doubt between two conclusions, and determine one way or the other without any reason. Can it not be said in such a case that we have acted on our own initiative without being controlled by anything?

We would answer this objection by inquiring if such a case cannot be explained in another way without recurring to the doctrine of the free will. If we attempt, as is usually done, to explain our acts by the motives, alone, of which we are conscious, we shall certainly be compelled to admit that we cannot explain such a case. But an attentive study of psychic phenomena shows us that unconscious elements play also an important part by the side of conscious ones in the mind, and that these unconscious forces will furnish us the explanation sought. If it is true that we are unconscious of the motives which press us to act in such or such a way, this is not to say that our wills act without any motive at all. It means only that the determining motive was an unconscious one.

Thus, the sole objection which the partisans of the free will can raise, our alleged consciousness of it, would disappear. It is no more serious than all the others which have been examined previously and whose weakness has been shown.

Section 40. *Society and the Individual*

The essential distinction which we have shown between society and organisms does not lead us to exclude social phenomena from the principle of causation. The characterizing quality of society consists in its psychic nature, but if we recognize moral phenomena generally and those of the will in particular as subject to the law of causation, we must recognize social phenomena also as subject to the same law.

All the factors by which social life is controlled are determined in advance. They are all subject to the law of causation. This is why the social phenomena which they cause must also necessarily be determined. But if this is so, if social and moral phenomena are themselves subject to the law of causation, can the individual[1] be opposed to society? Can there properly be any talk of independence on the individual's part? The question is double. From the point of view of modern psychology can the existence of an individual consciousness be explained in such a way as to set this consciousness over against the rest of the universe? Again, can a certain independence on the individual's part in his relations with society be established?

The law of association of ideas which serves as a basis for the whole doctrine of modern psychology explains what this individual consciousness is. It shows us that

[1] Since Cicero's time "individual" has indicated something such as Aristotle meant by the expression "*αδιαιρετος*," "indivisible." But already in Boethius this is not the precise meaning. "Individuum" means with him what is original, unique. Commentar. ad Porphyr. ed. Basil. 1570. p. 65. "Individuum autem pluribus dicitur modis. Dicitur individuum quod animo secari non potest, ut unitas vel mens; dicitur individuum quod ob soliditatem dividi nequit, ut adamas; dicitur individuum, cuius prædicatis in reliqua similia non convenit, ut Socrates." This last is also Leibnitz's meaning.

all our impressions from without are accompanied by a series of impressions which revive in the memory. This second set of impressions is not as lively and clear as the first. It does not depend upon the present external *milieu*, for these internal impressions remain the same whatever exterior changes may supervene. We can, as we choose, strengthen or weaken, revive or remove them. They are not outside of, but in us. They connect every distinct particle of our experience into a single whole, into an uninterrupted chain. Thus, we reach the consciousness of self and come to oppose it to the external world. The negation of the will does not interfere with the opposing of self to exterior things nor does it prevent the explaining of individual consciousness.

It may still be objected that the opposition of self to the world outside, of me to not-me, does not by any means embrace the whole notion of individuality. It may be said that such an antithesis gives only a negative idea of the individual and that his existence is something positive. He is his own proper end. We represent the individual to ourselves not only as a being opposed to all the rest of the universe, but also as one which is its own supreme end and not serving merely as a means for the realization of the purpose of some other creature than itself. If we deny the freedom of the will do we not deny at the same time that the individual is his own proper end? If we do not separate the individual from that chain of phenomena which indissolubly connects them together as causes and consequences, do we not reduce the individual to a state of complete submission where he ceases to exist for himself and where he is a mere single link amid all the links of that unbroken chain?

Whether the will is free or not, it is an error to believe that it is of decisive importance for the solution of the question as to whether or not the individual is an end unto himself.

The solution of this question depends entirely upon the significance which we give to the ideas of causation and finality. If we admit, just once, the existence of an objective end for which the universe was created and which has guided its progress through the ages since, everything in the world, and by consequence the individual also, is inevitably reduced to the condition of a means. If the universe exists with view to some other end than itself, all which it contains, of course, is but a means for reaching that end. The existence in the universe of a single phenomenon which was not brought about as a means for attaining that end, would render the teleological explanation of the world impossible. The question of the freedom of the will has no importance here. Under the teleological conception every individual, however endowed with a free will, would, none the less, serve merely as a means to bring about that end towards which the entire universe is working.

On the other hand, the explanation of the existence of the universe by the principle of causation, in denying the existence of an objective purpose for the whole world, does away with this idea, that the universe and all which it contains are but a means. If there is no general purpose, there is, then, no question of means. All is explained, then, by the causal connection. Everything is a product or a cause. The explanation furnished by the principle of causation allows only subjective ends. These subjective ends are but our ideas. They exist only in our consciousness and nowhere outside of us. There is no objective purpose, but, outside of ourselves, only causes and consequences. With such a conception, evidently, the individual cannot be recognized as only a means towards an end to which he is a stranger, for the existence of such an end cannot be admitted under the doctrine of causation.

Whatever are the ends towards which the individual compels himself to strive, they exist only in him, in his consciousness. They are ends which he conceives and whose elements he finds in his own head. From this point of view, the individual is objectively neither a means nor an end. Subjectively, it may be said that he is his own end, in the sense that every end which he conceives is a product of his own consciousness, of his own intelligence.

The consciousness of the individual in receiving phenomena which present themselves to it from without compels itself to group them into harmonious and satisfactory combinations. The imagination, the fancy, fills out pleasingly the rigorous facts of dry science; and hence arises the variety in the powers of different individuals. Each of us has a more or less different conception of the universe, one more or less embellished. Each individual, then, makes his own universe distinct from that of others and which perishes with him. As long as he lives, it is in this universe which he has made. All which he receives from without has more or less of an effect, a place which he assigns it in this world of his own creation, and it is the individual that is his own end.

The question of individuality, of the independence which the individual has in the face of the universe, is not altogether exhausted by these considerations. It may be claimed that if we do not admit the freedom of the will, the individual, even if he does not appear as a means for the realization of an end exterior to himself, nevertheless plays no part in the universe, his independence quite disappears, and is lost in the infinite chain of causes and effects.

If every act of the will is determined necessarily in

advance by some other antecedent act, as in the case of all the facts of the outer world, what is there to distinguish the individual man from external phenomena? Naturally, I would not maintain the individual's independence so far as to assert its completeness with reference to the conditions of the world which surrounds him. The principle of causation cannot be reconciled with such an independence as that. Nobody can say that the individual brings into the world anything absolutely new. This would contradict the principle of the conservation of energy. Only relative independence can be asserted. The difference is only in the more or less. Just as living beings exhibit an example of quite complete independence, as compared with inert matter, so the individual endowed with consciousness would appear very independent if his condition were compared with that of other living beings.

The question as to the relations of the individual and society shows that the mechanical and the organic doctrines result in two equally inadmissible conclusions. The mechanical theory subjects society absolutely to the individual. The organic theory, on the other hand, considers the individual as merely a subordinate part of the social organism, a part completely determined by that organism, one which would seem to be at the same time the product of that organism and designed to serve for the realization of the latter's purpose.

The psychic theory is equally remote from each of these two. It would recognize the influence of society upon the individual. It admits, even, that he is essentially a product of society, but at the same time it does not see in the individual a mere subordinate part of the great whole which society is. It does not agree with this idea to regard the individual as only a means for the accomplishment of social ends. According to the psychic theory the individual keeps his independence; his independent existence and his special ends, differing from those of society and not subordinate to these latter.

The conception which this last theory sets forth is that society, being a psychic union of men, admits, thanks to that fact, of the union of one man with several different societies.

The individual is the product of society,—this is not disputed, but of several societies and not merely of one. To the influence over him of one of these societies the individual opposes that which several others are exercising upon him at the same time. In this dependence in which he finds himself upon different societies, the individual often finds in some other a counterpoise to the influence of each particular one. Neither state, nor church, nor race, nor social class, nor community, nor family, can entirely subject the individual, precisely because they each tend to exercise such a subjection.

So, too, though the individual is a product of society, he is never a simple product of it, never the simple reflection of the principles which set in motion a given collectivity. Every individual is the product of the simultaneous influence of several societies and in each man can be seen combinations of distinct traits from many social influences.

Each individual in society forms a distinct independent principle which is not completely adapted to the environment around it, which is never completely fused with that society, so as to reach an entire identification with it.

The individual with characteristics fixed is constantly in movement, stirred by collisions and struggles. He tends to transform society little by little and so becomes himself a source of life and energy, and contributes to the progress of the social life. The mechanical theory of society regards the development of social forms only as a manifestation of the wills of individuals and that will as not being determined or limited by any objective principle. Social progress under this view depends upon the free will of those who are in control.

Under the organic theory, on the contrary, social development is a rigorously objective organic fact which constrains individuals, even against their wills, to group themselves according to immutable laws.

From our point of view social development is the resultant of all the conscious tendencies and efforts of individuals (the active element), which are reacted upon, also, (and this is the passive element) by an order of things which is the result of a long historic evolution. The objective social order is therefore formed, not only under the influence of the tendencies and efforts of individuals, but also, under that of objective factors which do not depend upon man's will and which act throughout every moment of his existence. The conception which we hold does not permit us to suppose that society will become in time a mere product of human art and will then clothe itself in a purely conventional form.

Section 41. *Law and the Social Order*

KORKUNOV. The Social Sphere of Law, 1892.

The existence and especially the development of every organism supposes the preservation of its essential parts. This is true, indeed, of every aggregate, organic or inorganic. If the action of some part of the mechanism destroyed the other parts, the mechanism could not act. If in a living being some organ develops at the expense of another, as by depriving the latter of necessary nourishment, the development of the organism as a whole is arrested.

This is equally true of social phenomena. There, too, the life and development of the combination depends upon the preservation and due development of the separate factors which make up society. An exclusive development of one of the factors may easily take place in a way to be injurious to the activity of other factors and interfere with the regular functions of the society as a whole.

So far as concerns a mechanical aggregate the bond connecting its parts is a material one. It is a mechanical arrangement which co-ordinates the functions of the several parts. But as regards society, whose principle of unity is psychic, the activity of its different elements must be co-ordinated by some different process. The factor which institutes and controls this co-ordination in society is no other than law. Everybody recognizes that law plays the regulator's part in society, but opinions divide when it comes to determining what the order is that law sets up.

If we regard society as a mechanical aggregate of a given number of individuals, and do not consider the individual as a product of social life, but, on the contrary, this society is looked upon as the result of a voluntary agreement of individuals, in a word, if we accept the mechanical conception of society, the sole active factor in social life must be the individual and his conscious will. Under this theory, the social order can be nothing but a delimitation of the manifestations of separate individual wills.

The limits assigned to each individual for the exercise of his freedom of will, limits within which that will rules unchecked, must constitute his right, his law in the subjective sense. The rules themselves, establishing the limits for individual wills, make up the objective law.

Law, in the mechanical theory of society, is something opposed by the individual to society; something which the individual, entering into society, brings ready made with him and with which he seeks to restrain the pretensions of social authority. The development of the organic notion, on the other hand, leads us to recognize in law a social order to which the society subjects the individuals who make it up. Subjective rights are not from this point of view opposed to social authority, but are bestowed by it. Law, consequently, is regarded as made by society itself in its own interest and at the same time in that of individuals. If we adopt the psychic theory of society we can accept neither of these two views.

If society has only a psychic bond we cannot regard law as simply an order imposed by society upon individuals who are only passive beings. The final basis of law is the individual consciousness. It is there that the ideas as to the means to be employed for the delimitation of conflicting interests take their origin; and, consequently, from thence arise all ideas as to juridical norms. It is only little by little that the notion of right, originally subjective and individual, has been taken up by others, has spread into constantly greater communities and has taken the form of customs, juridical practice, and finally, legislation. Reaching this point in its development, the primitive conception of right has become an objective factor in social life. In the same way, too, it is in the individual's consciousness of his obligations that a solid foundation, a firm basis for the action of law, is found. Law takes effect, subordinates to itself the activity of individuals, not, however, in such a way as to be by itself objectively the sole essence of order in the social life. The actual course of social life never coincides precisely with its existing laws.

From a rigorously objective point of view, if we are satisfied with generalizing actual phenomena, the real social order would consist of law, and of violations of law. The significance and power of law consist simply in this, that it is recognized by all classes as the necessary order of social relations. Wherefore, law is much less an objectively established subjection of the person to society than it is a subjective conception by the person himself of a necessary order of social relations.

We must not conclude, however, that law is always an exclusively one-sided product of the personal individual will. The mental fashioning of the necessary order of social relations is not a conscious and arbitrary matter. It is only little by little that the individual comes to a consciousness of such an ideal, and the process is mostly unconscious. So, he is disposed to consider it as not a subjective creation, but as a reproduction of an order of vital relations already existing in an objective way independently of himself. The more primitive the individual's intellectual culture, the less he comprehends the subjective nature of his social ideal, and the less he distinguishes between his own subjective conceptions and the reality which surrounds him.

To go still farther, the individual's conceptions not only have no arbitrary character. They are not entirely the act of the individual. The unconscious processes of their formation are determined not merely by the subjective qualities of the individual, but also by his environment. Moreover, even as regards his subjective qualities, they commonly are formed under the double influence of heredity and environment.

The social ideal of one individual is usually that of his neighbor in the same society, at most there are only differences of detail.

In the beginning personal peculiarities were fewer, the forms of human action and of social relations were not nearly so numerous. State and social life embraced the whole circle of human life, all the interests of mankind. Religion itself was a state institution. Under such conditions the whole of the development of the individuals who composed the state was fixed solely by their mere environment. There was then no possibility of meeting, as today, individuals belonging to different social groups. The various societies and differing churches did not exist. The individual ideal was naturally the same in all. So before the acquiring of individual conceptions as to what ought to be the regular legal relations between members of the society, the general rules governing these relations had become fixed and were known to all the world. Shaping itself in the course of time the individual conception of such legal rules showed already a partial deviation from the immemorial uniformity characteristic of primitive law.

At the same time law does not simply render possible the coexistence of individuals in some degree of liberty. Law constitutes, also, an important condition of human progress. The circle of social life constitutes a combination of interests of the different individuals who make up society. These interests are very variable and changeable, like those of individuals in that respect. According to the times, in fact according to the different situations in which he finds himself, the same person is controlled often by entirely contrary interests. So, in the general advance of social life there may come the same contradiction of interests. Under different political religious or economical conditions societies are dominated by turns by various interests which concern all and put in action the whole social activity. If there comes a change of conditions, a new orientation directs the social mind, and with it come new interests which overturn the old. In the absence of law to fix the bounds for these striving interests the predominance in the society of certain interests would quickly ruin the weaker ones and by consequence deprive the society of conditions indispensable to its further development. The future would be sacrificed to the exigencies of the present.

Regular social development would be seriously endangered, if indispensable future interests are sacrificed to the controlling one of the moment, for example the one which seeks to assure public order, when, in seeking to prevent the dissemination of dangerous doctrines, it would stifle all manifestation of ideas. Order would perhaps be restored more quickly, but in the end society would suffer a grievous calamity if all liberty of the tribune or of the press were taken away.

Law in delimiting the interests which make up the social life removes the possibility of such harm. Any interest which has gained a legal standing will always find some minority to defend it. If the rule of law is accepted in the society and the legal rights of minorities respected, the contemned interest will be upheld by this minority and the society's future vindicated.

Section 42. *The Form of Human Groupings*

MOHL. Geschichte und Literatur der Staatswissenschaften, 1855. 1. s. 67 ff.

The arrangement of men into social groups may take place under very different forms. The chief distinction among them consists, however, in their origins. Do they arise voluntarily on the man's part, or independently of his will? Of course, in the first case we have a voluntary, and in the latter, an involuntary group. The state and the family may serve as examples of the latter. Stock companies, clubs, and learned societies are instances of the former.

This distinction based on the origin of the grouping is very important in the organization of society. The modification of the man in respect to the society into which he has come of his own free will cannot be very extensive since he can always leave it. Vastly greater, however, is his subjection to the society of which he is an involuntary member.

Societies of the latter category, the so-called necessary groupings, present three different types. They can be based upon unity of origin (family, or tribe), upon unity of territorial location (commune, state), or upon unity of interests (associations, companies). A certain solidarity, of course, there is among the members of every grouping, but in some societies this results from the collective life, instead of producing the collectivity, in the family and in the state, for example, while in others it is the basis and not the result of the grouping. It is easy to see that this classification of necessary groupings corresponds to different epochs of the social life.

In the groupings founded upon unity of origin it is the influence of the past which holds the first place, in those based upon life in the commune it is the present, while in the groupings which rest upon unity of interests it is the future.

For a long time social science recognized the existence only of the first two classes and especially among them the family and the state. Only towards the end of the XVIII century did the idea arise that at the side of the state were other forms of groupings, that men while being citizens of the same state could also be members of other associations and could even enter into such relations with citizens of another state.

Scheltzer first advanced this idea in his treatise on political science. He indicated the need there was for a distinct science for the study of those associations springing up outside of the state and which he called, by analogy to metaphysics, metapolitical,—a science of social phenomena outside of the state and of political life. He limited himself to this observation. The practical consequences which he drew from it were of little importance, and it was only after the appearance of the new socialistic school that the learned were led to examine more closely the questions arising as to the groupings. The socialist school brought forward the conception that a political reorganization is not sufficient, that there must be a social reorganization.

The socialists by the side of the conception of a political revolution have developed the idea of another, a social revolution, concerning itself only with social phenomena which they say exist independently of any particular organization of government. They have thus given a new impulse to the study of social groupings among mankind, groupings which exist along with the state, and must have a place at its side. This was the practical result which they derived from the doctrine of the independent social existence of these groupings.

Almost at the same time as the appearance of these

socialistic teachings, Hegel, the renowned German philosopher, tried to establish an intermediary link between the individual and his family on one side and the state and its government on the other side. He recognizes in the development of social life not merely two phases, but three. The family is not for Hegel what it was for everybody else in his time, the immediate basis of the state. The family, according to him, is the thesis, whose antithesis is not the state but civil society, which is the result of the partial disruption of the family. Civil society is in opposition to the unity of the family and is an intermediate step between the family and the state. The state personifies and combines the unity of the family, together with the diversity of civil society.

Hegel, meanwhile, though recognizing clearly enough that the study of society cannot be, as tradition had to that time made it, limited to the family and the state, did not define the form of this "civil" society and has not left us a clear notion of what he thought it was. Hegel's general dialectics, in fact, admit the existence of only transitory forms. All phenomena are for him momentary transitions from thesis to synthesis. In conformity to this, civil society, also, assumes with him the character of antithesis. All the processes of social development consist merely in this, the opposing to the unity of the family the variety of other social forms and in this method leading to a higher social form, the state. In this manner his doctrine as to civil society does not have in Hegel's system an independent value. It appears as merely an intermediate moment of the development of social life and must be completed by the appearance of the state.

Under Hegel's influence and especially under the doctrine of socialism, Lorenz Stein in his critical study of socialism and communism, L'histoire des mouvements socialistes en France, tried thus to set forth his theory of society. Following Hegel's example in his dialectical method, he asserts distinct movements, one succeeding to another, the series embracing the entire development of social lie. At the same time he comes nearer to setting forth the contents of social life. Examining the socialist doctrine, he asks what is society? What is this social reform the socialists are talking about? It should be said in passing, that the life of the modern state at the moment when the socialists raised these questions was such as to call especial attention to economic questions. The revolution, in breaking the absolute power of the kings had given more freedom to the third class in society, the bourgeoisie, the capitalists, but the fourth class which constituted the greatest part of the nation were totally ignored and left out of all these political reforms. For the members of this last class the economic question is of the most importance, for, aside from the guaranty of his menial existence, the law has for him no value. Stein puts himself at this point of view for his examination of society, almost solely the economic point of view.

Therefore, following Hegel's general method and yielding to the direct influence of socialism, Stein gives only a one-sided view of society. With him, also, the family appears as the representative of unity, civil society of the diversity introduced by economic life between which two the government stands as that which establishes the unity and national well being of economic interests. No such narrow conception of society can satisfy the mind. It was quickly observed that harmonious and seductive as Hegel's and Stein's systems appeared, they presented grave defects. They leave, in fact, entirely at one side certain social forms which cannot, however, be regarded in modern times as incorporated into the state's government. The question of the freedom of associations is raised practically by the religious societies. Religious dogmas furnish a basis for a social grouping which is at the same time extensive and independent, an association which does not have as a basis any definite frontiers, nor for its mission any of the ends proposed by the state.

In the middle ages, when the church herself exercised political power, there was no occasion to raise the question as to the independence of the great society she built up. The church at that time appeared everywhere as a political body. The same must be said of the Protestant churches. They were everywhere state institutions, and instruments of government were at the same time organs of the church. But in the same degree that principles of religious liberty developed, to the extent that the church separated itself from the state, the identification of church and state were condemned, and the question of the independence of religious associations was once more raised. It is easy to see that the church plays no economic part. It remains by the side of the state without forming an integral part of it, since the same church embraces several states, adopting different types of social organization, of which the state cannot be considered either as a part or as the whole.

German philosophers have sought to give to the theory of society a wider development and with a double point of view. On one side the representatives of the organic school have applied their theory to that of society. In examining the different manifestations of individual activity, they have thought that the distinct forms of grouping ought to correspond to special needs of human nature. In this way the university satisfies the need of education; economic associations and the church correspond to some definite needs. The representatives of the organic school thus have come to recognize a series of collective groupings each of which is an independent organ satisfying certain needs. Such is the doctrine of Ahrens.

This doctrine cannot be precisely maintained. R. Mohl in his interesting article, The Social and Political Sciences, whose main subject is the nature of society, as also in his Geschichte und Literatur der Staats Wissenschaften, propounds a serious objection to Ahrens' doctrine. This doctrine, says he, shows us a mass of groupings, schools, churches, economic associations, etc., but does not show us any general conception of society in distinction from the state.

Meanwhile, if we take the church and those various combinations born of a country's economic life, we discover an essential resemblance among them. The ecclesiastical societies arise out of the common interests of the members because a given group of men holding the same religious dogmas have need of identical religious ceremonies. So they form themselves into a society. The same thing is true as to the associations having an economic purpose. Laborers', merchants', land holders', farmers', and bankers' associations are created by a common interest. Between these groups and the church the difference is said to be only in the basis, but that basis is found to be identical, a common interest. In the economic groupings the basis is an economic common interest, in the church a religious one.

Mohl, continuing his observations and study of different forms of groupings, observes that there are at the same time numerous variations among the forms which these associations take. In every state, besides the church and the associations for economic purposes, there are classes and ranks which are also groupings of men combined for a common interest. The nobility, the townsmen, the peasants, are three distinct orders, each associated together by common interests. Castes arise later out of classes, but these latter are already established on the basis of a common interest,—community, culture, instruction, etc. If we consider the internal organization of the modern state we shall see that its different parts —provinces, communes, etc.,—have also their common independent life, their common interests independent of the state at large; with which latter they may even come into conflict. These common interests have as their basis the communal life realized upon a certain territory. In modern states the distribution of population by no means corresponds to nationality, but national unity appears as an important factor in international matters.

In this way Mohl comes by observation to the conception of a category of social groups united by reason of a community of permanent interests. Each such group is distinguished from others essentially by the point in which lies unity of interests. These interests may or may not coincide with the state's interests. Cities on the different sides of the borders of two states may have common interests, as matters of hygiene for example. So different states may have common interests in regulating the navigation of a stream flowing through both. Society which took its birth from the fact of joint residence on the same territory cannot have the same limits as the state itself. The different lines of collective grouping which have been mentioned permit the ranging in the same category all the groupings other than those of the state and family. Society, according to Mohl's definition, is a combination of human groups whose basis is a common permanent interest.

Mohl's ideas as to the independent existence of society as distinguished from the state are now widely held. In the article which we have noted he tried to study society independently of the state and organize a system of social sciences comparable to the political sciences. As a whole his theory may be accepted, but requires some corrections in detail.

It is impossible, for example, to agree with him that the nation whose members are connected together by community of origin and that the communes whose inhabitants are united by the fact of neighborhood can be classed together and both regarded as social groups having for basis the unity of their interests. If the citizens of the same nation or the members of the same commune have common interests it is none the less true that the community of interests is not the basis, but a result of this association. The nation or the commune exists before the individuals who make it up recognize the unity of their interests. The church, on the contrary, is created only by the unity of faith, and the economic groups are formed only by and because of the community of economic interests.

Among the different forms which society may take is that of the state, which is of the highest importance for us since the state is the chief factor in the development of law, and in the enforcement of its authority against law-breaking. We therefore stop here in a special way to study the nature of the state, the political society.

CHAPTER II

THE STATE

Section 43. *The Concept of the State*

MOHL. Encyclopedia of Political Science, pp. 23, 49–64.
ZACHARIAE. Deutsches Staats und Bundesrecht. 3 Ausg. 1886, BI. s. 40.
GUMPLOWICZ. Philosophisches Staatsrecht, 1877. s. 15–19.
HUGO PREUSS. Gemeinde, Staat, Reich. 1889.
KORKUNOV. Russian Public Law, I., pp. 1–48. 6th ed., 1908.

Among the different forms of human association, chief importance must unquestionably be given to the state. There was a time when it took up into itself all the activities, without exception, of human life. Throughout classical antiquity the man was completely swallowed up in the citizen of a state. In our day, while at the side of the state there are a good many other social groupings, the state succeeds in making its influence felt at all points of the social life. Under all circumstances the history of humanity develops itself chiefly under the form of political activity.

So in studying social phenomena of any sort one collides constantly with questions of the organization, or of the forms, or of the activity, of the state. For a long time, as we have already said, the theory of the state, politics, embraced all the science of social phenomena.

Under such conditions it would seem that a definition of the state ought to be easily agreed upon by all the world. It has not been so. If, in truth, we meet with a great diversity of definitions in literature, this is explained by the fact that in most of them is included matter not pertaining to its purpose.

Thus, first of all, a good many in defining the state have in view to indicate how it must be in order to be in harmony with their own views; that is, they transform the definition into a criticism of the state. Mohl, for example, defines the state as an unique and permanent organism of institutions which, "guided by the general will, sustain and put in operation the general force, and have for their end the aiding of a given people upon a given territory in all its social activity, internal as well as external." It is certainly impossible to affirm that all states which exist or have existed have pursued only these permitted ends allowed by this definition, and have thereby contributed to the development of human life.

Welker's definition goes farther yet. He defines the state as "a personified, sovereign, living and free human association. Within the limits of its constitutional pact this combination under the direction of an independent constitutional government, aspires to liberty under law and within its limits to the realization of the destiny and happiness of its numbers."

To the same category, it would seem, belong those definitions which indicate the end which the state ought to serve. No such definition can satisfy us if we are seeking one which will apply to all states.

Other definitions are limited to indicating the place in a given philosophic system which the conception of the state should occupy. Hegel, for example, defines it as "the reality of concrete liberty."[1] To comprehend this definition it is necessary to know what Hegel means by the terms reality (*Wirklichkeit*) and concrete liberty (*Konkreten Freiheit*). This definition offers no meaning apart

[1] Hegel's Philosophie des Rechts. Werke B. VIII. s. 314. "Der Staat ist die Wirk lichkeit des konkreten Freiheits."

from Hegel's system of philosophy. By itself it is nonsense.

Schelling's definition is of the same character. "The state," said he, "is the harmony of liberty and necessity." Such definitions are too subjective despite their wish to indicate not what the state ought to be but what it in fact is. They are subjective because they rest upon a given philosophic conception, which, never having been objectively proved, depends always upon subjective conviction.[1]

Finally, very often writers feel compelled to give a definition which shall settle in advance all the most important political questions, all the problems which political science raises, so that the whole doctrine of the state can be constructed as a series of logical consequences of the given definition. But since many of the most important questions in political science are still in our time matters of controversy, it results that we are given in the definition contested matters for ascertained facts. Such are the definitions of the state as an organ of, or as personifying a will. There is hardly need to say that the definitions, thus settling in advance all these disputed matters, are far from getting any unanimous assent.

Universally, in studying historic forms of human societies, the political character of certain groupings are hardly ever in doubt. In a good many cases there is complete unanimity as to the question of whether or

[1] Here are some more definitions of the same kind:—

Ahrens. Der Staat is in dem allgemeinen Gesellschaftsorganismus der jenige besondere Organismus, welcher durch das Band des Rechts und vom Mittelpunkt einer centralen Macht, aus alle gesellscharten Kreise zu einer rechtlichen Einheit und Ordnung verknüpft.

Bluntschli. Der Staat ist der politische organizirte Volksperson eines bestimmten Landes.

Schulze. Der Staat ist die Vereinigung eines sesshaften Volkes zu einem organischen Gemeinwesen unter einen bestimmten Verfassung, zur Verwirklichung aller Gemeinswecke des Volksleben, vor allem sur Verstellung der Rechtsordnung.

not they are or were states. If there is sometimes a doubt, such as Finland now presents, nobody attaches to its solution any question as to whether its nature is organic or personal, or as to the end for which it is organized, but the one question is whether we can recognize in it the existence of an independent force-using authority.

But the power of the state is exhibited with special clearness. Among all the social groupings the state is the dominating power *par excellence*. In antiquity the state embraced man's whole social life and all the other forms of groupings were only parts of the state, and subject to it. The state at that time would be defined as the typical society, as the grouping which had need of no other and depended upon no one. It is thus that Aristotle defines the state.

In the middle ages the state's authority was severely pressed upon by the great landholders with their tendency to make of the state a mere contractual union between the representatives of the feudal proprietaries, and also, by the tendencies of the Roman church which wished to take power into its own hands. When at the time of the renaissance authority began to recover its former rôle, preoccupied, as it then was, with setting aside all influences capable of upholding the feudal tradition, there was recognized in the state a sovereign power, an absolute and unlimited authority. The sovereignty and supremacy of the state were then considered as its essential attributes.

This notion of sovereignty was set forth for the first time by Bodin (De la république, 1583), who defines sovereignty as an absolute, unlimited and independent authority. The same idea was stated in still more energetic terms by Hobbes, who styles the state "a mortal divinity." The conception of sovereignty thus understood was maintained until about 1870.

In our day a more careful examination of the conditions attending the organization of federal states and of the international relations of all states in general has compelled the late writers to reject the conception of sovereignty as a distinctive attribute of the state. For the most part, like Laband and Jellinek, they confine themselves to recognizing as possible the existence of both sovereign and non-sovereign states, and the autonomous existence of states which enter into the formation of a greater federal state. Others go farther yet and, like H. Preuss, reject entirely the notion of sovereignty, and affirm that there is in reality no sovereign state, exercising an absolute and unlimited authority. The authority of each state, they say, is in fact limited and depends externally upon international relations and internally upon the organization of the different groupings which compose it.

It is impossible to confute the arguments which Preuss brings forward. He shows in the course of them that the state's power is based upon the consciousness which men have of their dependence upon the state. But this consciousness cannot be unconditioned and absolute, because men recognize their dependence not only upon the state, but also upon a good many other societies as necessary as the state. If any society would pretend absolute dominion over men it would be the church.

For the real believer, the church's authority is certainly the greatest of all, for the holy writings teach us that it is necessary to obey God rather than men. The church, sole and eternal, does not, like the state, depend upon conditions of time and space. Finally, in it acts divine grace, the highest of all powers. So, it cannot be affirmed that the state is distinguished from the church by the possession of absolute and unlimited authority.

The distinctive attribute of the state is that "it alone employs, in an independent manner, coercive power." All other societies, however independent they may be in certain relations, use coercive means only by authorization and under the control of the state. If it sometimes happens that the church uses force, it is so used only within the limits allowed by local political authority. In the same way, too, the authority of parents over children, of husbands over wives, is established by political legislation and is exercised under the control of governmental agencies. There is always an appeal to the authority of the state from the abuse of coercion in the church or in the family. The authority of the communes and of the provinces is equally subject to this control.

The state, then, is to be regarded as the great dispenser of constraint. Political order is distinguished most of all by this trait, that it is a peaceful order which allows of no individual violence and only permits itself to enforce justice. Only organs of governmental authority have the right of constraint. Private persons and other associations are permitted to use it only within the limits where the state authorizes and controls it. Even in international relations, war is only authorized; that is, the various acts of hostile violence are performed only by agencies of the state.

Independent coercive authority, we would say again, is the characteristic attribute of the state; but this independence is not such as to be entirely unlimited and absolutely free. So, while the distinct states which make up the federal state and are, consequently, subject to the federation's authority, are of limited competency, they remain states in their own territory and are independent within the limits of their competency. Practically this independence is usually expressed by the fact that they create, themselves, the instruments designed to enforce their own authority without being subject in doing so to the federal authority.

On the other hand, communes and provinces in a unified state, even if they have a considerable degree of autonomy, never have such complete freedom in designating the personnel of their various organs. The central authority keeps the right of controlling the personnel of the various administrative circles by means of the direct nomination of some functionaries or, frequently, by approving their election, or frequently again by means of a right to annul an election and hold a new one, if the result of the last one was not in harmony with the wishes of the central administration. A federal government is never armed with such rights over the states or cantons which form the federal state. No federal authority is charged with naming state governors, with approving elections, or dissolving local assemblies in the states or cantons. The difference is an essential one.

So far as the central power has no control or direct influence over the make-up of local administrative bodies, the limitations imposed on these bodies have only an exterior and formal character. Their internal character, the precise orientation of their activity, cannot be determined in advance by formal disposition of law. When, on the contrary, the central authority takes in hand the composition of the local administrations, it augments so far its own influence as to supply, itself, the main activity of the local organs of power, inasmuch as it is after depriving them of their local attachment and independence that it makes them organs of the local autonomy.

It must be added, too, that the existence of a state presupposes, necessarily, an independent control exercised over free men. Otherwise it would be a constraint employed over slaves and not governmental control.

The state supposes always a fixed domination recognized by all. A mere fact of control, an establishment sustained by force alone, a military occupation, for example, over an enemy's territory is no state.

So, considering as a whole all that has been observed we may define the state as a social body asserting for itself independent, recognized, coercive, governmental control over a free people.

The attribution to the state of this exclusive right of coercion is of extreme importance for the whole social life. There results, first of all, a great reduction in the number of cases of violence and with it a great economy of force. The constraint exercised by the state according to law does not provoke resistance, because, for one thing, the preponderance of force is in most cases on the side of the government and leaves no chance of success in a struggle with it. This idea aside, the authority of government is submitted to voluntarily, from habit and duty. The change in the character of the constraint is something still more important. If the state assumes the sole right to constrain, it ought to exercise it in all cases of real need. It should be exercised, not only in cases where such use of it coincides with the state's own interest, but also in others. If it does not, then the citizen must necessarily enforce his own right. But to act for the interest of another is not the same thing as to act for one's own. The setting in motion of constraint exercised by the state with a view to prevent violence and private wars is not the consequence of an unreflecting spontaneous sentiment of government. The organs of the state to which the task of watching over the interests of individuals and of other societies is confided are moved in fulfilling this function solely by the sentiment of duty; that is to say, the action of power under such circumstances is tranquil, impartial, and taken after mature reflection.

The certainty of success, the consciousness they have of ability to compel obedience, adds to the calmness in action of the government's organs. The constraint which the state employs is not determined, therefore, by unreflecting violent natural feelings, but by more general considerations, better conformed to law and morals. The constraint is, so to say, disciplined by law. It is penetrated with ethical principles. This quality in constraint is shown at the beginning, only when the government has to repress violences which do not assail its own personnel. But little by little the state comes to apply the same principles even when it has to intervene to protect its own personnel. This movement comes out clearly when it becomes necessary to rigorously repress common law crimes on the one part, and political offenses on the other.

The controversies which arise over obtaining the extradition of a political offender are explained precisely by the doubt which is entertained as to the relations which there ought to be between the injured state and its neighbors. The manner of acting which is most equitable, most in conformity with moral sentiment, and which has been a long time followed, is generalized and puts its imprint on the whole coercive activity of the state, which subjects itself more and more to the requirements of justice.

Section 44. *Governmental Authority*

KORKUNOV. Ukaz i zakon (Decretals and Law). 1894.

We have defined the state as a social government invested with coercive and independent authority, but we have not explained in what that authority consists. From the days of scholasticism down to ours, the conception of authority was that of a single will, supreme mistress in the state. The authority of the state has been sometimes confused with the will of those ruling in it. Others have conceived the state's authority as the supreme will and those who hold power as the organs of that will, which must not be confused with the will of those governing.

At the first view the identification of the state's authority with the will of those governing seems to correspond well with the reality. The existence of will in government is an unquestionable fact, and the citizens are struggling together constantly over its manifestation. The existence, on the contrary, of some particular supreme will only appears as a quite vague hypothesis. It is manifested in practice in the orders and acts of those governing.

It is in this way that the existence in the political schools of a whole group of writers who identify the state's will with the concrete will of those momentarily governing it, is explained. The best representative of this class of writers in our day is Prof. Max Seydel of Munich. Such a conception of the state's authority may appeal to the realist because it rests upon no metaphysical assumption. The existence of governments and of their wills is something certain, real, but this alone does not explain the phenomena of the state's domination. Submission to political authority cannot be explained on the basis of the personal power of those who govern. Political history shows us by numerous examples that thousands of persons are obedient to the orders of one, and that one often destitute of intelligence, simply because that one person was recognized as representing the state's authority; and celebrated statesmen, on the other hand, have been compelled to shelter themselves behind a ruler who was of no importance from the intellectual point of view, but was the bearer of governmental authority.

Moreover, the submission to rulers is never absolute. They are obeyed only so far as they are recognized as representing something higher than their own personal will. If public opinion pronounces the activity of those who are at the head of the state to be arbitrary, obedience falls off very quickly, and a revolution becomes inevitable.

All this leads to the conclusion that submission to the state's authority does not depend upon any quality of the personal will of those who rule, and the dominating opinion in political literature considers them only as representatives of a higher will to which that of individuals ought to be subject. In the middle ages this sovereign will, manifest in acts of government, was said to be the divine will. XVIII century political ideas replaced this religious notion with that of the social compact.

The authority of the state is considered as the general will of the citizens who have decided to form a state and to submit themselves under certain given conditions to the government which they are establishing. Conformably to this theory, the power which the government has exists only so far as it is the expression of the general will in accordance with the social compact.

From about the beginning of the XIX century the contract theory began to be replaced by others. The state was no longer considered to be a thing of man's arbitrary institution, but as an objectively necessary form of human society and as the result of a preconceived progress of history. In these latter theories of the state's will, it is no longer the collective will of individuals nor the divine will. It is the abstract will of the state itself, regarded as a distinct and independent person which explains the state's authority. Most writers on constitutional law see in the state's power the expression of the will of the state itself, of which the government is only an organ. This explanation, meanwhile, will not answer the purposes of science. First of all, the state can be recognized as a person endowed with a distinct will only by means of a legal fiction. For being a person, the state lacks the prime condition, unity of personal consciousness. But fictions can only serve to simplify in our thought the complexity of real phenomena into a conceived and pretended unity, that is, into something we can grasp better. Fiction is powerless to furnish any genuine explanation of phenomena.

Power in a state serves precisely as the bond and recognition of its unity. Every state has its power, and where there are several such powers, there are several states. For this reason, if sovereign power is the expression of will, it must express only a single will. But it is impossible to explain all the manifestations of the state's domination as manifestations of one sole will. In history, the life of a state does not appear as the manifestation of one unique will, dominating all others, but, quite the contrary, it appears as a struggle between opposing wills. The legal organization of the state is most commonly the work of several independent wills, partly of some and partly of others.

We see this especially in constitutional monarchies. They are established precisely by a combination of the will of the sovereign and of that which is expressed by the national representation, and it is to be observed that very often it is the constitution itself which, so to say, divides the will of the state by charging different institutions with the performance of different functions which together constitute the state's sovereignty.

Evidently, unity of will is not here anything regarded as desirable. It would rather appear to be considered a danger to be guarded against. For the same reason, for example, the national representatives are divided into two houses. If the authority of the state lay in a single unique will, all the efforts of the state would tend towards the organization of unity in the expression of that will. It would, by consequence, be impossible to admit of the separation of the powers of government, of that decentralization which is deemed so necessary in modern times, and which supposes precisely that the main functions of the state can be exercised separately and independently of one another.

But there is another very important argument against the conception of the state as the embodiment of supreme will. Not only is it true that all the phenomena of state control cannot be explained as a manifestation of a single will; they cannot even be explained as manifestations of any will whatever. It is in legislation that the will of the sovereign most distinctly appears. It is, in fact, the legislator who gives orders, while the judge pronounces sentences, and the executive acts. Therefore if sovereignty and will were the same thing, legislation would necessarily be its prime function. But in the primitive states societies are governed by customary laws and have no legislation. On the other hand, the state never does without the administration of justice or without the executive power. We observe farther that not only the citizens, but foreigners too, if within the state's territory, are subject to the organs of its power. The authority of the state is shown over its own citizens not only in subjecting them passively to its control, but also in requiring them to contribute actively to its support.

The citizen differs from the foreigner in that he takes an active part in the state's life, its preservation and its development. He performs his duty of submission to the state not only when he carries out the orders of his government, but also when he forces himself to investigate and understand the true needs of the state and to strive to prevent faults and abuses on the part of his rulers. If the subjection of citizens in a state consisted merely in the obligation to carry out its orders, the state would not last long. It would inevitably soon fall to pieces. The authority of the rulers' orders does not have, as one might suppose, its basis in physical force and external constraint. The different organs of power in the state are always a minority of the citizens. Those bound to obey are always more numerous than their rulers. The obligatory force of government orders does not rest in the last analysis upon anything but their recognition, their tacit acceptance, by society. Every citizen taken separately is bound to yield to the orders of the state's officers, not merely because they require it, but above all because society, as a whole, has recognized these orders as obligatory upon each member. To recognize the authority of such orders, to be morally constrained to submit to them is not to be reduced to the performing the commands emanating from a stranger's will.

It should be added that in general the conceptions of authority and of will should not be confused. Will is not by itself authority. There are wills without force, and there is force without will. Authority is given to a will from the outside. It is something else, quite apart, and not to be confused with it. The will aspires to authority, is or is not invested with it. It serves as the object of will. Farther, authority itself does not presuppose necessarily a governing will. Take the simplest case of the use of authority, that by one man over another. This authority can exist without there being any dominating will. The man who exercises an ascendancy over another by holiness, genius, talent, or beauty, often does so without dreaming of it, without wishing for it, and is sometimes annoyed and troubled by it. The genuine ascetic, assuredly, mortifies his flesh from no aspiration for power. He crushes all his desires, and precisely on this account finds himself exercising a very great authority among men.

Thus, the conception of authority does not necessarily coincide with that of a dominating will. It happens that the will dominates, but this does not of necessity imply that every act of will is with a view to such domination. Divinities, which are a work of the imagination, nevertheless dominate. They surely have no actual will. Man is often subject to ideas which call out phenomena absolutely foreign to all will, as for example, the idea of an impending misfortune, that of a malady, or some superstition, etc. All these examples compel us to recognize that power does not necessarily presuppose the existence of a will directed towards the object of domination. Domination does not presuppose consciousness on the active side, on the part of the dominator, but on the passive side, the side of the dominated. All those things on which a man thinks he depends have power over him, whether or not they are capable of will. For the establishment of the domination it is not necessary that there be actual dependence. It suffices if there is the consciousness of dependence. In other words, authority depends not on the will of the ruler, but upon the consciousness of the subject.

If this is so, there is no need of attributing will to the state and of personifying it in order to explain the state's authority. Since authority is a force whose existence is conditioned only upon consciousness of dependence on the part of the subject, the state must have authority whether there is in it any conscious public will or not, so long as the people recognize their dependence upon the state. Governmental authority is not any one's will, but is a force arising out of the citizen's consciousness of his dependence on the state.

Section 45. *The Organs of Authority*

Governmental authority, as a force conditioned upon the recognition on the part of the citizens of their dependence with regard to the state, produces in the social life various phenomena, and, too, of a double kind. First, it urges the citizen to perform whatever seems indispensable to that state on which he recognizes his own dependence. On this rest the sentiments of patriotism, readiness to sacrifice for native land, fondness for political activity, etc.; in a word, all that united a people into one state and serves finally as supports for its power.

But this does not exhaust the activity of governmental control. It leads secondly to the citizens obeying the orders of certain persons who are recognized as organs of state authority. The different acts by which the state's functions are performed may assist or interfere with the realization of other human interests. Hence man's desire to advance the realization of his own interests by its means. He seeks to give to the state's activity a direction favorable to his own needs. How shall the man thus subordinate to himself this authority? Just like any other force, for example one of the forces of nature. He produces such forces where he needs them, where they will be useful to him. He is compelled, on the other hand, to paralyze or counteract them when they are harming his interests.

A force develops freely only when conditions favor the development. So, for the use of mechanical force a motor and tools are requisite. Authority, as has been shown, has its source in men's consciousness of dependence on the state. To incite authority to action needs only the ability to incite among the citizens this feeling of their dependence and give them a definite object. The man will best understand how to incite such action who interprets it best, sets forth most completely the situation and explains the dependence, the need of a higher power which is felt by all his fellow citizens.

If a man, for example, is filled with the idea of sickness or death, a sorcerer or physician in whom he has placed confidence will have almost unlimited power over him. So, a pious man filled with repentance for an act just committed will be in absolute dependence upon anyone whom he really accepts as an interpreter of the divine will, an intermediary between men and God.

In the same way our consciousness of dependence upon the state can be utilized by him whom we consider as the interpreter of the interests of society. Men acquire such a position in several ways, by success in arms, by the spirit of resolution which they have shown under pressing circumstances, by wealth, etc. He is never a sole interpreter. The complexity and diversity of relations in the life of the state always produce naturally a variety of interpreters for the different needs of the social life.

The authority of our fellow-citizens is not always a proof that they are regarded as the best interpreters of our needs. We often submit to a man simply because others have done so and because we think those others more competent judges of his fitness than ourselves. This submission augments his power and assures him that he can follow his designs. So, then, our dependence with regard to the state leads us to submit, not merely to the one we consider as the best interpreter of our interests, but more often to the one already holding authority over the majority of our fellow-citizens. Even when the submission has no political character; when, for instance, it is religious, it increases the political power of him who holds it.

We should not forget that purely personal qualities in the individual play a great part, too, in contributing to his authority; intellect, force, vigor, birth, wealth, are factors very important for all who adopt a political career.

Such are some of the reasons for which we submit as individuals of the same society to the judgment and the will of other men. Personal influence, authority over a greater or smaller mass of persons, these are for us determining motives which lead to the recognition of this or that individual as the best interpreter of our needs in our relations with the state.

But the wills of these individuals do not constitute the power of the state. Their wills only acquire the capacity of directing under certain circumstances the action of the state and controlling its authority. That authority is not simply the result of their wills, it is the result of that force which takes its rise from our consciousness of our relations towards the state, towards that social grouping which has for a mission our protection against other states without, and against violence of every kind within, by guaranteeing social peace.

The individuals whom we recognize as the representatives of the dominating idea are its representatives. The recognized savants represent science, the artists represent art; but we certainly do not intend thereby to personify science or art or to attribute to them a special will different from that of the savants or of the artists. In the same sense we should call representatives of the state those who interpret our social needs without for that reason, necessarily, attributing to the state any special will. The state, like science, can have representatives without being for that reason endowed with any distinct will of its own.

Each of us by different processes, individuals as well as whole social groups, must get some authority from the state as a force for the realization of our own private interests. This situation produces some conflicts for the possession and use of the state's power. There are, too, conflicts and struggles which arise over the possession of other things. Some conventions, some principles, some rules for determining interests necessarily spring up. They quickly become juridical rules which regulate the employment of the state's authority.

This juridical regulation gives rise to some rights and some duties in favor of and against each person. It brings thus into our relations with the state an always increasing complexity. So long as only *de facto* relations exist between the state and the citizen, the submission is not a duty but a fact. I submit, constantly, to anyone who produces in me a strong enough idea of submission. If the idea were to disappear the subjection would go with it. But in our relations with him who holds us under an obligation of duty imposed by a lawful governmental provision, this submission is a duty imposed by positive law and not resting simply upon our consciousness of dependence. Orders from a policeman are obeyed because important social groups are subject to him in certain ways. The submission is not to his personal prestige, but because the law has recognized him by conferring certain authority. This obligation and obedience arose first from consciousness of dependence upon the state and then from fear of punishment, or of some other disagreeable circumstances to arise from disobedience.

Those persons who have a recognized right of using within certain limits the state's authority are its organs; and since what an organ does is generally called its function, those acts of authority which fall within its legal competency are called its functions, and even, doing away with the connection between the organ and its acts, these last are regarded as functions of authority just as we call in general the functions of living beings, taken collectively, functions of organic life.

The realization of functions of authority, in view of the great diversity among them, requires ordinarily the activity of many persons and extensive material means. For this reason state organs are largely not individuals, but institutions, having a personnel and a more or less complex organization.

If now we examine the organization of these diverse institutions we discover that among the persons composing them, some decide precisely the direction to be given to the organ of authority, and others merely assist in the work of administration and are under the orders of the first. So, then, the different institutions in a state are themselves composed of two categories of organs, those which decide and whose which merely co-operate in the execution of decisions.

The organs which decide are the immediate and direct organs of power in the narrow sense of the word (*Amt-Pouvoir*). The co-operating organs are not immediate ones, but merely assist those which have the power of decision. Thus the judge or the tribunal renders justice, while the clerks, sheriffs, and policemen only co-operate in the work by getting ready the proceedings, making the arrest or executing judgments. The co-operation, too, may take three different forms. It consists sometimes in preparing the case or affair by co-ordinating the different elements involved,—preparation. Or it may consist in counsels given to the really deciding organ,—advice. Or, finally, it may consist in carrying out the conclusion reached,—execution.

So these co-operating organs are divided into the preparative, the consultive, and the executive ones. The preparative one procures the facts and materials from which the decision must be made; the consultive proposes a plan for the decision; finally, the executive puts in actual realization the effect of the decision by material force. These different functions are not all accomplished, however, by distinct organs. A single organ often unites many functions. Thus in the tribunals ordinarily there is no one distinctly charged with the consultive function. With the justice of the peace the preparatory assistance is almost wholly lacking. In other cases, on the other hand, these accessory organs may have an excessive, even almost abnormal, development. So among us (Russia) all the organs of the higher administration are co-operative ones. Such are the counsel of state and the ministry. This distinction between the different categories of organs is found in a greater or less degree among all the state's institutions. The absence of consultive organs in the administration of justice is by no means a necessary condition of those functions. At Rome there was in the tribunals a body of consultive officers, the assessors. But at Rome the judge was not a lawyer and must have recourse to skilled assistance, to the jurist, to get the rules of law covering the particular litigation in hand. The giving of such advice to the prætor was called *assidere.* The assessors gradually obtained official recognition.

In the organization of parliament we find also these different organs. The two chambers decide by their votes. The officers, clerks and secretaries prepare matters for submission. The committees are the consultive organs and finally the guards, sergeants-at-arms, etc., are the executives of the purely parliamentary functions.

In the ministries it is the minister himself who decides. The department constitutes the organ of preparation, while the consultive organ is the council of state and the different special advisers appointed for technical qualifications. The ministries being central institutions need no executive organs apart from the general executive of the state.

Examining the organs which decide we find three different groups. There are first those systems in which the power to decide is confided to a special organ. That organ may be a single person or a board. It is called unipersonal when the power of deciding is lodged in a single person even though that person is surrounded with agencies which co-operate in the manner above indicated. Thus, in an absolute monarchy the legislative power is unipersonal even though the ruler has at his side various councils whose advice he takes. The government is collegial when it consists of a combination of persons who decide by a majority of votes. The majority is absolute if the decision is by half of all the votes plus one. It is called relative, on the other hand, when the decision is reached by means of more votes than any competing proposition has, though less than half of all. It is called a qualified majority if at least a special proportion of the votes, as two-thirds, or three-fourths, is required.

The collegial form of government involves necessarily greater expenses and more delays, but offers a guarantee of impartiality and is preferable from this point of view. The unipersonal organization gives to the institution the greatest speed in acting upon different affairs. The most important point in selecting the form is to fix the responsibility with which the functionaries are charged. Such responsibility may depend upon the character of the function—legislative or judicial, for instance,—or upon the form of government—absolute monarchy, for example. In these cases it is necessary to obviate the troublesome consequences of lack of responsibility and to repress the abuses which might result. The collegial form best answers these conditions. Finally, the power of deciding may be given to one or several, the decision of one being conditioned upon the assent of the others, as at Rome it was conferred upon the two consuls. In our time, too, criminal jurisdiction is given to two boards at the same time, the judges and the jury. Between these last, of course, there is a division of authority, the jury passing on the question of guilt and the judges upon the extent of the punishment. The legislature, also, is commonly separated into two houses. Sometimes organs which together exercise the power of decision have a different organization so that they may each serve as a check upon the other. In this way in some constitutional states matters of legislation are entrusted to parliament and at the same time to the sole executive by allowing him the veto.

Finally, there is the system of several appeals. The decision which is entrusted to one organ is not necessarily final, and on the demand of the persons or establishments interested the determination can be revised by some other organ which in relation to the first occupies a higher place in the governmental scale. The organ of decision in the first instance is, as to this higher one, merely a preparative organ. It renders an effective decision, and if there is no appeal, that decision becomes final and the higher organ does not act. The number of tribunals in the series is commonly two or three and it is especially in judicial institutions that this organization is met with.

Consultive institutions are most frequently of the collegiate form, but when purely consultive have no power of decision. According to their character they present three different types,—first, the councils of state, whose members must have, above all, administrative experience; then, technical boards; and finally representative bodies which include representatives of local interests and of corporations of all kinds.

The function of the councils of state is generally to assist the organ charged with the final power of decision especially when this latter is a single person. The representative councils aid only those organs which have no representative quality themselves. The technical councils are found in connection with all state organs. The consultive organs had their widest development in the French Constitution of the year VIII, which applied the rule: "To act is the function of one person; to deliberate, of several." Such a system presents great inconveniences. It does not reduce the danger of arbitrary action. It does diminish the responsibility of the deciding body.

This observation has no application to technical boards. Their opinions have, or should have, a scientific value which sets them entirely apart. The preparative bodies are the bureaux or departments, but their organization is of no legal importance.

Executive organs assume extremely varied forms. The most impôrtant one is the army, which is under the immediate orders of the chief executive. But the other internal organs of the inner life of the state are numerous. Their organization is upon two different systems; either to each deciding organ there corresponds an executive one or the general executive power is confided to one and the same body, as, for instance, the police. The first is the English system; the other prevails generally on the continent and especially in Russia.

Such are the fundamental principles of the state's institutions. As for their personnel, it is very different according to the phase of development reached by the nation. Three principal epochs are distinguishable, in a general way, in the development of nations.

At the beginning there is no general system of regulating political organs. The task of government at that time is very simple and the people themselves, without much intermediary, perform it. The organ of legislative power, the consultive functions and the administration of justice are all confused. The people meet for all these purposes in general assembly and the army consists of the same people combined for war. The prince and the military chiefs subject to him are the only distinct organs at this time, and as yet are but slightly distinguished from the mass of the people.

The second epoch is that of organization by classes. The government of the state gets into the hands of a separate class, the nobility for example. This class holds all political positions, some of which become hereditary. Such an organization marks by contrast with the former an important advance. The class specially charged with the public service participating in all government action acquires, naturally, an increasing influence and capacity from generation to generation. The transmission of these duties, imitation of ancestors, family tradition, education directed from the earliest years towards political life, all this was for the young noble so much of guarantee of his political capacity and energy. His energy, zeal and devotion to public affairs would go on increasing because, to the ordinary stimulants of interest, duty, and patriotism, would be presently added that of class and family distinction.

The organization into classes, however, could not long stand in the face of general social development. It carried in itself the germ of its own destruction. In the first place functionaries drawn exclusively from among members of one single class of society would represent not merely the interests of the state but those of their class, and would surely provoke by their acts discontent among those excluded from power. As these latter became stronger they would grasp some part in the direction of affairs.

Then the ruin of this type of government was caused also by the very development of the specialization which the administrative function requires. So far as division of labor and variety of function grows up in the state, the general preparation, on which the class spirit depends, becomes insufficient and more and more the requirement of a special technical preparation becomes imperative. Presently there is formed a body of individuals to whom the state service becomes a genuine profession.

With the new organization of government which takes the place of the old two facts are of special importance. First, the tendency of influential members of society to enlarge their privileges as against the nobility and subject the latter to their control. Second, the formation of a distinct class of professional functionaries whose high position in respect to power is an unavoidable fact.

The task of government in all modern states requires a technical preparation. The rôle of functionary in the modern state requires so much of the individual's time as to make the state's service now a real profession. Moreover, that the government may not be exclusively in the hands of one class, it is indispensable to give the other members of society some influence and allow to them also some function in the state. It is for this last reason that the personnel of the different departments of government comprehends two elements,—first, a set of persons destined to the service of the state as to any other profession; second, a class of persons who are merely representatives of the interests of other classes of society.

In other words, in making up the modern establishments of states, there is a professional and a representative element both included. The first is to guarantee competent knowledge and experience. The second is to serve as a check upon routine and class spirit.

These two elements have to do with each of the different organs of the state. Legislation and the administration of justice equally require them. Their combination varies. Sometimes they are so wholly distinct that the same function is confided to two separate organs each composed of one of these elements. In most constitutional countries legislation belongs both to the popular assemblies and the so-called "government." The judges and the juries represent them respectively in the administration of justice.

In other cases these two elements enter into organs, but only one of them is charged with deciding, the other merely co-operating with the first. This happens when along with the deciding organ which is professional there is a consultive part which is representative. It is necessary to distinguish the system which organizes a separation of these two elements of the organ from that in which there is a combination of the two. As regards an organ in the form of a board, this is made up in part of persons appointed for professional character and in part of persons elected. In a unipersonal organization this combination is realized if the one individual unites in himself a professional and a representative character, as takes place, for example, when a functionary, appointed for an indefinite time, as a consequence is called upon to take part in a local council (Prussian Landrath, or Russian Chief of Division).

Section 46. *The Form of the State's Organization*

ZWEIREV. The Main Classification of States.
KORKUNOV. Russian Public Law, I. 8th ed., 1908. pp. 100–131.

The organization of public institutions offers a great diversity, which has its influence over the general structure, of states. One can always reduce this diversity to some leading types. The study of these types is also that of the forms of state organization, or, in other words, of forms of government. This study early attracted learned attention. The oldest classification of governments is that based on the number of those ruling. If the supreme administration is in one person the government is a monarchy; if in a considerable number, it is an aristocracy; if in all, it is a democracy.

This extremely simple classification is in Herodotus. It is still in our time the one with the most partisans even among the most modern schools, as witness Roscher, for example. Such a classification offers meanwhile some serious defects, as Aristotle already pointed out. These defects appear in all their force when the extremely complex organizations of modern states come under consideration.

First of all, who are to be designated as the rulers? If we mean by this term all those into whose hands any part of governing authority comes, so that all others are merely to be regarded as co-operating in the government, the term monarchy can only properly apply to an absolute one. In a constitutional monarchy, parliament is not restricted to co-operating towards a decision of the sovereign, and it is not from him that it gets its power. On the contrary, it constitutes an independent organ which limits the monarch's power and draws its own from the people's mandate.

If, on the contrary, we include as rulers those in whose hands is placed not the whole government in the large sense of the term, but only the executive power, most republics, since they have in our times usually a chief at the head of the executive, would be included under the name of monarchy. The name of democracy, too, if defined as government by the whole people, is not truthfully applicable to any existing state. Nowhere does the whole populace share in the state's power. Things presented themselves somewhat differently in antiquity because then those who were deprived of rights were usually deprived of them altogether and made slaves. In defining the government as that of all, all free men was understood. But in the modern world while everybody in this sense is free, everybody does not, anywhere, partake in the functions of public power. Even where universal suffrage, so called, really exists, it is only one-fourth of the population which has the right to vote and of these not more than two-thirds use the right. Consequently only a sixth of the population take part in elections and the choice is actually made by a majority of these; that is, by something more than a twelfth of the whole population.

The number of rulers is in general the result of chance and circumstances. If this is to be taken as the sole test of classification it would be necessary to say that Russia under Peter the Great ceased to be a monarchy and became an aristocratic republic. This error of accepting the number of rulers as the sole ground of classifying governments leads immediately to another one, that of seeking to find a criterion for classifying states which would serve to explain all the differences between one state and another. Thus Plato reduced the differences in the forms of government to that between the three virtues,—sagacity, courage, and temperance, of which sometimes one and sometimes another prevailed in the state. Aristotle counted as the principal distinction among governments their regular or irregular forms, counting as regular such as subjected the personal interests of their rulers, whoever they might be, to those of the state, and those irregular which placed higher the personal interests of the rulers.

Montesquieu specially undertook to exhibit the guiding principle in each case and he distinguishes several principles: virtue in democracy, moderation in aristocracy, honor in monarchy, and fear in tyranny. Heeren derives the distinction between forms of government from distinctions established between individuals. If the subjects are slaves despoiled of all rights it is a despotism. If individuals have only civil rights it is a monarchy, and a republic if the citizens have both civil and political rights. Lorenz, Stein and Mohl have sought chiefly to establish the distinctions between governments upon their relations not to the citizens but to society.

All these definitions have value for explaining the state's activity. To characterize completely a state there is need, certainly, to explain the connections which exist between that state and the moral principles and subjective rights of the citizens; but all this serves only to fix the interior life, the social life of the state, without furnishing a basis for the distinctions of its various external forms.

All states, it is today universally agreed, may be divided into monarchies and republics, but the basis of this distinction is not the number but the legal situation of rulers.

In the republic every one who holds any part or parcel of authority has also some responsibility and this is true of the humblest elector as well as of the president of the republic himself. In the monarchy, however, there is an irresponsible organ of authority, the monarch. This difference of responsibility in the first case, and lack of it in the second, is the characteristic in their functions. The difference is not in the number of persons exercising those functions. The President of the United States has more power than the King of England, but the President is responsible to Congress and so is not a monarch. The King of England on the other hand is not responsible and therefore, despite the narrow limits of his power, remains none the less a monarch.

The character of the state's organization cannot fail to be modified by the fact that a holder of power which he is exercising in his own right and not as a state mandatary is irresponsible. If there is in the state an irresponsible subject, some of the legal rules established with a view to assuring order become to that extent destitute of sanctions. They maintain a certain force and importance but they derive it, as against such privilege, from morals or usage, not from legal effect. So in a republic the legal organization of the state is more thoroughly wrought out than in a monarchy. But on the other side, the personification of the state's authority in the monarch is for the advantage, as Stein points out, of the state's independence in the exercise of its authority over powerful social classes.

These two conditions have compelled the recognition of the difference between monarchy and republic as a fundamental one among the forms of the state's organization. It is necessary to add further that the chief of the state, called upon to represent it at home and abroad participates more or less in all that is done in the state's name, in legislation, justice, or administration. This is why the independence of the monarch's power and his irresponsibility have a certain influence upon all the manifestations of the state's power. The monarchial principle requires that nothing be done contrary to or even aside from the monarch's will. In his name justice is rendered. He appoints all the high functionaries of government. To him belongs the right of veto and so of deciding upon the law and its promulgation. All these powers the president, too, has, but the difference is enormous. In the first case the laws are promulgated by an irresponsible sovereign, in the second by a functionary responsible for his acts before the people.

From the monarch's irresponsibility results finally the essential peculiarities of the monarchical government. It is possible, and such examples could be cited, that the government should be in the hands of several irresponsible individuals, but this is exceptional. The exercise of an irresponsible power is hard to reconcile with the division of that power into several hands. In a monarchy, therefore, we see generally that all manifestations of power tend towards the unipersonal form.

The republic, on the contrary, is better suited to a collegiate organization of government. It is better suited to the republican principle, which is always to subject more and more the powers of government to the people; and, so far as modern republics show a preference for unipersonal forms, it is because of the influence of monarchical ideas. Where, as in Switzerland, a republican organization has long existed, it is under the collegiate form.

In the same way hereditary power is conformable to monarchy and elective power to a republic. Only hereditary power is completely independent. Elective monarchies have always shown a transitory form, and today have all disappeared. Even in these elective monarchies the power of the monarch was always for life, and not for a limited time as in republics, and this because such limited power leads to a fatal dependence on the citizens. So, too, in republics the president is always elected for a definite time and usually a short one. The most common term is ten years. This was the term under the French constitution of the year eight for the consuls. The French president now is elected for seven years. So, then, irresponsibility of the monarch, who governs without being subjected to another organ, and by his own power, constitutes the essential distinctive mark of a monarchical organization of government, and establishes the fundamental distinction between it and the republican form. But both the monarchical and the republican principle may receive a more or less complete application.

Monarchies can assume different forms according as the state's authority is centralized in the monarch's hands and all the organs of government act only by his orders, or, on the contrary, according as there are other agencies outside of him, for example the popular representatives, which retain some portion of public power. In the first case when all the authority is in the monarch's hands it is an absolute monarchy, and is a constitutional monarchy when the authority is shared by the national representatives.

The multiplicity of forms of republican government cannot rest merely on different combinations of republican and monarchical principles. If there is monarchical power, however limited it may be, there is no place for a republic. Republics, however, are distinguished according to the degree, more or less advanced, of the realization of the republican principle, according to the greater or less subordination of all the organs of authority to the will of the people. The greater the participation of the people in public power, the less independent are the institutions and mandataries of the people. A distinction is made between true republics and representative republics. The first is an organization where the people participate directly in the legislative function. A representative republic, on the contrary, is one in which this right does not belong directly to the people but is confided to representatives, and the people have only the right of naming these.

Section 47. *Power and Law*

IHERING. Zweck im Recht. I, 1884. pp. 176 ff.

Whatever may be the state's organization, whatever powers it may have, the human conscience tends always to subject this power to legal rules. To the interests of power are necessarily opposed the principles of law. In submitting to the authority of the state the citizen requires of the organs of power a similar submission to law, because to whatever height the interest of authority of order may rise, it can never wholly annihilate and engulf men's other interests. In centralizing force into its hands the state thereby assures to all its citizens good order in all their mutual relations. In defending its international independence and external power the state assures at the same time the preservation and development of national culture and the social life of the country.

But however important the state's function may be in thus assuring the preservation and development of society there is a throng of other human interests which are liable to fall into conflict with those of the state. The individual who regards himself as his own supreme end cannot consent to the sacrifice of all his interests to sustain order and peace which are in his eyes only a means for reaching that supreme end. For this reason he opposes, altogether naturally, to the interests of power his own interests, and guards and defends them against the grasp of the state. This is the origin of those legal rules which delimit the interests liable to fall into conflict, the state's on the one hand and the individual's on the other. This limitation, applied to the rights of the state, goes on developing increasingly, keeping pace with social development itself, and has appeared at all epochs of history. No government denies the existence of these legal obligations and the greater the political development of the society the greater also is the circle of these obligations. But how explain this limitation applied to power by law?

For the partisans of natural law this question received one of the simplest of solutions. Certain rights, said they, are inherent in the individual, in his quality as a human being. They are independent of the state, existing outside of it, absolute and inalienable. By consequence they escape all action of authority itself. It is these rights which form the basis of the limitations upon political power. The existence of these limits is so much the more natural, as the authority of the state rests upon the free agreement of individuals.

But the question cannot today, when the doctrines of the school of natural law are no longer admitted, receive the same solution. Today, only the existence of positive law created by the historic development of human societies is accepted, and in it the authority of the state constitutes one of the most important factors. How then explain the birth and development of law in a society united precisely by a common obedience to the state? How could this law create the rules which limit the functions and powers of the state itself?

In the theory which identifies the power of the state with its will, dominating all, the restrictions which the law applies to this power can be explained only by the considerations of opportunity, or by the idea of the ends of the state. If power is the will which dominates all and there is no natural law to limit this will, the restrictions imposed by law upon the state's activity can be explained only as limitations to which that dominating will consents with a view to some personal end. It is the autolimitation of the state which is the source of constitutional restrictions. It is thus that Ihering explains the birth of this law.[1]

For Ihering, all law in a general way is created exclusively by the state's authority and is merely the product of the state's power. He shows first of all that conformity to law is the first condition of political force. Physical force can never take the place of one acting according to reason. The best politics, Ihering concludes, is conformity to law. This conception is very simple. In fact the state's power in becoming less extended, in limiting itself in order to act conformably to law, only strengthens itself; because this restriction makes the sentiment of law so much stronger in society. There is no room for doubt that the chief support of the state's power is only a strongly developed sentiment in favor of legality. Power in a state can never be supported solely upon physical force, because the ruling portion of a state is always a minority of the society. Consequently this feeling in favor of legality is so important a support. It leads the citizens to discharge the legislature's demands and guarantees the enforcement of the law by them, even in cases where such enforcement conflicts with their special interests. We can understand that this sentiment should be the principal force in government, for it induces the voluntary submission of individuals and restrains the power of the state within fixed limits; for despotic power is one of the leading hindrances to the development of the sentiment of respect for law. This sentiment makes necessary for all a rigorous observation of the law, above all for those charged with power, and particularly for the organs of the government.

[1] Die Gewalt gelangt zum Recht nicht als zu etwas ihr Fremden, das sie von ausserhalff vom Rechtsgefühl, entlehnen und nicht als zu etwas Höheren dem sie im Gefühl ihren Inferiorität sich unterordnen müsste, sondern sie treibt das Recht als Maas ihrer selbst aus sich heraus—das Recht als Politik der Gewalt.

At the side of this consideration which urges power to act in conformity with the laws, which assign limits to its freedom of action, another at the same time presses it towards the same result; it is the idea that a regular organization is the condition for successful discharge of the state's functions. Regular organization effects indeed a great economy of force and would seem, also, to be one of the bases of the state's power. But such a condition can be maintained only if the most rigorous equality is observed among the organs of power.

Thus, according to Ihering, there are two reasons which explain the self-limitation of the state's power: first, because in thus limiting itself it strengthens the sentiment of legality which is the principal source from which it draws its own strength; and then, because legal rules being recognized as obligatory, not only by the citizens but by the organs of power as well, the force of the state thereby gains a regular organization and effects an economy of strength.

Ihering's suggestions evidently contain a large part of the truth. If the representatives of power are well advised and understand their situation they will assuredly limit their activity with a view to their personal interest and in order to consolidate their authority. But all this does not yet explain how all the limitations imposed upon power for the juridical organization of the state are consequences of a conscious self-limitation of its power established solely for its own interest. This would, first of all, contradict Ihering's own doctrine according to which the law's development does but follow as a result of the conflict of interests. If law is such a result of conflicting interests there cannot be a simple self-limitation set up by power. The history of the development of constitutional government shows, in fact, that it is very rarely that the government consents voluntarily to submit to the restraint of law.

In most cases the restraints upon political power, applied by law, are the result of an embittered conflict between different elements of the society. These restrictions are not in all cases imposed solely because of considerations of advantage and, consequently, they do not present an optional but an obligatory character, as a result of being established independently of the opinions of the different organs of power. Our conception of political power, looking at it, not as a force which has its source in the will of the government, but rather as one arising from the feeling of dependence on the part of the subjects, furnishes a more satisfactory explanation of the law's control over the state's power. It explains this restriction as an objective fact quite independent of any calculations of advantage on the part of the organs of power themselves.

If political power rests upon the consciousness which the subjects have of their dependence upon the state, this is sufficient to determine the nature of the acts of power and the conditions of their realization. These acts cannot be determined merely by the will of the rulers. For an organ of power to draw its strength from the notion of dependence with regard to the state with which the citizens are penetrated, the acts of that organ must have a certain harmony with the ideas held by the citizens as to their relations to law and to individual and social freedom. The power of the state exists only to the extent that it is accepted by the consciousness of the citizens, and for this reason the notions which individuals have as to their own freedom and social liberty produce a corresponding restriction upon the state's power. Thus, the limitation of power by law arises not only from well-advised representatives of the state's power limiting it by the rights of the citizens, but also and especially from the fact that the idea which the citizens have of their dependence upon the state is never unlimited, and with the development of social life, with the creation of a throng of other societies at the side of the state and with the growth of international relations this feeling of dependence on the state becomes more and more restricted.

The power which the state has over us, and the limitations applied to that power by law, have a common basis, which is the notion which we have of our dependence upon the state, and also the consciousness which we have that there is a whole category of interests opposed to the interests of power and that they require that an ascertained limitation be applied to the state's activity.

Section 48. *Combinations of Governmental Powers*

VOROSHILOV. The Division of Powers, 1874.
FUZIER-HERMAN. La Séparation des Pouvoirs.
KORKUNOV. Decrees and Legislation, 1894, pp. 193, 227.

Men do not recognize themselves as subjected to the state in any unlimited and absolute fashion, and this is why in accepting the necessity of such subordination they recognize at the same time that the organs of power are also obliged to conform to legal rules which regulate the relations between the interests of power and those of individuals.

Such is the general and essential basis on which rests the limitation applied by law to the state's power. But even in a state of small extent there are so many and such complex institutions that this notion alone of the necessary existence of such limitations is not sufficient to secure that all the acts of power shall conform to legal requirements. In addition to this the organs of power must be disposed in such a way as to make difficult, if not impossible, encroachments upon the law's domain. It is only in our time, with our numerous political theories as to the state and the individual, that this question has been studied.

Montesquieu, in his famous theory of the separation of the powers, indicates such a separation as the only means for the guaranteeing of liberty. This theory is found in Book XI of his L'esprit des Lois, 1748, which has for a title, Of Laws with Regard to Political Liberty Considered in Relation to the Constitution.

The different states, says Montesquieu, pursue different ends. Rome pursued the augmentation of her territory, Sparta, war; Judea was wholly devoted to religion, Marseilles to commerce, China to peace, and

Rhodes to navigation. Savage peoples still seek natural liberty. Despotic states are given up to the sovereign's will. The monarchy seeks glory. Poland sought independence for each citizen and ended in general servitude. Finally there is one people all whose efforts turn towards the single end of political liberty. That people is the English. Their organization certainly comes the nearest to liberty.

In the whole state there are three powers,—first, the legislative; second, the executive as to international relations; third, the executive as to private law relations. The first promulgated the laws whether transitory or territorial; the second made war and peace, sent ambassadors and repelled invasions; and the third punshed crimes and executed legal process,—was the judicial power.

If the same individual or institution united at the same time legislative and executive powers, liberty would no longer remain, for it was to be feared that the same person would proclaim tyrannical laws and then execute them tyranically. Liberty would no longer exist if the judicial power were not separate from the legislative and executive; for then, laws over life and liberty would be arbitrary because the judge would be at the same time the legislator. If the judicial were combined with the executive the judge would readily become an oppressor.

In fine, all liberty would disappear if the three powers fell into the hands of the same individual so that the same person should hold all three. Such a government would have as complete a power of executing the laws as of making them. It could ruin the state at pleasure by its general dispositions and pursue and condemn each citizen by its special judgments.

All those who have power seek to abuse it. They seek always its increase so far as possible. To avoid arbitrariness it is necessary to confide the exercise of public authority to several powers so that one shall serve as a check upon the other. The judicial power ought not to be given to a permanent body but to be left to chosen individuals elected by the people to hold such a position for a short time.

In this way this terrible power not being given to a class nor to a given profession would become like something invisible, like zero. It would not be the judges which would be before the mind; one would look to the judgment and not to the judges. The other two powers, on the other hand, can be given to permanent bodies since they are not in direct relations with individuals.

In a free state every man ought to govern himself, and, by consequence, the legislative power should belong to the whole people; but in the great states this is an impossibility. Even in small ones this causes too much inconvenience. The people, therefore, must act by representatives.

In every state some men are distinguished by birth, by wealth or by glory. If they are confused with the mass of the people and have like the rest only the authority of their vote, liberty would be slavery for them and they would have no interest to defend it. Their participation in the legislative power ought to be proportional to the prerogatives which they have in the state; but they will be so only if they form a distinct chamber possessing the right to veto the conclusions reached by the house of representatives, and this latter should have the like power over the conclusions of the other house.

So the legislative power should be confided to two separate houses, the house of lords and the representatives of the people. This organization presents another advantage, also. Since the judicial having no permanent representative can be considered as null there would be left only the two, the executive and legislative powers; and these two have need of a third, a moderating power. The house of lords can fill this place, and the executive power be confided to the monarch; for this power requires prompt action and is better confided to one than to several.

Montesquieu's theory very quickly became popular. It received many applications and served as chief director for the American and European constitutions of the end of the XVIII and beginning of the XIX centuries. But presently the accuracy of the theory began to be doubted. A more profound study of the English constitution showed that this rigorous separation of the three powers which Montesquieu thought he had found in it did not in reality exist there.

The English parliament is not in reality limited to legislative functions. It extends its influence over every part of the government.

Different attempts have been made to correct Montesquieu's doctrine, and among these ought to be cited those of Benjamin Constant and of Hegel. Constant thought that only the ministers had executive power and that the king had none, but only a moderating power.[1]

The king occupies a peculiar place above all parties and has no other interest than that of maintaining order and liberty equally for all. The monarch's lofty situation ought to inspire him with an ardent desire for peace. His place, one might say, is above human passions and the *chef-d'œuvre* of the political organization consists precisely in this, that amid the discords and above them there is created an inviolable sphere of peace, of grandeur and of impartiality which permits all quarrels to end of themselves or else stops them in time by legal means. If the danger is caused by the ministers the king has the right to dismiss them. If the house of

[1] Benj. Constant Principes de Politique, 1875. Chap. II.

lords becomes a menace by an obstinate resistance, the king may name new peers. If it is the house of commons, he may dissolve it. Finally, against injustice perpetrated by the judiciary he may interpose his power of pardon.

Hegel, like Benjamin Constant, regards the king as a distinct power and believes that the judiciary and executive are only branches of one power. He distinguishes only two powers,—aside from the king's, the power of determining general principles or legislative power of bringing particular cases under a general rule, a power of government which is exercised at once in judicial and executive administration. These different attempts to modify Montesquieu's theory can hardly be accepted.

First of all the joining into one power that of the judiciary and the legislature cannot be accepted. The historic development of the social life furnishes us with the proof that the judiciary cannot be considered as merely a special branch of the executive power. It separates from the general executive before the legislative power itself does, and one should rather consider, placing himself at the historical point of view, the executive and legislative as two branches of a unique power of government. The delimitation between the legislative and the executive functions is much less rigorous than that between the judiciary and the other two. The legislative power constantly needs to resort to the executive to carry out its enactments. The judiciary scarcely ever experiences such a necessity.

The very character of the functions offers more resemblance between executive and legislative than between the former and the judiciary. Legislation and the carrying of it into effect both look to the future. Both are seeking to set up something new and assume a creative character. The judiciary, on the contrary, plays a part that has to do with the past. It brings forth nothing new. It merely protects existing rights. Its activity is essentially conservative. The administration of justice is guided in its activity solely by the principles of law. Legislation and the executive power on the other hand are guided principally by views of advantage, by opportunism. The law serves only as an external limit and not as an internal principle to guide their activity.

This distinction in functions exercises also a certain influence over the organization of the institutions charged with performing them. The organization of legislative and of executive institutions present much more resemblance to each other than do those of the judiciary and the executive compared as a whole. Judicial institutions rest entirely on the principle of their independence as regards both society and government. It is, in fact, on this condition alone that justice can be freely administered and the principles of law applied. The organization of the legislative and executive institutions rest on different principles. The national representation and local autonomy subject them constantly to the action of society. Ministerial responsibility subordinates executive power to the legislature. Finally, the whole organization of executive institutions rests upon the principle of monarchic control of different administrative organs. The lower power acts always in accordance with indications from above. Judicial institutions on the contrary, even in courts of first instance, act independently and upon no one's orders.

Judicial power offers some characteristics so distinct that a special science has been formed whose subject of study is judicial procedure and organization. The study of the legislative and of the executive departments of government on the contrary have always gone together and have constituted one science, that of constitutional law.

To complete Montesquieu's theory by adding to it a special moderating power is almost equivalent to denying his theory absolutely, so far as he proposes to accomplish this "moderation" by distributing the state's powers and functions among different institutions. Montesquieu affirms that it is precisely this distribution of powers which safeguards liberty without disturbing the harmony of social relations. There is, then, according to him no need of a special tempering function to unite the others. Harmony among political powers according to Montesquieu is the result of proper distribution among the different institutions, and to ask if a special moderating function among them is needful is equivalent to asking whether his theory is good or bad.

Since Montesquieu's time it has been quite the habit to teach that the separation of the powers, the distribution of the functions which make up the public power among several different holders, really constitutes the surest guarantee of the individual's freedom.

Montesquieu already gave to his theory a categorical formula by declaring that only the distribution of these powers in accordance with his principles could assure liberty. His successors have gone farther. Placing this separation upon a philosophic basis, while he only gave it a concrete expression, they declare it absolutely necessary.

Such attempts to split up the powers are false. The elements of public power cannot be reduced to a single absolute unchangeable principle. The elements out of which it is formed are developed little by little along with the social life itself. They are not the result of the dismemberment of an abstract notion of power, but they constitute the differentiation in the manifestations of that power as concrete phenomena. The three powers as Montesquieu distinguishes them, are not an indispensable attribute of every state.

At the time when the whole legal life was controlled by custom, there was no legislative power. The state did not fulfill that function. The legislative power only appeared later with the state's development. But the development of the state did not stop with the appearance of the three functions of power. The greater the state's activity, the more complicated its rôle, the more varied, also, are the forms of its power, its elements, and their functions. Once the power of the state did not speak through general rules. Today it is no longer satisfied with one form of generalization. Several are necessary for its use and it employs constitutions, legislation and general decrees and administrative rules.

If with the development of the state the functions of the state's power also develop, we cannot assuredly make the guarantee of liberty depend upon his particular division of the functions of power. Liberty is no longer guaranteed by a special distribution alone of power among these functions, but by a general distribution among different institutions. The distribution may vary from moment to moment.

These are not rectifications of detail; but, on the contrary, this general observation prevents the theory of Montesquieu from becoming one capable of truly explaining all the forms for the distribution of functions of power among different organs.

Montesquieu presents his theory as if the reciprocal limitation of organs of power were only possible if there is a distribution among them of different functions of power, and he takes no account of other functions than executive, legislative, and judiciary. At the start it cannot be admitted that this reciprocal check of the different organs of power is truly the result of a wise distribution of the functions of government among its organs for guaranteeing freedom. Why, indeed, should the mutual dependence and moderation of each other on the part of these organs assure liberty? Because, says Montesquieu, all holders of power are tempted to abuse it. That it may not be abused one holder must be able to check another. But the abuse of power consists in an organ's performing its functions not in the general interest of the whole state, but in some personal interest. With such a discharge of functions of power, dependence upon the state turns into a personal dependence upon the organs of power, and the citizens' liberty is no longer respected, since it depends not upon objective conditions of the social life, but upon subjective considerations in the mind of the person controlling the organ of power which uses for his benefit all the state's force.

It is, of course, impossible to assure the entire disappearance of such abuses. Power can only be exercised through organs composed of men who are subject to their own passions, their own aspirations, their own interests, real or imaginary. Collision between personal interests, therefore, and the state's are always inevitable and it is always to be feared that personal interests, being the warmer and the more directly effective upon men, will overcome the more remote and abstract interests of the state.

It is impossible to change human nature and uproot from the human soul its passions and interests. Some guarantee, then, of the state's general interests by means of such an organization that the different ambitions of men shall themselves neutralize each other, is needed. This object will be in a degree obtained if the different functions of power are entrusted, not to a single person, but to several, in such a way that each important act of power shall not depend exclusively on a single will.

Among several individuals personal interests ordinarily differ and those individuals seek each on his own behalf the realization of his own interest, so that contention promptly arises. This weakens the influence of private interests which may come to nothingness by mutual opposition.

The general interests of the state have equal weight with all individuals and are not paralyzed when entrusted to several persons because they tend in the same direction, but they are thus, on the contrary, freed from the effects of individual interests.

Such a result is reached not only by entrusting the different functions of power to different organs, but by giving the same function to different ones at the same time. It is not simply the legislative, judicial and administrative organs that modify each other's action, but, also, the two Roman consuls, each possessing equally the same powers, mutually checked and limited each other in exercising them. Each of them, exactly because he had power equal to his colleague, could annul the orders and acts of the other and though both exercised the same functions, between them as individuals there was an opposition of powers that produced a reciprocal limitation.

It is at bottom the same principle which is found under the modern organization of the legislature into two houses, with this difference always, that a conclusion by either one is in no case sufficient, and an agreement between the two chambers is required for a valid act.

In all these examples the same function is performed by several organs at the same time, all of them having equal authority. There is no subordination among them. It may happen, however, that the various organs charged with the same function may be subordinate one to another. This happens in the case of appellate courts. The higher ones can arrest the action of the lower ones. The converse is not true, and it is to be observed that the action of these courts is not simultaneous but successive. Naturally different ones, having more or less power, but possessing equally jurisdiction, moderate reciprocally each other's activity.

In this way the mutual moderation of each other's action by the organs of power in a state is sought not only by entrusting its different functions to different organs, but, also, by giving the same one to different organs. There are, however, other means for moderating the wills which direct the state's power.

The organs of power are ordinarily represented by institutions composed of a number of persons. Even in the unipersonal organization of institutions it is unusual that the power of decision, properly speaking, belongs to a single person. He is commonly aided by others charged with co-operating in these functions. The organ of decision is thus surrounded with consultive organs, advisory boards, executives, etc., always composed of a good many persons. The special influence of each person depends as much upon the organization (collegiate or unipersonal) as upon the procedure adopted for dispatching of affairs.

This influence depends, too, upon the way in which questions are voted upon, whether unanimity, or only a majority is required, and if the latter, whether an absolute or only a relative one must be had. Must there be a public or only a secret inspection of the vote? The same affairs may be voted on in different ways in the same council with different results according as one or another method of procedure is followed. So, too, the different ways in which all the organs participate, organs of co-operation, consultive or advisory, have also an influence upon the action of the deciding organ. In Russia, for example, although all matters belonging to the supreme administration are to be resolved by the monarch, in fact, however, it is of much importance for an affair's determination to know who has prepared it, the council of state, the council of ministers or some particular minister.

Then, too, different procedures applied by the same organs influence the decision of any given question. The setting in motion of a special procedure of course favors the action of the will of the agent who has charge of that process. Well, it is precisely in the influence of procedure upon the direction of governmental activity that guarantees of impartiality must be sought. The government, in setting in motion for its purposes of administration the activity of its agents, compels them to conform to precise rules, makes their wills impersonal and impartial.

There is, too, a certain separation of powers not only between different institutions, but in the same organ between different aspects of its activity. Such a separation of powers in the same organ having for its object the limiting of the action of power there is, for example, in the case where the same organ, following the same procedure, is charged with establishing constitutional measures and with passing ordinary legislation. It cannot be said that the omnipotence of parliament has in such a case suffered any loss by the setting up of the new constitutional rule. The revision is not entrusted to any special organ, yet, always, the modification of constitutional provisions is more difficult and by this fact the legislative activity of parliament finds a certain limitation.

The same distinction exists, too, under an absolute monarchy when there is adopted for the promulgation of general legislation a special procedure, distinct from that followed in the case of decrees of the emperor. The absolute monarch is omnipotent like the parliament which is also the constituent assembly. But, if only those acts of the emperor which are put out in a certain form, have the force of law, his power is none the less limited in a certain degree. The consultive council, for example, if there is one, ought to be advised before the promulgation of the law.

The power of the state can then be limited in three different ways, and not simply by the separation of the powers; first, by distributing different functions among different organs, then, by executing the same function by different organs, and finally by giving several functions to the same organ but requiring under differing conditions different procedures.

All these forms can be brought under one conception, that of the combination and collaboration of powers. The mutual checking brought about by this adjustment of acts of power, results, always, in the combination of powers in some one of the three forms just indicated.

These different forms do not apply the same checking effect to all the forces which make up the state's power. This check appears most of all in the execution of the same function by several organs. In this case each organ has an absolutely equal power with its associate organ, and every act which it performs can be set aside by an act of the other. When the different functions are discharged by different organs their mutual moderating effect is less direct. Each organ in the discharge of its own function is entirely independent, and their action on each other is only indirect, and is caused by the fact that they depend upon one another for the functions with which they are charged. Thus, for example, when the legislative power is separated from the executive the latter would be limited only in the degree that it would depend upon the legislature. In the performance of its own discretionary powers there would be no limitation.

This reciprocal limitation is still more reduced when it is the same organ which is charged with different functions, each following a special form of procedure. In this case the limitation does not assume the form of opposition between independent wills but that of mutual influence, as the two cannot of course be at the same time equal and one subordinate to the other; the one being charged with deciding, the other only with co-operation.

These three forms of combinations of power can be joined to one another, and form new combinations which would create a greater variety in the functions of the different organs of the state. The functions of power can be subdivided in various ways among different organs and also the same organ can perform various functions. Such an adjustment is in contradiction to the specialization of the organ's activity, but would not do away with the reciprocal limitations to which they are respectively subject. We have already shown that the combination of powers is a principle altogether opposed to that of the division of labor. This is why such a mode of activity does not necessarily suppose specialization of the organs of power, and each organ may not always perform the same identical function. The complex combination of powers only supposes the resolution of different acts of power into their integral elements and the performance of different elements of the same act by different organs, so limiting one another.

It is quite possible that the same organ in different cases performs different functions. If, for example, a legislative organ has the right of sanctioning a budget, and also that of calling a minister to account, these functions quite naturally become very diverse, and the organ's specialization is reduced; but the cases in which the different organs limit each other become more and more numerous because an agreement between the two powers, legislative and executive, becomes more necessary, needs to be more permanent. We would say the same so far as concerns the part of the chief executive in preparing laws, when he possesses the right of veto. His functions become more varied and less specialized, but the reciprocal limitations of the legislature and the executive go on enlarging.

So, when the principle of the separation of powers is raised up to the more general one of the combination of powers, the facts of political life which were found to be incompatible with the principle of the separation of powers, are found to be explained completely by the more general principle of their combinations and collaboration.

There is no state in which the three powers, executive, legislative and judiciary, are wholly and rigorously separated from each other. Even in states whose constitutions proclaim an absolute separation of them, such separation cannot in fact be accomplished. The executive power does not stop with enforcing the law. It makes, itself, some general rules of procedure which are legal norms. The legislative bodies do not merely promulgate laws, properly so called, but they put out, also, administrative orders under the form of legislative acts, and so encroach upon the domain of the executive. All of these facts contradict absolutely the principle of the separation of the three powers. The principle of the combination of the powers, on the contrary, explains these facts as special cases of collaboration.

BOOK IV

POSITIVE LAW

CHAPTER I

THE SOURCES OF POSITIVE LAW

Section 49. *Positive Law*

The permanent connection between men leads us to make our conception of law objective. Legal rules primitively elaborated by the subjective consciousness find an objective expression under the conditions of social life in customs, which are a result of juridical practice, and in legislation, the instrument of governmental power. All these external forms of law do not depend for existence merely on the subjective consciousness. Customs, judicial practice, legislation, present themselves as something objective. The very changes which occur in customs and in law and which go to make up the phenomena of social life, are not caused according to the laws of mental phenomena, but according to the special laws of social life. However, the subjective conception of rights is not destroyed by customs, by judicial practice, nor by legislation. This conception goes on developing as a necessary manifestation of the individual's psychic life and as it is more mobile and not so subject to laws of its own, it can hardly fail to develop differences from the law which is expressed in objective forms.

Hence a division of law into two parts: the legal rules on the one side expressed under the forms of customs and of legislation constituting the positive law, and the law, "right," on the other side, under its subjective form which develops freely. This division exists not only in law but throughout the whole domain of human activity under the influence of the conditions of social life. Doubtless, in spite of the subjective conditions of human activity, despite all individual qualities, knowledge, and experience, the social and intellectual life go on developing more and more. They have grown unceasingly by the labor of former generations and may be considered as the capital of human activity. But all this culture thus obtained cannot destroy the individual factor and is at the same time a guarantee of the development of the race. A fruitful activity is impossible for any one unless it is conformed to this social culture which has been slowly elaborated, but the creative factor remains always the individual. This social culture is, like capital, the fruit of labor, and powerless to produce new values unless new labor comes to its aid. So, the development of human life depends upon subjective conditions.

Positive law is only one element of this social culture, and, as each social stage is only a heritage from past generations, it results that it can neither destroy nor replace that subjective conception of law and right which springs from the immediate needs of the present life and upon which depends the further development of the positive law itself.

To imagine a juridical life which should be absolutely determined by positive law alone, without any participation of the subjective conception, is something as impossible as to imagine a religion without any religious sentiment, morals without conscience or feeling of moral duty, or a nation without the individual's productive activity.

Positive law depends necessarily upon the subjective conception of right, but, at the same time, as it consists in a heritage from the past it can never be in perfect correlation with the subjective conception of the present generation. In positive law there is always an element, already grown old, which does not answer to modern needs or to modern conceptions of justice. This is why positive law has sometimes been regarded as an hereditary malady of human society.[1]

In all cases the subjection of human relations to the rules of positive law is something vexatious and troubles somewhat the free development of social life. Some such considerations as to positive law are mingled, however, with others much more favorable.

First of all positive law offers the same advantages as are possessed by society. In using the positive law to regulate our mutual relations we are using something which has been modified and elaborated by a whole course of generations. The individual's subjective conception cannot embrace the infinitely varied and multiplied relations of the law. I might elaborate, myself, voluntarily, a number of cases in which my interests would conflict with those of my fellows, but these cases, relatively few, might easily fail to fit some circumstances of which I had not dreamed. Positive law, being a product of the experience of many centuries, is always much more complete than any possible conception of subjective right.

The idea of doing without positive law, constructed by successive generations, might be held at a time when it was believed that there was a natural law, a system of legal rules created by nature herself. This eternal and absolute law must appear as more complete than the gradually developed positive law. But if we no longer recognize the existence of natural law, we can no longer set up against positive law any but a subjective conception of right and law, a conception itself gradually devel-

[1] "Es erben sich Gesetz und Rechte
Wie eine ewige Krankheit fort."—*Goethe*

oped under the influence of multiplied conditions and which cannot possibly replace positive law.

If positive law is more complete, it is also more general. Juridical norms regulate our interests, all the interests of men. This is why they ought to be known by all. To be sure, since the subjective conceptions of law also spring up, as a result of social conditions, it, too, presents a certain generality; but this generality is altogether conventional and limited by numberless individual peculiarities and a great diversity of human consciences. So, the generality of the subjective conception of law is limited to a very small circle of individuals. Society, on the other hand, grows unceasingly, and a constantly increasing number of men must be taken into the circle of legal relations, and this is why legal rules must be known of all men and be recognized as obligatory by everybody. Only positive law can answer such a requirement.

Positive law itself, also, is very diverse and much varied. It, too, depends upon conditions of time and place, but this dependence is expressed by external signs. For this reason positive law is distinguished by great precision.

The changes which take place in the subjective conception of law arise in an intangible way, which very often shows no outward indication. On the contrary, changes in custom, in judicial practice, or in legislation are manifested by facts which are external and easily recognizable.

It is, then, only the positive law which can furnish these principles which are assumed to be known to all within the sphere of its action. It is on this principle that the doctrine rests, that no one may claim not to know the law, and no man's ignorance of it shall do away with his responsibility. *Error juris semper nocet.*

Section 50. *Foundation of the Positive Law's Action*

The foundation for the law's action rests in general among the vital conditions of society. With this thought one can say that law acts upon humanity as the sole and indispensable agency for establishing some kind of harmony among the constantly clashing individual interests, not permitting the overthrow of society, nor sacrificing to social order the independence of individual people and their freedom. Starting from another point of view as to the very essence of law we would reach an altogether different statement of it. Thus Stahl says: "*Gottes Ordnung ist der Grund des Ansehens des Rechts.*" According to Kant the foundation for the obligation of obedience to law is the latter's accordance with reason; according to Bentham it is in the possibility of betterment, the advantage of the greatest number of people.

Just now we shall not enter upon this question. In speaking of the foundation for the action of legal norms, I have in view the question of why in a given government, a given society, there acts inevitably some given system of positive law, with all its peculiarities and differences from other systems, acting with it in the relations of time and space.

The need of some juridical order is universal in human societies which have attained a certain degree of development. As a matter of fact, this immutable law shows itself under very various forms because in each society it is not merely law in general which has effect, but a system of legal rules fashioned for that very society. Law, in furnishing order to the social life, subjects the state to the conditions of time and space.

It is for this reason, in order that it may always answer

its purpose and not become a dead letter that the law must always assume a form adequate to its epoch and environment. Subject to this reservation, laws act in an independent fashion, whether or not they harmonize with divine precepts or with the results of reason. The rules of positive law act with the same independence. All this leads to the question as to the foundation for this relative independent action of each system of positive law.

Law is not something which, like natural and physical forces, exists independently of human action and may be opposed to this latter. It is, on the contrary, an order established by men and for themselves. It does not matter, so far as concerns this, whether the man acts according to the law of causation or acts freely. Whichever it be, law established in accordance with the principle of causation, or by uncaused voluntary action, it is always the work of man. It is also a rule for the mutual relations of men to each other. It is a social order. This is why the need of law and the possibility, even of its creation, is out of the question apart from society. Law can exist only as there exists union among men. Law, therefore, is nothing foreign imposed upon men from without. It is a product of human consciousness and for it to exist there must be association, a social life, among men. Law, born with the society, is created by that society as the rule governing the relations of the associated. In each society it acts as if created to bring about the union of all the members.

So the foundation for the action of positive law consists in the fact that it is made by the society itself, and in each society has no force except in so far as it is the work of that society.

It sometimes seems that there are exceptions to such a rule. It sometimes happens that there is found in a society a law which originated outside, in some neighboring society. In this case it is important to distinguish between the law of the country itself and that which comes from the neighbor. We have in mind at this moment, not any distinction in the material, but only a distinction according to the form, according to the basis, for the action of the law. Consequently, if the legislator takes his material in part from foreign laws and in part from native ones and local customs and makes of the whole one common law, no distinction from our present point of view will be left between the national and the foreign law. But it may happen that a foreign law as a whole has effect over a country. Ought such a case to be considered as an exception to the principle that the positive law is to be considered as always the product of the society where it is applied? In the German Empire of the XIII and XIV centuries Roman law, without being fused with German law, has weight of its own and a power independent of local law.

It might seem at first sight that such a fact would completely destroy our thesis that law acts only in the society in which it was made. To settle this question, however, it is not enough to show the force of Roman law in Germany in those centuries. The route by which it got there must be examined.

The *corpus juris civilis* is a legislative compilation. Three compilations, all three the work of legislative power, have gone to make it up and give it all the force it has. But, carried into Germany, it became a customary law. By consequence of such custom, by connecting with such a basis of action, it renewed itself completely. In Germany the *corpus juris civilis* acted not as the will of the emperor of Rome but as German custom. Consequently, in fact, while certainly derived from a foreign source, this law so far as it was German positive law, manifests itself as the work of the German nation. This is why in Germany Roman law is recognized as acting only within the limits of the usage which applies it, absolutely as German customary law. Its appropriation was based on the work of the glossators, but they did not interpret all parts of the *corpus juris civilis*, and the parts they laid aside were never applied in Germany.

This appropriation of Roman law offers for Russia a practical interest since, thanks to it, Roman law acts still as a subsidiary law in the Baltic provinces which were once under Livonian rule, a fief of the Holy Roman Empire. Roman law has left its mark on nearly every state in Europe. In France it never ceased to act in the southern part, and later the lawmakers brought it into the northern provinces also. Even in England and Russia, which are among the states most distinguished by a special legal development, Roman law has had great influence, at least upon the practice of special tribunals. Thus in England, aside from the church, which according to one jurist's expression, *vivit lege Romana*, Roman law has found application in the admiralty jurisdiction. It has, in fact, formed the basis of international customs, known under the name of Rules d'Oléron, which is mostly made up of rules from Roman law.

In Russia, Roman and Byzantine law were frequently placed under contribution by the church tribunals, and it is truly to be said that the ecclesiastical jurisdiction was formerly quite extended. Roman law received among us the form of a canonical law and its influence has been very great over the development of all law and especially that of the family.

Greco-Roman modifications of the *jus civile* have penetrated even into the Caucasus and into Georgia. The second part of the Georgian code, that of Bachtang V, who lived at the end of the VII century, contains some laws of Leon the Wise, of Constantine, and of other

Byzantine emperors, relating to the administration of justice. Georgian law is distinguished by large borrowings. Besides those indicated there are many from the Pentateuch and from Armenian legislation. Since Georgia's subjection to Russia it is the code of the Council of 1649 and the military code of Peter the Great which is in force.

Foreign law may be adopted by legislative act. Thus, for example, the French code was adopted in Poland, Belgium and Italy, etc. Such an example is found too in the mediæval history of the cities on the Baltic. Thus, the city of Rega took from its founder, Bishop Albert I, the law which was in force in Visbi, a town distinguished for its mixed population so that every nation had a street in it. The city of Revel is of interest juridically. The Danish King Erik V in 1228 bestowed upon it the legislation then in force in Lubeck. According to the ideas of that day the Lubeck magistrate was the highest court for Revel. So the Revel magistrate in cases of doubt betook himself with his question to Lubeck and got there a determination. Lubeck law prevailed in Revel not merely as it was when adopted, but with later additions and changes. At the same time similar relations prevailed between Revel and Narva.

In southwest Russia prevailed in the same way the law of Magdeburg which had been bestowed by the kings of Poland and was continued in force by the Moscow Czars.

In all the preceding examples foreign law prevailed without change of form, controlling unchanged the foreign society by its adoption, but special action in that society introduced it, the will of the local government. Consequently this borrowed law, none the less on that account, presents itself as taking its force from the act of that same society in which it is in force.

Section 51. *The Sources of Law*

PUCHTA. Gewohnheitsrecht, I. ss. 143–148. Vorlesungen I.
SAVIGNY. System, I. ss. 6–57.
MUELLER. Die Elemente der Rechtsbildung. ss. 427–443.
AUSTIN. Lectures, II, pp. 526 ff.
ADICKES. Zur Lehre von Rechtsquellen, 1872.
REGELSBERGER. Pandekten, I. Sec. 82 ff.

We have already said that the correlation of the positive law with the subjective law, the sense of right, is not complete, that this was to be regretted; but it must, however, be recognized that the positive law offsets this by its precision and the ease of knowing it.

In considering the origin of law we showed that it had been first established as a determinate order of the mutual relations which men have with each other. Each individual expects his neighbor to observe the same conduct under the same circumstances, and if it happens that this expectation is not realized, then he will require of the one responsible for the injurious act compensation for any wrong which he suffers. Under such conditions each of us asks the same question, how to distinguish the general rules of law, which are obligatory upon all, from those rules which have only a subjective force.

It is highly important for each of us to determine beforehand with all possible precision what are the rules which govern us, and what are the rights they give us, and the obligations they charge us with. An exact reply can be made only as to rules which have become objective. To do this they must assume some specific form. This is why the theory of the forms which make up the objective character of a law has such importance for the jurist.

These objective forms of legal norms which serve to indicate the obligatory character of the rule are called "sources of law." To understand the doctrine of the sources of law, it is very important not to confuse the technical meaning of the phrase with that ordinarily given to it. We must distinguish, in fact, the meaning here given to the expression "sources of law" from that of mere means of knowledge, *fontes ex quibus notitia juris hauritur*. Sources means also historic monuments, and the word is used in this sense in the historic sciences. These notions can be applied in part to the very matter now under consideration, but never by more than an altogether superficial analogy, due to accident. If, for example, we have the authentic text of an enactment, we may say that we have the source of the law in the technical sense of the word and that we have at the same time its source in the meaning that we have the means of knowing it. But if such a text is not to be had, if we have the law only in the same indirect way as we do, for example, the twelve tables, or the law of Voconia, or others, such original laws are still sources of law without being any longer in any sense sources of knowledge of the law. In the same way if we learn of some rural custom in Ephimenko's or Pachmann's collections, these collections are the source of our knowledge of it, but the custom itself is the source of the law or of any effect upon law thereby produced.

These different conceptions have been often confused, especially in antiquity. So among the Romans it is, thanks to a confusion of these two notions of source, that there arose a distinction into written and unwritten law. (*Jus scriptum* and *jus non scriptum.*) This distinction was rigorously applied and the written law included, besides legislation, the prætor's edicts and the *responsa prudentium*. It was required that the law be at its origin written down (*inscriptum quod ab initio litteris mandatum est*). From this it resulted that a custom written down after its establishment, remained, notwithstanding, unwritten law, and the jurists established a new distinction between a law created by written enactment or establishment, and one already existing which is then set down in writing. Despite the slight importance of such a distinction it was sedulously preserved, and was even developed by later jurists. Thibaut puts this distinction at the head of his classification of sources of law, and Glück developed it very far. He accepts like a good many others the distinction between the *jus scriptum sensu grammatico* and the *jus scriptum sensu juridico*, which latter includes only law consciously established by means of written language.

A later confusion is that which has arisen between the source of law considered as the mark which distinguishes it as obligatory, and the source considered as the matter from which the content of legal rules is drawn. Such a confusion grew out of the fact that before the time of the historical school it was thought that law was the legislator's creation pure and simple.

The will of the legislator was then recognized as the sole cause of legal rules. The command, laid down by sovereign power, to observe a given rule was according to the opinion of that time the sole authority for saying that the rule was obligatory. We, on the other hand, are able to recognize that legislation is one force for creating rights, but that it is only one of the forms under which right, the work of conscience, law, is expressed.

The legislator does not create the law arbitrarily. He has no power to make rules which are not prepared for by the march of social advance. Legislation passed in any other way remains a dead letter and totally unapplied. The question of the sources of law thus put is totally different from that which we are seeking now to examine. For this, it would not be important to know whether or not a rule is obligatory upon all, but merely to know what factors participate in its establishment.

If we understand the question in this last fashion we may admit with Adickes that the general source of law is subjective reason, or, better said, the subjective consciousness. All the other factors affect the formation of law only through our consciousness. Divine orders, the nature of things, reason, conformity to an end, moral duty, all this can induce the formation of legal rules, only on one condition, which is that all these motives are admitted by the human consciousness. The general consciousness is only the sum of individual ones, and this is why it can be said that the subjective consciousness is like a hearth where concentrates the action of all the creating factors of law. But this subjective consciousness cannot be admitted as the source of law in the technical sense, because the subjective consciousness of a norm is not the index of its obligation over us and is not the form of its objectivity.

In the practical meaning of the term only custom, judicial practice, and legislation can be recognized as sources of law. It cannot be admitted that the nature of things is a source of law, for such nature is very differently understood among men. The conception recognized by enacted and established law, customs, and judicial practice, is the only one obligatory for all the world. It is necessary to say this much as to the conception of justice which is held by all, but in such different fashions, and which receives objective precision only on condition of being expressed through the sources of positive law above indicated.

Finally, and for the same reasons, we must place in this category of false sources, the science of law. The numerous controversies, which the question as to what are to be considered sources of law, has given birth, come most of all from wrong notions as to the action and function of the sources of law.

Before the appearance of the historical school, when positive law was still considered as a voluntary human institution, it was believed that legislation, expression of the creative will of law, was the sole force in setting up positive law. Therefore legislation was then recognized as the sole source of it because there was no other creating force to produce it.

The historical school taught a diametrically opposed theory. The force creating law is for them the genius of the people which embraced all positive law even before it was externally expressed by the "sources," which were then considered as only sources of our knowledge of the law, living in the genius of the people. In this way these authors considerably enlarged the notion of the sources of law by adding to it the science of law, which certainly serves as a source of our knowledge of law, but which cannot furnish the quality that makes these rules obligatory. The definition which we have accepted of sources of law, the recognition of what they are as necessary juridical forms for setting up objective law and serving at the same time as the mark of the obligatory character of the rules, this definition holds the mean between the two other definitions we have discussed.

Therefore the source of law has importance only as a test of the obligatory character for us of the given rule. Legislation or custom are not forces which create law, but merely forms by which we decide that a law is obligatory. Any rule may have its effect, but one which is not expressed through legislation, custom or judicial usage is of slight effect and supposes for its completion the enactment, custom, or judicial acceptance. Its action has little precision because it lacks the external index of an obligatory character. It is impossible to show in advance what its action will be or to indicate to what particular cases it will apply. Its application to each case must be shown. On the contrary, a rule expressed in the general sources of law can be precisely limited in advance. In such precision there may be a distinction of more or less, but this is nonessential. Only the action of legislation can be exactly delimited. It is only of it that we can say in a general way, accurately in advance, to what cases in both space and time it will apply. The same precision cannot be reached as to customs and judicial usage. The precise moment when the action of a rule of custom or judicial usage will commence cannot be foretold. Custom is established little by little, and it is hardly possible to fix the exact boundary between the established custom and the one only forming. Judicial usage presents a form a little better ascertained, notably so as regards decisions of a given time; but the existence of a rule in a decree or judgment supposes that it was previously recognized as obligatory, for the judgment always rests on anterior facts.

To this peculiarity of precise action which legal rules have, another should be added. They are presumed to be known to all. No one may claim not to know the law; it is presumed always that each individual can easily take knowledge of rules contained in any of these sources. If he does not know, his ignorance is his own fault. There is no need to prove to the tribunal the rules of positive law. It knows them. *Jura novit curia.* Only facts are proved. Laws are not.

This doctrine that the laws are known is not justified by facts as to all kinds of rules. It may easily happen that the judge does not know the common law or local legislation. The common law is precisely one in which jurists have taken no part. It is established without them and independently of their activity. It is not the jurists who are familiar with the common law, but those who create and follow this law derived from custom. This law presents the peculiarity of changing with locality and with classes of individuals. So, the parties can more easily than the judge, who is placed outside the *milieu* of these customs, bring together the proofs of the actual existence of this law. In the same way the judge cannot know the law of all foreign states. The conscientious study of the law of only one country takes up a good deal of time. It is to be added that the cases for the application of the laws of foreign countries are rare. So, for customary law and for foreign law the principle of *jura novit curia* is not rigorously applied.

As for customary law its application was, according to some jurists, a question of fact, always to be proved by the party in order to warrant its application. Without this the judge would not apply it even if he knew it. In such procedure the judge knew only what was produced during the hearing. *Non refert quod notum sit judici, si notum non sit in forma judicii.* This was Hofacker's and Wenning-Ingenheim's opinion. It was the logical result of the conception then held of the natural law as the mechanical theory held it. If the action of a rule of customary law depended solely upon a simple definite observation of a given custom, certainly the existence of such a custom is only a question of fact, as is admitted today in cases of trade usages. These latter are distinguished from juridical customs in that they carry in themselves no *opinio necessitas.* They are the result of simple observation of a given fashion of acting, and are only questions of fact and not of law.

The customary rule thus considered as a mere fact depending upon circumstances, harmonizing badly with certain rules of procedure, several authors, Thibaut (1722–1840) and Hönner (1746–1827), the celebrated opponents of Savigny as to codification, introduced a modification of this idea and demanded that a thoroughly notorious custom be regarded as a law. If accepted by only a small number of persons it might be regarded as a question of fact. Such a distinction is, nevertheless, entirely abstract. How, indeed, can this transformation of a question of law into a question of fact be explained according to the greater or less notoriety of the custom?

Puchta and Savigny produced a more accurate conception. They recognized that the existence of norms of customary law is always absolutely a question of law, that customary law is, like all others, always supposed to be known to the tribunal *ex officio*, and that it is only in case of actual impossibility for the court to know the custom that it is permitted to expect a party to set up the custom and prove its existence. But if they claim a custom known to the judge there is evidently no need of requiring proofs as to the existence of such a custom.

The same rules are applied to foreign law. The question of its application is absolutely one of law. And since it is impossible for the judge to know the law of the whole universe when the question is one of applying a foreign law the proofs of it ought to be brought by the parties claiming under it.

Section 52. *Customary (Common) Law*

GLUECK. Ausführliche Erlauterung der Pandektem nach Hellfeld, ein Commentar, 2 Ausg. B. I., 1797. s. 442, n. ff.

KLOETZER. Versuch eines Beitrags zur Revision der Theorie vom Gewohnheitsrecht, 1813.

PUCHTA. Das Gewohnheitsrecht, 2 B., 1828, 1837.

BOEHLAU. Mecklenburgisches Landrecht. B. I., 1871. s. 315.

ADICKES. Zur Lehre von Rechtsquellen, 1872.

SERGEIEVICH. Essay upon the Study of Customary Law. In the Observer, St. Petersburg, 1882. Nos. 1 and 2.

SCHUPPE. Gewohnheitsrecht, 1890.

Customary law is the primitive form of positive law. None the less, the recognition of custom as an independent source of law was scarcely established before the second quarter of the nineteenth century. Up to that time legislation was thought to be the sole independent source of law. However, few went so far as to wholly deny the obligatory force of custom. Of those who did so the most celebrated in the eighteenth century were Thomasius and Grolman. They admitted custom only as a reason for affirming the existence of a contract or of legislation compatible with it. Most writers recognized the existence of customary law-making without attributing to it any independent force. In democratic states, where the legislative power belonged to the people, customary law was deemed merely a special form of such popular legislation. The obligatory force of the law and of such custom was thought to be the same. In both cases it was the people's will, in one case directly expressed and in the other by facts leading to an *a posteriori* conclusion of its existence (*facta concludentia*). This exception gave birth to the notion of a silently established law, *lex tacita*, and it was this idea that under republican *régimes* replaced customary law. Such an explanation could not be admitted for monarchical states, especially for autocratic ones such as most European states were in the XVIII century. In those states legislative power did not in fact belong to the people. So, to explain the obligatory force of customary law recourse was had to the idea that the legislator gave to custom its obligatory character. It was held that the custom became obligatory as a result of the legislator's assent (*consensus imperantis*). There was dispute as to whether this consent applied to all the customs in general (*consensus generalis*) or only to all those which were specially for some particular cases (*consensus specialis*). Some required a special consent for all customs without distinction. Others like Hufeland, Thibaut, and Glück required such a consent only for those which derogated from legislation. Others like Heffner, Baltzen and Kestner, admitted as sufficient in all cases a general consent. Special consent was supposed to be given silently by the very fact that the custom could be applied. It was thought, on the other hand, that general consent came directly from the *corpus juris civilis*.

The weakness of all these theories is evident. They are all based upon absolutely arbitrary fictions, and all turn in the same vicious circle. The doctrine of the identity of the will of the people as expressed both in the customs and the legislation of democratic states is wholly fictitious. In the most favorable cases the national assembly includes only one generation. Custom, on the other hand, is slowly formed, and is the work of many generations. Only will expressed in determinate forms can create legislation. Customary law is built up outside of all forms. It furnishes form to the formless.

The famous sanction of custom supposed to be given

by the legislator is also clearly a fiction, for it is not legislation which precedes customs in the historic sequence, but quite the contrary. Customs appeared long before legislation. It is therefore impossible to maintain that legislation serves as the basis of customs. The precise contrary is the truth. Sovereign power at the beginning rested entirely upon custom. As to the general consent which some authors think to find in the *corpus juris civilis*, it is sufficient to recall that the *corpus* itself cannot be considered in our time as having anywhere legislative force. Accepted in practice, but having behind it no executive force except some text of legislative enactment, it must be considered itself as merely customary law for modern nations.

The historical school, and especially among the authors of that school, Puchta, gave the finishing stroke to all these theories. His Das Gewohnheitsrecht remains to this day the best study of the subject. In it Puchta established the new theory. He not only recognized for customary law a wholly independent significance, independent of any harmony with the legislative will, but that it is an antecedent condition for legislation. The foundation of customary law, said he, is the natural generality of the conviction of the nation's purpose. This immediate national conviction finds expression in customs, and its realization in laws is therefore by the establishment at the beginning of customary law.

Manners and customs form the primitive law of peoples, just as some kind of a system is the primitive law of jurists, and verbal expression of the legislator. If customary law stands in such strict and necessary connection with the natural conception of the nation, and is the immediate result of the latter's activity in the legal direction, can it be asked, then, whether custom has independent force as law, or why it has? Customary law, if this is the case, acts for the same reason as all law does, the reason which produces this conviction of nationality and that there are such things as peoples. If the existence of a unified people is in fact recognized, some activity must be attributed to the genius of that people, and consequently some conception of moral and legal freedom be formed, and since customary law is nothing but this conviction in its immediate and concrete form, the existence of customary law is inseparably bound up with the people's existence.

There is still less need of direct proof that the force of customary law does not come from connection with the other sources of law; for the establishment of law immediately through legislatures and the activity of jurists, presupposes an immediately established law through custom giving them authority. For if there were no nation and no immediate consciousness of nationality there would be no state and no jurists, and by consequence no juristic or enacted law; so, the very essence of these forms of law affirms the force of previously established customary law, and there can be no doubt as to this point.

So Puchta attributed to customary law an absolutely independent capacity, but only so far as related to the customs of an entire people. Customs of this kind are always relatively rare. Local customs, on the contrary, are quite numerous. This observation was made by Unterholzer in his critique of Puchta's theory, and by Muhlenbruch. Savigny, also, thought to correct Puchta's doctrine by recognizing the unity of the people as a necessary common basis for the formation of the custom and a ground for its force as law; but that just as legislative power can promulgate laws at the same time for the whole state and for special localities in it, in the same way the people's immediate consciousness of law may take the form of customs for distinct localities, as well as for distinct classes, which are considered as organic parts of the nation.

Savigny in formulating this theory started with this idea, recognized by the historic school, that the unity of a people is not a result of historic evolution but something innate and which existed from the beginning. This, however, is not what history teaches us. As Sergeievich has shown, it is not general customs which are found at the origin of nations, but rather special ones, and only little by little do they become general. And again, as is admitted elsewhere, Savigny's theory does not explain the formation of certain customs, as in ecclesiastical law, and certain international customs which cannot in any way be admitted as customs taking their origin spontaneously from the general unity of the people.

For all these reasons the doctrine of the historical school ought to be regarded as insufficient. In very recent times the birth of a new conception is to be observed, one which considers that customs are obligatory simply by the fact of their long standing. This is notably Adickes' opinion. According to him, the very long existence of a custom compels us to recognize its obligatory character. This is explained first of all by the fact that for a legal judgment the existence of *some* definite rules is generally the most important point and it matters relatively little just what the rules are. Besides this, it is necessary to consider that in most cases customs are conformed to some end, since they are the work of individual interests. Finally, time has, in general, the quality of giving a special stability in man's eyes.

This opinion, however, cannot be accepted. In seeking to escape the too exclusive result of the historic doctrine, Adickes has fallen into the opposite extreme. The historic school believed that the creation of obligatory customs was only possible as a result of the unity of a people. Adickes did not regard the fact that the custom, considered altogether as law and not as habitude, is not simply a manner of conduct long observed but it is only such a particular manner as is observed in a given human society as obligatory.

The existence of unvarying habits among the men with whom we are in relation presents this advantage, their fixedness compels us to accept them as they are, even if this causes some trouble. But a mere individual habitude is not a custom, and its duration cannot be considered as the index of the obligatory character of a rule. Custom, as we have already shown, is one of the forms of consciousness of a law which has become objective. A man in expressing himself uses the forms of grammar and rules of style elaborated by a people's common life, and at the same time his language becomes not merely the expression of his own ideas but, also, a part of the popular language and a vehicle for expressing the ideas of that people. In the same way a man expressing his ideas as to law uses forms elaborated by the common life in society; these forms are taken up and become the expression of the collective consciousness of law, that is to say, they are transformed into juridical customs. When I act conformably to custom, because it is custom, my consciousness of law is thereby expressed in a manner which conforms to the consciousness of law on the part of others who, themselves also, observe the same custom. If it were otherwise there would be no custom. For this reason the custom exhibits a juridical norm which is accepted not by me alone, but by all who are members of the same society with me. In other words, not because the practice is ancient is it obligatory, but because it is common in that character to all the society.

Some analogous discussions have arisen, also, as to the

origin of customs. Customary law forms little by little through the very life of society and outside of fixed forms, and for this reason controversies about it are so numerous. We cannot directly observe the formation of custom. We can determine its origin only by more or less complex considerations. Till Puchta's time the mechanical theory of the formation of customs prevailed. This theory explained the origin simply by the observance of the same rule in several identical cases. At that time any other explanation was difficult, as we recall that the obligatory character of the custom was supposed to be due to the legislator's recognition of it. The juridical character of the custom was considered in this theory as coming from above, from the legislator's will; but the legislator can give obligatory force to a set of uniform rules drawn up at hazard and which have nothing to do with customs.

This explanation fell of itself with the recognition in customs of an independent capacity as laws. It was necessary to find in the custom itself and in the conditions of its formation the basis of its obligatory character. Instead of the mechanical theory, Puchta set up a spiritualistic one of the origin of customary law, absolutely opposed to the old conception. He affirms that the observance of a rule does not make of it a customary law. Its observance is only the material expression which shows us its existence. The rule existed before it was followed, and was already regarded as an obligatory norm. The juridical custom is distinguished from the simple habit in that it is an external and conscious expression of the rule which existed already in the national consciousness of legal rules. Simple habits are those created by a chance uniformity unconsciously introduced into the conduct of individuals in identical cases. Savigny early showed that Puchta's theory could not be admitted without some reserves. There are, said Savigny, some customs whose formation cannot be explained by the conscious application of an already formed juridical conception.

Such, for example, are the terms to be used in making a formal contract, and the number of witnesses necessary. The juridical idea can only indicate that it is desirable to have the terms and the number of witnesses appropriately fixed, but cannot itself precisely determine either. It is evident that no legal principle can determine just how many witnesses should be present at a given act. For this reason Savigny thought that, besides customs born of the conscious application in private cases of a rule existing already in the popular consciousness, there were other juridical customs, established, notwithstanding their obligatory character, by the fortuitous and unconscious observance merely as habits of some particular fashions of acting.

It is easily understood that Savigny's correction of Puchta's theory does not correct, while it shows clearly the impossibility of explaining the origin of juridical customs by this theory. The theory in reality explains nothing. It considers the juridical norm as the external expression of a norm already existing in the consciousness of the people, but does not explain how any such popular conscience is formed or exists. Has it more reality than the legislator's assent?

If the general explanation of the origin of law before given in this book, is accepted, that of customary law is very simple. In setting forth our conception of the origin of law, it was not possible to lay aside customary law which is its primitive form. We were compelled to recognize that the commencement and the continuance for a time of the custom resulted unconsciously, and that it became "juridical" only when to its observance was added the consciousness of its obligatory character. The consciousness of its obligatory character would appear as a consequence of the tendency we have to believe that identical conditions always produce identical acts. As ndividuals, people so believe each time, in advance of observation, of the order already established, and whenever this order is violated, it produces reaction. If this opinion is accepted, the explanation of the origin of all customs is easy. They are inevitable.

The history of the theories as to the marks of the existence of a juridical custom is equally interesting. The glossators required only two conditions, a long enough time, and reasonableness. Then the number of conditions became greater. Barthol counted three, *longum tempus, tacitus consensus populi, frequentia actuum.* Their successors indicate, besides, *quod consuetudo sit introducta non erronea sed cum ratione et quod sit jus non scriptum.* The number of required conditions went on always increasing, and at the commencement of this century they counted eight, *rationabilitas, consuetudinis, diuturnitas temporis, consuetudo contradicto judicio firmata, pluritas actuum, uniformitas actuum, continuitas actuum, actus publici, actus consuetudinis introductivi, opinio necessitatis.*

The modern *jurisconsulti,* like Böhlau for example, require, as formerly Placentin, only two conditions,—first, the custom must express a juridical conviction; second, it must be old enough. The controverted question is to know what is the connection between custom and law. Can or cannot the custom abrogate the law? Has it that force which is called derogatory?

No law, no rule, being able to claim eternal existence, the possibility must be recognized of applying derogations by future rules, legislative or customary. But there is sometimes in legislation a prohibition against applying customary law either general or outside of the cases indicated. Can such a prohibition take away the derogatory power of customary law? Such prohibitions make very difficult, to be sure, the development of customs derogatory to the law. Tribunals as well as interested parties can by supporting themselves with such a prohibition very easily prevent the application of customs. But if the custom developed all the same despite the prohibition, it could not be denied obligatory force.

It goes without saying that the formation of such a custom is admissible only where the violated law is in the general opinion unreasonable and unjust and with the condition that such opinion is absolutely shared by everybody, by the tribunals, as well as the persons interested. On these conditions surely no one can doubt the obligatory force of a custom which abrogates an unjust law recognized as such by everybody.

Section 53. *Judicial Usage*

IHERING. Unsere Aufgabe. Gesammelte Aufsätze I, 1881. ss. 1–46.

MOUROMTZEV. The Courts and the Civil Law. Juridical Messenger (Russian), 1880. pp. 337–393.

MAINE's Ancient Law. pp. 25–34.

UNGER. System des Oesterreichischen allgemeinen Privatrechts. 3 Aufl., 1878. B. II. s. 151–257.

BUELOW. Gesetz Richteramt. 1895.

FRANKEN. Vom Juristenrecht. 1889.

Judicial usage offers a good many resemblances to custom. Just as in customs, in judicial usage legal rules are not expressed under any general form but only under a form applicable to special and distinct cases. It, too, supposes that the rule before being expressed in judicial conclusions was obligatory. It, no more than custom, fixes the period of the rule's action and it is not surprising that for all these reasons a good many authors, perhaps a majority in our time, have considered judicial usage as a special form of customary law.[1]

There are serious objections, however, to such a conclusion. Judicial usage and precedent occupies an intermediate place between custom and legislation. It presents points in common with each. Like legislation, judicial usage is consciously shaped. While, primitively, custom would appear as simple habit, wholly unconscious of legal relation and entirely outside of all regulation, judicial usage and decision is, like legislation, the result of a conscious effort towards the ap-

[1] Wächter, "Pandekten," I. 1880. s. 112. Stobbe, "Handbuch des deutschen Rechts," I. 1871. s. 146. Malichev, "Course in Russian Civil Law," I. 1878. p. 85. Lüders, "Das Gewohnheitsrecht." Böhlau, "Mecklenburgisches Landrecht," I. 1871. s. 320.

plication of a legal rule. The custom, too, does not become a "legal" one, a law, until to the observance of the rules which it prescribes is added the consciousness of its utility; but the matter of the custom is furnished always by habit. It is formed unconsciously. The legal consciousness which transforms a simple habit into a juridical custom finds a material ready made. On the contrary, the judgments of courts which make up judicial usage are absolutely conscious acts. The matter of each judgment is elaborated consciously and precisely in order to regulate the relations of the parties by law.

Another difference between judicial usage and custom is that, like legislation, judicial usage is not created by society or by some distinct class, but by an institution. This is why, differing in this respect from custom, judicial usage has, like legislation, a recognized authentic legal form. There are recorded authentic orders and judgments. Let us observe, too, that like legislation, judicial precedents ordinarily appear in a written form, while custom, in the beginning at least knows nothing of writings.

There are, then, between customs and judicial usage such differences that it is impossible to class them together and regard judicial usage as a special form of custom. But in refusing to identify them are we not compelled to deny the existence of judicial usage as an independent source of law? Is not the sole mission of the tribunal to declare and apply existing law? Charged with determining special cases, ought it not to limit itself merely to applying the legislation in force when the action was brought before it? To recognize judicial practice as an independent source of law, is this not entirely the same thing as to recognize a right in the tribunal to judge, not according to law or custom, but according to its own will, and to establish thus the uncontrolled arbitrament of the judges instead of a general obligatory rule?

If there is no doubt that the tribunal ought not to decide at its own pleasure but according to law or custom, we cannot on that account deny all creative value to judicial usage and precedents. The government in constitutional states is itself limited to the terms prescribed in the legislation put out by the two legislative houses. However, its acts, decretals, orders, rules of procedure, are an independent source of law. In the same way in many states the two houses have their power limited by constitutions which they have no right to change, and meanwhile the ordinary laws are recognized as a source of law. We see the same phenomena develop in connection with judicial practice. Just as ordinary laws or administrative rules have of necessity a creative capacity, the tribunals themselves are not strangers to the creative genius. The tribunal which decides practical cases, problems which require very often extremely varied and diverse legal conceptions, applies necessarily the legislation in force. Otherwise it could never find the directing thread in the casuistical labyrinth.

But, in fact, legislation is not formed *en bloc*. It is formed gradually, and its parts have been shaped under the influence of diverging, even of opposing ideas. The same thing to a certain extent is true of the different parts of the same legislative act, since all laws are results of compromise between the extremely divergent tendencies which control government or parliament. A legislative act is very rarely the complete expression of a single idea. If logical unity is to be found in it, it is the tribunal's part to develop that unity. This is certainly a creative activity. Legislative institutions have their field, a comprehension in which propositions vary greatly. The same thing which under one conception might be a general rule, might very well under another view be regarded as only a stringently limited exception. Independently of this, in all legislation we find contradictions. They can be dealt with in various ways, and the choice made by judicial usage among the methods has also a certain creative force.

To bring legislative institutions into a logical whole, to avoid the contradictions which they present and complete their *lacunæ*, the tribunal uses general principles of law and supports itself by scientific reasoning. This has led a good many writers, particularly among the ancients, to regard legal science as an independent source of law. But in this branch of law contradictions were numerous, and it became necessary to set up a more general rule that the judge must base his decision upon the combined voices of the most general opinion (*communis opinio doctorum*).

But how find out this opinion? What is the common opinion of all the learned? For this purpose there were several rules of an essential mechanical character. The *communis opinio doctorum* was that which was held by seven savants, or better yet, that which Barthol and the Glosses, that is to say, the *glossa ordinaria*, admitted. If this means gave no result, then the opinion of the oldest savants was to be admitted. A jurist then, had more authority the older he was. Such rules adopted in the middle ages could not remain in force. Most authors, perceiving how impossible it was to replace them with other rules for getting an infallible means for choosing between contradictory scientific opinions, have very logically concluded that science was not an independent source of law.

The historical school, however, found this to be an extreme opinion. The naïve rules of the middle ages, based upon the assent of a greater or less number of jurists, must assuredly be set aside. It was not necessary, however to conclude from this that science in general could not be regarded as a source of law.

The representatives of the historical school have not found any rule for choosing between such contradictory opinions. If there is no possibility of a correct choice, the rules established by science alone have no direct application. Consequently, science cannot be recognized as a source of law in the technical sense in which customs, judicial usage and legislation are; that is to say, as an absolute index to the obligatory character of a rule. It is only judicial application which furnishes the mark of an obligatory norm. In other words, it is not theory, but the practice that embodies a given theory, which is an independent source of law.

In recognizing judicial practice as an independent source of law we must observe that it is not necessary to conclude that a decision once rendered binds the tribunal forever. If every law can be replaced by a new one, surely judicial usage on its side cannot be condemned to perpetual rigidity. But on the other hand, the rigidity which judicial practice has and the precision of its rules have certainly a great value.

One of the first conditions of justice is that the laws be applied equally for all, but such a thing would be impossible without a durable and steady, uniform system of administering justice. For this reason the tribunal is always ready to apply again a principle previously accepted. It requires very important reasons to produce a change in the jurisprudence which a given tribunal has recognized, and it ought to be admitted on principle that a rule once established should be followed in later judgments of the same tribunal.

Section 54. *Legislation*

SAVIGNY. System I. ss. 16–20.
ZACHARIAE. Vierzig Bücher vom Staate. B. IV. s. 1.
BOEHLAU. Mecklenburgisches Landrecht. B. V. s. 283.
JELLINEK. Gesetz und Verordnung. 1887.
SELIGMANN. Der Begriff des Gesetzes. 1886.
HAENEL. Gesetz im formallen und Materialen Sinne. 1888.
KORKUNOV. Executive Orders and Legislation. 1894. pp. 227–228.

The expression of legal rules in customs and judicial determinations has always a casuistical and indefinite character. Legal customs as well as judicial precedents are gradually formed to the extent that there is call for the application of legal rules to special and definite cases. Legal rules cannot therefore find in these forms an expression which is at the same time precise and general. These are defects that become more and more strongly felt as the developments of social life become more complex and varied. Governmental power, designed to uphold and protect law, cannot accept such forms as legal rules. To the degree that it becomes strong enough and firmly enough established, it proceeds to replace these indefinite principles of customary law and judicial precedents by more precise and fixed rules of legislation.

At first this is done only as regard rules that especially concern the government and its organs which are charged with applying them. The relations of individuals with each other, those having to do with property, those of the family, such are the things which customary law controls the longest. But gradually as legislation goes on little by little increasing in scope, it comes to subject to itself all the branches of the law, and thus becomes the general form in which the law clothes itself, and custom and judicial precedent become only subordinate principles of law, secondary and almost exceptional.

Legislation, in the large sense of the word, is every legal rule established by direct action of governmental organs. It is defined often as the will of the organs of governmental power, or of the state. Such a definition is too broad. The organs of the state's power may express their will without any intention of giving to the emitted rule the force of an obligatory norm for all the citizens. Such, for example, are the words which terminate the manifesto announcing the enfranchisement of the peasant. "Make the sign of the cross, believing people, and call down upon you the blessings of God upon your free labor, with the prosperity of your house and your happiness among your fellows."

On the other hand, the definition of legislation as a direct expression of will cannot be accepted because it is too narrow. Even if the legislative act contains only one general rule, it cannot be said that all its special consequences are equally contained and expressed in the law. Even if it interdicts such and such actions in carefully determined cases, the same actions are authorized in all other cases. The law acts, then, not only within the directly prescribed limits, but also within the limits of that which is the natural consequence of the orders put forth, that is, in many cases, beyond any human foresight or any human will.

Very many writers have thought it worth while to put back into the definition of legislation, the idea that it is promulgated only after a procedure instituted precisely for that purpose. This is entirely superfluous. If the required procedure necessary to make what will be recognized as an obligatory rule is not followed, there will be no law, but only a personal command of the person or persons emitting it as representatives of governmental power. If such representative has not observed the required forms, he cannot be recognized as acting in the name of the state. The definition we have given of legislation as a rule established by governmental organs, supposes as already established regular forms for acts in the name of the state. In this definition we have said nothing about publication, which has been by many writers recognized as an essential attribute of legislation. But, in truth, history shows us many examples of unpublished laws. Among ourselves today the fundamental laws provide a category of legislation which remains secret.

As to the question of what is the basis of the obligatory character of legislation, there is no firmly settled theory recognized by the whole world. The representatives of the natural law school have recognized as such basis an implied agreement among men. Every citizen, they say, ought to obey the law because he holds a part in such a contract. Certain ones, like Hobbes and Grotius, add, also, that such an agreement might operate to confer upon some given person or institution the right to make laws.

This opinion in the second half of the eighteenth century was replaced by another according to which each distinct legislative act was regarded as the expression of the general will. Rousseau and Kant and their successors shared this opinion. This theory supposes that every agreement is obligatory in itself and that there is no need of proving this obligatory character, since it is *a priori* evident.

In reality, we often see facts wholly the other way. All agreements are not obligatory, but only those which conform to the law's requirements. By consequence, it is precisely the law which furnishes the basis of their obligation. In all cases to attribute to the law's obligatory character such a foundation as contract, is a pure fiction, and quite often we see laws which do not at all have the approbation of society.

The historical school considered as the basis of the law's obligatory force the legal consciousness of the people. But this, too, is a fiction, as much so as that which made the obligation rest on contract. We cannot deny the existence of a conception of law, common to the nation, but it is impossible to affirm that all laws express only this conception which the people have as to law. Legislation may not agree with this conception, and may even contradict it.

In states whose population comprises different races not yet united by political life, such a contradiction between legislation and the notion of law, prevailing among some of the populations in the state, are even necessary. For all legislation independently of its matter has obligatory force.

A basis for the obligatory character of legislation remains, then, to be sought. Legislation is set up by the organs of power who can on the one side constrain individuals by force to submission, and who have on the other hand an authority in the eyes of the public which often suffices to make their rules observed.

Legislation is established for the most part by those organs of governmental power which have under their direction the organs charged with practically applying it. The same state has usually several sets of organs, and we can thus distinguish legislation into groups according to the organ which produces it.

The most important juridical rules are confided to a special legislative institution, which concerns itself only with legislation and the care of the administration. The less important rules are the work of the executive power properly so called. We shall divide, then, into two groups the rules established by these two branches of authority: legislation (*zakon*, *lex*, *loi*, *Gesetz*) and rules or orders (*ukazi*, *décrets*, *Verordnungen*). Since the directions of the executive power must be carried out in conformity with legislation, and such execution is subordinated to the legislative body, executive rules and orders are subject to enacted law. The order is only valid as long as it does not contradict law.

This formal distinction of legislation and "orders" according to the different powers which establish them, is found at the bottom of the matter out of which they are made. The most important legal rules, those which relate to the most important interests of the citizens, should have their assent, or at least that of their representatives. The details may be arranged by the executive or its departments more competent for such technical questions.

This distinction, however, between laws and orders cannot be formulated in a precise manner, since it is impossible to find any external measure, any absolute outside mark for distinguishing the more important from the less so. So, everywhere in constitutional states, it has been established in practice that an executive order cannot nullify a legislative act. By consequence, all matters already held by the legislative remain within its exclusive competency, at least so far as it does not authorize the executive to regulate such matter by orders.

For all those questions, on the other hand, which have not been regulated by legislation, it is the executive's duty to provide as need arises, by orders. This general rule establishing the relations between legislation and executive orders, suffers, however, one exception. In case of extreme necessity, when the safety of the state is endangered, it is impossible to employ the legislative method. In such a case the executive can take measures and make orders contrary to law, but the ministers are responsible to the houses of the legislature. Legislation and executive orders can each in their turn be divided according to the organs producing them. In a good many states legislation, properly so called, the rules made by organs other than those of the executive, are subdivided into ordinary laws and constitutional provisions which are elaborated either by special organs or by a special procedure. Executive orders are also distinguished according as they are made by the chief executive or by inferior organs of administration, departmental or municipal.

Since this distinction between laws and executive orders is a distinction resting purely upon form, in opposing them to each other, we are advancing a conception resting purely on form. Legislation in the formal sense is merely acts of a legislative body, and this definition can, in a way, be opposed to the one already given of legislation as legal rules established by an organ of governmental power whether under the form of a legislative act or an executive order. The conception with which we are now dealing of legislation relates purely to the form it takes on. The executive orders, so far as they contain legal rules, can be considered as legislation in the only important sense of the word.

The preparation of laws is divided in constitutional states into several parts clearly distinct. For example, in all states where legislation is the work of the executive and legislature combined, there are distinguished: 1st, the initiative; 2d, the discussion; 3d, the sanction; 4th, the promulgation; 5th, the publication of the law. The initiative is the power to propose a law for discussion before the legislature. It can be organized in four ways: 1st, the government alone can have it, as in France under the second empire; 2d, parliament alone, as in the United States at the present time; 3d, the government and the legislature, as in most constitutional states; and 4th, the whole people, as in Switzerland today.

The discussion of the law is the chief function of the national representation. Wherever there is popular representation in the legislature, it performs this function. But the right may have two forms essentially different. It may be simply a right to accept or reject the projected law without right to offer any amendment or modification. Such a situation necessarily supposes that the initiative belongs only to the government.

In modern states a broader right is established which consists not only in accepting or rejecting the project, but also in proposing amendments to it. If parliament is composed of two chambers as happens in most modern states, each of these two chambers has equally the right of discussing projects of law and these projects of law can be sanctioned by the chief executive only after they are passed by the houses, or by one of them.

The sanction or confirmation of projects of law belongs always to the chief executive. The right of sanctioning supposes the right of rejecting, that is, of the veto, which may be absolute or suspensive. An absolute veto is an absolute right existing in some monarchical states of stopping all projects of law after they have been adopted in the legislature. The suspensive veto only checks the project for the time being, but if the chambers insist, the project may become a law under certain conditions in spite of the chief executive. This form of veto is found in republics and in some monarchical states, Norway for example.

The law accepted by the chambers and sanctioned by the chief executive may then be executed by promulgating, and is finally published that everybody may have knowledge of it.

In most constitutional states, as we have said, legislation in the narrow sense of the word is divided into ordinary laws and constitutional provisions. These last are those which establish the fundamental principles of the organization of the government and by consequence are more complete than the others. In some states the right to make constitutional provisions belongs to the same institutions as the right of passing ordinary legislation. The provisions as to their discussion, however, call for more complicated forms, designed to insure maturity of consideration. Such is the case in Prussia and in France. In other states the power of establishing constitutional provisions, which may be called the constituent power, is separated from the ordinary legislative power, and is regarded as the special privilege of the whole people and not of their representatives. In Switzerland, for example, this is the means in use for making a constitutional provision.

Legislation is distinguished, essentially, from the other sources of law, in that it is not an act of application of a rule, like custom, or judicial usage, but an act which lays down a rule.

Therefore the action of legislation is precisely determinate not only as to relations of place, but also in relations of time. Legislation acts only from the moment when it is promulgated and all projects of legislation prior to that are not law. It can also be arranged to have force only during a given time. In any case the action of the law ceases when it is abrogated, or replaced by a new law, or by custom.

The moment when legislation has the force of law is ordinarily that of its publication. The publication of a law is by means of its insertion in a paper specially designed for such service, but the law may not be known on the very day when its text is published in the journal; it requires a certain time for the journal to reach all the towns and villages of the state, and become generally known. So it is reasonable to require, as is done in Germany, that legislation be not enforced until a certain number of days after the publication. If the term is long enough, it ought to be the same for the whole state and all its cities. This gives the advantage of having the law in force on the same date throughout the state. In Germany the time fixed is fourteen days for the mother country and four months for the colonies.

The action of legislation ceases, either by the expiration of its term, if the law was made for a fixed term, or because of a new law abrogating the preceding one. The promulgation of a new enactment abrogates the old one only as to those parts which were actually designed to be replaced. The other rules, set up by the old law and which are not replaced by the new, keep their full force. They can no longer, however, be considered as constitutional provisions. At least, this is so in France.

Legislation is made up of a succession of dispositions, one after the other, at the requirement and according to the degree of needs. Such a diversity presents very grave inconveniences which make the study of legislation more and more difficult, but these inconveniences are further aggravated by the fact that special dispositions arising at quite different epochs are often the expression of totally opposite principles, according to the epoch in which they arose and according to the interest controlling the government's action. As a result there are grave contradictions in the several parts.

A systematic re-enactment of legislation, a complete revision of different laws in order to form a systematic whole, is an extremely practical and necessary thing. Such unification can be obtained in two different ways,—either by incorporation or, better, by codification.[1] Incorporation is a means of codifying law, but merely for those in force, without change of form, so that at bottom they are not modified. It is the unification of the legislation in force. It produces, therefore, only an

[1] Zhinuliak. "As to codification and its influence on legislation and the science of law." Legal Messenger (Russian), 1876.

apparent unification. It does not remove the numerous contradictions which the existing laws previously contained.

Codification does not limit itself to a mere change in the forms of law. It permits the obtaining of a systematic unification from the very bottom of the law, and for this reason the codifier is not limited to working upon actually existing legislation. He can draw from customary law, from judicial decisions, from foreign law, or from the science of law. The code is not simply ancient legislation under a new form, it is new law in the most complete sense of the word.

CHAPTER II

THE SOURCES OF RUSSIAN LAW

Section 55. *The Relations Between the Different Sources*

GRADOVSKY. Principles of Russian Constitutional Law. I. p. 11.
ZITOVICH. Course in Civil Law. I.
TAGANTZEV. Course in Russian Criminal Law. Part I. p. 141.

The sources of Russian law, like those of all positive law, are legislation, customs, and judicial usage. The 47th article of Fundamental Laws says also, it is true, that the Russian Empire is governed by the positive laws, the institutions and the regulations made by autocratic power, as if this text would exclude all other rules than those created by legislation. Article 65 of these same Fundamental Laws provides in its terms that the law should be applied according to its exact and literal sense without any possibility of admitting "the fallacious uncertainty of a voluntary interpretation." It seems, then, that legal rules can be created among us neither by customs nor by judicial usage. In reality, however, judicial usage and, above all, customs play an exceedingly important part in Russia.

This absence of correspondence between the fundamental laws and the truth is explained in the first place by the fact that the editors of the code were under the influence of old conceptions, and they thought legislation was the sole source of law. Customs and judicial usage had no importance in their eyes. Independently of this first reason, at the time when the code was established the people almost universally lived under customs. Serfdom then prevailed and legislation up to that time had hardly touched upon private relationships. As to the judicial power, it was not then yet separated from legislative power and the highest judicial tribunal, the Council of State, was at the same time a legislative institution. For this reason judicial usage had not then been recognized as an independent source of law. If the tribunal found in legislation some obscure or incomplete places, it went for explanation to the court one degree higher, and thus in hierarchical order before the Council of State, was then disposed of according to the opinion of this council, on the order of the Sovereign, that is to say, legislatively. These opinions of the Council of State as to special litigation have played a very important rôle in the development of our legislation. A great many dispositions, still today in force, had no other origin. There was in such state of things no reason why the editors of the code should consider judicial practice as an independent source of law. Judicial sentences at that time constantly turned into legislative decretals. There was no rigorous delimitation between the two. There is none even up to this day, and our code itself brings some attenuation to the principle formulated in Article 47.

Our modern legislation recognizes an extensive enough application of juridical customs by the tribunals. Legislation permits, first of all, to the justices of the peace to guide their decisions by local customs known to all, but only in the precise cases in which this application is authorized or in such cases as the law has no provision for (C. pr. civ., Art. 130). Certain special tribunals have equally the right of employing customs. These are district tribunals, courts of commerce and certain indigenous tribunals.

The application of customs by the district tribunals has special importance, since they are the ones which control almost all the peasants' civil affairs; that is to say, those of the largest part of the Russian population.

Judicial reform in 1864 separated the judicial power from the legislative and at the same stroke suppressed the prohibition against interpreting the law. Today the tribunals are required to decide the actions submitted to them according to existing legislation without being able to assert that the law is obscure, incomplete, defective or contradictory. The tribunals find themselves, then, given the right to interpret the laws. Judicial matters can no longer be carried before the Council of State to be there resolved by legislative methods. The judicial power must itself resolve all the questions submitted to it. In fact our judicial usage, especially that of the Court of Cassation, as a result of the numerous imperfections in the texts of the law, exhibits very often a creative character.

Legislation, however, in Russia, as in all other states at the present time, is the chief source of law. All the legal rules established by the organs of power are so by the sovereign power. The organs of administration have also in an important degree the right of creating legal rules by their own acts on the condition, well understood, of not contradicting the law. It is thus that such a right is given to governors, to municipal councils, and to the provincial assemblies of departments as well as to different ministers through a special delegation. Article 47 of Fundamental Laws must then be interpreted in a restricted way. The laws made by supreme power are not, in Russia, the only legal rules having obligatory force. Legislation itself admits, to a certain extent, that customary law, judicial practice, and the lower organs of executive power are also makers of rules having an obligatory force for the citizens. So Article 47 must be interpreted with the meaning that laws made by the supreme power are the higher form of the rules of positive law in force in Russia. These laws fix the conditions and the limits of the obligatory force of legal rules. Customs, judicial usage, the directions of inferior functionaries,—all these rules are subject in their action to the laws created by the supreme power.

Section 56. *Russian Legislation*

GRADOVSKY. Principles of Russian Constitutional Law. I.
KORKUNOV. Russian Public Law. II. pp. 28 to 88. *Id.* Executive Orders and Legislation. pp. 289 to 357.

The Russian Emperor like all autocratic monarchs has unlimited power, and the legislative function which he performs is not limited in any way by any other organ. His sole will governs all legislative questions.

A good many writers have concluded that every order emanating from the Emperor is a law. From the fact that his power is unlimited, obligatory force has been attributed to all his orders. All manifestations of the supreme will, say they, have necessarily equal force and there can be no distinction between laws and executive orders of the Emperor if the latter are not in contradiction with some law. This is Speransky's opinion, and from his time was the dominating one in Russian literature.

The fundamental laws, however, show no such complete confusion between laws and other acts put forth by the supreme power. The preparation and abrogation of laws, as well as their forms, are determined by special rules which are not applicable to executive acts. As regards the making of law, for example, Article 50 provides that all proposed laws shall be examined by the Council of State. As to the form to be given to them, Article 53 fixes their number and Articles 54 and 55 distinguish between new laws and those which are only complementary to those already put forth. The new laws must be completed by the Emperor's signature; for the others, on the contrary, a verbal assent suffices. Finally, Article 73 prescribes the rule that laws must be abrogated with the same formalities.

After having in this way distinguished between laws and other sovereign acts, the fundamental laws provide in Article 77 for the possibility of contradictions between laws and orders, and it is the senate first, the supreme power afterwards, which is to judge of them.

Do all these rules in the fundamental laws express, then, only a tendency which cannot be carried out practically under the rule of an absolute monarchy? Such a conclusion cannot be admitted. Whoever has unlimited power, can, if he pleases, give to his different acts different effects, and the difference in the general principles controlling special acts in administering the state make such difference in effects of acts necessary. A monarch who has unlimited power, who controls at the same time the general principles of the state's activity and the special concrete customs relating to separate individuals, even such a soveriegn cannot escape such a necessity, and he must establish a difference between his acts which have a directing influence and those which have only a momentary effect.

It is necessary to apply to all these acts, legislative and administrative, rigorously determinate forms in order to distinguish them readily. No man could, in dealing with a multitude of individual cases, with the most special and various questions, apply to all of these cases the same general principles, if those principles were not established under a special form, under the form of law. If the distinction between legislative acts, strictly so called, and administrative acts, properly so named, were not drawn, there would be reason to fear that both would be frequently neglected. It is by no means easy to always apply to the cases of all men impartially the same general principles once for all adopted. Strong interests of every kind struggle constantly together and numerous difficulties rise up at every instant. In a state, by reason of the extreme complexity of the facts, and the diversity of human activity, this difficulty of applying always the same principles is still greater. The absence of a preorganized system is then still more dangerous in the state's administration than in individual activity.

In an unlimited monarchy, as in every other government, the need of distinguishing certain acts having a certain form and possessing absolute force as legislative acts is none the less strong. The distinction is still possible though the monarch's power is unlimited, because he can manifest that power under different forms. He has less reason for departing from the rigorous observance of these forms than has the constitutional monarch. If his power over legislation is limited by that of the national representatives, there is a strong temptation on the monarch's part to enlarge more and more the sphere of application of his orders to which no parliamentary consent is necessary. The constitutional monarch is not assured of the consent of parliament for the projects which he submits to it. There are measures which he thinks it absolutely necessary to take which may raise a lively opposition in parliament. It is quite otherwise with the action of the absolute monarch. In legislation as in administration his power is equally unlimited and complete. Then, too, he has no interest in refusing to observe the forms of legislative acts which he has himself instituted. In observing them he remains always free, as they are his own work. It is only among counselors of the monarch, who seek to subject him wholly to their own influence, that there can arise an interest in setting aside these more complex forms of discussion of legislative acts, which call for a great number of counselors.

As to the monarch himself, a rigorous observation of the established forms of legislation would not seem to be troublesome. His power will be manifested so much the more freely as the preliminary discussion of his projects is complete and fully reasoned. After having heard the observations of many counsellors, he will the more easily raise himself above the petty quarrels or interests among the counsellors. The personal interests which surround the monarch certainly urge upon him a certain confusion of matters of legislation with those of administration; but unlimited power in the monarch does not of itself require any such confusion.

We must, then, recognize that all sovereign acts are not laws; but among them, those only are laws which have been promulgated in accordance with Article 50 of the Fundamental Laws, that is to say, after discussion before the Council of State. The Council of State, however, performs a function wholly consultative. It does not, itself, decide any question. It merely gives its opinion as to any matter submitted to the Sovereign. The opinions are unanimous or by a majority of votes, but whichever way it is, the result is not binding on the Emperor. The Emperor after hearing, or as the manifesto of Alexander I says, "after having taken into consideration the opinion of the Council of State," takes a resolution according to the majority or minority opinion, or one according to his own personal ideas.

Notwithstanding Gradovsky's great authority, we may not compare the distinction which has been taken between verbal and written acts to that between laws and executive orders. On the one hand the laws, even those made with the concurrence of the Council of State, do not always have the Emperor's signature. Quite frequently the sanction is in the Emperor's handwriting, but with the signature only the words, "Let it be so"; and sometimes there is only an oral assent.

Article 54 of the Fundamental Laws which prescribe that every new law must receive the Emperor's signature, has its corollary in the following Article 55, which provides that complementary laws need not have such signature. With the development of modern legislation there are few laws which cannot be considered as complementary to some existing one.

The Emperor's signature under Article 66 may be appended to acts of sovereign power which have no legislative character; for example, to acts conferring titles and appointments to higher offices. The Emperor's signature proves in such cases not that the act has been discussed in the most profound manner, but merely that it has the character of highest authenticity. This signature belongs, then, to quite different acts, some of which are by no means legislative.

Gradovsky's opinion is based chiefly upon a wrong printing of the text of Article 77 in the edition of 1857. The true text of this article, that of the editions of 1832 and 1842, spoke of the law for removing contradictions contained in sovereign orders, whatever form those orders may have had; as a result of a mistake in the text of 1857, there was no question of errors except those in laws which had the Emperor's signature.

So far as concerns the elaboration of legislation in Russia, as a result of the absence of all national representation, the right of initiative belongs solely to the government, and first to the Emperor, then to the senate and to the synod, which can bring before the Council of State the discussion of legislative questions; but the privilege of legislative initiative does not belong to the ministers. They have to get the Emperor's authority for the bringing before the Council of State of any projected legislation. The Council of State itself does not have the right of initiative. It can discuss projects for legislation only when laid before it.

The discussion of projects of legislation takes place at first in one of the sections of the Council, a sort of commission of preparation, then in a general gathering which includes, besides those specially designated by the Emperor, all the ministers. The conclusion reached by the Council is submitted to the Emperor under the form of very brief reports, which are called Journal of the Session, or Memoirs. The conclusion of the Emperor is then expressed, according to the importance of the question, either in writing or merely orally in various forms, according to whether it is the majority or the minority opinion of the Council, which the Sovereign adopts. If the Emperor confirms the majority opinion, he indicates it merely by the words, "Let it be so," or by a statement of the decision reached by the Emperor, signed by the president of the Council. In the opposite case the sovereign will is expressed either by an act signed by the Emperor or by an oral order of the Emperor declared to the Council by its president.

The external forms of law are very diverse. They may be distinguished into complete and abridged forms of legislative acts. The complete form has three parts: first, the text of the law; second, the opinion of the Council of State; third, the order for its publication and putting in force. The text of the law carries different names: regulation, decree, edict, ordinance. These different names do not correspond to any clear distinction of fact. The order which the Emperor makes for the publication of the law and the putting of it into effect is contained in a decree which he signs and sends to the senate. In the case of law which is specially important, the Emperor, in addition to the formalities which we have just stated, makes a proclamation to his subjects in which he explains the motives which led him to take such action.

This complete form is rarely applied. The manifestoes of the Sovereign directly to the people are few. Very often, even, the decree sent to the senate is suppressed. In this case the legislative act contains only two parts: first, the opinion of the Council of State; second, the text itself of the law. If the law is of little importance, its text is included in the opinion of the Council of State. It happens, too, that some laws consist only in orders, signed by the Emperor, and addressed to the senate. The order contains, then, the text itself of the law and a direction to the senate to publish and put it in force. The publication of law is brought about by means of the senate, which sends the new laws, with notices, to all the institutions required to apply them. It also causes them to appear in the Collection of Laws and Ordinances of Government, so that all may have knowledge. Government institutions, functionaries, and the general public, can thus learn of new laws.

The rules with regard to the putting in force of laws are, with us, still very vague and unsatisfactory. Dating from the XVIII century, they call for knowledge of new laws only on the part of governmental institutions, and not of the whole population. Articles 57 and 58 of the Fundamental Laws seem to prescribe a rule according to which laws must be published twice. Article 57 provides that this duty be entrusted to the senate, and Article 58 assigns to the provincial administration the task of publishing the law in each department, but since the whole Empire is divided into departments it will be asked what is the senate's rôle in the publication. Article 59 says that the different administrations can apply the law before it has become obligatory upon individuals. Each tribunal, consequently, including the senate and the departmental administration, should apply new laws from the moment of their reception. They can only be published after they have been received, and the day of reception cannot be the same as that of publication. Meanwhile, the law has obligatory force both for individuals and the tribunals which are charged with ascertaining rights and obligations.

The absurd consequences of a literal interpretation of the text of the Fundamental Laws is explained only by the fact that these texts are not designed to speak of the application of laws except so far as such application shall be made by the different administrations. But how ought law to be promulgated in order to come to the knowledge of all?

It is in a very general way that Article 59 tells us that law has no executory force except so far as it is published. But it does not say what is meant by the expression, "The day of publication." The general regulations of the senate, it is true, in its Article 19, says that this day is determined by the senate's order. The publication of the law in the Collection of Laws is equivalent to an official one, and it might properly seem that this publication fixes the moment from which the law should begin to be obligatory upon individuals. This interpretation leads us, however, to some consequences which cannot be admitted. If we should accept it, it would be necessary also to recognize the law as obligatory for individuals before it is for tribunals, since it is through the Collection of Laws that the tribunals learn of new ones. It must, then, be admitted as a general fact in practice, and in legal literature, that the law becomes obligatory at the same time both for individuals and for tribunals, and in becoming so, it becomes obligatory before reaching the knowledge of the people generally. This inconvenience also must be added, that for each tribunal the starting point from which the law becomes obligatory is different. With the great distances which separate certain cities from the capitol this is an important point, and the difference between the dates of application of the law in different places is sometimes very wide.

We cannot, then, simply by recognizing the moment of publication of the law in the Collection determine the time at which it becomes obligatory. For this it is necessary to know at what time each local tribunal receives it.

Section 57. *The General Code of Laws*

HISTORIC DEVELOPMENTS OF THE CODE OF 1837

Besides the Collection of Laws and Ordinances of Government published every year since 1863, we have in addition two other collections of laws,—the Chronological Collection, complete with all legislative acts since the code of Czar Alexis, and the Systematic Collection of present legislation, more simply styled Code of Laws. These are all collections of laws already promulgated, of original laws, but they present very important differences between each other. In the first place they are not final collections, like, for example, the Code of Justinian. They are, on the contrary, collections of legislation actually in force and always susceptible of revisions and changes. The Complete Collection does not, like the Code, present a tableau of our legislation at a given moment of its historic evolution. On the contrary, it is designed to show us all the successive changes in that legislation. Then these collections are not prepared by the legislative power, but by an institution having no such power. At the beginning, this institution was the second section of the Emperor's chancellery. It was transformed in 1882 into a section charged with codification of laws, and since 1893 it has become a special section of the chancellery of the state, a section of the Code of Laws. Gotten up by this institution, the new volumes of the Complete Collection, the same as new editions or supplements of the old Code, are not subjected to the action of the Council of State, as is required in the promulgation of fresh laws.

Under the reign of Nicholas I were put out for the first time this Complete Collection and the Code.

What is appearing today is merely the succession of these different publications. Therefore, the last edition of the Code, that of 1893, bears still the same title, Code of Laws of the Russian Empire prepared by Order of the Emperor, Nicholas I.

Several times it has been attempted to publish other codes, that of Alexis in 1648, and under Peter I at the beginning of the XVII century, as well as at the commencement of the XIX. All these attempts failed, and Nicholas I decided to compose, instead of a new code, a collection made up of laws then in force. He entrusted this work to Speransky.

Such an enterprise offered a good many difficulties. The laws were, up to that time, published on separate sheets; there was no collection at all complete, either official or private. So, to determine upon and classify the laws then in force it was necessary first to collect all since 1649 and classify them simply in chronological order. This was done in 1830, when appeared the first complete collection of laws, a collection of forty-five volumes, which includes all the legislative acts put forth from 1649 to December 12, 1825, that is to say, up to the day of the first manifesto of Nicholas I, a total of 30,220 acts.

All these acts were inserted in the Collection just as they had been promulgated, without any changes and in the chronological order. The day of publication of the law was sometimes indicated, but not always. This Collection, in order to facilitate researches, includes besides, two indexes, a chronological and an alphabetical one, and a systematic table of contents. At the same time with the appearance of this first "Complete Collection" there began the publication of a second collection which was to include all legislative acts newly promulgated and to begin with the first manifesto of Nicholas I. This second collection is composed on the same plan as the first, but numbered in a different order.

With the coming to the throne of Alexander II there arose a question whether this second collection should not be terminated and a third commenced with the first manifesto cf that Emperor; but Alexander II refused to undertake the publication of a new collection. It was only on the twenty-fifth anniversary of his reign that a third collection was commenced, February 19, 1880. After the accession of Alexander III, October 19, 1883, the second collection was continued up to that date so as to embrace all the acts of the preceding reign, and it was from this date only that the third collection commenced with the first manifesto of Alexander III. The second collection at the present time terminated includes, then, all the legislative acts of two reigns, that of Nicholas I and of Alexander II, a total of fifty-five volumes.

The publication of the Complete Collection was brought about by the dispersion of the laws, which were all published on separate sheets. Since 1863 the publication of new laws has taken place through the Collection of Legislative Acts, which is also a complete collection provided with a chronological and alphabetical index. The inquiry is made if there is any necessity for continuing the Complete Collection when there is another Chronological Collection which always appears long in advance of the Complete Collection. This question has been several times raised, notably in 1882, by the Council of State. The publication of the Complete Collection has nevertheless been maintained.

The reasons for keeping up the publication of these two collections are interesting from several points of view. It has been explained before that it is only in the Complete Collection that the laws are placed in a definite chronological order. In the Collection, on the contrary, the order is merely that of chance. The laws in this collection are inserted, not according to the date on which they are sanctioned, but according to the date on which the senate has discussed them. But it is necessary to say that the chronological order according to the time of their publication which has been selected by the Complete Collection is not very important.

For a jurist the important thing is to know at what time a law became obligatory, not when it was sanctioned. This last date can interest only the historian. Then it is observed that there are numerous defects in the Collection inevitable in such hasty publication. To be sure, there are defects, also, in the Complete Collection, for such there are in all human works, but they are not in great number. These defects should be corrected as promptly as possible by the same institution which has created the law. It must be added to these considerations that the Complete Collection and the Collection do not coincide in all their parts. The Complete Collection contains a much greater number of acts. Volume 41, for example, of the Complete Collection has 1242 orders, while the corresponding volume of the other collection comprises only 893. This is explained because the second section of the chancellery charged with the publication of the second collection followed the same rules as those which had served for the first. They were not satisfied with reprinting the published orders to which the senate had refused publication because they had not been rendered according to the forms required by general law. The section of codification recognized how badly ordered was such a publication, and since then, by order of the Emperor, the Complete Collection includes only acts published in the Collection. We may therefore question the importance of continuing these two collections which have become identical.

The existence of these two official collections may give rise in practice to serious inconveniences. Two independent collections, prepared by different institutions, can never be completely identical. There will be differences between them, and besides, the director of the Complete Collection asserts the right of correcting faults in the text of the other collection. It can happen, then, in this way that the same law will present a different text in the one collection from that of the other. Which of the two texts, then, would have obligatory force? Since the insertion of the law in the Collection is an essential element in its publication, it must be admitted that the law is as it has been put forth in the Collection and this has obligatory force, and that in case of conflict with the text of the Complete Collection it is the text of the Collection that ought to prevail.

Section 58. *The First Editions of the Code*

The publication of the Complete Collection was considered as a necessary preparation for the publication of The Collection of Laws Actually in Force, that is, the Code. This Code is distinguished from the Collection first of all by its contents. It does not contain all the laws, but only those which still have obligatory force. Then, the laws in force are not inserted in the Code in their entirety and under the form in which they were promulgated at the beginning. The Code includes only extracts under the form of distinct articles with references to the orders which served for their revision. Finally, the order of the legislative dispositions contained in the Code is not chronological but systematic.

The Code was composed in seven years. Commenced in January, 1826, it contained at the end of 1832 the laws in force up to January 1st of that year and on January 19, 1833, it was presented to the Council of State at a memorable sitting over which Nicholas I presided. The manifesto was signed January 31, 1833, but this first edition was called from the year of its publication, the edition of 1832. The date of its going into effect was January 1, 1835, in order to permit the tribunals to fully understand it.

At the publication of the Code it was first of all necessary to exclude all laws which had been abrogated by later ones. All repetitions were also set aside and instead of several laws as to the same matter, the Code never contains more than one. Finally, the very text of the ancient laws is preserved as far as possible "because in law it is not elegance of style which must be considered, but its force, and its force is so much the greater the older it is." Finally, diffused laws, too much extended, were abridged and for this purpose it was decided to recall for what object the law had been established without setting forth too extensively the particular cases.

Made up in this way, the laws form different articles of the Code, and for each of them dispositions have been found which have served as a basis. The object of giving to these articles a greater certainty was not the only one, but also to make the reading of the Code more comprehensible. There are here some indications necessary in order to determine precisely the field of the law and to understand its true meaning in case of doubt. They are the best means for gaining a good interpretation. They form a system based, not upon arbitrary conclusion, but upon the comparison between the two forms which are given to the same law.

Besides the references to the orders which have served as their basis, some articles of the Code include in addition notes and supplements. The first edition contained under the form of notes, some explanations, which, containing neither command nor prohibition, were not laws. The supplements contain different forms and tables which would have obscured the meaning of the leading articles and would have broken their connection if placed in the text itself. In later editions the same rule was, unfortunately, not observed, and under the form of notes and supplements, true laws have been inserted modifying entirely the articles to which they are added. It is observed, moreover, in these last times, there is a tendency to give to notes and supplements the same effect which they had formerly.

The articles of the Code are arranged in a systematic order.[1] This system rested upon the following principles· All laws are divided into constitutional and civil.

[1] The edition of 1832 contained 36,000,—with supplements, 42,198.

The constitutional laws are those which determine the rights and duties of the individual towards the state. They are of two kinds. The one kind fix the very essence of the organization of the state; the others merely protect the rights which result from it. The laws of the first group are subdivided in their turn,—first, into fundamental laws which regulate the sovereign power, its organization and its action as to both legislation and administration; second, into organic laws which regulate the organs of power; third, into governmental laws, which determine the means by the aid of which power acts and which arrange the forces of which power disposes (personal duties, military service, taxes); and, finally, fourth, those laws of the classes, laws which fix the rights and duties of subjects according to their degree of participation in the state's power.

The public laws of the second group are divided into preservative laws and criminal laws.

Civil laws fix the rights and duties arising from the family and from the possession of property. Speransky, however, has divided them into two categories by another mark of distinction. He has combined together the laws of the family and patrimonial ones under the name of general civil law, and he distinguishes from them the special civil laws, that is to say, those which fix the rights over goods in their relation to the state and to commerce, industry, etc. These special civil laws are called, according to their main purpose, the economic laws of the state. The whole Code is thus divided into eight leading sections comprised in fifteen volumes:

I. The Fundamental Laws of the State, Vol. 1, Part 1.

II. Institutions: *a*, central, Vol. 1, p. 2; *b*, local, Vol. 2; *c*, rules as to functionaries, Vol. 3.

III. The Laws Organizing the State's Forces: *a*, regulation of requirements, Vol. 4; *b*, regulation of imposts and rights of the state, Vol. 5; *c*, regulations of import duties, Vol. 6; *d*, regulation of money, mines and salt, Vol. 7; *e*, regulation of forests and domainal receipts, Vol. 8.

IV. Laws with Reference to the Classes, Vol. 9.

V. Civil Laws and Concerning Boundaries, Vol. 10.

VI. Laws as to Good Order in the State: *a*, credit, commerce and industry, Vol. 11; *b*, ways for communication, constructions, fires, rural economy, police of village and colonies, police of foreigners in the Empire, Vol. 12.

VII. Laws of Police: *a*, public assistance and medical laws, Vol. 13; *b*, passports, criminal arrests, Vol. 14.

VIII. Criminal Laws, Vol. 15.

Each of the fifteen volumes in the Code constituted a separate whole, a distinct code, devoted to a special institution, having its own numbered order and separate pagination. This system includes all the law in force with the exception, first, of local law; second, legislative acts as to public instruction and the control of the state; third, legislative acts as to the control of religious worship; fourth, some laws concerning the administration of the court and certain benevolent institutions placed under the special auspices of the Emperor or of members of the imperial family; fifth, some laws as to the army and navy. It forms a code of laws in the material, not the formal sense of the word. It includes all the legal rules created by the sovereign power and also those which emanate from inferior administrative organs, especially from the ministers and from the senate. In including in the Code the orders of the senate or of the ministers it was not intended, however, to give them for the future the force of law. In the Review of Instructions as to the Code, p. 176, it is said, on the contrary, that all these orders have been carefully distinguished by a reference to the order itself, in order not to confuse them with the law.

According to the opinion of the Council of State of December, 1834, an opinion confirmed by the Emperor, it was understood that the Code would comprehend, first, the circulars of the ministers bearing upon the execution of the law, if these circulars were confirmed by the senate; second, the explanations furnished by the administration ratified and published by the senate, on condition that they conform to the laws in force and that they do away with the doubts which might arise from reading the text, without, however, giving to that text any modification.

Section 59. *Later Editions of the Code and Supplements*

Since our Code is a collection of laws actually in force and is intended to reflect all the changes brought forward in legislation it was necessary to take measures that it be always in conformity with the actual state of legislation. To reach this end two different means are employed,—first, new editions of the Code are published; second, supplements are added from time to time. After the first edition of 1832 there were two others in 1842 and in 1857 and then a great number of editions of separate volumes and distinct parts in 1883, 1885, 1886, 1887, 1889, 1890, 1892 and 1893.[1] All these editions, however, do not fully replace that of 1857, certain parts of which are still in full force.

At the beginning it was hoped that new editions could be made upon the precise plan of the old one, maintaining its least details. With this object, the Council of State put out on December 15, 1834, the opinion that the preparation of a new statute ought always to conform as far as possible to the leading arrangements in the corresponding article of the Code. It was thought then that whatever changes were subsequently brought into legislation, they could always find place in the Code. In the meanwhile, however, when this question was discussed in the Council of State, Count Kankrine expressed some doubts as to the possibility of always placing under the Code's rubrics the new laws, which introduce notable changes, and to which, in consequence, there would be no corresponding chapters already existing. This was what, in fact, happened at the editing of the new Code of 1842.

[1] No mention has been made of the reprints of 1833 and of 1835, though both these reprints were entitled in printing them, as new editions.

After the first edition of the Code a good many important institutions were created. There were some very useful instructions on this subject addressed to the governors. There were some laws as to the matter of a regency in the government, as to police of districts, etc. As it was impossible to place them in the midst of existing articles, they were put at the end as supplements to the articles which they superseded. Their position has no relation to the importance of the new laws. The original plan put in the supplements only some articles bearing upon modifications of detail; instead of this there are now some orders fixing the entire local administrations which find place there.

In the second edition of the Code in 1842 it was thought to set aside so troublesome a disposition, and that it could be done without essentially modifying the arrangement of the different volumes. It is in this way, for example, as Count Bludov explained in his report to the Emperor of December 10, 1842, that Vol. II was made over and entirely composed anew in this second edition. One might almost say that every part in this volume has recived modifications as a result of new laws. The same thing happened in other volumes, but in less degree.

Besides this, there is an important innovation in all the volumes, one which appeared at first to have no purely external results, but which has, however, absolutely changed the general character of the Code. In the first edition each volume was one of a series with a general numbering. The Code was then a systematic collection of articles forming fifteen volumes. For the indication of an article two numbers were required, its volume and the article. The place of an article was determined solely by its place in the Code and not at all by the chapter in which it first appeared. There was thus obtained a complete unity between the different parts of the Code. In the edition of 1842, on the contrary, the different institutions and the different articles have all received a separate numbering. Count Bludov gave a reason for it, basing it upon considerations of an external, practical sort. It was necessary, he said, to make the sale of different parts of each volume possible. In fact, this change had consequences which were important in another way. In rendering easier the preparation of the new edition it permitted the new laws also to find a place in it, while still keeping its original system for the Code as a whole. This happened, for example, in the articles regulating the Council of State, and the one as to instructions addressed to the governors.

The second edition is larger than the first, the number of articles is greater by more than twice that of the edition of 1832; it is 59,396 articles. On the first of November, 1851, the Emperor directed the preparing of a third edition. The Count Bludov, who had always charge of these codification projects, hoped, according to his report of November 1, 1851, to introduce some very important changes into this new edition. He wished to put in all the laws which had not appeared in the first two editions excepting always the military and naval codes, the laws as to the Emperor's domain lands, as to the government of the Baltic, and as to the orthodox religion. The number of volumes would be raised in this way from fifteen to twenty. In his report of December 16, 1854, he decided to keep the same number of volumes and to do this he divided Vols. 2, 8, 11, 12, and 15 into two parts each, and Vol. 10 into three, and so the third edition has fifteen volumes in twenty-two parts. The whole Code is divided into eight principal parts and since certain volumes are divided into parts that word has to be understood in two meanings. Count Bludov's idea of putting into this new edition all the laws then in force was not fully carried out. There were introduced only the statute as to finances, Vol. 8, Part 2, those relating to foreign religions, Vol. 12, Part 1, and those as to the post and telegraph, Vol. 2, Part 2. The third edition comprises about ninety thousand articles.

The edition of 1857 was the last of the whole Code. Up to 1876 there was no new edition. A new edition was then made up of the first parts of Vols. 2, 3 and 8, the second parts of Vols. 10, 11 and 15, and since that time there have been various editions of separate volumes.

All these new editions compromise badly the original unity. Beside volumes of the edition of 1857, still in force today, must be put editions of 1892 and 1893, which were composed after the appearance of the very important reforms of the XIX century. Our Code has never had an internal unity. It has not lost its external unity, and has ceased to be the work of a single hand, or even that of a single epoch. It now no longer presents a tableau of the legislation of any given historical period.

The different statutes become from day to day more diverse and more independent. We have already seen that in the edition of 1842 the different Codes contained in the same volume had received a distinct numbering. In the most recent editions, each volume formed a distinct collection of codes, regulations and institutions without having any connection with a preconceived general plan, and without being attached to any given system. Each new legislative act, however unimportant, forms a new integral part of the volume coming the nearest in matter to that of which it treats. The numerous changes which have taken place in our legislation in these last sixty years have completely altered the original system of the Code. The number of volumes, even, is no longer the same.

The Code gave no distinct place to the judiciary and the administration of justice. The tribunals formed the subject of a chapter among those treating of the other state establishments. They were subdivided into Central Tribunals, in Vol. 1, and Local Tribunals, in Vol. 2. The laws for the administration of criminal justice and of civil justice have been joined to criminal and civil law. In the regulations of justice by Alexander II, the judiciary and the administration of justice were completely modified, and became a separate whole. For this reason after the attempt of Prince Urusov to place the regulations as to the administration of justice in distinct parts of different volumes of the edition of 1876, it was decided in 1892 to make out of these a new volume, Vol. 16. The number of parts in certain volumes was changed. Vol. 10 had no longer three parts, but only two, the civil laws and laws as to boundaries, and Vols. 2 and 15 were reduced to one part each.

With regard to what the Code should include, it was decided in 1885 to put in only legislative acts, and ordinances of the Emperor addressed to his subjects, which were connected with texts of the Code, and as to which there were no existing legislative texts. It was decided, also, to put in explanatory orders which had been sanctioned by the Emperor. Orders of the senate were to have no place, unless presenting something specially important for the explanation of a law, and on condition that each such order should be authorized by the Emperor to be inserted in the Code. The ministers' circulars were not to be inserted except those of the Finance Minister in regard to import duties. In our time the Code is made up, therefore, of sixteen volumes, Vols. 1, 8, 10, 11, 12, and 16 having two parts, and Vol. 9 containing a distinct supplement with regulations as to the peasants. These volumes include the following matter:

Vol. 1, Part 1: Fundamental laws of the state. Part 2: Statutes of the Council of State, of the Council of Ministers, of the Council of Siberian Railroads, of the senate, of ministers, orders as to petitions addressed to the Emperor, as to recompenses decreed by the Emperor, as to different titles of nobility (editions of 1892, 1893 and 1895).

Vol. 2: The general organization of the provinces, laws as to provincial institutions and districts, cities, Poland, the Caucasus, Trans-Caspian territories, Turkestan, as to the province of Akmolinsk, of Semipalatinsk, of Semiretchinsk, of Uralsk, of Turgaïsk, of Siberia, and laws relating to foreigners (editions of 1892, 1893 and 1895).

Vol. 3: Provisions with regard to nomination of functionaries, subventions and pensions (editions of 1876, 1890, 1891, 1893), regulations as to civil service in distant localities, in western governments and Poland (editions of 1890, 1891, 1893), as to funds of the civil department (editions of 1886, 1890, 1891, 1894).

Vol. 4: Provisions as to military service (edition of 1886, 1890, 1891, 1893), those relating to land taxes (editions of 1857, 1890, 1891 and 1893), and to provincial institutions (editions of 1890, 1891, 1893).

Vol. 5: Provisions as to direct taxes, as to the rights of the state, receipts, lodgings, taxes (editions of 1893, 1895).

Vol. 6: Provisions as to imports, the general tariff on imports in European commerce (editions of 1892, 1893, 1895).

Vol. 7: Provisions as to money and mines (editions of 1893 and 1895).

Vol. 8: Provisions as to forests, payments due the state, administration of state domains in western and Baltic governments (edition of 1893, part 2), provisions as to accountability (editions of 1857, 1890, 1891, 1893, and 1895)

Vol. 9: Provisions as to ranks, special supplement to Vol. 9 (editions of 1876, 1890, 1891, and 1893).

Vol. 10, Part 1: Code of civil laws, regulations as to markets and matters furnished for the account of the state (editions of 1887, 1890, 1891, 1893, and 1895). Part 2: Provisions as to boundaries (editions of 1893 and 1895).

Vol. 11, Part 1: Provisions as to foreign religions (editions of 1857, 1890, 1891, and 1893), as to educational establishments under control of Minister of Public Instruction (editions of 1893 and 1895). Part 2: Provisions as to credit, bills of exchange, commerce, consuls, industry (editions of 1893 and 1895).

Vol. 12, Part 1: Provisions as to the administration of roads (editions of 1857, and 1893), as to railroads (editions of 1886 and 1893), as to posts and telegraph (editions of 1876 and 1893), constructions (editions of 1887 and 1893), regulation of fire insurance (editions of 1886 and 1893). Part 2: Laws as to rural economy, field labor, taverns and hotels (editions of 1893 and 1895), police of villages (editions of 1857, 1890, and 1891), Cossack villages and foreign colonies in the Empire (editions of 1857, 1863, 1864, and 1868).

Vol. 13: Provisions as to public food supply and public assistance (editions of 1892, 1893, and 1895).

Vol. 14: Provisions regulating passports, the censorship, the press, persons detained and deported (editions of 1890, 1891, 1893, and 1895).

Vol. 15: Criminal and correctionary laws, the rules as to punishments by justices of the peace (editions of 1885, 1890, 1891, 1893, and 1895).

Vol. 16, Part 1: Judiciary regulations. Part 2: Organization of local tribunals, laws as to the administration of justice and civil penalties (editions of 1892, 1893, and 1895).

As the successive editions of the Code are separated

from one another by a considerable interval, there have been enacted every year supplements, which, without citing the whole contents of the Code, contained only the changes brought about.[1]

These supplements are of two different kinds; one includes only the laws adopted since the publications of the preceding supplement, the others include all which have appeared since the last edition of the Code. The supplements actually in force are those of 1890, 1891, 1893, 1895, and it is only for laws in regard to the Cossacks and colonies of foreigners (Vol. 12, Part 2) that the supplements of the editions of 1863, 1864, and 1868 preserve their force.

The laws inserted in the Code, or in the supplements, should be cited by notes indicating references to corresponding parts of the Code. That is the way the senate regulation has provided. These references should include, first, the date of the edition or of the supplement; second, an indication of the volume, or the part of the Code if the volume has more than one part; third, the title of the law and the abbreviation commonly used to designate it; fourth, the numbers of the article; as one should say,—Code of 1892, Vol. 11, Statute as to Cities, Art. 1. As we have already indicated, certain branches of our legislation are not included in the Code. They may be found only in the supplements to later editions. This is the case with the laws as to scientific establishments and foreign religions. There are some laws which have not gotten into the Code at all, but form distinct codes. Such are those relative to the region of the Baltic and the military and naval codes.

The military code appeared in 1838. It consists of five parts, is divided into twelve volumes in fifteen

[1] The Code of 1832 included six supplements of this kind, those of 1834, 1835, 1836, 1837, 1838, and 1839. The first included 823 corrections. The Code of 1842 had nineteen supplements, and the Code of 1857 also nineteen.

books. The first part, Vols. 1 to 4, contained the organization of military institutions; the second, Vols. 5 and 6, the laws as to the service; the third, Vol. 7, as to instruction of troops; the fourth, Vols. 8 to 11, the laws as to the amendments; the fifth, Vol. 12, as to military crimes.

On the same plan was the second edition in 1859, which had six supplements up to January 1, 1869. The military reforms of the last reign, however, were so important that his plan became impracticable. So in 1869 came a third edition on a new plan. It consists of six parts,—first, military administration; second, regular troops; third, irregular troops; fourth, military establishments; fifth, military economy; sixth, military discipline and justice. The new edition, however, is not yet complete. Only parts one, four and six have fully appeared, the second and fifth in parts only, and the third not at all. There are three supplements, issued in 1874, 1879, and 1881.

The code of marine laws of 1886 includes eighteen books: 1st, administrative rules of the naval ministry; 2d, equipage and detachments; 3d, establishments of instruction; 4th, medical establishments; 5th, technical establishments; 6th, hydrographic establishments; 7th, prisons; 8th, matters of service; 9th, pay and aids in money; 10th, maritime laws; 11th, police of ports; 12th, instructions on economy; 13th, pay of functionaries; 14th, equipage of ships; 15th, regulations of finance; 16th, punishments on ships of war; 17th, discipline in general; 18th, justice.

There are special laws for the governments of the Baltic Region,—first, organization of local institutions; second, rights of classes; third, civil laws. The code of laws of the government of the Baltic contains only these three parts. The two first appeared in 1845, with a supplement in 1853. The code of civil laws was published only in 1864.

In the government of the ex-kingdom of Poland, the French civil code, introduced in 1808, prevails down to the present time. There have been, however, important changes, notably as to marriage. The official Russian translation of this code appeared in 1870 under the title, Collection of Civil Laws of the Governments of the Kingdom of Poland.

Finally, in Finland, there is still a special legislation in force, which has grown up through the activity of a special legislative organ, the Finland Diet. The basis of this legislation is the Swedish Code of 1734, published in Russia with changes and supplements in 1824, under the title of Swedish Code Accepted by the Diet of 1734 and Sanctioned by the Emperor for the Grand Duchy of Finland. The new laws were printed in the collection of decretals of the Grand Duchy of Finland which appeared in Swedish in 1808 and was printed in Russian in 1860.

Section 60. *The Importance and Force of the Code*

From the appearance of the Code it was the intention to condense into one systematic whole the body of laws then in force, but there was no intention of replacing the former legislation by new. It may be asked, then, what the legal compass of the Code was designed to be. Ought it to be regarded as a new law abrogating all former ones, or only as a new form given to the old laws and merely intended to make their comprehension and application easier? If the Code is recognized as new law the legislation in force before will keep its force only in so far as it shall have found a place in the Code itself. And if there is any contradiction between the Code and former decisions, the articles of the Code will control it, since the Code in its quality of new law will abrogate previous contradictory laws. If it is considered merely as a reproduction of the old laws which keep their force, then it must be admitted that the articles of the Code are obligatory only so far as they correctly reproduce that law on which they are founded.

To recognize the Code as new law abrogating all anterior ones was, in practice, the most convenient way. The question of the relations of the Code to anterior laws would thus be solved in a very simple way. Only the Code had the force of law. On the other hand, to resolve it in this way was to depart from the very purpose of making the Code, which was to combine all the legislation in force without bringing in any change. Like all human work, it had certainly made changes. To count it new law, abrogating what went before, was to ratify and establish all the changes and omissions unconsciously made by its redactors.

The determination of the legal effect of the Code is,

then, a practical question of great difficulty. How has it been determined in our legislation?

The manifesto of January 31, 1833, which announced the first edition of the Code, in its second and fourth articles determines this question. The second article indicates the legal force of the Code in requiring its citation and application in governmental and judicial matters. In all cases where laws are applied and cited, at large or by extracts, a reference and citation to the Code, where it treats of the matter, must be added. The fourth article says that the Code is not designed to change the law but merely to combine it under one form and order, when the law reproduced by the Code shall not be sufficiently clear it shall be explained as it has been hitherto.

These directions are not very explicit. On the one side, it is recommended to always refer to the Code only, without looking at the laws themselves, and it seems that the Code abrogates all previous decisions; but, on the other hand, it is claimed that the anterior law is unchanged and only uniformity is sought. What conclusion is to be drawn from this as to the weight of the Code?

Zitovich,[1] and after him Tagantzev, affirms that the Code has the effect of new law and abrogates anterior laws. He even adds: "The fourth paragraph of the manifesto is not entirely exact," and he relies, to show it, upon the report of Count Karl and upon the opinion of the Council of State as to the weight to be given to the Code. The demonstration leads him to some conclusions precisely opposite to what takes place in judicial practice. According to him each article of the Code is a new law, which has been in force since January 1, 1835, and has such force, even if the article is not drawn

[1] Course of Russian Private Law, Vol. I. Sources of Law. Odessa, 1878. pp. 8 to 11.

from any previous law or decision, or even if it was put in by error or misunderstanding as an extract from a decision.

But it was decided to apply the articles of the Code of 1832 not only for affairs which have arisen since January 1, 1835, but also to prior ones, when the only law was the decisions and rules which are the basis of the Code's articles. So, now, the supplementary articles are applied to matters which arose before their publication, provided they sprang up after the laws which served as a basis for the new articles of the Code. This practice is directly supported by the fourth section of the manifesto of January 31, 1833. So, too, our judicial usage never recognizes as law evident errors in the redaction of the Code. Law not correctly reported in the Code is not regarded as changed, and omitted laws are not treated as abrogated.

It is true that the manifesto of January 31, 1833, does not expressly indicate that it is not necessary to conclude that a law changed in the Code, or omitted from it, is changed or abrogated, but the opinion of the Council of State affirmed this and the Emperor sanctioned it January 30, 1836. This opinion declares that every time the minister of justice shall learn that during the consideration of an affair some difficulty has been raised because the law has not foreseen the case, or has done so incompletely, the minister can take the matter in hand and charge Section 11 with furnishing a resolution of it to be placed at the end of the Code. In case of disagreement between the minister's opinion and the section, the Council of State decides. This rule was not published, for it was found to completely settle the relations of the minister and Section II.

The Code, therefore, cannot be considered as new law, but only a new form given to pre-existing law, a form that permits the ascertainment of the sense of the original text and which has been sanctioned by the legislative power.

Certainly the possibility of citing inexactly the laws which have served as a basis to the articles of the Code, and the necessity in consequence of always comparing the articles of the Code with the original text of laws, presents serious practical inconveniences. But they can be avoided by inserting in the Code the literal words of the original law and merely reprinting them. This is the means used, as we have seen, in recent years.

CHAPTER III

THE APPLICATION OF POSITIVE LAW

Section 61. *Criticism*

UNGER. System. I. Sec. 12, s. 73.
SAVIGNY. System. I. Sec. 38, 39.
PUCHTA. Pandekten Vorlesungen. Aufl., 1863, I. Sec. 12, 13 (customs), 15 (legislation).
REGELSBERGER. Pandekten. I. ss. 134–140.

The study and application of the rules of positive law supposes first of all the criticism of sources,[1] that is to say, the determination in advance of what is to be understood as the genuine rule of the positive law. Such a rule cannot be set apart nor understood without knowing in what it consists. The word criticism is supplied by historical science, but presents, when applied to jurisprudence, some peculiarities. Criticism, critique, understood as the determination of the genuineness of the rule or of its existence, is properly applied to all the sources without distinction.

The existence of rules of customary law is ascertained by direct observation of the customs, by legal maxims, by the testimony of learned persons, by published collections of customs, and finally, by decisions based on customary law.[2] The first two, direct observation and maxims, give direct knowledge of customary law. The whole matter is reduced to distinguishing between legal customs and mere habitual usage. The last three,—testimony of the learned, collections, decisions,—on the con-

[1] Ordinarily in speaking of a criticism of laws, only law in the sense of legislation is spoken of, but there is no foundation for such a limitation.

[2] Puchta, Gewohnheitsrecht, ss. 12–150. Salza, Gewohnheitsrecht, Weissek's Rechtslexikon.

trary, furnish only second-hand knowledge. When these means of knowledge are employed, therefore, independently of the distinction between habits and customs, it must be asked how reliable is their testimony, and it must be ascertained to what extent the jurist, the editor of the collection, or the judge, had the ability or the will to formulate into an accurate rule the customary law. Judicial decisions are a more sure source of knowledge of the customary law, because they are ordinarily the result of a minute verification of the custom by the judge, usually a person well equipped for the task. The same qualifications must be allowed in a degree to those tribunals in which the judges are not jurists, but representatives of the people's sagacity. Such a popular tribunal is, to be sure, less apt to find an exact and clear formula for a legal rule than is a tribunal composed of jurists, but from the persons who make it up, the popular tribunal has an immediate knowledge of customs.

Less confidence is to be put in the conclusions of tribunals whose personnel consists of men equally strangers to the popular conception of law and to legal instruction. Such are, for example, the clerks of local courts, who can scarcely read and write, but have, however, great influence over the judicial usage in the communal tribunals.

The popularity of a collection of customs is the best proof of its authority as to those customs. If the collection enjoys an authority recognized by every one, confidence may be put in its assertions.

The testimony of competent persons may be given under three different forms. It may consist in the first place of testimony by individuals chosen by the tribunal or by the parties. There can be, also, testimony from the populace by means of general interrogatories. This is a method of ascertaining the existence of customary law which was in force in France up to 1667, when such inquiries were stopped. Finally, the testimony can also be that of some institution, as for example, commercial deputations, or committees from the Board of Trade.[1] Formerly in France the notary's certificate, especially as to commercial customs, had great favor.

In conformity to the edict of 1700 the opinion of merchants confirmed by the Chamber of Commerce had the effect of so-called acts of notoriety.[2] Like custom, legislation and judicial usage can be known to us in two ways, at first or second hand. Its immediate force is derived from the authentic text of the law or from judicial decisions. Both are considered as authentic texts, that is to say, both the copy which carries the signature of the chief executive or that of the judges, and also the official editions of the laws and of judicial opinions. To be sure, the original has a greater authority than the official edition, because there may creep into the latter some defect in the printing, but defects are possible, too, in the original. They may result from carelessness in copying or in printing, for nowadays the original is usually printed. Defects in copying or printing which are noticed in the original are sometimes corrected in the official edition. So, the difference between the original and the official edition is trifling.

The opinion that there can be no criticism of official editions[3] is widespread, but, as Puchta has shown, entirely erroneous. If no criticism applies to official editions, it would result that each page of printed paper, if it came from the government printing office, would pass for a law. A critical examination even of the text of the originals is necessary. It may happen, too, that

[1] Zitovich, Commercial Law, p. 91.

[2] Merlin, Répertoire, voce parere.

[3] See, for example, Unger, System. I, s. 73. Böhlau, Meklenbürgisches-Landdrecht. I, 1871. s. 320. Malichev, Course in Private Law. I. p. 291.

the governmental order goes beyond the limits of the governmental authority in that respect and has disposed of some matter which ought to be regulated only by legislation, that is to say, in constitutional states, by parliament. In this case the ruling is illegal and has not the force of a law for any tribunal. It may happen, too, that the law contradicts some provision of the constitution, in which case it has no effect.

But criticism can be employed upon the official editions not merely in countries where constitutional powers are separated, but in all countries, because, whatever be the government organization, there are everywhere definite forms for the publication of laws. Criticism is applied to determine whether these forms have been properly observed. Just as it can be applied to official editions of laws, so it can to reports of decisions. A judgment that has already been enforced and would regularly be placed in an official edition can be suppressed if, after an examination, a personal object and interest on the part of the judges has been shown. Evidently such a judgment cannot be considered as an expression of principles accepted in judicial usage. When there is no official edition, the criticism of sources uses the same general process as historical criticism does, the jurist employing absolutely the same principles.

Where the jurist has to do with manuscripts, besides this general criticism, he is led to use another sort of inferior criticism which has been styled diplomatic criticism. Its object is to ascertain the text, to correct the defects left by the copyist or printer, to complete it, add signs of punctuation, etc. These operations, as relates to old manuscripts, require much labor and ability. Such a manuscript presents ordinarily an uninterrupted series of letters with no separation between them. To group these letters into words, and separate them by signs of punctuation into propositions, is criticism's first task. The texts which present numerous differences with each other are successively corrected. There are distinctions between the processes employed in this task, and this criticism is divided into comparative, resting upon the comparison of different texts and editions, and into conjectural criticism, the following out of suppositions independent of the text (*emendationes ex ingenio*).

Section 62. *The Correlation of Laws of Different Places and Times*

SAVIGNY. System. B. VIII.

BAR. Lehrbuch des Intern. Privat und Strafrecht. 1892.

SCHMID. Die Herrschaft der Gesetze nach ihren räumlichen und zeitlichen Grenzen. 1863.

GRADOVSKY. The Effectiveness of Law in Respect to Time (Journal of Criminal and Civil Law). 1873, No. 4 (Russian).

KORKUNOV. Essay as to Construction of International Criminal Law. *Id.* 1889, No. 1.

If the same rules of positive law were always and everywhere in effect, criticism alone would suffice for their practical application, but in fact positive law is variable with time, and differs according to states. For this reason it is necessary to have definite rules for its application to avoid conflict between different laws. Such conflicts are possible only between laws of different epochs, places or states.

Law, of course, can be applied only to the facts which bring about its action. There can be no talk of the application of a foreign law with regard to a transaction which took place in Russia, for example, and is brought before Russian tribunals; or again, of the application of the penal laws in force before the regulation of 1845 to a fact which arose and is passed upon under the new penal code of that date. There would be no reason for such an application. Whether a fact has arisen within the sphere of a certain law's operation or not, has always to be determined.

But it may happen that the same fact falls under the action of two different laws, the one with regard to the place and time of its happening, the other to the time and place of the judgment. This would happen, for example, if a criminal has committed his crime abroad but is tried in Russia. There are two possible principles for settling such difficulties. Supremacy can be given to the law in the sphere of application where trial is had, or, equally, to the law of the sphere of application in which the facts arose, and we are liable to get two absolutely different results according to which is used.

There are arguments in favor of each of these two methods. In favor of the application of the law of the tribunal in which the given fact is heard, this general consideration may be first of all advanced,—that of knowing definitely that the tribunals are guided by laws which are in force at a given place and during a given time. An organ of local power, and performing its functions as a result of such power, the tribunal cannot support itself upon foreign laws, for foreign legislation may sometimes present a complete denial of the principles upon which local legislation rests. In replacing old laws by new ones the governmental authority recognized that the old ones were unjust and useless; otherwise, it would not have changed them. So the tribunal, organ of this power, cannot continue to apply the old laws whose injustice is openly recognized. To this fundamental argument considerations of practical convenience are added. If the courts of the Empire apply always its own law to the facts brought before them, it will have to do with only one law and that one well known. It will ignore foreign laws, as well as those formerly in force, and since abrogated. It is only on this condition that the old laws lose their force, and there results an incontestable clearness and simplicity of judicial usage.

Despite the force of these arguments, science as well as practice has accepted the opposite theory, according to which that law should be applied in whose sphere of domination the facts arose. This opinion rests everywhere upon the fact that it is only by the guarantee of the law's authority that the acquisition of a right becomes fixed. A law cannot, in fact, be followed, if it is believed that, when the facts are produced before a court, some other law will be applied to them. Rights can be settled only if, on each new discussion before a tribunal, the same law is always applied to them. If it were otherwise, the same right might belong to me and at the same time not do so. It is necessary to note, also, that the time and place of the trial depend either upon a combination of fortuitous circumstances or upon the will of interested persons, but can have no connection with the fact itself. That fact remains the same, whether the tribunal be Russian or French, or the trial take place this year or next. On the other hand, the time and place of the origination of the facts have great influence over them. The very character of the act depends greatly on the environment in which it is done, but this is determined by time and place. One may say that the law within whose sphere the given fact arose is like a part of the social atmosphere which surrounded the fact and helped determine its performance. Being a human action, it would be very unjust to pass upon it in accordance with a law which the man could not have had in view when performing it.

The principle according to which the new law ought not to be applied before it has been published, or, in other terms, the principle according to which a law ought not to have retroactive effects, rests upon still other considerations. If the state should refuse to apply to facts laws which it was prescribing at the moment when those facts arose, such a use of power would reduce the authority of the state and deprive its laws of all obligatory character. The making of laws, and giving them a retroactive effect, would deprive them of any general objective, impartial character. When laws are made applicable only to the future, it is quite uncertain to what facts they will be applied, whose interests they will serve or harm, and so subjective considerations of a personal kind yield to others of a more general and objective character. If, on the contrary, the law is made to apply to already accomplished facts known to all the world, subjective considerations would take the first place, and the law might easily become a personal weapon for this or that individual.

As to laws of different states, it is enough to say that the simple application of the law of the state in which the judgment is rendered would be an absolute contradiction to the interests of the international community. A stranger in a country other than his own would be, in fact, deprived of all his rights, since the rights which he has in his own country he surely does not hold at the will of foreign legislation.

Such are the arguments which compel us to accept, for the determination of the correlation between the laws of different epochs and different states, the principle that the whole fact ought to be judged according to the law under which it was produced. This principle in itself is very simple, but to comprehend the whole extent of its application, its whole use in special cases, it is necessary to give it a very careful study. The notions of law and of its sphere of action are already known to us. Law, moreover, means here every general legal rule, whether created by legislative act or not; the product of customs and of judicial decision, for example. We shall stop only to analyze some notions of legal facts and of their origination.

The universe which surrounds us presents an unbroken connection of different changes, which we recognize by grouping them in some way as distinct facts, each having a scientific bearing or an historic, moral, economic or legal one. This grouping is not determined in any objective way and this notion of a distinct fact is not absolute but relative. We consider the same succession of phenomena sometimes as a combination of several facts, sometimes as one distinct fact. It all depends on the purpose which guides us.

What is a distinct legal fact? It is a combination of changes such as taken together have a legal effect, but since the legal effect of a fact depends exclusively upon the application of a legal rule which it sets in motion, one can say in a more precise way that a distinct legal fact is the combination of changes which taken together bring about an application of law.

The legal fact may be quite complex; it may consist of several acts or circumstances. A crime, as a legal fact, may be composed of different elements whose common presence is necessary to make it a crime. Taken separately these elements will not constitute a legal fact, because they will not bring about any application of the criminal law. The intention, taken separately, is not yet a legal fact, and it may be connected with any other fact.

Legal facts are very different from each other and can be differently grouped. It will be more convenient for us to group them conformably to the questions which form the subject of judicial decision. We shall thus more easily reach our end, which is to know what laws, indigenous or foreign, old or new, ought to control the tribunal.

The question which a tribunal is charged with settling can be reduced to four different categories, 1st, Is the indicated law established? 2d, What are the conditions for the application of that law? 3d, Is that law still in force? 4th, What are the forms established by law for passing upon the given affair, and have these forms been observed?

The criminal tribunal is charged, first of all, with settling the following question: Is there a right to punish?

Then it settles the condition for applying the penal law and fixes the penalty. If there is doubt as to the question whether the law is not extinct by prescription or by some other alteration, it is necessary to settle the question anew.

The question of knowing if the forms instituted by law have been properly observed is of little importance in criminal jurisdiction, but before the civil tribunal is often the principal question, since each contract is connected with an obligatory form whose non-observance produces the nullity of the contract.

Each of these four questions must be resolved in conformity with the corresponding group of actual circumstances which form, from this point of view, a distinct legal fact. We shall regard as distinct legal facts the circumstances which bring about the establishment, the application, or the cessation of the law, and also the observance in legal action of legally required forms. Each of these facts ought to be treated in accordance with the law under whose control it was brought about. Quite frequently each of these distinct facts in the course of a single affair requires to be discussed according to different laws, because the establishment, the realization, the cessation, of the same right can very easily have taken place under different laws.

The notion of legal facts which we have thus isolated is very important in explaining the question now under examination. After having explained it, it will be easy to understand that the realization of a right is the work, not of the time and place of the acquisition of the right, but of the time and place of the realization itself, because the acquisition and the realization are distinct facts and each is to be judged according to the law of its accomplishment. Thus, all the owners in a given time and place can realize their right of property quite independently of the place or moment of its acquisition.

It results that the criminal character of an action is decided according to the law of the time and place of the action itself, but the fixing of the penalty by the tribunal, so far as it is a distinct legal fact, is the realization by the state of its right acquired over that person by reason of the action which he has done. It is to be considered according to the time and place of the tribunal.

Since the form of legal action has also a legal weight, its observance or non-observance is to be regarded as a distinct legal fact and ought, consequently, to be treated according to the law of the time and place where the act is performed. For this reason the form of judicial action, in other words, the administration of justice, is fixed by the law of the tribunal, and not by that of the place and time in which the act was performed. This is the more evident from the fact that in the same judicial matter one is very often compelled to consider very different facts, connecting them with times and places also very different, while it is impossible to apply to the same process different forms of the administration of justice.

Since legal facts are very complex, it may be asked at what precise moment a fact is to be considered as accomplished. Considering that the fact receives a legal effect only after the performance of its final element, the time and place of the accomplishment of the last element must be regarded as that of the legal fact itself. It may happen, still, that the performer of the act finds himself in one jurisdiction while the result of his act appears in another. Where, then, is the act considered as performed? The criminalists, disposed to give to the subjective element the leading rôle, determine this question by saying that it is the place in which the doer finds himself, which is to be considered as that of his act. The civilists turn to the opposite opinion. The realization by a person who finds himself within a state of his right over property, over immovables situated in another state, ought to be discussed according to the law of the place where the property is. Rights to obligations are discussed according to the law of the place of the debtor and not of the creditor. It would, perhaps, be more equitable to hold to the same opinion in criminal matters, since in such cases crime is not committed except when it has produced some results which manifest themselves outside of the jurisdiction in which the criminal is found. When a man on one side of a frontier shoots at another man on the other side, the realization of a criminal intention, the deprivation of life, takes place where the man is slain.

The determination of the mutual relations between the laws of different epochs and different places can be reduced, it is seen, to a single common principle, but these relations are none the less very complex. They depend upon two circumstances of fact.

In the submission to action of laws of different epochs the legal relation is effected by the action of the laws in a single fixed order, first, that of the old law, and then that of the new. The inverse order is impossible. In case of conflict between laws of different states, the difficulty is much greater. The same relation can, turn and turn about, be transferred from one country to the other, and vice versa. This permits interested persons to move from one country to another in order to avoid the requirements of the laws of one or the other country.

A more important complication results from the following fact: When old laws are replaced by new ones these extend their action necessarily, at once, over all the elements of legal relationship. It may happen, however, that the subject of a relationship falls under the action of the new law while the object of it remains under the old. Very often it happens that the subject of the relation is in one jurisdiction while its object is in another. Conformably to the rule above indicated, each realization of right in this case is considered as taking place where the object of the right is.

We ought to observe, in conclusion, that in practice, thanks to different political considerations, some infractions are admitted in the application of the general principle which determines the correlation between the laws of different epochs and of different places.

Section 63. *The Interpretation of Laws*

SAVIGNY. System. Band I. s. 206.
GRADOVSKY. Judicial Interpretation of Laws. Journal of Criminal and Civil Law (Russian), 1874, No. 1.
TAGANTZEV. Lectures on Russian Criminal Law. Part I. p. 346.

Criticism fixes the authenticity of the source of laws as a whole and of their several parts. The principles of the correlation of the laws of different times and places settle precisely what laws are applicable to special cases. But it is not enough to know what laws are to be applied. It is necessary besides to apply them. For this, it is required first of all to explain the meaning and the field of application of the legal rule, and this is the task of interpretation.

Since positive law must come from some of the sources of law the will of the legislator is law only so far as it is found in the legislative act. If by accident or ignorance the legislator has expressed his will in a law of a form more restricted than such will would require, the law nevertheless remains within the limits of the expression. On the other hand, the law serves as a source of rights only within the limits of the expression of the legislator's will. If by chance the expressions employed are more extensive in parts than he intended, that cannot be considered as law which goes beyond his real intention. A defect or irregularity of language cannot be considered as a source of law. The task of interpretation is, then, that of explaining the will of the legislator within the limits of its expression in the legislative act.

Interpretation like criticism is not an exclusive attribute of jurisprudence. It is found in all science which has to do with written sources,—in history and theology, for example. Rules might be given applying equally to the interpretation and to the criticism of legal science and of historical manuscripts or of religious books; but criticism in jurisprudence presents some peculiarities, as, for instance, the question as to whether or not a law is constitutional. There are, then, two elements in juridical interpretation, the general and a special one.

The general element consists in the ordinary logical and grammatical processes of interpretation. Each written source contains a human idea expressed in words, but the idea and the words are subject to certain logical and grammatical rules. To understand what is written or said it is necessary to know these rules. The interpreter should, as Savigny says, reproduce all the means, the whole progress, of the composition of the law; and he should use for this purpose the corresponding logical and grammatical form. Grammatical rules vary with epochs. The interpreter should apply to each given law the rules of the time of its composition. Moreover, just as each writer has his own peculiarities of language, every legislator has his also, and it is an additional task of the interpreter to study the individual peculiarities in the style of the law-giver.

Logical rules do not change, but the conceptions which they express may be stated in various ways. So, in the interpretation of legal rules, heed must be given to the changes in the conceptions which they embrace. The legislator, it is said, observed the rules of logic and grammar in expressing his will. This is only a supposition (presumption). Therefore, if we are satisfied that in a given case the legislator has committed some logical or grammatical fault, as very often happens, this doctrine loses all its force and we cannot then accept the interpretation it would give to the law. It is the same way when the logical and grammatical interpretation leads to results evidently absurd.

To explain how it is necessary to understand the law conformably to the spirit of the legislator, and perhaps in spite of logical and grammatical rules, the history of the law must be known. The first scheme of the law must be reported, and then the different changes to which it was subjected, the debates before the legislative body. These are so many materials for explaining how a given proposition of law came about and consequently may be very useful in case of doubt as to its meaning.

Comparison between the articles of our Code and the sources from which they come is also very important. In composing the Code the legislator wished to express in his articles the same rules as those which are contained in former laws, and not to make new. So legislative dispositions according to which the Code has been formed have all the value of legislative materials. With us, it is true, it is a custom to consider the comparison between articles of the Code and the previous enactments which gave birth to them an historical interpretation. This opinion, as we shall see later, is entirely erroneous.

The special element in juridical interpretation presents much greater interest than the preceding. It rests upon a special correlation of succeeding rules and of those simultaneously existing. This correlation is not at all identical with that which exists, for example, in historical or literary memoirs. The combination of historical memoirs, connecting with a given epoch, do not form a whole. Each of them can be separately interpreted, and the appearance of some new ones makes no change in the meaning of those in existence before. To be sure, these new memoirs may assist in getting the meaning of the old ones, but do not thereby change that meaning.

The combination of legal rules existing in a given society at a given date, exhibits, on the contrary, the whole juridical order of that society, and the manner in which each rule is to be applied. To the same subject there cannot be applied at the same time, several conflicting rules. So the combination of legal rules forms a whole, a system. The birth of new rules changes it, either by limiting or enlarging the scope of the system. Legal rules resemble in this respect religious dogmas, which also form a systematic whole.

As to the correlation between the successive rules, here, too, an essentially peculiar character is observed. A new rule always abrogates as to the matter which it determines, any rule which may have previously prevailed.

This correlation of successive rules presents another original peculiarity. It cannot be said that an earlier historic memoir has not of itself the force of a later one, and if it relates to the same historical event, the old is preferred to the new. As to religious dogmas, they do not present these exclusive relations. God in his wisdom does not contradict himself nor the New Testament abrogate the Old. The correlation just indicated between legal rules gives to their interpretation a peculiar character, and because of this fact there must be a careful distinction made between systematic interpretation and historical interpretation.

Historical interpretation is the explaining of the meaning of a rule by comparing it with the rule which was acting as to the same matter at the moment when the new rule was promulgated. If it is thus defined, the explanation of the articles of our Code by means of comparison with the rulings cited under these articles is not historical interpretation. The article does not replace the rules which are cited by it, because it is only a new expression of the same rule. There is lacking here the prime condition for all historical interpretation the comparison between two successive rules. The comparison between the prior legislative acts and the articles to which they serve as source, presents absolutely the same character as that between the original of the law and its official edition. In both cases we compare the two official forms of the expression of a single rule.

The necessity for historical intrepretation often arises from the fact that very frequently the conception of the new law is wholly fixed by the law which it abrogates. Just as it is impossible sometimes to understand the answer without knowing the preceding question, so sometimes a law, which abrogates another, can be understood only when the abrogated law is understood. If sweeping legislation, embracing a whole branch of law, is under consideration, only an attentive comparison between the old law and the new can decide whether or not the new completely abrogates the old, and this especially because it may happen that the basis of the two laws is quite different. The new law, by connection with the old, may have several results,—it may abrogate it completely and replace it by a new act (*abrogatio*), or, may modify it in part only (*derogatio*), or, again, may complete it (*subrogatio*).[1] By systematic interpretation we mean the explanation of a rule made by comparing this rule to the whole system of law. Thus, the explanation of the rule by comparing it with the title of the section of the law which contains it, is only a special form of logical interpretation. The system of the legislative act, the arrangement of its different articles, are a result of the logical development of the thing determined upon, but we must not confuse the plan of the legislator, subject, like all men, to the rules of logic, and the system of legal rules acting in a given society,

[1] Glück, Commentar, I. s. 5–14.

which has its basis in the law of solidarity between coexisting phenomena. This last system can serve as a basis for systematic interpretation. If such a distinction is not recognized, the explanation of the law will be in accordance with the plan of the whole article, considered separately, and this will be logical interpretation; but the explanation according to the arrangement of the articles considered as an entire succession will be systematic interpretation.

So far as the article formulates no principle peculiar to itself it is permissible to the editor to combine several into one, or, on the contrary, to make several out of one. This is why the order of exposition of a distinct article must be considered, and even the order of disposition of several articles, as the basis of logical and not systematic interpretation.

This is not a mere question of words. Since with us the interpretation according to titles of chapters is ordinarily a systematic interpretation, we neglect to search for another. Besides the distinction of interpretation according to different processes, there was formerly a distinction, according to subject, between doctrinal and legal interpretation. The first is interpretation by persons charged with applying the law, who derive their influence from the science of it. The second is an interpretation based on habit, or even on legislation itself, and has the authority of custom or that of legislative power; but, as Savigny has indicated, doctrinal interpretation should be considered by itself. The pretended interpretation by practice is only custom. Authentic interpretation is itself only law. The force of that strange expression, legislative interpretation of the law, is sometimes under the cover of a legislative interpretation to make the former legislator say the contrary of his original thought. We must not confuse with interpretation the application, which is sometimes made, of a rule by analogy. Interpretation is the explanation of a rule. Analogy is the application of this rule to some case which was not foreseen in the law, but which presents judicially an analogy to the cases for which the law was made. As often as we apply a rule drawn from some distinct enactment or from some separate system of legislation we distinguish between the analogy of this legislation and the law.

Section 64. *The Scientific Study of Law*

IHERING. Geist des rōmischen Rechts. II. 2 Abth. 3 Auf. 1875. s. 309–389.

KORKUNOV. Scientific Study of Law. Journal of Civil and Criminal Law, 1882, No. 4, pp. 1–29, and No. 5, pp. 194–195.

Interpretation explains the meaning of different legal rules. If such meaning is not understood the rule can get no application. So, interpretation is an indispensable condition for the application of legal rules, but interpretation alone does not answer. It cannot give complete meaning to the law. Interpretation, in the first place, being the explanation of a single meaning of the indicated rule is connected too intimately with the law of a given country and a given time. When we need to apply a foreign law, or even a newly promulgated law of our own country, the interpretation of the old laws is useless. If the study of law were limited solely to interpretation, the jurist of each state and each new generation would be compelled to begin anew the complete study of law, for laws change more than once in the course of a single generation. Despite the variety and number of changes in the law, there are permanent elements, or at least some so stable that they do not change at the same time with any definite new legislation. Legal rules as to relations change much more quickly than the relations themselves and their fundamental elements. For this reason, if we accept as the basis of legal studies not legal rules, as happens in interpretation, but legal relations, we shall get more stable and solid conclusions.

Another consideration, too, leads to the preference for the study of relations over that of the interpretation of rules. We have seen that legal rules cannot be considered separately, even for the purpose of pure interpretation. Since they act together in society, the rules necessarily constitute a whole, and on this fact is based systematic interpretation.

This system does not result from the external form of legislative collections, but from the organic combination of the relations to which legal rules are applied. For this reason the study of legal relations is necessary to the construction of such a system.

This study leads to something unified, something systematic in law, that is, to something exclusively scientific, and it is in this sense that Ihering could call interpretation inferior jurisprudence, and could oppose to it as superior, analysis, the construction of systematic relations. In what consist the processes of scientific study of law? Science generalizes our perceptions and replaces the immediate but superficial concrete observation by a more abstract and general knowledge. It studies the separate perceptions only as necessary means for generalization. It presses forward to conclusions applicable to whole groups of like phenomena and thus it replaces the knowledge of all special phenomena by the general study of groups. But generalization cannot operate upon the facts themselves. These, at least, immediate observation furnishes. In comparing the facts of immediate observation, before they are decomposed into their integral elements, we can observe only faint resemblances, which may lead us into error and bring about the combining of phenomena which have almost nothing in common.

To make generalizations more certain, the materials, the facts, which present themselves to our observation, must be considered beforehand. For this purpose we analyze our notions, decompose them, to find out their general elements and the different combinations they make. Then we combine together these general elements and the notions which we have found by analysis just as all true scientific research requires, and we thus construct some juridical conceptions, original ideal constructions, such as all science tends toward. Finally, these scientific combinations, collected together, we classify, guiding ourselves by their common resemblances and differences in grouping them.

All these processes, observations, analysis, construction, classification, are the general processes of all scientific research and do not belong exclusively to the science of law. This, however, has not always been understood by jurists, at least so far as regards analysis and construction. Thus Ihering in his theories of analysis and judicial construction refers for his explanations, not to general principles of scientific method but to the alphabet to explain analysis, and to organic bodies to explain construction. Mouromtzev connects directly all the processes of juridical construction "with peculiarities of the juridical conception,"[1] which, says he, "has only a practical, conventional sphere and cannot serve as a means for scientific explanation."

We shall try to prove that neither in construction nor in analysis, can be seen merely peculiarities of juridical conception, but that, on the contrary, we are here in the presence of a special application of the ordinary scientific principles of all generalization. We will take first juridical analysis.

The jurist, contrary to current ideas, does not regard each legal case as a complete whole. On the contrary, he separates the whole question into several elements, seeks to distinguish these from one another, and applies a solution to each of the distinct elements of which the question is composed. Where every other savant sees an indivisible question, admitting of only one answer, affirmative or negative, the jurist finds, on the contrary,

[1] Definition and Fundamental Divisions of Law, 93.

a series of questions of which each requires a distinct solution. Such a decomposition, such an analysis, applied to isolated practical questions, might certainly often appear as a useless complication of the question. But if, not limiting ourselves to the study of one case, we consider a succession of them, we shall then understand that legal analysis confuses nothing and complicates nothing. The analysis, in fact, leads to a small number of identical fundamental elements, which go to make up the whole infinite variety of juridical cases. Thus, we replace by the study of some essential elements the study of all possible cases, and get in this way, —is it not true?—a great economy of time and labor.

Can this process of juridical analysis be regarded as an original peculiarity of jurisprudence? To show the contrary a very little reasoning will suffice. The process of analysis, which we make upon juridical conceptions, can be considered as the general processes for the formation of those conceptions. Sigwart considers such an analysis as the fundamental question in every theory of methods.[1] In the old treatises on logic, it is true, the process of the formation of our conceptions was explained in a more exclusive fashion. It was explained as if we formed all our general conceptions always in the same way, by the successive omission of signs, and the correlation of genus and species was recognized as the general form of correlations between conceptions. This is evidently what leads Ihering to search for an explanation of juridical analysis, not in the general processes of logical analysis, but in the analogy which it presents to the alphabet. In the old treatises on logic, indeed, it would be hard, perhaps, to find a suitable formula for explaining the distinction between concrete and abstract elements, between dependent and independent elements. Ihering explains this distinction by comparing

[1] Sigwart. Logik. B. II. Methodenlehre, 1878, s. 5.

it to that between vowels and consonants. The vowel of the juridical alphabet is that which is found in life existing in an independent way, that is, a transfer of property, a will, etc. The consonant is what is incomprehensible except as an attribute of some other thing, such as, for example, the notion of holding over a term. Well, for this distinction, I repeat, it will be difficult to find in the old treatises on logic a suitable explanation, but the recent German logicians, Sigwart, Lotze, Wundt, do not recognize the omission of signs as a sole general process for creating generalizations, as a sole general form for their correlation. According to Wundt the correlation of genus and species is only one of the possible forms for the correlation of notions, and generality is the essential attribute of notions, only in the sense in which each of these notions includes elements entering equally into the formation of other conceptions, from the combination of which depends solely the distinction of different notions.[1] So, it cannot be said that from the more or less abstract character of the notion depends always its greater or less generality. For example, the notion of obligation is less abstract than that of injury, but one cannot say that it is at the same time less general. It is not, then, the omission of individual signs which is the process of generalizing, but the analysis of these notions into their elements out of which they are formed. There is no need of seeking outside of logical rules for the explanation of analytical processes in jurisprudence. Effort has been made in German jurisprudence to profit by the results in logic obtained by Sigwart and Lotze, so as to explain the formation of juridical conceptions.[2]

What Ihering calls logical concentration of notions is also a process derived from general logic. It acts here

[1] Wundt, Logic, I, 1880, pp. 8, 96.
[2] Rümelin, Juristische Begriffsbildung, 1878.

in determining the mutual relations between notions. It should be observed that Ihering does not attend to the variety of forms of this correlation. The correlation of notions can be not only a relation of subordination, but it can also take different forms; for example, reciprocal opposition (the fortuitous and intentional case), correlation (right and duty), contiguity (*dies incertus, certus quando, conditio*), alternation (right to things and to services), etc.

But this logical concentration of Ihering gives unity only in a restricted degree. In order that this unification may include also general elements obtained by analysis there must be a synthesis by means of juridical construction. Like analysis, juridical construction is no special peculiarity of legal science. It is a general process of scientific unification. It is not required that we regard scientific generalizations as simply copies of reality. Such copies are necessarily obscure and indefinite. They are like the confused impression we receive in looking at several diaphanous pictures placed one upon the other and held towards the light. Their colors and contours are mingled and no longer precise.[1] Certainly generalizations like these confused impressions do not answer the purposes of science. Perhaps they can answer the purposes of ordinary life, for often, in fact, it is by the assistance of confused and obscure notions that we are guided in life. But science requires before all things, exactness, clearness and precision. In truth, scientific generalization is summarizing, rather than making copies of reality. All scientific generalizations are ideal constructions presenting original combinations between general elements of conception obtained by analysis. These combinations are not a servile copy of reality. They are made up freely, conformably to the scientific generalization, and for this reason they depart

[1] Lewis, Problems of Life and Mind, Vol. I, 272–300.

somewhat from all reality. Such is the character of generalizations in all sciences without exception. They are none of them a copy of reality. They constitute, on the contrary, an ideal construction. For example, when it is said that the moon moves in a fixed orbit around the earth, we do not intend that for a simple description of the fact. It is merely an ideal construction, designed to make the moon's movement understood. In fact the moon does not describe any ellipse around the earth, and if it were to leave behind it a visible track, that track would not appear as an ellipse or any other form of a closed figure, but as a waving, unclosed line. We speak in the same way in studying crystals. In order to study and explain their phenomena the savants imagine that in each one there is a certain axis, a certain line by which the nature of the crystal is determined. In certain classes of crystals four such axes are counted; in others, three only. They may be of equal length or all perpendicular to each other. According to the number of these axes, their length and their inclination, crystals are divided into seven categories which have as their basis their geometric form or their physical properties. These axes, however, are purely imaginary. All crystallographic science rests, then, on a purely ideal construction.

Juridical constructions have a similar value, not merely from the practical, but also from the scientific point of view. Between them and astronomical or crystallographic constructions there is no essential difference. Of course the methods used are different, but this is all which separates them. The fundamental process of juridical construction consists in this, that the juridical relations which exist between men are objective, that is to say, are considered as independent things, arising, subject to variations during their existence, and disappearing, precisely like animated beings. They are distinguished, besides, in their organization, their structure, their subjects, that is to say, the individuals, between whom these relations exist, and their objects, that is to say, the forces which serve for the formation of relations. In every legal relation one recognizes finally a right corresponding to an obligation.

Just as by the determination of the number of axes of their length, and of their position, one reaches a determination of the properties of different crystals, so the determination of the properties of different legal relations permits of determining their subject and object and the conditions of their establishment. The construction of legal relations resembles that of crystallographic systems. It is an ideal construction, employed for the purpose of legal research, and for this reason criticism of legal construction has not exhausted its rôle when it has answered the questions as to whether this legal construction corresponds well in all its parts to reality. The axes of the crystal, the ellipse which the moon describes, exist only in our heads. We only imagine them, but this does not prevent such constructions from having great scientific value.

The estimation of every juridical construction ought to depend exclusively on the following idea: Is it, or is it not, a useful form for the reproduction of legal phenomena and for the determination of their mutual relations? The utility of a process of juridical construction is proved when one can put this process into practice. Worked out by the civilians, properly so called, this process becomes from day to day further applied. It is absolutely useful for the reproduction of juridical phenomena, however different they may be.

That this juridical construction may answer the purpose for which it was devised it must fulfill certain general conditions, which Ihering called laws of juridical construction. The first is that it be complete. It must include all possible cases. They must all find a place in its different pigeon-holes. The second condition is that it be logical. The whole construction must be consistent with itself. It must not be out of harmony with juridical institutions of the more general kind. It ought to conform to them. It ought, farther, to be such that the solution of all questions, having regard to the relation indicated, should be derivable from it as a logical and necessary consequence. Finally, it ought to be simple and natural. Anything otherwise would not facilitate the conception of the law, but have quite the reverse effect.

When the construction of different institutions of law is accomplished, it remains to classify them. Conformably to the distinction in the logical correlation of notions, which subordinates, or sets them into opposition, two forms of classification are possible, by system and by rank. The first is the work of a comparison between different notions which are subordinated, the one to the other. It seeks not merely to divide into several groups the classified phenomena, but also to make of each of these groups a whole and bind them together so that they shall be presented as all one branch of the fundamental notion, and thus make it a systematic classification, which can be represented under the form of a trunk with branches and subdivisions, all co-ordinated with each other.

Jurists apply almost exclusively the classification by system. It is, however, only a special kind of classification. If we compare these notions of law according to the degree of their mutual proximity we shall have a system based upon position and such a comparison does not create ramification. We shall have, then, a series of several notions presenting themselves, as might be said, like links in an indefinite chain. Such a classification has special applicability to the phenomena of the juridic life passing successively across the ages.

INDEX

Published by

Facsimile Publisher
Ashok Vihar, Delhi-110052 (India)
Website: www.facsimilepublisher.com

Distributed by

Gyan Books Pvt. Ltd.
5, Ansari Road, Daryaganj, New Delhi-110002 (India)
E-mail: books@gyanbooks.com, Website: www.gyanbooks.com

2 222000 011048